Agents and lives offers a new and important rethinking of the traditional 'humanist' view of literature. That tradition's valuation of literature for its 'moral import' is extended in a wider, more complex, open and exploratory understanding of those terms. Literature, not simply in a didactic or exemplary sense, represents a kind of moral thinking in its own right – a kind necessary to our moral understanding, and which moral philosophy has spoken of, but cannot itself supply. Goldberg demonstrates the way in which literature combines a sense of people as voluntary agents and as moral beings whose lives extend well beyond the voluntary and deliberate, manifesting themselves in everything the individual feels and suffers, as well as in everything he or she does.

The book argues that this double way of thinking about people corresponds to traditional literary criticism's most vital insights into the way works of literature both depict and themselves manifest modes of human life. Such criticism avoids the need for separate 'aesthetic' judgments (since all literary judgment becomes moral) and for treating a work of art as if it were simply the voluntary expression of a conscious and responsible moral 'self'.

Goldberg's argument ranges across English literature since the Renaissance, focusing on central examples from George Eliot's novels and Pope's poetry. A final chapter assesses the relationship of his argument to recent accounts of literature offered by moral philosophers such as Iris Murdoch, Bernard Williams, Martha Nussbaum and Richard Rorty.

AGENTS AND LIVES

AGENTS AND LIVES

Moral thinking in literature

S. L. GOLDBERG

*Formerly Senior Fellow, Institute of Advanced Studies,
Australian National University*

CAMBRIDGE
UNIVERSITY PRESS

Published by the Press Syndicate of the University of Cambridge
The Pitt Building, Trumpington Street, Cambridge CB2 IRP
40 West 20th Street, New York, NY 10011–4211, USA
10 Stamford Road, Oakleigh, Victoria 3166, Australia

First published 1993

Printed in Great Britain at the University Press, Cambridge

A catalogue record for this book is available from the British Library

Library of Congress cataloguing in publication data
Goldberg, S. L. (Samuel Louis), 1926-
Agents and lives: moral thinking in literature / S. L. Goldberg.
p.   cm.
Includes bibliographical references.
ISBN 0 521 39468 6
1. English literature – History and criticism – Theory, etc.
2. Literature and morals.   3. Ethics in literature.   I. Title.
PR21.G65   1992
820.9 – dc20   92–7580   CIP

ISBN 0 521 39468 6 hardback

For Peter, Richard and Kate

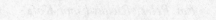

Contents

Sam Goldberg died in December 1991.

Agents and lives was by then nearly ready for editing.

The whole project of the book was clarified and enriched by conversations Sam had over the years with many friends and colleagues: Stanley Benn, Michael Black, Robert Brown, Graham Burns, Myles Burnyeat, John Casey, Del Chessell, Christopher Cordner, Frank Cioffi, Keith Campbell, Stefan Collini, Frances Dixon, Alan Donagan, Dirk den Hartog, Richard Freadman, Robin Grove, Jenny Gribble, Heather Glen, Simon Haines, Michael Holquist, Loraine Hugh, Frank Jackson, Rob Jackson, Dan Jacobson, Nick Jose, Fred Langman, Ann Loftus, David Parker, Christopher Ricks, Peter Shrubb, Lee Shrubb, Michael Slote, Barry Smith, Maggie Tomlinson, Jock Tomlinson, John Wiltshire, Iain Wright. Both Michael Black and Stefan Collini were particularly generous with their help in reading and commenting on the whole manuscript.

Much of the book was written in the History of Ideas Program and the Philosophy Program in the Research School of Social Sciences at the Australian National University, and while Sam was a Visiting Fellow of Clare Hall, Cambridge, and Gonville and Caius College, Cambridge. Earlier versions of chapters 3–7 appeared in *The Critical Review*, 1980, 1981, 1982, 1983 and 1986.

At Cambridge University Press, Jeremy Mynott, Josie Dixon and Helen Spillett gave special care to the book's publication. In preparing the text and seeing the book through the press I have also been most grateful for the help given at proof stage by Frances Dixon and Sue Fraser.

Jane Adamson

Preface

If the basic aim of moral philosophy is still to answer Socrates' question, 'how to live?', the contribution that 'poetry', imaginative literature, might make to answering it has been in dispute at least since Socrates asked the question. I must confess that I have never found the dispute particularly exciting or relevant to my interests as a literary critic, mainly because the dispute has usually been conducted by philosophers, who naturally assume that moral philosophy is the centre, so to speak, the place where truth and reason are to be found, and that literature is simply the application of moral ideas and feelings, somewhere on the periphery. (A surprising number of literary scholars and critics assume this too; we are a trusting – not to say credulous – lot when it comes to thinking.) True, some philosophers in recent years have questioned this assumption on philosophical grounds; but having grown up in the English tradition of evaluative literary criticism (which has, incidentally, very little to do with the New Criticism and other American schools of literary study), and so not having shared this assumption in the first place, I began some years ago to think about the relationship of literature and moral philosophy, but in a different way, from the literary critic's side, as it were. Coming among philosophical colleagues, I found myself trying to explain to them how and why I think literature and literary criticism form a distinctive and irreplaceable way of thinking about certain crucial aspects of Socrates' question – a way which is outside the scope of philosophy but complementary to it, which is no less subject to requirements of truth and reason, and which makes some kinds of literary judgment not just like

xiii

moral judgments, nor just connected with them, but actual moral judgments in their own right.

There are, I realize, serious risks in using the term 'moral' as freely as I do, since many people still think of morality as a code of right and wrong conduct ultimately derived from God or from one of His more popular substitutes. I can only hope that it will relieve more readers than it will disappoint to say at the outset that I have no such moral code or doctrine to teach, no scheme of moral salvation to preach, and nothing so substantial and grand as even a moral philosophy. In fact, my conception of the 'moral' is altogether loose and baggy. For example, I do not assume that moral judgments are restricted only to expressions of fault-finding or resentment or righteousness or the desire to bestow guilt; I do not even think that all moral judgments are prescriptive, or universalizable, or directed only to what people intentionally choose to be or to do, as distinct from what they cannot help being or doing. In my view, moral judgments range over much more ground than that – just as Socrates' question does.

To a philosopher – even one as liberal as Bernard Williams about the range of matters that can reasonably be called moral, and as sceptical about the power of moral philosophy to deal with every one of them – all that literature and literary criticism can offer is perhaps no more than a kind of phenomenology:

> There could be a way of doing moral philosophy that started from the ways in which we experience our ethical life. Such a philosophy would reflect on what we believe, feel, take for granted; the ways in which we confront obligations and recognize responsibility; the sentiments of guilt and shame. It would involve a phenomenology of the ethical life.[1]

To those who are not proposing to do moral philosophy, however, but just want to reflect on how to live, I think literature offers much more than this; but as Williams suggests elsewhere, a major stumbling-block is the remarkable assurance with which people think they already know what moral questions are about, and consequently what can and what cannot be called 'moral'. Nor does it help matters that every moral outlook prescribes, explicitly or implicitly, what is to count as 'moral'. This is why I do not even try to delimit the term. Indeed, I even want to question Williams's own phrase, 'the ethical life', which seems to suggest what I doubt he believes himself: that there is only one such life-pattern (or a small number of them), and that we already know what a human 'life' consists in, and what its 'moral' or 'ethical' elements or aspects are, before we apply these ideas to any particular life. (How would, say, Jane Austen's conception of 'ethical life' be applied to, say, the Karamazovs?) This is not to deny, of course, that we can consider a particular life morally only if we have some pre-conception of a 'life' and some pre-conception of 'the moral'; but as I try to argue, literature is (and always has been in our culture) a special kind of moral thinking in that it continually re-opens such questions. What must count here as 'moral' or 'ethical'? What does this or that individual 'life' consist in? As I see it, literature does its moral thinking in the particulars it imagines, and it has to: not, however, because literature aspires to, but cannot reach, the universals of moral codes or moral philosophy, but because literature can do something that moral codes and moral philosophy cannot. It can think morally in the widest, most inclusive sense of the term – which means, I argue, thinking about people (whether as individuals or as social groups) in a double way.

On the one side, literature does consider people much as moral codes and moral philosophy do, as voluntary agents, each of whom is like any other in having passions, desires, rationality and will, in confronting recognizable moral problems, and in exemplifying recognizable moral concepts and rules of conduct. But at the same time, literature also considers people as lives: as individual unique forms of life – or better, to avoid the specifically Wittgensteinian sense of that phrase, as individual, unique modes of human life – whose particular qualities and trajectory in time are, in quite crucial ways, not like others', nor by any means entirely a matter of voluntary actions, and yet no less morally important for that. What is more, I argue, it is (and always has been in our culture) the distinctive power and importance of literary criticism to make moral sense of 'poems', of literature itself, and so to evaluate it, in this same double way. Indeed, this double kind of moral thinking applied reflexively to literary works seems to me essential to the traditional institution and practice of literature and evaluative literary criticism; or to put it another way, that to consider any text – lyric or memoirs, realist or fantasy, mythic or post-structuralist – as manifesting a mode of life as well as embodying voluntary intentional actions *is* to regard it as 'literature'. In the hands of traditional evaluative criticism, one might say, 'literature' is in the final analysis as much a way of considering texts as it is a body of texts that have been considered in that way.

The order of the chapters that follow is pretty much the order in which they were written. Some originated in essays (published in different form in *The Critical Review* at various times between 1980 and 1986) on literary works I happened to be interested in at the time: works in which, and through which, I found myself thinking about the moral thinking of the particular author, but progressively thinking about more and more complex issues. This is why I discuss a rather odd collection of works, and also why the terms of my argument vary slightly from chapter to chapter as I consider different aspects of literature or literary criticism. Originally, I thought that the whole argument would come to centre in a study of Shakespeare's *Antony and Cleopatra*, which (along with *King Lear*) seems to me to manifest the most ranging and powerful moral life, and some of the most searching moral thinking, in English literature; but for various reasons (including the one mentioned at the end of chapter 8) I have kept that study for a separate book. However, I hope that the sequence in which the chapters of this book were written forms an argumentative sequence for the reader too. I should add that I have deliberately tried *not* to discuss works in historical order, so as to avoid any suggestion that I think the issues I am concerned with are only a matter of personal maturation, of growing into a fully 'adult' moral understanding, or of historical 'systems of thought and belief which have had their day'. And I have also deliberately *not* arranged the general chapters together at the beginning and the more specific literary-critical chapters after them, so as to avoid any suggestion of a theory thought out in the abstract and then applied from above, as it were, to illustrative examples. My argument is largely about the inability of that kind of thinking by itself to make moral sense of people and of poems: this, indeed, being my main point of difference with some of the contemporary Anglo-American moral philosophers who have discussed the moral import of literature in ways that in many respects converge with mine, but whose limits (as a literary critic sees it) I try to sketch out very briefly in the final chapter.

CHAPTER I

'*Perpetually moralists*' ... '*in a large sense*'

I

Various interested parties keep saying that the traditional 'humanist' critical study of English literature – centred on, though not of course confined to, imaginative moral under-standing and literary evaluation – is on its last legs, but I very much doubt if they are right. For one thing, their conception of that tradition is little more than a caricature of its real complexity and openness; and for another, it is hard to see any of the alternatives on offer becoming popular outside the walls of academic professionalism. Admittedly, in matters like this one's reasons inevitably involve a good many calculated guesses and unverifiable judgments – moral probabilities, as they used to be called. But it seems to me that, given a reasonably free, open and cohesive society, people are more likely than not to go on being 'humanist', at least in the sense of being interested in people, and interested in them at least as much as in abstract theories and ideologies, or impersonal forces, or structural systems, or historical information, or even the play of signifiers. They are also more likely than not, I think, to go on wanting literature to be interested in people too, to go on valuing those writings that they judge best help them to realize what the world is and what people are, to persist in distinguishing between those ideas, utterances, fictions and texts that they believe enlighten or deepen or enrich their minds and those that do not; and also persist in thinking that this is still a good ground for preferring some books to others. Moreover, I think that as we still face certain intractable questions, so they will too: the sort of questions, I mean, that people have always disputed most bitterly – whether with others, or themselves, or with the gods – precisely because they have to be answered and yet no answer to them can be known to be right. For the questions are not so much, 'What do we really know about the world and ourselves?' or 'What shall we do with what we know?' but rather, 'What is most important for us to know?', 'What is most worth our deepest and fullest attention, as having most bearing not only on what we are and do, but also on what we might become?'

Something like this, I take it, was what Bacon had in mind in saying that 'in this theatre of man's life, it is reserved only for God and Angels to be lookers on';[1] and what Arnold had in mind in saying, of the fundamentally 'moral' bent of English poetry, that 'a large sense is of course to be given to the term *moral*. Whatever bears on the question, "how to live", comes under it.'[2] It is also evidently what Johnson meant, repeating a point that is at least as old as Aristotle, in saying (apropos education in the 'Life of Milton') that 'we are perpetually moralists, but we are geometricians only by chance. Our intercourse with intellectual nature is necessary; our specu-lations upon matter are voluntary, and at leisure.'[3] In its context, Johnson's word 'moralists' is bound up with his particular kind of Christian faith, but his general point is not. People may or may not happen to understand geometry, or need to. They may choose to occupy themselves with science or not. But it is not a matter either of chance or of choice whether they are 'moralists' – at least in one basic sense of the word. For in *that* sense, being a 'moralist' is not a particular, dispensable activity of mind, nor a particular vocation or 'choice of life' (to use a key phrase from *Rasselas*). It is not even to live 'the ethical life' or 'the moral life'. It is to be alive as a human being among other human beings. In other words, the key fact is not moral *choice* in itself; it is rather the value-shaped, value-shaping nature of all inter-human mental activity. Choice is only one mode of such activity, one place on the whole spectrum of feeling, noticing, foregrounding, selecting, heeding, realizing, respecting, delighting, preferring, ranking, loving, valuing, deciding and all the other modes of reflective and unreflective judging. To regard people as 'perpetually moralists' is therefore to hold a certain view of human nature and of the status of certain questions. It is to see us as creatures necessarily engaged in intercourse with material nature, but no less so with intellectual nature – our own as well as other people's (living, dead and unborn), not to mention that of God and the angels.

Johnson, of course, would certainly have mentioned that of God. Just before the sentence I have quoted, he remarks that, for the 'great or frequent business of the human mind',

the first requisite is the religious and moral knowledge of right and wrong; the next is an acquaintance with the history of mankind, and with those examples which may be said to embody truth, and prove by events the reasonableness of opinions. Prudence and Justice are virtues and excellencies of all times and all places; we are perpetually moralists...

We today would hardly speak so confidently about 'religious and moral *knowledge* of right and wrong' or 'examples which may be said to embody *truth*'. We are more likely to think of moral judgments as 'opinions' and moral values as inter-subjective, or as having only a provisional objectivity and universality. But this area of moral probabilities, of the 'reasonableness of opinions', is all the ground that traditional criticism and the critical study of English literature require; and their footing in it is made no less secure by realizing that, if no intercourse with intellectual nature can be value-free, this also applies to what Johnson himself said about it or what I am saying about it now. All *that* means is that every one of us is in the same boat, and that even the most erudite, rationalistic, or speculative, supposedly non-evaluative 'literary science', for example, is as value-laden as *The Great Tradition* or last week's *London Review of Books*. Indeed, one could argue, as I would, that the values with which 'literary science' is laden generally prove to be drearily conventional, predictable, not to say complacent – and largely because they are disguised as 'science', *Wissen-schaft*, and not brought out into the open and argued for against other possibilities. Either that, or they prove no less drearily crude, not to say formulaic, no more than the unself-critical application of some theory, or public ideology, or 'ism'.

Similarly with attacks on any kind of authoritative 'centre' – on an established 'canon' of literature, for example, or on the very concept of 'literature' as something different from, and 'privileged' over, other writings. What the attacker sees as the imposition of an authoritarian, quasi-religious orthodoxy, is actually the necessary cultural process of sifting out those writings that retain interest and value for different readers at different times in different social formations.[4] And of course the anti-canonist is also taking part in this process, using the unmasking of 'values' – other people's values, that is – as an evaluative strategy. Anti-canonists are rarely without alternative texts or interpretations or judgments that we ought to find more interesting than the 'canon', more 'valid', more deserving of time and energy. In practice, they are no less perpetually and necessarily moralists than the rest of us.

All of this is obvious enough, I suppose, though it is worth reminding ourselves occasionally of the sense in which any traditionally critical study of English literature is, and must be, 'humanist'. Its central concern is with the human or moral significance of literature – 'moral' in every sense of the word, I would claim; and this is why critical evaluation, the judgment of such significance, is as essential a part of that concern as is understanding – the point being, in fact, that in moral thinking and discussing 'the reasonableness of opinions' in moral matters, understanding and evaluation are not separable, even if they are theoretically distinguishable.

Yet if all this is obvious, acting on it, or sometimes just saying it, is likely to produce an amazing degree of hostility from some academics, and not just from those with anti-'humanist' ideologies to push. They suppose that one must want literature – and criticism too – to be perpetually teaching or preaching some moral doctrine, or pronouncing stiff moral judgments, or pestering people with reminders that they are no better than they should be. Some academics seem to think that any interest in the moral dimensions of literature is merely a fashion that went out years ago. Others seem to believe that morality is essentially a matter of performing or refraining from certain external actions – a matter of visibly conducting oneself according to the code prescribed by God, or the Church, or the Law, or some other inscrutable (and usually patriarchal) authority, or perhaps by Utilitarian calculations instead. Where morality is conceived like that, it is hardly surprising if 'moral' becomes a 'dirty word' for many people.[5] But then why conceive morality and the sphere of the moral so crudely and reductively? Perhaps, as one philosopher has suggested, it is the influence of English philosophers like John Stuart Mill and G. E. Moore that is to blame; perhaps it is also the effect of English schoolmasters and American preachers. In any case, it is a surprisingly common conception of morality, and a surprisingly common attitude to the word 'moral', even now and even among people who might be expected to know better.

Sometimes, of course, this academic hostility towards evaluative judgment has powerful personal reasons behind it. It may well come from a deep and quite sincere lack of moral curiosity, for instance; or from a wholly authentic incapacity to *see* differences of quality, even between arguments, let alone works of literature. Then again, it may come from the kind of political zeal that regards any form of 'discrimination' as élitist or an assertion of mere 'privilege'; or from the kind of political faith that regards critical understanding and judgment as nothing but ideological warfare carried on by other means. Then again, the hostility may come from the warm, foggy 'pluralism' which supposes the critical study of literature to be only a matter of applying some preconceived 'approach' to it, and every 'approach' to be just as good as any other; and which therefore supposes critical evaluation to be merely 'the evaluative approach' or 'the moral approach' – one that unfortunately sometimes questions the 'validity' of other 'approaches'. Or the hostility to critical judgment may come from the kind of academic quidnunckery that supposes 'critical' thinking and keeping at the 'leading edge' of the subject consist in picking up 'ideas' from other disciplines, and then finding literature on which to apply these 'ideas'. Evaluation tends to be dismissed as naive, old-fashioned and not worth doing.[6]

On the other hand, it must be said that the ways of the righteous have not always been especially winning. Given the legal-religious (and highly questionable) conception of morality that has dominated our culture for so many centuries – the conception of it as a necessarily single, coherent, and objective system, with a higher authority than that of any individual, imperative in form and function, prohibitive and punitive in effect, applicable to everybody, and designed to ensure the best all round – it has always offered a useful and not unenjoyable opportunity for anybody who likes bossing people about, even if only himself. And of course, there has never been a shortage of volunteers. On the whole, their efforts seem to have contributed more to the history of mankind than to its righteousness; but one notable result of their good work has been a wide and persistent confusion between morality itself and the rigid and domineering style of some of its chief proponents. It would help reasonable discussion a good deal, for example, if we could always keep in mind the difference between being *moral* and being *moralistic*. The latter is a derogatory term; to use it is itself to make an adverse moral judgment about certain ways of being moral or certain ways of making moral judgments. In fact to describe someone as 'moralistic' is to make exactly the kind of moral judgment – the kind we cannot help making, whether we realize we are doing so or not – that illustrates how we are 'perpetually moralists'.

Related to this are some other pretty off-putting habits to which moralists are prone. One is identifying morality with the particular moral emphases of one's own society or class. There is something of this in Johnson, of course, and it is also quite obvious in Matthew Arnold, even in the essay on Wordsworth where he warns against it: 'Morals are often treated in a narrow and false fashion; they are bound up with systems of thought and belief which have had their day; they are fallen into the hands of pedants and professional dealers; they grow tiresome to some of us.' All too true, of course, even today. Yet Arnold evidently thinks that morals really consist in the specific duties and ideals he then spells out: 'You have an object, which is this: to get home, to do your duty to your family, friends, and fellow-countrymen, to attain inward freedom, serenity, happiness, contentment.'[7] Very worthy, no doubt, but it does sound rather like one of Her Majesty's Inspectors of Schools boarding the train after a hard week in Coketown. Certainly, as a summary of 'how to live', or as the basis on which to make moral sense of, say *Antony and Cleopatra*, it seems not wrong exactly, but too limited, too 'Victorian' or 'bourgeois', too bound up, as we might put it, with 'a system of thought and belief which has had its day'. But of course the kind of judgment we are making in saying this is one we all have to risk; even our own deepest thoughts and beliefs have to stand the siftings of time.

Another bad habit of moralists is to suppose that moral judgments must be, explicitly or implicitly, prescriptive – that is, tell us how to act. I say 'bad' habit because those people to whom morals have grown 'tiresome' do have a point – indeed, several points. For one thing, there are many personal predicaments, and many social, economic and political ones, that seem impossible to change just by applying to them prescriptive moralizing and the good deeds that might go with it. As some people see the matter, the only way to deal with such cases is to act in a suitably radical manner on their root causes, no matter how high the cost might be to various individuals – and to blazes with 'bourgeois morality'. And sometimes, perhaps, that is the best that can be done. Then again, even those of us who live in happier circumstances seldom feel so faultless that we positively want to be morally judged; and if we do have to be judged, we might well prefer to leave the matter entirely to God (if He exists – or come to think of it, even if He doesn't). There is probably no one who does not feel, sometimes at least, that the less we could hear about 'morals' and 'standards' and 'values', the better life would be. Yet if these are understandable attitudes, and sometimes thoroughly justified, they are hardly non-moral. On the contrary, they once again represent the sort of judgments – this time about the relative importance or value of certain kinds of moralizing in the whole fabric of human life – that makes us, willy-nilly, 'perpetually moralists'.

But there is another sort of reason altogether why people fear and shun moral judgments: they are bothered and confused about the nature and force of such judgments. Whenever they cannot apply a single, specifiable, objective and authoritative criterion (or set of criteria) along with clear-cut procedures of judgment – for example, the sort of commandments and procedures that Religion once supplied, and for which Science, Law, and Ideology now seem the only alternative sources – they become afraid to judge ('who am *I* to judge?'). On the other hand, they believe that the absence of any such specific, objective and authoritative criteria and procedures makes moral judgments entirely 'subjective' and therefore so easy to make that anybody can do it off the top of his head – or off the top of his 'feelings'. So why bother making them anyway, unless it is to lean on others? Thus any claim on people by standards higher than their own makes them either afraid ('what *authority* has the judge got?') or resentful ('who is *he* to judge, anyway?'), or most commonly a bit of both.

This is not the occasion to explore the jumble of moral attitudes and moral confusions that mark scientifically-advanced, secular, liberal-democratic societies in our time; but, given that jumble, it is not hard to understand why people try to reduce moral judgments – of situations, or people, or books, or whatever – as far as possible to some *other* kind of judging that makes them feel less uncomfortable. They try to turn judging moral issues into something like judging heights, for example, or (to take various other kinds of judging) something like judging horse-races, or gymnasts, or Persian cats, or washing-machines, or wines, or cricketers, or legal actions – that is, any other kind of judging that involves certain (either more or less) specifiable, 'objective' criteria and is capable of some (either more or less) definite and (either more or less) authoritative decision.

I suppose that everyone teaching the critical study of English literature has found as I have that one almost always has to try to untangle some of these confusions and fears in students before they feel able even to try to read and think critically for themselves. If you ask them for a literary judgment – what they make of a poem, for example – they will usually propose such absurdly high criteria for 'objectivity' that any judgment, moral, political or literary, is bound to fail the test. As teachers of political philosophy have also found, students need to be shown what is inadequate about the very subjective/objective dilemma that can freeze them rigid.[8] They need to see that literary judgment, like moral and political judgment, involves understanding much more than one can express verbally or even be fully conscious of. It also involves one's own qualities of character; a responsibility to, and commitment of, one's self; and a willingness to be part of a community – an ongoing social and cultural tradition or 'form of life' – to which one appeals for other views of the object, a similar concern for its nature, and that 'pool of criteria from which we draw justification for our judgments'.[9] Above all, I have found, students need to be reminded that, whether or not people can explain how they do it, they do somehow manage to judge political candidates or policies, for example, or religions, or possible marriage-partners, or friends, or social causes to commit themselves to and how far to commit themselves. Nor only these, but a host of other matters that involve conflicting and often incommensurable moral values, potentially endless debate about the 'reason-ableness' of any opinion, but not any single, clear, specifiable, indisputably 'objective' and authoritative set of criteria and procedures. For all one's fear, one can (and does) make such moral and critical judgments – in fact, one has to.

Such judgments do not (as is often supposed) depend on a set of abstract moral or political truths which is simply applied to the institution or situation being judged, so that the correct judgment can be read off by anyone capable of elementary deductions. Rather, they depend on, and bring into play, a more difficult capacity: what Aristotle called 'practical wis-dom', and many later writers (including Dr Johnson) called 'prudence'. Indeed, literary students might do well to read some of the classic accounts of political judgments, since the same applies to literary-critical judgments too. What they require is not a set of abstract truths about poems – a valid literary or critical 'theory' – which is simply applied to poems to produce a (or the) correct reading, but rather the equivalent of 'practical wisdom': what might be called 'practical criticism' if that term had not been annexed (probably irredeemably) by

a particular academic routine of minute 'explication' associated
with I. A. Richards and the American 'New Criticism' of a
generation ago. But the 'practical judgment' required by the
literary critic is 'practical' in the same sense as in 'practical
wisdom': the word signifies the same kind of rational but
unformulable process, the same kind of difficulty in developing
it and learning how to exercise it, and the same necessary
involvement in the long, continuous, many-stranded, pluralistic, and ever-changing 'conversation' (or debate, or 'form of
life') that is our socio-cultural tradition. Our participation in
that tradition is what enables us to understand language, which
is also to understand the various forms of human rationality,
speech and action; and it is that understanding which both
presses and enables us to evaluate, to form judgments. Thus, for
academics to reject 'practical judgment' in the study of English
literature is, to that extent, to shut the door on that socio-
cultural tradition – and to prevent students from entering it as
well. In fact, it is to 'politicize' not just culture, but judgment
itself – to replace it with conformity to some supposedly better,
more 'valid' (or 'pragmatic') ideology; and it is important that
we realize this as clearly as possible.

II

In speaking of the characteristic concern of English poetry with
'moral ideas', Arnold was clearly right to add that the term
'moral' here was not to be taken in a limiting sense,

because moral ideas are really so main a part of human life. The
question, *how to live*, is itself a moral idea; and it is the question which
most interests every man, and with which, in some way or other, he is
perpetually occupied. A large sense is of course to be given to the term
moral. Whatever bears upon the question, 'how to live', comes under
it.[10]

Arnold's echo of Johnson ('perpetually moralists') is perhaps
deliberate, but there are some characteristically Arnoldian
confusions in the way he handles the point. One is visible in this
passage itself. Inasmuch as moral ideas are a *part* of human life,
however 'main' a part (and Arnold's famous calculation

estimated that 'conduct is three-fourths of life'), then the term 'moral' *is* limiting. It has, we might say, a smaller sense, in that 'moral' ideas – presumably moral doctrines, considerations and values – are distinguished from other kinds of normative doctrines, considerations and values that also play a part in human life. In this smaller sense of the term, it might well be said that people are 'most interested' in asking the Socratic question, 'how to live', and in some way or other are 'perpetually occupied' in answering it. But in this case, 'interest' would mean conscious attention, 'perpetually occupied' would mean frequently explicitly engaged with, and 'moral' would mean whatever *answers* (or seems to answer) the question. As Arnold sometimes put it, the sphere of the moral in this sense is that of righteous action and conduct. On the other hand, if 'moral' in its large sense means whatever 'bears upon' the question, then 'interest' would also mean something like having a vital stake in the matter, whether one realizes it or not; 'occupied' would also mean implicitly engaging with the question and implicitly answering it, whether one realizes it or not; and 'perpetually' would mean always, and 'always' because engagement with the question is a necessary constituent of human life, whether one realizes it or not. After all, there is hardly any aspect of human life that, if we think about it, does not bear upon this question in some way or other. Thus in the smaller sense, it would not be a *moral* judgment to say that a man has the sensibility and taste of a Philistine; in the large sense, it certainly would be.[11]

Another, related, confusion in Arnold's thinking appears in a passage shortly after the one quoted above. He now begins to speak not of moral ideas in poetry, but of morals, without noticing his slide of attention or the difference it makes:

We find attraction, at times,... in a poetry of revolt against them [i.e. morals]; in a poetry which might take for its motto Omar Kheyam's words: 'Let us make up in the tavern for the time which we have wasted in the mosque.' Or we find attractions in a poetry indifferent to them; in a poetry where the contents may be what they will, but where the form is studied and exquisite. We delude ourselves in either case; and the best cure for our delusion is to let our minds rest upon that great and inexhaustible word *life*, until we learn to enter into its meaning. A poetry of revolt against moral ideas is a poetry of revolt against *life*; a poetry of indifference towards moral ideas is a poetry of indifference towards *life*.

Arnold seems to have let his mind rest rather too easily here. The sentiment he attributes to Omar Kheyam is certainly in revolt against the morals of an Ayatollah, say, or those of a Christian teetotaller; but considering what frequently happens when people spend too much time in mosques, we might well think it would be better for everyone if they spent it in taverns instead. In the long run, the drunk is probably less of a menace to the world than the fanatic. But in any case, the sentiment surely *is* a 'moral idea', whether we think it a good one or not. Similarly, with Arnold's conception of an 'indifference' to morals. As he himself tries to insist in this same essay, moral ideas are not only a matter of 'content', nor is 'style' ever morally null. Why then is a care only for 'studied and exquisite form' not itself a moral idea, even if one that usually amounts to no more than a vapid, self-conceited conventionality? It is one thing to say that, as human life is inescapably permeated with norms or values, a poetry hostile or indifferent to them is hostile or indifferent to life. Such a poetry might devote itself to describing the world scientifically, or to illustrating acknowledged Truth, in a rhetoric suitable to the occasion. It might inform us about Nature, for instance, or celebrate an eternal spiritual world transcending the imperfections and strife of the natural one. It might justify the ways of God, or represent the class-struggle, or illustrate the insights of psychoanalysis. All of these have provided material for what an earlier age called 'delightful teaching', and also for what our own age calls 'critical approaches', even if such poetry (let alone the commentary on it) generally leaves many readers feeling what Johnson felt about *Paradise Lost*: a 'want of human interest'. That is presumably what Arnold thought he was getting at, but it is something very different from identifying, as he actually does, 'moral ideas' with ideas in accord with a specific substantive morality, a particular set of moral ideals. To do this is to suggest that a particular moral outlook can be a critical criterion – an essential feature, and yardstick, of good poetry.

In effect, Arnold seems to make two quite false assumptions. The first is that 'moral' is not a *radically* problematical term. Whatever it is taken to refer to, Arnold supposes, must be compatible with what cultured and right-minded people (like you and I and Epictetus, say, but notably not Omar Kheyam) know to be good, right, worthy, serious and so on.

The second assumption is more fundamental. Arnold takes it as self-evident that moral conduct ('morals') is at least three-fourths of 'life', and that a poet who deals with moral matters (in the smaller sense of the term) is therefore dealing with 'that in which life really consists'. The right normative conception of 'life' is, for Arnold, pretty much that of a life focused on the question, 'how to live', and in effect answering the question with the right feelings, ideals, duties and actions. But there is a still further assumption. Since a 'truly human' life is one that instantiates a certain set of moral principles, even a certain moral doctrine (in the smaller sense of the term), so a 'true' – i.e. a normative – idea of everything encompassed by the term 'moral' in its large sense must, it is supposed, have the same kind of intellectual structure, and the same kind of constraining and prescriptive force for us, as do the principles of moral conduct. Indeed, the main moral idea with which English poetry has been concerned seems, for Arnold, to be this last idea itself: that since 'moral' life (in the large sense) consists predominantly in being or becoming properly 'moral' (in the smaller sense), there is a right conception of 'how to live', a correct ideal of human life, which has the same kind of prescriptive claim on us as do the principles of good morals. It is an idea that is likely to strike us nowadays as not so much moral as moralistic.

Interestingly enough, the passage from Johnson's 'Life of Milton' that Arnold seems to have been echoing ('perpetually moralists'...'perpetually occupied') also moves between the large sense and the smaller one, though with less confusion of the two. In the smaller sense, Johnson speaks of 'the religious and moral knowledge of right and wrong', of 'the principles of moral truth', and of the 'virtues' such as justice, all of which he distinguishes from plainly non-moral scientific knowledge on the one hand, but also, on the other hand, from 'axioms of prudence', 'opinions', and 'excellencies' such as prudence. But although Johnson does not recognize the large sense of 'moral' in his Dictionary, it is the sense in which we are all, whether we realize it or not, 'perpetually moralists'. It is also the sense in which Johnson himself was a great moralist. As he puts it here, our 'intercourse with intellectual nature' is not merely the frequent and the necessary 'business of the human mind'; it is also our 'great' business. In other words, the 'moralist' is a being who lives in a way that is distinctively, and therefore normatively, human. Moreover, as a person's 'intercourse with intellectual nature' engages, so it 'immediately' manifests, his or her 'moral and prudential character' – presumably in both senses of 'immediately': straight away, and without any mediation.

To be 'perpetually moralists' (in the large sense of the term) we require, of course, much more than the 'principles of moral truth' (in the smaller sense of the term). We require, in fact much more than Johnson allows here: the 'axioms of prudence', a knowledge of 'the history of mankind' to see 'by events the reasonableness of opinions', and sufficient 'materials for conversation'. True, Johnson here at least allows that a normatively human life includes conversation as well as action, and being 'pleasing' as well as 'useful'. Yet when he ends this passage by endorsing Socrates' 'opinion' – that 'we are placed here' (in this theatre of man's life, so to speak) in order to discover 'how to do good, and avoid evil' – the stress seems to fall predominantly on moral conduct in the smaller sense of the term. As Johnson puts it here, it would seem that our entire life as 'moralists', all of our 'intercourse with intellectual nature', is (or ought to be) dominated and shaped by the observance of moral right and wrong. Indeed, the value both of literature and of education can be virtually reduced to their specifically moral function: of informing and encouraging 'right' thought and conduct. For what is right socially and prudentially (i.e. in the large sense of 'moral') is also right 'morally' (in the smaller sense). 'Those authors, therefore, are to be read at schools that supply most axioms of prudence, most principles of moral truth, and most materials for conversation; and these purposes are best served by poets, orators, and historians.' This does not represent the whole of Johnson's conception either of human life or of literature, any more than it represents the whole of him as himself a moral being, a 'perpetual moralist'. But it does represent, as does the passage from Arnold, a persistent source of confusion in the traditional, humanist, moral view of literature and in the literary study based on that view: its need of both a smaller and a large sense of 'moral' so as to move between them.

III

This need is nicely illuminated by John Stuart Mill in his essay on Bentham (1838) – an essay interesting in this context for two reasons. In the first place, one of Mill's chief points in it is precisely the disastrously limiting effect of Bentham's emphasis on the 'moral' in the smaller sense, even while it is Mill's own shifting between a smaller and a larger sense of 'moral' that is one of the essay's chief points of interest for us. And in the second place, the essay, we might notice, is itself a notable piece of traditional, moral literary criticism, even though its subject was anything but an imaginative writer: that, indeed, being the nub of Mill's criticism.

A key passage of the essay is worth quoting at length:

He [i.e. Bentham] is chargeable also with another error, which it would be improper to pass over, because nothing has tended more to place him in opposition to the common feelings of mankind, and to give to his philosophy that cold, mechanical, and ungenial air which characterizes the popular idea of a Benthamite. This error, or rather one-sidedness, belongs to him not as a utilitarian, but as a moralist by profession, and in common with almost all professed moralists, whether religious or philosophical: it is that of treating the *moral* view of actions and characters, which is unquestionably the first and most important mode of looking at them, as if it were the sole one: whereas it is only one of three, by all of which our sentiments towards the human being may be, ought to be, and without entirely crushing our own nature cannot but be, materially influenced. Every human action has three aspects: its *moral* aspect, or that of its *right* and *wrong*, its *aesthetic* aspect, or that of its *beauty*; its *sympathetic* aspect, or that of its *loveableness*. The first addresses itself to our reason and conscience; the second to our imagination; the third to our human fellow-feeling. According to the first, we approve or disapprove; according to the second, we admire or despise; according to the third, we love, pity, or dislike. The morality of an action depends on its foreseeable consequences; its beauty, and its loveableness, or the reverse, depend on the qualities which it is evidence of. Thus, a lie is *wrong*, because its effect is to mislead, and because it tends to destroy the confidence of man in man; it is also *mean*, because it is cowardly – because it proceeds from not daring to face the consequences of telling the truth – or at best is evidence of want of that *power* to compass our ends by straightforward means, which is conceived as properly belonging to every person not deficient in energy or in understanding. The action of Brutus in sentencing his sons was *right*, because it was executing a law essential to the freedom of his country, against persons of whose guilt there was no doubt: it was *admirable*, because it evinced a rare degree of patriotism, courage, and self-control; but there was nothing *loveable* in it; it affords either no presumption in regard to loveable qualities, or a presumption of their deficiency. If one of the sons had engaged in the conspiracy from affection for the other, his action would have been loveable, though neither moral nor admirable. It is not possible for any sophistry to confound these three modes of viewing an action; but it is very possible to adhere to one of them exclusively, and lose sight of the rest. Sentimentality consists in setting the last two of the three above the first; the error of moralists in general, and of Bentham, is to sink the two latter entirely. This is pre-eminently the case with Bentham: he both wrote and felt as if the moral standard ought not only to be paramount (which it ought), but to be alone; as if it ought to be the sole master of all our actions, and even of all our sentiments; as if either to admire or like, or despise or dislike a person for any action which neither does good nor harm, or which does not do a good or a harm proportioned to the sentiment entertained, were an injustice and a prejudice. He carried this so far, that there were certain phrases which, being expressive of what he considered to be this groundless liking or aversion, he could not bear to hear pronounced in his presence. Among these phrases were those of *good* and *bad taste*. He thought it an insolent piece of dogmatism in one person to praise or condemn another in a matter of taste: as if men's likings and dislikings, on things in themselves indifferent, were not full of the most important inferences as to every point of their character; as if a person's tastes did not show him to be wise or a fool, cultivated or ignorant, gentle or rough, sensitive or callous, generous or sordid, benevolent or selfish, conscientious or depraved.

Connected with the same topic are Bentham's peculiar opinions on poetry... [H]is ignorance of the deeper springs of human character prevented him (as it prevents most Englishmen) from suspecting how profoundly such things [i.e. the arts] enter into the moral nature of man, and into the education both of the individual and the race.[12]

It is not quite clear whether 'the moral nature of man' at the end of this passage means only 'man's capacities for right or wrong action'; but assuming it does, we can take the whole passage as a claim for taking 'moral' in a smaller sense and as an illustration of that sense in operation. Given Mill's view of morality (which he partly shares with Bentham) it is not unreasonable to deal with the sort of qualities or dispositions of character listed at the end of the quotation – which are hardly matters of right and wrong conduct to be enforced by society – by removing them from the field of morality altogether and giving them some other name instead, like 'aesthetic' or 'sympathetic' for example. We may admire or dislike such qualities, but (on this view of the matter) they are obviously well outside the legitimate area of legal or religious compulsion.

Nevertheless, there are difficulties about restricting the sphere of 'moral' considerations thus far and no further. It is actually to claim (by a bit of pre-emptive definition) that the moral sphere ought not to extend any further – a claim that has some strategic point if we are considering, as both Bentham and Mill himself often were, the moral grounds of social – i.e. legal and religious – compulsion. But without that polemical and legislative intent in mind, it would seem more reasonable to distinguish (as Mill himself later tried to do, for example in *On Liberty*) different kinds of consideration and judgment and activity within the sphere of the 'moral', some of which are matters of right and wrong conduct, or dispositions to right and wrong conduct, while others are not. That is more persuasive than implying that, say, folly, ignorance, roughness, callousness, sordidness, selfishness and depravity, are not at all, as everyone supposes, 'moral' qualities but really 'aesthetic' ones – though certainly Mill is right to insist that we make judgments about such qualities. They are not, as Bentham supposed aesthetic matters are, just a matter of idiosyncratic 'taste'.

In any case, what else but 'moral' could we call Mill's own principle that 'the *moral* view of actions and characters...is unquestionably the first and most important', and that it is 'sentimental' to regard one of the others as paramount? This is hardly an 'aesthetic' or 'sympathetic' judgment. Then again, why is it not a 'moral' judgment to decide whether, and how much, a person is *worthy* to be admired, despised, loved and so on? More obviously relevant to literary criticism is the proper relationship between Mill's three modes of viewing actions, characters and sentiments. They are not only separable, he claims, but they ought to be kept separate. Yet one obvious effect of doing so is something like that 'dissociation of sensibility' between thought and feeling which T. S. Eliot saw as a moral and critical catastrophe, and of which Mill's own essays on 'What is Poetry?' and on 'The Two Kinds of Poetry' (1833) are perhaps the classic expression. On the one hand, Mill assumes, there is thought ('moral' judgments, for example), and on the other hand, there is emotion and feeling ('aesthetic' and 'sympathetic' reactions), the object being to combine them in an appropriate way. But if it is a moral precept that claims, as Eliot does, that we ought to *avoid* any such 'dissociation', it is no less a moral precept to say, as Mill does, that we ought not to 'confound' the three separate ingredients. Or to put the point more generally, what else but a moral issue is the manner and the extent to which we ought to be 'materially influenced' in any particular case by Mill's so-called 'aesthetic' and 'sympathetic' considerations?

Similarly, of course, with Mill's judgment on Bentham and other 'professed moralists', and with the conception of 'human nature' he uses in making it. Significantly, it is not clear whether Mill thinks Bentham (like other professed moralists) is 'chargeable' with the wrong action, the 'error', of 'entirely crushing' (by an act of choice) the 'real' human nature in himself, or whether Mill is here only repeating a point he makes several times throughout the essay, that Bentham's moral philosophy is 'one-sided' because Bentham's own nature was – that Bentham was a natural Philistine, simply unaware, blank, about certain kinds of things that human beings ought to be aware of and feel about, even if it is not a matter of their own choice or action whether they have the relevant capacities. Such capacities, we might add, do not make a man's character merely more 'beautiful' or more 'sympathetic' or 'genial'; as Mill insists elsewhere in the essay and suggests even here, they make him a better human being. Thus a person might be criticized for lacking them by nature, even though he can hardly be blamed or censured. All we might blame is his refusal to 'cultivate' them – supposing, that is, he had the capacity (as Bentham evidently did not) even to see what it was he needed to cultivate.

In other words, what renders Mill's restricted conception of the 'moral' finally inadequate in the passage quoted above is the very point he stresses ('in a spirit neither of apology nor of censure') earlier in the essay: that Bentham's error or one-sidedness lay *not* in confining himself to the 'moral' sphere alone, but in conceiving the 'moral' sphere itself in altogether too isolated and restricted a way.[13] Bentham 'recognizes no such wish as that of self-culture, we may even say no such power, as existing in human nature'. His philosophy 'overlooks the existence of about half the whole number of mental feelings which human beings are capable of, including all those of which the direct objects are states of their own mind'; consequently, it has nothing to offer concerning 'the nicer shades of human behaviour, or for laying down even the greater moralities as to those facts in human life which tend to influence the depths of the character … such, for instance, as the sexual relations, or those of the family in general, or any other social and sympathetic connexions of an intimate kind'. (So much for the clear separation of the 'moral' and the 'sympathetic'!) Even on the obviously social level, Bentham's philosophy 'will do nothing (except sometimes as an instrument in the hands of a higher doctrine) for the spiritual interests of society; nor does it suffice of itself even for the material interests'. What causes anything to *be* a society, Mill argues, is 'national character': it is this 'which causes one nation to succeed in what it attempts, another to fail; one nation to understand and aspire to elevated things, another to grovel in mean ones; which makes the greatness of one nation lasting, and dooms another to early and rapid decay'. (So much for the clear separation of the 'moral' and the 'aesthetic'!) In short, Bentham's philosophy can do little more than help with 'the merely *business* part of the social arrangements. Whatever can be understood or whatever done without reference to moral influences, his philosophy is equal to; where those influences require to be taken into account, it is at fault.' In this sense, Bentham's error was to suppose that the 'business part of human affairs' comprised the whole of the 'moral' – 'all at least that the legislator and the moralist has to do with'. It was not that he disregarded 'moral influences' when he saw them. Nor was it that he looked only to the 'moral' view of actions and characters 'as if it were the sole one'. It was rather that 'his want of imagination, small experience of human feelings, and ignorance of the filiation and connexion of feelings with one another', made him all too rarely *see* the relevant 'moral influences'.

In those judgments, Mill's use of the term 'moral' clearly shifts towards a large sense, and it does so even more in yet another key passage of the essay, where Bentham's error is now said to have consisted in 'overlooking' the 'moral part of man's nature, in the *strict* sense of the term [my italics] – the desire of perfection, or the feeling of an approving or of an accusing conscience', and in but faintly recognizing as 'a fact in human nature, the pursuit of any *other ideal end* for its own sake' [my italics]. It would seem that there is also a less strict sense of the term 'moral'; and it is hard to think what else but moral anyone reading Mill's list carefully would call them: the sense of honour and personal dignity; the love of beauty; the love of order; the love of 'the power of making our volitions effectual'; the love of action – i.e. 'the thirst for movement and activity'; and the love of ease. These, says Mill, are 'powerful constituents of human nature', which Bentham never adequately recognizes among his 'springs of action'; nevertheless, as Mill describes them, they are not just psychological 'springs', not just objects desired by men, but ideal – good, desirable, worthy to be desired – 'ends' or indeed forms of human life.

Even under the head of *sympathy*, [Bentham's] recognition does not extend to the more complex forms of the feeling – the love of *loving*, the need of a sympathising support, or of objects of admiration and reverence. If he thought at all of any of the deeper feelings of human nature, it was but as idiosyncrasies of taste, with which the moralist no more than the legislator had any concern, further than to prohibit such as were mischievous among the actions to which they might chance to lead. To say either that man should, or that he should not, take pleasure in one thing, displeasure in another, appeared to him as much an act of despotism in the moralist as in the political ruler.

Mill's point here can be generalized, I think: those who judge morally only in terms of particular actions and quantities of 'pleasure' will certainly be among those who will think an evaluative or prescriptive judgment about different kinds of pleasure is an act of despotism; and those who think *that* will certainly be among those who insist on the smaller sense of 'moral' as the only true one.

On the other hand, there are those who think that human nature, or any individual's entire mode of life, has a complex coherence, and that its value (and limitations) need to be discriminated in the operation of all the 'springs of action', in every end pursued, indeed in every form in which human nature, or a particular human's nature, manifests itself. For such people as these, the large sense of 'moral' is just as necessary and just as valid as the smaller one, even if they designate it by another term. Johnson's key phrase in *Rasselas*, 'choice of life', is such a term; significantly, Johnson constantly draws attention in the book to the fact that any mode of human life is not more 'chosen' than it is determined by the individual's nature and circumstances. The phrase that Mill used in the later editions of his *System of Logic*, 'the Art of Life', is another such term:

For the purposes of practice... there is need of general premises, determining what are the proper objects of approbation, and what the proper order of precedence among those objects.

These general premises, together with the principal conclusions which may be deduced from them, form (or rather might form) a body of doctrine, which is properly the Art of Life, in its three departments, Morality, Prudence or Policy, and Aesthetics; the Right, the Expedient, and the Beautiful or Noble, in human conduct and works. To this art (which, in the main, is unfortunately still to be created,) all

other arts are subordinate; since its principles are those which must
determine whether the special aim of any particular art is worthy and
desirable, and what is its place in the scale of desirable things.[14]

While we wait for this art of life to be perfected, we can only
practise it as best we can, of course, and it is worth noting what
it actually consists in. For although Mill here regards it as
having three departments rather different from the triad in the
essay on Bentham, it is in fact 'moral' evaluation that he means,
in just the same 'large' sense of the term as Arnold speaks of.
Indeed, with an eye to the ways that a Shakespearean drama –
Macbeth or *Coriolanus*, for instance – can enact a process of moral
thinking, it is worth emphasizing how natural and appropriate
is the term 'moral' for questions about 'the nobleness of life'.
And all the more so when Mill goes on to claim

that the cultivation of an ideal nobleness of will and conduct, should
be to individual human beings an end, to which the specific pursuit
either of their own happiness or that of others (except so far as
included in that idea) should, in any case of conflict give way...The
character itself should be, to the individual, a paramount end, simply
because the existence of this ideal nobleness of character, or of a near
approach to it, in any abundance, would go further than all things else
towards making human life happy;...in the...sense...of rendering
life, not what it now is almost universally, puerile and insignificant –
but such as human beings with highly developed faculties can care to
have.[15]

Mill's essay on Bentham is itself a piece of 'moral' criticism in
just this large sense of the word. It aims to characterize and
assess Bentham's moral significance as a thinker; and in order to
do this, Mill traces the 'filiations and connexions' between
every aspect of Bentham's activity as a moral being that seems
relevant: his theories, his perceptions, his feelings, his sensibilities, his sense of 'right' and 'wrong', and his fundamental
lack of human (or as we say, moral) imagination. In other
words, Mill's understanding and judgment of each aspect (or
element) of Bentham's thought, and his understanding and
judgment of Bentham as a whole – of Bentham as a particular,
unique human being living in a particular social and historical
context – continually inform and substantiate *each other*. The

result, in which Mill carefully traces out both Bentham's strengths and his limitations, is in its way a classic illustration of how a traditional moral literary critic might work. One of the best-known passages in the essay is the following paragraph, which nicely illustrates what Mill does on a larger scale in the essay as a whole:

By these limits, accordingly, Bentham's knowledge of human nature is bounded. It is wholly empirical; and the empiricism of one who has had little experience. He had neither internal experience nor external; the quiet, even tenor of his life, and his healthiness of mind, conspired to exclude him from both. He never knew prosperity and adversity, passion nor satiety: he never had even the experiences which sickness gives; he lived from childhood to the age of eighty-five in boyish health. He knew no dejection, no heaviness of heart. He never felt life a sore and weary burthen. He was a boy to the last. Self-consciousness, that dæmon of the men of genius of our time, from Wordsworth to Byron, from Gœthe to Chateaubriand, and to which this age owes so much both of its cheerful and its mournful wisdom, never was awakened in him. How much of human nature slumbered in him he knew not, neither can we know. He had never been made alive to the unseen influences which were acting on himself, nor consequently on his fellow-creatures. Other ages and other nations were a blank to him for purposes of instruction. He measured them but by one standard; their knowledge of facts, and their capability to take correct views of utility, and merge all other objects in it. His own lot was cast in a generation of the leanest and barrenest men whom England had yet produced, and he was an old man when a better race came in with the present century. He saw accordingly in man little but what the vulgarest eye can see; recognised no diversities of character but such as he who runs may read. Knowing so little of human feelings, he knew still less of the influences by which those feelings are formed: all the more subtle workings both of the mind upon itself, and of external things upon the mind, escaped him; and no one, probably, who, in a highly instructed age, ever attempted to give a rule to all human conduct, set out with a more limited conception either of the agencies by which human conduct *is*, or of those by which it *should* be, influenced.

IV

To see Bentham in that way is of course to see him morally, as distinct from historically, say, or psychoanalytically. The passage is directed, that is, to characterizing Bentham as a moral being – to defining the distinctive character of the person whose activities are to be seen as characteristic as well as important enough to prompt analysis and explanation from the historian, the psychologist, the sociologist, the legal or social philosopher, and so on. And I have spent so much time on Mill partly because he thus illustrates very clearly the kind of subject-matter and judgment that is moral-in-a-large-sense, and partly because he also illustrates the difficulty of replacing the term 'moral' here with a better one.

It might seem better, for instance, to call the moral-in-a-large-sense 'ethical', and keep 'morality' and 'moral' for the stricter sense. And it is true that the term 'moral' does suggest that there is some positive code of right and wrong conduct behind it somewhere, which is just the opposite of what its large sense is usually meant to suggest. Some philosophers have actually tried to use this ethical/moral distinction in their discourse, but so far it has not reached into non-professional discourse, and very possibly never will.[16] In ordinary discourse, the main distinction between the two terms seems to be that 'moral' is used in reference to the conduct of anybody and everybody, while 'ethical' is used in reference to the conduct of a particular profession. (As the cynic observed, when doctors lose their morals they tend to become all the more concerned with their ethics.) This is presumably why the ugly term 'ethicist' is coming into use for a moral philosopher employed by a hospital or some similar institution to advise on questions of specifically medical conduct. Ordinary usage simply does not support the distinction between 'moral' for the strict sense and 'ethical' for the large sense. It would only sound odd, I'm afraid, to speak of 'the moral and the ethical aspects of literature'.

Another possibility is to call any basic, general, moral-in-a-large-sense outlook a *Weltanschauung*; but this is no improvement

either. Quite apart from the obvious difficulty of naturalizing
the term into English at all, especially in adjectival form, the
fact that it is most easily translated by words like 'picture' or
'visualizing' raises an even larger difficulty. For it misses, or
catches too little, the extent to which a person's moral being is
realized and his or her moral values are manifested in forms of
activity. Such forms of activity include characteristic patterns of
motivation (the 'springs of action'), and the ways people feel,
speak, desire, work, respond, love – even the way their sensibility works – as well as the forms of their awareness, their
ways of 'visualizing' life, their characteristic 'picture' or
'vision' of the world. Thus it would hardly be adequate to say
that Mill, in the passage on Bentham quoted at the end of
section III above, is criticizing Bentham's *Weltanschauung* or
'picture of life', or that he is placing his own *Weltanschauung* or
'picture' over against Bentham's. 'He was a boy to the last':
that judgment, which is so finely pitched in tone and substance
(for a boy is not a wholly bad thing to be), is not a matter of
Bentham's 'world-picture', nor is such a term adequate to the
way that, as Mill actively ranges over various considerations, his
own larger moral activity not only defines and articulates, but
actually helps to validate, his crucial limiting judgment of
Bentham's.

There are difficulties too with another possible alternative to
moral-in-a-large-sense: 'spirit', as in the usage that distinguishes the spirit from the letter of the law, for example, or that
in which we speak of the spirit of a writer or the spirit in which
something is said or done. That is certainly part of moral-in-a-
large-sense; and yet 'spirit' becomes less rather than more
convincing, I think, as we ponder forms of it like 'spiritual', or
consider the fact that Mill's German translator rendered the
term, the 'moral sciences', as *Geisteswissenschaft*.[17] The trouble is
simply that both 'spirit' and 'Geist', for all that various
nineteenth-century writers used them in something like the
relevant sense, have contracted altogether too many dubious
metaphysical attachments elsewhere to form a happy marriage
of semantic convenience with 'moral' in the narrower sense.[18]

And yet, as we have seen, Mill's own term 'aesthetic', even

helped out with 'sympathetic', is no better. Given the human qualities he is concerned with in the Bentham essay, in the last chapter of his *System of Logic*, and (most especially) in *On Liberty*, 'aesthetic' actually seems rather odd, almost beside the point. It is true that, as Mill sees, certain human qualities can strike us as fine or noble. It is also true that we judge works of art – or at least works of literature – partly in terms of such qualities: a point that Bentham, of course, with his notorious 'opinions on poetry', could never grasp. It is also true that such judgments are not concerned, as Mill thought specifically 'moral' judgments are, only with assessing a particular class of actions and conduct, but rather, as one of his commentators has put it, with 'trying to visualize life in a certain way'.[19] And once more it is true that some imaginative literature (as Mill well knew from his own experience), together with what he calls elsewhere our 'artistic impressions',[20] can make us sharply aware of certain important qualities or aspects of human lives. Nevertheless, whatever 'aesthetic' and 'sympathetic' capacities are engaged by Mill's so-called 'aesthetic' judgments, and however such capacities are developed by art or literature, the kind of judgments he means are still value-judgments about personal lives and social *mores*, about more or less valuable ways of being human – about matters of such absolute seriousness, indeed, as to make this relegation to the 'aesthetic' seem almost bizarre. This is perhaps especially so nowadays, after Aestheticism has made 'aesthetic' usable precisely to *exclude* the sort of qualities and judgments Mill is concerned with. Indeed, to call these qualities and judgments 'aesthetic', as if people were somewhat like pots and poems, seems to me to get the point exactly the wrong way round. The truth, as I want to argue later, is rather that works of art – or at least, works of literature – are somewhat like people.

V

But Mill is not the only one to turn to the 'aesthetic' as a category for human qualities and judgments that do not fit happily into the writer's moral categories, nor is he the only one to assume in doing so a pretty curious conception of art and of literature in particular. Henry Sidgwick, for instance, was presumably following Mill in *The Methods of Ethics*:

It is, however, necessary to distinguish between the ideas of *Moral Goodness* and *Beauty* as applied to human actions: although there is much affinity between them, and they have frequently been identified, especially by the Greek thinkers. No doubt both the ideas themselves and the corresponding pleasurable emotions, arising on the contemplation of conduct, are often indistinguishable: a noble action affects us like a scene, a picture, or a strain of music: and the delineation of human virtue is an important part of the means which the artist has at his disposal for producing his peculiar effects. Still, on looking closer, we see not only that there is much good conduct which is not beautiful, or at least does not sensibly impress us as such; but even that certain kinds of crime and wickedness have a splendour and sublimity of their own. For example, such a career as Caesar Borgia's, as Renan says, is 'beau comme une tempête, comme un abîme'. It is true, I think, that in all such cases the beauty depends upon the exhibition in the criminal's conduct of striking gifts and excellences mingled with the wickedness: but it does not seem that we can abstract the latter without impairing the aesthetic effect. And hence I conceive, we have to distinguish the sense of beauty in conduct from the sense of moral goodness.[21]

This is somewhat less than persuasive to anyone who (like myself) remains sceptical about the need, the importance, or even the inner coherence of any such category as 'the aesthetic' or 'the beautiful', especially if it is conceived in such terms as Sidgwick's; and even more sceptical about moral theories that predetermine the existence and scope of something called 'aesthetic value'. All too often, 'aesthetic' theories require us to believe that such generic characteristics as are shared by, say, pots and poems must be more important than those that are not, which is a highly implausible story in itself. In practice, talk about the 'aesthetic' properties and 'aesthetic value' that pots and poems are supposed to manifest often seems, to a literary critic's eye, to amount to little more than some variety of formalism – a way of conceiving poetry that seems almost designed to evade the need or the effects of critical value-judgments.

With Sidgwick, for example, we can grant his general point

here straight away: to judge human actions or conduct
'beautiful' in his sense of *this* term is not the same as judging
them morally good in his sense of *that* term; nor is judging
them 'criminal' or 'wicked' the same as judging them as
'aesthetically bad' in his sense of the term. But granting this is
not at all to grant that our critical judgments of poems – works
of literature – are normally or properly expressed in terms of
more or less 'beauty' or more or less 'aesthetic value'. They are
not; they are normally and quite properly expressed in terms
of particular qualities; and once we start to specify what
is valuable about a particular work, the qualities we point to
are no different in kind from those we point to in making
value-judgments of human conduct or character.

Thus the 'splendour' and 'sublimity' of some criminally
wicked conduct is not, as Sidgwick supposes, an 'aesthetic'
quality, a kind of 'beauty', rather than a moral quality in a real,
if large, sense of the term. To treat such splendour or sublimity
as a merely 'aesthetic' quality rather than a moral one does
avoid an obvious threat of conflict within our moral thinking,
and many people find it hard to live with such unresolved, and
perhaps even unresolvable, inner moral conflicts. But if we
consider, say, Shakespeare's Macbeth as an example here, or his
Antony (in *Antony and Cleopatra*), avoiding conflicts within our
moral judgment of the character is really evading some crucial
moral aspects of the drama itself.

For one thing, Macbeth's 'striking gifts and excellences' (or
Antony's) are exhibited not just in his 'conduct', as Sidgwick's
phraseology would suggest, but also in the very way he sees and
feels and imagines. We are speaking of a quality of his whole
moral being. The same is true of Macbeth's 'criminality' and
'wickedness' or of Antony's weaknesses and vices; and it is also
true of each character's 'splendour' and 'sublimity', which are
qualities not just of his criminality or wickedness or vices, but
again of his moral being as a whole. Moreover, the drama in
each case is so deeply moving, indeed tragic, partly in its
bringing us to realize that the 'gifts and excellences' of the hero
(as also with other characters in the drama) are not just
'mingled' with wickedness or weaknesses in a merely unlucky,

contingent way. Nor do we ever seriously suppose that such human qualities are just an 'aesthetic' means used by Shakespeare for 'producing his peculiar effects'. Of course Sidgwick is right in implying that Macbeth's wickedness or Antony's weaknesses could not be 'abstracted' from the drama; but this is not because abstracting them would 'impair the aesthetic effect', whatever that means, but because it would completely nullify the very substance of the drama. The whole dramatic action brings us, forces us, to see each man's wickedness or weaknesses as related to his gifts and excellences in an obscure, but an internal and perhaps even necessary, way. All of the moral characteristics of each man, we come to realize, are symbiotic elements of his nature as the particular man he is – a being whose fitful splendour, even sublimity, is a *moral* property that is *morally* inseparable in him from wickedness or weakness. As for the 'aesthetic effect' of each play, that is basically our sense of the depth, clarity and energy of its moral insight – along with other qualities no less moral.

The category of 'the aesthetic' can serve to protect or to confine 'the moral' in other ways than Mill's or Sidgwick's, of course. A small recent example is an article 'On Aristotle and Thought in the Drama'.[22] This argues that while drama uses ordinary moral and metaphysical categories for its aesthetic purposes, its artistically 'worked world' is so different from the real world that within the aesthetic realm such categories are only '*quasi*-moral' and '*quasi*-metaphysical'. And indeed it is a mistake, one must agree, to regard drama – a Shakespearean tragedy, say – as philosophy speaking in examples. But once again, to grant this is not to grant what the article then claims: that the dramatic world is so distinct from the real one, that it is equally a mistake to regard the 'quasi-moral' and 'quasi-metaphysical' categories of drama as anything but formal. We should not, it seems, make the mistake of applying those 'aesthetic' categories directly to life – the mistake of supposing, for instance, that the lives of real people could have 'aesthetically ordered destinies and tragic flaws'. But why on earth not? – especially since we do not see such destinies as Macbeth's or Antony's as merely '*aesthetically* ordered'. Presumably, to think of real people in terms of 'destinies' and 'tragic flaws' is not really *moral* thinking; and neither it is – unless, that is, one understands 'moral' in a large sense. Indeed, unless it has a large sense, it is difficult to understand why we, as moral beings, should be interested in understanding human lives in this so-called 'aesthetic' way in the drama.

A similarly constricted view of 'the aesthetic' appears even in a more cautious philosopher, R. M. Hare, who regards the large sense of 'moral' in terms rather of a 'parallel' or a 'resemblance' with the 'aesthetic'.[23] The large sense of 'moral' he has in mind is that which refers to personal ideals, for example, and to the questions one might ask oneself in certain quandaries about 'what a man should *be*'. Such questions are 'very like aesthetic ones': 'it is as if a man were regarding his own life and character as a work of art, and asking how it should best be completed'. All the same, Hare insists, the parallel is no more than that: 'I think it is inadvisable to confine the term "moral" so narrowly' as to exclude such issues from its scope.

The problem about this, however, is Hare's conception of both 'moral' and 'aesthetic' questions. If, for example, one were to ask oneself the question 'what a man should *be*' as Macbeth and his wife do ask it, or again as the Prince asks it in Johnson's *Rasselas*, finding an answer (as these works make very clear) is not a matter of freely choosing among a number of objective, equally possible alternatives. This applies to art too. It would hardly have been a matter of choosing among objective, equally possible alternatives if, for example, Shakespeare ever did ask himself how *Macbeth* should best be completed, or Johnson *Rasselas*. As Hare says, the question can have many good answers if it is considered theoretically, but it is essentially a particular question for each person who asks it seriously, or for each literary work it is seriously asked about. To answer it seriously, therefore, may well be to realize what has brought one to ask it, to discover what inward need of meaning or understanding it represents; and to realize *that* is to realize that what one is seeking is already implicit in, or already determined by, what has gone before. In these cases, to answer the question is to find the 'logic' one can feel the presence of, but cannot yet quite grasp, in the whole span of one's life or in the whole span of the work requiring completion. Or to put it another way, a serious answer is not necessarily a possibility one can freely propose and select from among others, but rather a possibility one has to discern and realize: in a literary work, something rather like the completion of a sequential process of thought or argument; or in personal life, something like the discovery of a vocation (as it is, for instance, for Joyce's Stephen Dedalus in *A Portrait of the Artist as a Young Man*), the realization of a life-informing 'destiny' that one *has* to choose in order to be the only moral being that one can be.

This sort of point is not prominent in Hare's conception of the moral, even in its large sense, and it does not get into his disabling superficial conception of the aesthetic either. But while a good deal might be said about both conceptions, and none of it favourable about his conception of literature at least, it is hard not to conclude that his 'parallel' of the moral-in-a-large-sense with the aesthetic clarifies neither side of the parallel. It tends only to obscure what is not all that complicated anyway. For I think he is right about one distinctive feature of the moral-in-a-large-sense, but it applies directly to literature and traditional literary criticism as well. Where the moral-in-a-narrow-sense is concerned with regulating and judging human actions or conduct, the moral-in-a-large-sense is concerned with the evaluation of 'lives or men'.[24] It encompasses those principles and considerations engaged by the evaluation of lives or people that (in Arnold's phrase) 'bear upon the question, "how to live"', that (in Johnson's phrase) are required by 'our intercourse with intellectual nature', and that (in Mill's phrase) are necessary to any 'art of life'.

VI

Before taking the distinction between the narrow and the large senses of 'moral' any further, it is probably worth noting two or three other distinctions that in some respects are like the one I want to draw, but are not quite the same.

I want to distinguish between two different ways of con-

ceiving the subject-matter of moral thought – ways that underlie the differences between judging specific actions on the one
hand, and judging people or lives on the other. I use the term
'lives' in both a lateral sense – the whole span of a life through
time; and a vertical sense – the whole depth of a life as it is lived
at a particular time. I do not mean exactly the distinction Hare
draws 'between two distinct grounds on which we can commend
or condemn actions, one of which is connected with the interests
of other people, and the other with ideals of human excellence',
but both of which are properly called 'moral'.[25] It is not just
'grounds' of judgment that I have in mind; it is rather different
basic conceptions of a moral being – differences that are
psychological as well as social, for instance, and extend to the
very nature, scope and even point of the moral judgments we
might make, as well as to their grounds. Indeed, these different
conceptions apply to our sense of ourselves as moral beings,
which is perhaps why they may well seem to be not so much
different conceptions or perspectives, which can be changed at
will, as different aspects or dimensions of human life or of moral
beings. But I do not mean to tie my distinction to specific
moralities, for example, those that focus on the interests of other
people, or those that specify the 'true' and sufficient virtues or
excellences. I mean no more than different conceptual frame-
works (or different dimensions) that various moralities fill in (or
measure out) differently. Our judgments of lives or men are
connected with our norms and ideals of human excellence; and
the way we hold and use these norms and ideals raises questions
that are moral in the largest sense. The way that we judge
actions, on the other hand, may or may not be connected with
such norms or ideals, or with 'the interests of others', or with
maxims or a code of right and wrong conduct. My distinction
itself is not committed (I hope) to a particular morality or a
particular set of moral principles.

The distinction I want to draw is therefore not simply one
between (on one side) moral philosophies and judgments that
employ concepts of right and wrong, say, or obligation, or duty,
or happiness, and (on the other side) those that employ concepts
of human well-being, or virtues and so on. Both actions and lives

can be judged in any such set of terms, however morally adequate or inadequate we judge the judgment to be. (I take up this question again in the last chapter.) Nor is the distinction I want to draw quite the familiar one between a narrow and a broad sense of 'morality' – the distinction touched on by Hare, but described by another recent philosopher, J. L. Mackie.

In the narrow sense, a morality is a system of a particular sort of constraints on conduct – ones whose central task is to protect the interests of persons other than the agent and which present themselves to an agent as checks on his natural inclinations or spontaneous tendencies to act. In this narrow sense, moral considerations would be considerations from some limited range, and would not necessarily include everything that a man allowed to determine what he did.

As against a morality in this 'narrow' sense, a morality in a 'broad' sense

would be a general, all-inclusive theory of conduct: the morality to which someone subscribed would be whatever body of principles he allowed ultimately to guide or determine his choices of action... no-one could, in his choices of action, deliberately overrule what was his morality in the broad sense, though he might diverge from it through 'weakness of will'.

That is like a point made by Hare; and in much the same way as Hare, Mackie also thinks that

[t]here is no point in discussing whether the broad or the narrow sense of 'morality' is the more correct. Both are used, and both have important roots and connections in our thought. But it is essential not to confuse them, not to think that what we recognize as (in the narrow sense) peculiarly moral considerations are (jumping to the broad sense) necessarily finally authoritative with regard to our actions.[26]

The distinction I want to draw attention to is rather like this one – indeed, it overlaps it to some extent – but it is both simpler and wider. It is simpler in that it does not claim that moral considerations directed to *conduct* necessarily form 'a system ... of constraints', or have such a 'central task', or 'present themselves to an agent as checks on his natural inclinations or spontaneous tendencies to act'. It is wider in that it does not limit moral considerations only to those that are directed to 'principles' a person has deliberately 'subscribed' to, or has 'allowed ultimately to guide or determine his choices of action', but extends to such considerations as the agent's 'natural inclinations or spontaneous tendencies', to his or her activities as well as his 'choices' and 'actions', to the unchosen patterns as well as the 'principles' of those activities and actions, to his 'natural' virtues as well as those he has cultivated, and to factors he could neither have allowed nor disallowed but which also helped to guide or determine his activities and actions.

The point of drawing the distinction as I do is precisely to avoid the supposition that moral judgments are properly concerned only with human *actions*, even if the actions are as implicit and diffuse as Mackie's 'subscribed' and 'allowed'.

When we are morally assessing an agent we tend to discount things that it was not within his power to control. That we do so, it is plausible to say, is a distinctive mark of a moral assessment of an agent... In moral assessment, we may say, it must be entirely up to the agent whether or not he gets a high rating; in other kinds it is not.[27]

I realize that most people, including most moral philosophers past and present, would subscribe to this as a general principle. In practice, however – in dealing with particular lives or people – it is often overridden by a different kind of moral thinking: a kind which is quite common in Western culture but which very few people 'allow' (or disallow), mainly because they do not notice that they are using it. To hark back once again to the passage from Mill's account of Bentham quoted at the end of section (III) above: Mill's judgment there is entirely typical of countless such judgments all of us make about particular lives or people, even if it is also shrewder and deeper than most. Even so, I cannot see how it can be called an 'aesthetic' judgment, or a 'sympathetic' one, or perhaps a 'cultural' one, or some 'other kind', or anything other than a moral judgment on a moral thinker. But it is certainly not confined to Bentham's actions or 'choices of action', or to principles that Bentham could be said in any real sense to have allowed, proximately or 'ultimately', to 'guide or determine' his choices of action. Mill is concerned with Bentham's distinctive characteristics as a man, most of which did not derive from anything Bentham ever did or anything it was in his power to control (though they manifested themselves in what he did, as in other aspects of his life). Nevertheless, those distinctive characteristics are crucial in any evaluative account of Bentham's life, and consequently any evaluative account of his norms and ideals of human life and human excellence.

CHAPTER 2

'How *to live*' *and* '*how to* live'

I

'How to live': that is, how should we live, how is it best for us to live. In discussing Plato's phrase, Arnold left aside the particular nature of the claim that morality makes on us (as distinct from manners, say, or laws), but he did put succinctly the substantive question at the centre of moral thinking. On the other hand, he also managed to overlook a crucial ambiguity in the question. For it makes an important difference whether we emphasize the word 'how' or the word 'live': *how* to live, or how to *live*. Being perpetually moralists we ask both questions, of course; but to ask the former is to have in mind the moral-in-a-narrow-sense, whereas with the latter it is the moral-in-a-large-sense. With the former, we are asking about the difference between right and wrong (or good and bad) in human actions: that is, in what we call *moral conduct*; or between dispositions to, or habits of, right and wrong (good and bad) conduct: that is, in what we call *moral virtues and vices*; or between the sum total of a person's virtues and vices: that is, in what we call *moral character*. When we ask 'how to *live*' however, we are asking about the inner coherence of various modes of human life, and how to evaluate them *as* modes of life, individual or social; about the value of the manifold capacities, potentialities, wants and needs of human beings; about what is 'truly' human, or what the 'perfection' or 'well-being' of a life consists in, or what the finest and fullest modes of human vitality. And very often we are also asking about how such 'perfection' and 'vitality' can be realized: that is, about the truth of what the priest, the

36

prophet, the sage, the politician, the revolutionary, the psychoanalyst, or the guru, claims to teach us.

Since there are no agreed names for these two kinds of moral thinking, I shall take a couple from Arnold himself, and in particular from his famous calculation that 'conduct is three-fourths of life'. Sometimes he meant by this that conduct is *not more* than three-fourths of life, and that human perfection requires 75 per cent of righteousness plus 25 per cent of sweetness and light derived from Culture. At other times, he meant that the figure was *not less* than three-fourths, and that 'the sense of *life*, of being truly *alive*,... accompanies righteousness' – for three-fourths of the time, that is.[1] Whatever we think of Arnold's formula, the distinction between 'conduct' and 'life' does catch the distinction I want to draw between the moral-in-a-narrow-sense and the moral-in-a-large-sense. At its simplest it is no more than a difference in the primary object of moral consideration – though many people (including Mill, Arnold and George Eliot at times) have tried to make the distinction unnecessary by telescoping one sense into the other. But that is matter for another chapter.

Conduct-centred morality – or 'conduct-morality', as I shall call it from now on – is the more familiar of the two. Its primary object is the voluntary intentional actions of a moral agent; and it usually presents itself to the agent as an impersonal, regulative claim or imperative: that of the obligation of reason, or of duty, or of benevolence, or of maximizing happiness, or of altruism, or (as in Aristotle, for example) of *the* ideal virtues, or whatever else – different moral theories offer different accounts of the claim. Of its very nature, moreover, the claim is addressed equally to all agents; indeed, it is usually conceived as a set of universal principles, or a universal code of rules, or a universal 'Moral Law', which derives from God, or Reason, or the Nature of Things, or Human Nature, or from some other ultimate foundation.

Human beings cannot live in a society without *some* accepted code or principles of conduct-morality, of course; and in the codes and principles that European societies have drawn from the Bible and the classical world, one of the most important injunctions – perhaps, as some have thought, the central rule – is that one's actions should be regulated by a regard for others that is no less – perhaps even more – than for oneself. But in every age in every society, conduct-morality includes much more than this. It spreads out to cover a vast range of public, private, and intra-personal relationships, customs, habits and laws. And in every age in every society, people have naturally contested not only which actions morality enjoins or forbids, but also how far it properly extends; whether particular laws, customs, institutions, and actions are truly right or wrong (or good or bad); how people actually come to recognize the claims and principles of morality, and then come to follow them in conduct, and how they can best be brought to do this; – and so on. The disputes of conduct-morality are as various as they are inevitable; and if (as I suspect) the amount of moral indignation in the world is always pretty constant per head of population, the disputes are likely to be endless as well.

Life-centred morality – 'life-morality', as I shall call it – is also concerned with voluntary intentional action or conduct, but now it is conduct seen as part of the whole range of a person's active existence (or that of a group or a class or a society). Indeed, the very scope of moral attention now makes it seem possibly misleading to speak of a life-*morality*. The noun may suggest, not an 'art of life', but rather a craft of life – an already fixed code, a body of rules or ideals, to be always and everywhere followed throughout the *conduct* of one's life. Or it may suggest something like Dilthey's *Lebensphilosophie*, or a particular doctrine about seeking 'Life', or some large amorphous 'philosophy of life'. *I do not mean any of these.* Nor do I mean a quasi-Lawrentian conduct-morality that enjoins us to do what 'makes for life' or 'vitality' – as if it were self-evident that an ideal human 'life' or 'vitality' is what the moralist says it is, and as if we might choose instead to do what anyone can see makes for death. By a life-morality I mean a person's (or a society's) operative norms or ideals of 'human nature' or of human 'perfection' or 'a good life' or 'well-being'. In the terms of Arnold's question, it is what we should mean if we spoke of 'truly *living* our lives'. There are a number of familiar though competing terms for the substance of a life-morality.

But to speak of life-moral 'ideals' can be misleading as well. For one thing, Coleridge's remark about the art of poetry also applies to the art of life: 'Could a rule be given from *without*, poetry would cease to be poetry, and sink into a mechanical art.'[2] In other words, life-moral ideals cannot be formulated as a set of regulatory rules, which anyone need only accept and follow. This would betray their very point as ideals of *life*, which for most people includes much more than accepting and following rules. Sometimes life-moral ideals or norms are formulated in that way, however, but generally for a particular group or caste that chooses to live a special kind of life: monks, for instance, or Samurai, priests, English gentlemen, Brahmins, courtly lovers, and so on. In these cases, people choose to identify living with conduct. They also choose to identify life-morality with a specific ideal, and to identify the ideal with a 'rule given from without' which needs only to be accepted and obeyed.

But there is also another way that speaking of 'ideals' can be misleading. If it is not sufficient for poetry to follow a rule given from without, neither is it sufficient to imitate a *model* given from without. Many apparently life-moral ideals are really a supposedly sufficient set of conduct-rules that are amalgamated and exemplified in an ideal figure, to whom everyone should approximate as closely as possible. As I shall argue in a later chapter, the difference that such ideals ignore – the difference between a person living his or her life, and a person trying to imitate an exemplary model – is crucial in understanding the moral dimensions of literature. For certain kinds of literature do present us with exemplary models: idealizing stories or biographies, legends, fables, parables, allegories, utopias, masques and so on. These set out to depict what one philosopher, P. F. Strawson, calls 'ideal images' or 'pictures' of 'a human life, or of human life', which can be taken as 'the core and substance of a personal ideal' of a 'form of life'. But as Strawson points out, such ideals can 'capture the ethical imagination' in various forms of discourse: as 'general descriptive statements about man and the world', for instance or as 'incorporated into a metaphysical system', or as 'dramatized in a religious or historical myth', or as the 'truths' of such unsystematic moralists as 'Pascal or Flaubert, Nietzsche or Goethe, Shakespeare or Tolstoy'. At some times, such a picture or ideal

may present itself as merely appealing or attractive; at others it may offer itself in a stronger light, as, perhaps, an image of the only sane or non-ignoble human reaction to the situation in which we find ourselves. 'The nobleness of life is to do thus' or, sometimes, 'The sanity of life is to do thus': such may be the devices with which these images present themselves.

And, Strawson argues, it is 'this readiness, which a great many people have, to identify themselves imaginatively at different times with different and conflicting visions of the ends of life ... which partly explains ... the enormous charm of reading novels, biographies, histories ...'.[3]

But Strawson's allusion to Shakespeare's *Antony and Cleopatra* ('the nobleness of life is to do thus ...') is more to the point here than Strawson perhaps sees. The dramatic action of the play does not present us with an 'ideal' figure (Antony) that serves to show us that the nobleness of life is (or on other interpretations of the play, is not) doing 'thus'. Strawson's point, of course, is not that the play does do this, but only that anyone may take 'nobleness' as an ideal, as it was taken so by Shakespeare's Antony. Nevertheless, the play's dramatic action does bear pretty directly and critically on the key terms here. For one thing, it brings us to regard any such distinction as Strawson's, between the personal ('ideals') and the social ('rules'), as pretty shaky, to say the least. The outcome of battles, for instance, the history of Rome, indeed the history of the world, all of which are social enough, turn on the 'ideal', the 'form of life' that Antony represents. For another thing, Strawson's term 'image' seems inadequate. The dramatic action of *Antony and Cleopatra* brings us to see *any* 'form of life', Antony's or those of other characters, as a matter of a person's physical existence as well as his or her social existence and his or her mental, self-directing existence as a moral agent. Any account of Antony's 'nobleness of life' has to include his so-called 'natural' virtues as well as his 'moral' ones; his sensory capacities, desires and pleasures as well as his mental ones; his characteristic style of speech and of command; the facts of his aging; the sheer force of his presence; and so on. It is his mode of *life* that we are trying to characterize; and such a term as Strawson's 'image' or 'picture' seems too static, too flat, for our accumulating sense of dynamic, unpredictable natural and psychological forces at work in Antony, of natural energies released in him and gradually exhausting themselves over time, which are essential elements in our sense of him as a mode of life. But two other facts about the drama are even more important here.

One is that it does not give us in Antony simply an image of nobleness (or the lack of it). Rather, it explores and *questions*, in the very process of presenting him, what 'nobleness of life' might appear to be in him (or fail to be) as he is seen by this and that character in the play; it explores what, to this and that character's eyes, the 'thus' is exactly; it explores what 'life' can (and cannot) be to these or those eyes, and what it might be to us, who see the life *in* this and that way of seeing. The second important fact about the drama follows from all of this. The sheer physicality of the drama – in its language, its movement, its noise and silences, the presence (and absences) of its characters, the varying speed of its plot and so on – makes the term 'ideal' seem rather too intellectual, too mental, for what it presents us with. The term has too much of the philosopher's stamp on it. It suggests that life-moral 'ideals', while they may be embodied (for the purpose of 'attracting' us) in artistic 'images' and 'pictures', can quite readily and quite properly be formulated in general, abstract, and perhaps even propositional terms. More than that, however, the term 'ideal' can also suggest that life-moral 'ideals' are, or could be, *conscious* ideas or images to the fictional character who supposedly exemplifies them, just as they can be for us who respond to the character and try to define him or her as a mode of life. Yet if *Antony and Cleopatra* forces any moral point on us, it is the vital difference between acting in accordance with a conscious 'ideal' of nobleness, and actually being noble. In the former case, nobleness tends to become an ideal of conduct, a set of dos and don'ts, which in its turn tends to stultify the very thing it seeks to realize. For unlike conduct-moral ideals, life-moral ones exist in the whole texture and rhythm of a life – for example, in that 'interpenetration of passion and of will, of spontaneous impulse and of voluntary purpose', which Coleridge thought characteristic of poetic life.[4] In short, the life-moral ideals a man represents to others are not likely to be only those he is conscious of seeking – nor even, perhaps, will they include them at all.

To put the point another way, a person's actual, operative life-moral values are not normally held or formulated explicitly by the person himself, even if they include ideals or norms he does hold explicitly. Indeed, outside the teachings of religion, of philosopher-sages, gurus, and so on, life-moral ideals or norms are generally unspoken, implicit in actual forms of life, personal and social. Moreover, given any degree of cultural complexity in a society, such ideals or norms are bound to be various, sometimes even incompatible, embedded in very different modes of life, and appearing openly in people's relative preferences and their delicate mutual adjustments of values, rather than in clear-cut, black-and-white choices or decisions. The spirit of the life-moralist is consequently rather different from that of the conduct-moralist. When the conduct-moralist becomes merely moralistic, for example, he or she usually becomes self-righteous, not to say sanctimonious – something of a prig. When the life-moralist becomes merely moralistic, however, he or she usually becomes an ideological zealot – something of a fanatic. (Some people manage to become both, of course.) Similarly, if the conduct-moralist is merely superficial or formalistic, he tends to identify morality with social respectability; if the life-moralist is, he tends to identify morality with social good manners or fashion or 'style'. And of course once again some people manage to be both: as Dr Johnson said of Lord Chesterfield's *Letters*, 'they teach the morals of a whore, and the manners of a dancing-master'.[5]

Another important difference between conduct-morality and life-morality is in the generality of the main objects of attention. The main object of conduct-morality can be specified quite satisfactorily in very general terms: it is this or that kind of action or conduct, a kind for which we have a general name, as performed at any time in any place by any moral agent – keeping promises, for example, or malice. The main object of life-morality, on the other hand, can usually be specified satisfactorily only with some reference to the particular historical, social, and cultural conditions that make it a unitary mode of life rather than a mere sequence of actions and events: it is such and such a life lived within these or those particular social institutions, practices, beliefs and attitudes, for example, and within these or those personal, sexual and familial relationships.

As with conduct-morality, every society and every age in European civilization has naturally disputed the substance of life-morality, but the main questions are different from those of conduct-morality. What does a truly 'human' life consist in? – or a truly 'civilized' one? or a truly 'polite' one? What are the distinctive elements of human nature, and the kinds of 'good' it seeks? What are the most valuable qualities of this or that human being? How are the 'natural virtues', qualities, capacities, needs and values of a human being to be ranked in importance? What is the best mode of life possible for this individual, or for this society, given these and those constraining circumstances? What place should conduct-morality have in a life? Are the finest possibilities of a human life actually incompatible, except perhaps in the 'play' of imagination? How far does a person's moral consciousness enable or limit their realization? How many various possibilities of life can this or that person realize without disintegrating; how few without withering? How is a moral self to be located among all its possibilities of life, those realized and those that remain partly or entirely unrealized? – And so on. Disputes about how to *live* are just as inevitable and endless as those about *how* to live.

It is worth noting, incidentally, that the existence and the nature of such life-moral disputes do support Arnold's basic point about Culture – or rather, the basic point he fumbled. The operative terms and content of our life-moral thinking are created in, and by, Culture as well as Religion – Culture not quite as Arnold thought of it, however, as a given and authoritative corpus of 'the best that has been thought and said in the world', which we need only 'get to *know*'.[6] What he should have meant is rather the process, and the results of that process, by which people in their own times and places are perpetually discovering and re-discovering, judging and re-judging, what *is* the best that has been thought and said – and created – in the world. In other words, the moral import of Culture is not just the sweetness and light it can add to our religiously-based righteousness. It is the content we find we can give to life-moral terms like self, nobleness, grace, heroism, fulfillment, human dignity, moral intelligence, moral courage, greatness of spirit, unity of being, maturity, joy, imaginative power, genius, mediocrity, meanness of spirit, maiming, nar-rowness, alienation and so on. And along with all this it is also the content we find we can give to the moral language – the terms of what some philosophers rather sniffily refer to as our 'folk psychology' – in which we speak and dispute about such matters.

Any actual conduct-morality is (to say the least) likely to have implications for life-morality, and vice versa. The two are often in what we might call a drunken-sailors' relationship, each incapable on its own but propping the other up as they stagger back to their ship. And it hardly needs saying that for most of us both kinds of morality are necessary. If we require an acceptable conduct-morality to be part of any acceptable life-morality, we similarly require an acceptable life-morality to complement conduct-morality. The former requirement leads us to object to certain life-moralities: those that involve the exploitation of other people, for example, or those of antinomian cults, whether their emphasis be religious, political, artistic, or all-round Nietzschean. For such cults, man's sole good *and* his sole duty is to be 'illuminated', or nobly 'free', or 'authentic', or 'creative', or 'vital', or 'revolutionary', or whatever; and what he does apart from expressing or realizing this life-morality is, morally speaking, a matter of indifference. The objections to this, of course, are those we make to any immoralist or amoralist. On the other hand, we also object to those who regard conduct-morality as sufficient in itself, as Mill objected to Bentham's moral blanknesses and Arnold to those of the righteous British philistine. Those blanknesses, as Mill and Arnold quite rightly (and, alas, still appositely) argued, are really human imper-fections, which show themselves as a carelessness about matters that people are better for caring about and judging well. In fact, even if one cannot do much about such imperfections, they amount to a kind of immorality: the kind that debases feelings or deadens consciousness.

But although we require any adequate life-morality to accommodate an adequate code of conduct, and any adequate conduct-morality to accommodate some adequate normative conception of human life, the precise inter-relationship between the two is not at all obvious. In fact, it is seen differently from within different moralities and different theories about moral-ity. As some see it, for example, what I call conduct-morality is grounded in what I call life-morality. For others, it is vice versa. For others again, they have only a contingent social or psychological connection. To some people, they are merely different ways of making the same basic recommendations; or merely different shades in the one moral spectrum; or merely different functions of the same moral system; or correlatives, held together by the actual content of a moral system. Most of us nowadays, I suppose, see the matter pretty much as Bernard Williams does:

I am far from thinking that considerations about human nature, what men are, what it is for men to live in society, do not contribute to a correct view of morality. Of course they do: one could not have any conception of morality at all without such considerations. In par-ticular, they help to delimit the possible content of what could be regarded as a morality. Just as obviously, differing views of human nature (as, for example, some psycho-analytical view) must have differing effects on what views one takes of particular moral requirements and norms. Not merely scientific or semi-scientific views must have this effect but also views in the philosophy of mind. Thus a proper philosophical understanding of the nature of the emotions should have a discouraging effect on Manichean views about their management, and philosophical considerations about the nature, indeed the existence, of something called the will must have a direct

effect on moralities which find in the exercise of the will (against the
desires, for instance) a central clue to moral worth.[7]

To the scientific and philosophical insights Williams mentions
here, we certainly need to add artistic and cultural insights too;
but even as he puts the point, it suggests one reason why the
meaning of 'moral' has extended, since the eighteenth century
at least, to 'whatever bears on the question, "how to live"'. It
has come to denote, that is, whatever pertains to characteristically human behaviour which (directly or indirectly)
comes within the scope of normative conceptions of human
nature or human life.

Most of us, I suppose, are probably, like Williams, life-moral
pluralists as well. As he goes on to say,

> there is no direct route from considerations of human nature to a
> unique morality and a unique moral ideal. It would be simpler if there
> were fewer things, and few distinctively human things, that man can
> be; or if the characters, dispositions, social arrangements and states of
> affairs which men can comprehensibly set value on were all, in full
> development, consistent with one another. But they are not, and there
> is good reason why they are not: good reason which itself emerges from
> considerations of human nature.

But leaving aside the philosophical issues here, there are some
important implications in all of this for literature and traditional
literary criticism that are worth noticing.

II

In the first place, it is obvious to us, as it was not obvious to
earlier periods, that the traditional accounts of human nature
have had their normative elements built into them, and into
their psychologies and moral language, from the start. Nevertheless, this does not mean that we ourselves can think morally
without some such normative conceptions. It only means that
we need to be aware that we have normative conceptions –
conceptions that embody a vast range of judgments about what
we find to be the best that has been thought and said in the
world, and that engage the subtlest, non-conscious values of our
lives as well as the values we know, or discover, we believe in.

A second implication for literature and literary criticism is that in every cultural period, including our own, life-moral ideals and norms tend naturally to converge, to hold together for mutual support. As E. H. Gombrich has pointed out, psychological needs and moral values, personal and social, are usually so 'intertwined' with 'aesthetic taste' – that is with critical evaluation – that each aspect of life becomes the source of normative terms (usually metaphors) for the others. Indeed, all such values, he suggests, 'spring from that living centre where the "good", the "clean", the "noble", the "true", the "healthy", the "natural", the "sincere", the "decent", are but the facets of one untranslatable experience of a plenitude of values that speaks to the whole man – as great art has always done'.[8] Gombrich directs his argument to the *content* of life-morality from age to age, and in particular to the way that changes in critical evaluation have reflected the value that different ages have placed on the restraint of easy sensuous and emotional gratifications; but his point about the 'convergence of values' applies generally. All through the history of European civilization, every society and cultural period has tried both to distinguish and to reconcile opposing norms and opposing 'ideas' of the kind that A. D. Lovejoy traced in his book *The Great Chain of Being*. This is why the opposition Lovejoy saw between 'otherworldliness' and 'this-worldliness', for example, ramifies much further than he remarked, and tends to group ideals and norms into opposing sets. Not only has the One been set against the Many; order against plenitude and diversity; peace and concord against competition and strife; universal reason against individuality and idiosyncrasy; and so forth. Because these 'ideas' have all had life-moral import, they have been accompanied by other opposites. The natural has been set against the artificial; the simple against the sophisticated; the civilized against the barbaric; the noble against the vulgar; force against elegance; contemplation against action; retirement against public life; country against city and court; the individual self against the fragmentations of society; self-sufficiency against involvement and dependence on others; self-preservation, withholding, against giving and self-consumption; 'character' against sensibility; sincerity against prudence, tactfulness, accommodation; the integrity of the self against fluidity and the manifold potentialities of the self – the capacity (which Coleridge saw in Milton) to 'attract all forms and things to himself, into the variety of his own IDEAL', against the capacity (which he saw in Shakespeare) to 'dart…forth, and pass into all the forms of human character and passion, the one Proteus of the fire and the flood'.[9] As Lovejoy suggests, each opposition has usually been taken as exhaustive of all the possibilities, and the writer (or the age) has usually valued one term over the other, or tried to reduce one to the other, or tried to transcend the opposition between them. But it is also true, and no less significant, that the oppositions themselves have usually been taken as an inter-related *set*. And each set has seemed more united, more coherent, precisely to the degree that a 'truly human' life has been regarded as morally one and indivisible.

Yet another implication relevant to literature and literary criticism is that, as we need both conduct-morality and life-morality, so we must be prepared to move mentally from one to the other and back again – not confusing the two, or privileging one over the other, but recognizing the place of each in our moral thinking and judgment. We need two different eyes with which to judge distances well, and two different legs with which to get from one point to another. Moral insight and the process of moral thinking are sometimes rather like that too – though not always, of course, nor perhaps even most of the time. Arnold may have been right in estimating that three-fourths of the moral issues we find ourselves engaged with are matters of conduct; perhaps he would have been more obviously right in his own day. But certainly many moral issues are issues of right and wrong (good and bad) actions, choices, or decisions; or matters of duty or responsibility; or of moral virtue or character; or of moral agents following (or not following) specifiable principles or rules in their voluntary intentional conduct. Certainly, this is the sort of issue with which moral philosophers often illustrate their theories and arguments. But sometimes the issue we have to judge and act upon is not like this; and in these

cases, the usual sort of examples discussed by moral philosophers, or the exemplary models they set before us, are very
much less helpful than, say, a drama or a story or a poem can be.

Indeed, considered from this standpoint, some moral philosophy seems a relaxing, if charming, kind of light fiction. It
enables us to enjoy the niceties of moral discrimination and
argument, and with none of the distracting bewilderments and
strains of our ordinary moral lives. It transports us to a world
where all the relevant circumstances of a moral problem can be
laid out quite definitively; where the moral issues can be
pinpointed unmistakably, and the range of choices fully
specified; where people's feelings, motives, desires and intentions (including the agent's) can all be accurately known,
named, and so evaluated with assurance; where people's
characters, human virtues, even human dispositions, present
themselves with the correct labels already attached to them;
and where the agent's thoughts can remain undisturbed even by
the possibility of far-reaching, perhaps dismaying, implications
in the issue for his whole sense of the world, of other people, of
himself, or of the relationships between these.

In 'real life', as we say, it is not always so agreeably simple.
Even with many conduct-moral issues, we often find ourselves
having to judge not one issue, but a complex tangle of issues
which is intractable to analysis and reduction, in which every
aspect is radically connected with all the rest, in which our own
relationship with the issue may itself be a major problematical
factor, and in which all the key judgments seem to be about the
most basic things of all. What, among all the various beliefs,
actions, claims, desires, intentions, ends and even the tones of
voice and personal manners of the people concerned, are those
we ought to evaluate? Which, among all the manifold circumstances, are those we should regard as most important?
Why? Should we judge this or that aspect at all? Do the issues
exist for the people concerned (including ourselves) in the way
they do only because each is the particular person he is – and if
so, should one be that sort of person? *Can* one be another sort of
person – and if not, what difference (if any) should this make?
In what sort of terms should we conceive the people involved,

not to mention their attitudes, motives, dispositions and characters – in the sort of terms that, say, Plato might have recognized, or Nietzsche or Jane Austen, or Aquinas, or William Blake, or Freud? What is the best way of reasoning about this situation – if any ethical philosopher or teacher can help us here, for example, which of them should we consult? Should we not perhaps alter or qualify our own basic attitudes, about the world or other people or ourselves, in the face of this situation? Exactly how much weight ought we to give this aspect or that, this value or that – and in any case, should we treat them as commensurable? How should all these questions and considerations be related to one another? And so on, and so on.

I have in mind here the kind of questions that present themselves in morally understanding and judging something like the situation in the first scene of *Antony and Cleopatra*, for example, or in the first scene of *King Lear*. And yet even those are simpler than many of the things we have to judge in reality. It may be that many of the questions that crowd in on us are analytically reducible to simpler ones. Nevertheless, the situation we are judging is not reducible to anything simpler – except, that is, by a specific judgment on it: as something (for example) that we *ought* not to regard as a single entity, but only as a mere bundle of features requiring only a series of different kinds of judgment, 'moral', 'aesthetic', 'sympathetic', social, psychological, political and so forth. In other words, although many of the issues we are faced with seem to be conduct-moral ones, the key issues are often life-moral ones, and our basic problem is to form a moral judgment that answers to the intrinsic *inter-relatedness* of all the features and aspects of the object being judged – that is, to judge something which inevitably engages our normative conceptions of human nature or of human life in its inter-relatedness.

Many of the things we make moral judgments about are of this kind: not just states of affairs (like a lovers' morning-after, or a family crisis, for example), but the state of a society, or a political system, or a religion, or a culture, or a moral code, or a philosophical 'stance' (like Bentham's), or an individual's entire life, or his or her distinctive mode of life. Thus what we choose as the salient characteristics of a mode of life, for example, or what we decide is its 'essence' or 'spirit' or 'soul', and how we describe it, are themselves major parts of our judgment. The very terms of our description and analysis are often what are decisive in our thinking and judgment, and therefore most contestable. Nor can we decide in advance what considerations will or will not enter into our thinking and judgment. The process may well engage our psychological conceptions, and metaphysical ones, and social, cultural, anthropological, political, religious ones and so on; it will certainly engage our conduct-moral ones; and in addition to all these, it will quite directly engage our conceptions of how all these are inter-related. Our judgment, embracing (as it must) many if not all of these, and directed at an object conceived as also morally indivisible, cannot but express a life-morality.

However indirectly, all of our life-moral judgments involve our conceptions of what human nature and human life *are* (as well as what they should be) – 'descriptive' conceptions, that is, which need to be at least plausible, not demonstrably false or inadequate. This is why it is important, especially with literature and literary criticism in mind, to remember as well something that Peter Winch has pointed out:

Putting the matter briefly, and therefore, over-crudely, what I want to say is this: what we can ascribe to human nature does not determine what we can and what we cannot make sense of; rather, what we can and what we cannot make sense of determines what we can ascribe to human nature. It is indeed precisely for this reason that the concept of human nature is not the concept of something fixed and given; i.e. the reason for this is a philosophical, not a sociological one.[10]

The point is well taken, though people in every age have tended to overlook it – including literary critics. Moreover, it helps to explain why 'moral change' (or 'moral development') can mean two different things. When the conduct-moralist is concerned to change people's moral attitudes it is usually because he or she believes that the principles of right conduct, which involve a fairly stable conception of human beings as moral agents, really apply (or really do not apply) to certain kinds of action that were previously supposed to lie outside them: to owning slaves, for instance; or to the way one treats employees or the mentally ill or minorities; to censoring speech or writing; to the disposal of waste materials; to bear-baiting, or to wearing swords. When the life-moralist is concerned to change people's moral attitudes, however, it is usually because he or she believes that various aspects of human experience 'make sense', cohere, in ways not previously seen, and that this coherence so alters our conception of what human beings *are* that it alters our conception of what the full, or best, or most perfect, or most adequate, or most proper, realization of human nature may consist in – what 'life' in its normative sense properly includes and assimilates.

In other words, the life-moral reformer is concerned to change the very terms in which we think about people or human life. He or she introduces new principles into our mental universe, as it were – as with terms like righteousness, for example, or *hubris*, or *caritas*, to mention only some of the oldest in Western culture. There are a great many others, however, each of which expresses and enables a particular way of 'making sense' not just of what people are, but of what they should be. For example, the word 'heart' as Shakespeare uses it in *King Lear* and in *Antony and Cleopatra* is such a term; so is 'nobleness' in the latter. And like all the important terms of life-moral discourse, it cannot be wholly reduced or even fully translated into other terms – though we may have to try to translate it in 'making sense' of *it*. The same applies to a term like 'wit' in its seventeenth and early eighteenth-century senses, for instance, or a little later to terms like 'politeness', 'benevolence', 'sensibility', 'genius', 'energy', Schiller's '*Spieltraub*', or later still, to 'alienation', 'individuality', 'will-to-power', 'authenticity', 'the Unconscious'. These are only a few obvious examples – and the fact that they were each born at some particular time, and that this was obviously not entirely by chance, makes it easy to understand why people have supposed that 'human nature' is a concept open because of sociological reasons, rather than a concept that is open because of philosophical ones, yet which is constantly being filled in (partly at least) because of sociological ones. Many such terms die away, or get pushed aside, or become absorbed in others, but many do not; a language is as full of them as its cultural roots are wide and vigorous. And learning a language, including one's own, is largely a process of acquiring this sort of moral vocabulary – which is to say, acquiring this sort of life-moral understanding and capacity for judgment.

This is one reason why life-moral ideals are often expressed in the form not of 'images' so much as stories, and why even at the most general level the life-moralist usually has to make some reference to social facts, or psychological facts, or history, in order to identify the mode of life he is talking about, and to specify what makes it a unitary mode of life. Mill's *On Liberty* is an obvious case in point:

on the Calvinistic theory...the one great offence of man is self-will...'whatever is not a duty, is a sin'. Human nature being radically corrupt, there is no redemption for any one until human nature is killed within him. To one holding this theory of life, crushing out any of the human faculties, capacities, and susceptibilities, is no evil: man needs no capacity, but that of surrendering himself to the will of God: and if he uses any of his faculties for any other purpose but to do that supposed will more effectually, he is better without them. This... theory...is held, in a mitigated form, by many who do not consider themselves Calvinists...

There is a different type of human excellence from the Calvinistic; a conception of humanity as having its nature bestowed on it for other purposes than merely to be abnegated. 'Pagan self-assertion' is one of the elements of human worth, as well as 'Christian self-denial'. There is a Greek ideal of self-development, which the Platonic and Christian ideal of self-government blends with, but does not supersede. It may be better to be John Knox than an Alcibiades, but it is better to be a Pericles than either; nor would a Pericles, if we had one in these days, be without anything good which belonged to John Knox.

It is not by wearing down into uniformity all that is individual in themselves, but by cultivating it and calling it forth, within the limits imposed by the rights and interests of others, that human beings become a noble and beautiful object of contemplation; and as the works partake the character of those who do them, by the same process human life also becomes rich, diversified, and animating, furnishing more abundant aliment to high thoughts and elevating feelings, and strengthening the tie which binds every individual to the race, by making the race infinitely better worth belonging to.[11]

The very curious phrase in the last paragraph of this passage, about human beings becoming 'noble and beautiful objects of contemplation', presumably descends from Mill's earlier term, 'aesthetic'; it certainly repeats the earlier mistake of regarding people as if they were works of art – a mistake that was to be subtly explored in many of Henry James's fictions. And of course the argument about self-abnegation versus a life 'rich, diversified, and animating' is more closely related to George Eliot's novels, for example (and perhaps most especially to the near contemporary *The Mill on the Floss*), than to any novels of our own day, when 'Pagan self-assertion' is in full swing and few people would dream of modelling themselves on John Knox. But however persuasive we think Mill's argument, it is worth noticing the specificity required in order to identify a mode of life. In this respect, *The Mill on the Floss* seems to me actually a better medium than Mill's abstract argument in which to think out what is really inadequate about self-abnegation, and what a legitimate 'self-assertion' might or might not be precisely. But this is also matter for a later chapter.

III

Our need of both kinds of morality has at least two other significant implications for literature and literary criticism.

The first is that the two kinds of moral consideration, pulling in different directions as they do, often become twined around one another in our thinking and judgments, and yet there is no single formula for their relationship. Sometimes they simply oppose one another in irreconcilable conflict; sometimes one reinforces the other; sometimes they 'deconstruct' one another, or seem to; sometimes one serves not to deny the other, but to sharpen our need of it.

To take a small literary example of their opposition, we can easily understand why Pope's 'Elegy to the Memory of an Unfortunate Lady' ends by referring to the poet himself as well as the (fictitious) lady who committed suicide for love. One of the main points of the poem is to present the lady, not as wicked for killing herself, but as one of those 'who greatly think, or bravely die', who 'aspire / Above the vulgar flight of low desire'. That 'ambition' in her was the 'glorious fault of Angels and of Gods', which on earth usually 'glows' in the 'breasts of Kings and Heroes' – but also (we are to understand) in some poets. In other words, the poem offers us a high life-moral view of the lady – a view that only the poet can properly appreciate and express – to displace the obvious but commonplace conduct-moral judgment of her suicide by 'vulgar', commonplace souls. But it is interesting to see the critical response to this offer from a man to whom Christian conduct-morality was more important than anything else, and who was not willing to relax it for a mere poem, even if the poet was himself a Christian and a genius. Dr Johnson insisted on a conduct-moral view of the poem, and in those terms he seems unanswerable: 'Poetry has not often been worse employed than in dignifying the amorous fury of a raving girl.'[12]

For literary examples of how the two kinds of moral consideration and judgment are entangled it would be hard to find a better case than Shakespeare's *Antony and Cleopatra*, or, in less complicated ways, his *Henry IV*. But for a small example, we might perhaps take a famous moment in *Paradise Lost*, where the issue is not unlike that of Pope's 'Elegy': Adam's silent response to Eve's confession that she has eaten the forbidden fruit. As so often, the most complex relationships between conduct-morality and life-morality turn on the nature and value of human love (alias 'amorous fury'); and in this case, because of the obvious moral and religious implications, the episode has attracted an enormous amount of critical commentary: Why exactly is Adam's action wrong? What exactly is his sin or moral failing? How is such a sin or moral failing reconcilable with his prelapsarian perfection? Is his will entirely free? – and so forth. But what is most in question, of course, is not just Adam's moral thinking and judgment; it is also our own as we consider his:

> Speechless he stood and pale, till thus at length
> First to himself he inward silence broke.
> O fairest of creation, last and best
> Of all God's works, creature in whom excelled

Whatever can to sight or thought be formed,
Holy, divine, good, amiable or sweet!
How art thou lost, how on a sudden lost,
Defaced, deflowered, and now to death devote?
Rather how hast thou yielded to transgress
The strict forbiddance, how to violate
The sacred fruit forbidden! Some cursed fraud
Of enemy hath beguiled thee, yet unknown,
And me with thee hath ruined, for with thee
Certain my resolution is to die;
How can I live without thee, how forgo
Thy sweet converse and love so dearly joined,
To live again in these wild woods forlorn?
Should God create another Eve, and I
Another rib afford, yet loss of thee
Would never from my heart; no no, I feel
The link of nature draw me: flesh of flesh,
Bone of my bone thou art, and from thy state
Mine never shall be parted, bliss or woe.[13]

At this point in the poem at least, Milton creates Adam
dramatically by realizing in him a kind of love so serious that it
makes a good deal of love poetry seem merely self-centred, even
self-absorbed. For the force of this poetry here is such that I
think we have to agree with those who see Adam here as
thinking and acting out of love of Eve, and not just succumbing
to the 'temptations' of Eve's previous speech (lines 856–85) or
as just succumbing to 'female charm', or irrational 'desire' or
'passion', or pride, or uxoriousness, or to any other sin or
weakness of conduct-moral character. Nor is his love self-
regarding, as Eve's was when some similar considerations came
to her mind (lines 827–33); nor is it cosily 'conjugal', nor a
merely subjective state of excitement. Like King Lear's love for
Cordelia at the very end of Shakespeare's play, Adam's is
entirely concentrated on seeing and responding to its object,
attending to *that* with his entire self, and loving it in the very
anguish of his attention. In short, I think we see Adam's
'resolution' as what I call a life-moral one, and in the most
literal sense of 'life'. He both discovers and commits the whole
of his being – or to speak more accurately, the whole of his being
commits itself – to what he sees standing before him: this

particular person in these particular circumstances, to whom
and to which he must answer with all of himself:

> for with thee
> Certain my resolution is to die.

One of the profoundly right things about Adam's silent
soliloquy is the way the stresses in this line and a half fall on
'thee', 'certain', and 'die', welding the three words together as
the heart of his resolution. Another is the absence of any pun on
'die'; in fact, Milton's seriousness here makes a lot of the
seventeenth-century play with the word look rather cheap. But
probably the most profoundly right thing about the passage is
the way Milton imagines the resolution coming to Adam. It
comes, that is, before Adam is conscious of having reached a
decision, even before he is aware of reasons for and against it, let
alone weighing those reasons and exercising his famous free will.
The resolution comes unheralded and yet as somehow inevitable, as if it has somehow formed *itself*, almost *un*willed, as
the answer to reality that Adam, being what he is, discovers he
had to make. The point is quite crucial, though some of Milton's
critics seem not to notice it. For what it means is that, although
Adam may be said to make a decision here, he could also, no less
accurately, be said to come, or even to be brought, to one. In
short, the standard, apparently natural view of Adam here as
actively choosing, actively making a decision, is brought into
question by a rather different view of him.

Nevertheless, this does not mean that the standard view is
wrong. Adam does decide. Moreover, it seems hardly worth
debating that, in so far as Adam performs a voluntary
intentional action, it is – or must be judged to be – morally
wrong. On Christian premises, it is wrong, and wrong, I think,
not because of some complex view about moral Reason, or
moral measure, or virtue and sin, according to which Adam's
motives are bad or impure, but for the simple blunt irreducible
reason that, out of whatever motives, Adam does something
that was expressly and unqualifiedly forbidden by God irrespective of any or every other moral consideration. There is no
higher Reason here about the prohibition or the transgression,

nor any subtle theological point. God said not to do it – it does not matter why – and Adam resolves he will do it, and again it does not matter why.

Thus Adam chooses, and his choice is a particular act of will that consciously transgresses, out of whatever motives it happens to have at the time. But he also comes to a resolution: a state that seems (causally) to arise spontaneously and yet inevitably out of, and yet seems to be (morally or rationally) required by, his very existence, past, present and future. There is nothing contingent about the grounds of such a 'resolution' as Adam's – or, in a situation not unlike Adam's, the 'resolution' of another unfortunate lady, Shakespeare's Cleopatra. Nor is such a resolution simply an act of will. In such situations as theirs, the resolution is a discovery-and-confirmation of the shape of their whole being and experience – the unfolding shape, as it were, that forms their existence into the life they now find, make, wish and accept as their own. The resolution defines the distinctive identity and fate each has been given and then chooses.

Moreover, the word 'resolution' is very much to the point. It suggests harmonizing and integrating as well as deciding; and yet paradoxically (though very relevantly) it also carries an ominous sense of reducing, atomizing, disintegration. And it has a double application. It applies to a sharpened moral definition of the object being considered – the 'resolution' of the nature and significance to Adam of Eve, her action, and her life; and it also applies to the moral actualization of the person considering and judging – the 'resolution' of everything Adam is, as he recognizes and acknowledges what the object of his moral thinking really is.

Thus on the one side, Adam recognizes and acknowledges (as he must) Eve in conduct-moral terms, as a fellow member of the community of God, as a part of the order from which she has been beguiled to cast herself away; 'How art thou lost, how on a sudden lost'. His own resolution is partly implicit in the very way he sees her as that; and this is because what he sees answers to something essential in himself: his own capacity to die, to be morally lost or to lose himself, to be a mere dispensable part of God's world. On the other side, he recognizes and acknowledges her (as again he must) in life-moral terms, not as a member of a class of beings, but as the particular, unique moral being in front of him, now and here. And once again, if his eventual resolution is implicit in the very way he sees her as this, what he sees answers to something essential in himself, which he does not become aware of but which the passage certainly discloses to us: *his* particular, individual moral being. As he ponders, he realizes what is really and inescapably there in Eve: not just the 'fairest of creation, last and best / Of all God's works', not just a creature now lost to the Enemy, though one that God might replace with another of the same general class of creature; but this unique person, Eve, whom he loves precisely because she *is* Eve, and whose loss is therefore irremediable: 'yet loss of thee / Would never from my heart'. The stress in the one case falls on 'lost': 'How art thou *lost*, how on a sudden *lost*'. In the other, it falls on 'thee' and on the correlative of that word: 'yet loss of *thee* / Would never from *my heart*'.

There is no way Adam can escape the conflict, and no right way he can resolve it out of existence. It is true that he shapes his own fate by (in some sense of the word) choosing what to acknowledge as real and inescapable in the world (and thereby expressing and disclosing to us what is real and inescapable in himself). Yet that fate can also be seen as one he cannot avoid, since it shapes *itself* in what he, being Adam and having this life to live, cannot but acknowledge and answer to. For the particular fate here is (to borrow a phrase)[14] nothing less than 'the fate of loving' – the need and the capacity for love and loving-kindness which, as Milton presents the case at this key moment, lie at the very 'heart' of Man. They form an essential part of his very 'perfection' *as* a man; they are central to his 'humanity' in the full normative sense of the word; and yet they are also the very source of his fall. As we see it (and we do so, of course, in a way that Adam cannot), Adam's 'true' life as a man partly consists in his being a creature within a universal Order, and conducting himself as an instance – a free, participating, consciously affirming instance, it is true, but only an instance nonetheless – of God's goodness, creative power, providence and (above all) absolute moral authority. But his 'true' life as a man also partly depends on his being an individual, *this* unique being with this particular 'heart' – with this particular need and capacity for love that can be satisfied only in loving this particular individual human being, as well as loving God. Thus for him fully to realize Eve's nature and her meaning to him here is not a matter of his just seeing with his mind that she is lost, and also just seeing with his mind that he needs her. (Nor, I would add, has it anything to do with a statement like 'I feel / The link of nature draw me', the very self-consciousness and abstraction of which are dramatically – that is, humanly – incoherent with the rest of his thoughts here, and betray it as a touch, not of Adam's mind as it is being really imagined by Milton, but of Milton's theological thumb wandering into the moral scales.)[15] Adam's love of Eve *is* the way he sees her, the way he *has* to acknowledge her specific identity – a way that claims his own and determines it, since his 'heart' requires he acknowledge her as that. His love of this particular human being is a necessary condition of his own nature, and of any life he would think worth living. This is why the loss of her would be real and total, and one that not even God Himself could remedy. In short, it is an unresolvable conflict in being human that Adam has to resolve; and there is no reason to suppose that the whole unfortunate fall would never have happened if only Adam had chosen the right thing to do. A crucial life-moral issue was also involved, and such issues rarely, if ever, have a single, straightforward, rationally-deducible right answer – which is why life-moral judgments are usually more like *coming* to a resolution than *making* a decision.

All of this applies equally to our judgment of Adam here. In so far as his resolution is a voluntary intentional action, it is, given the premises of the poem, a morally wrong action. But this does not require us either to find a sinful motive to be the cause of his action, or to judge his resolution, in so far as it is caused by his love and loyalty, to be a morally right action. In the relevant sense of 'action', it is not so much an action based on rational considerations, as a pattern of perceptions and feelings that this particular human life finds itself committed to. This is why it does not seem to me quite accurate to say, for instance, that the poem is deeply flawed because it 'asks from us, at one and the same time, two incompatible responses... to believe that Adam did right... and to believe that he did wrong'.[16] What the poem presents here is rather something that Adam did: a choice that has to be judged in conduct-moral terms as wrong, as transgressing the only categorical imperative given him; and at the same time it presents something that reveals and crystallizes what Adam *is*: a confirming discovery of what he cannot help seeing and feeling, an anguished but spontaneous, unhesitating, undeliberated, and therefore truly natural self-commitment of his moral being. That self-commitment has to be judged in life-moral terms. And in those terms, his resolution is no less fine, no less responsive to the particulars of 'intellectual nature', and (to risk the term) no less noble than we would want a truly, a normatively, *human* being to be.

Thus it is not mere word play, I think, to see the poem here as presenting us with the need for a resolution of our own: a judgment of Adam that is also a discovery of our own moral lives. And I also think it is hard not to discover that, for us, the Adam whose moral nature could show itself in this soliloquy is a better, a higher, human creature than one who could have acted here strictly by God's commandment. There is no call to write off such a judgment as sentimental or romantic, or to deny it because Eve in her fallen self-regarding way praises Adam in terms rather like those of Pope in his 'Elegy': 'O glorious trial of exceeding love, / Illustrious evidence, example high!' (lines 961–2). Adam himself, we might note, did not see his resolution in that way, nor should we. In fact, its *lack* of conscious virtue or nobleness, like its lack of calculation, is one of the main things that makes us value it as truly noble.

The hypothetical comparison with a totally righteous Adam brings out the way that conduct-moral judgment here pulls us in one direction, and life-moral judgment in the other. And we can begin to appreciate how much tighter and more stubborn this makes the knot by asking ourselves whether we would be much engaged, or even much interested, in the fate of an Adam who could and would have acted rightly here, or who could have measured his loyalty to what he had to love, against reasons that, good as they must be, would nevertheless always favour his own preservation as against Eve's. The fall of Milton's Adam is so moving that it is almost insupportable both to heart and mind. For it is 'the nobleness of life' that manifests itself in Adam's resolution – or rather, manifests itself *as* his resolution – which makes his fall so strange and enigmatic; but it is also what makes his fall in the fullest sense *matter* to us in every word and detail. Unless conduct-moral and life-moral considerations were at odds here, we would hardly care what happened to Adam. On the other side, without that conflict there would be nothing by which we could discern the importance and value of love and of loyalty to love. And of course there would be no recognizably complex, painful and crucial object to resolve here unless, as perpetual moralists, we needed both kinds of morality.

But as we can also see in this case, our need of both has a still more basic implication for literature and literary criticism. It requires us to think of people in two different ways, in two different kinds of terms: both as agents and as lives.

CHAPTER 3

Agents and lives: making moral sense of people

I

My basic contention is that imaginative literature has traditionally been, and still is, a distinctive and irreplaceable form
of moral thinking. Compared with philosophy in its various
branches, or history, or psychology, or biography, or any
combination of the 'moral sciences', it has a unique capacity to
look at human experience with, as it were, stereoscopic moral
vision. Literature does not necessarily have to do so, perhaps,
but on the whole it has, and in many literary modes and genres
and forms, not just those that might be called 'realistic'. But by
'stereoscopic moral vision' (to repeat the point once again), I
do not mean seeing or trying to see human experience, or
'criticizing life', by the light of two different codes of morality
(for example, Adam's action is wrong/Adam's action is right),
but rather combining, so long as it is not confusing, two
different but equally needed ways of thinking about human
experience and evaluating it (for example, Adam's action is
wrong/Adam's action shows him to be (among other things)
loving, and noble in his loving).

To put it baldly, I think that the moral thinking characteristic
of imaginative literature can proceed, if a work is to do anything
more than unquestioningly reiterate and exemplify accepted
moral attitudes and ideals, only by walking (to borrow a
metaphor of A. E. Housman's) with both the legs on which our
moral conceptions stand. Of course, the moral consideration of
somebody's voluntary intentional actions (Adam's, for example,
or Milton's, come to that) can, if it goes deep enough, itself bring

the mind to swivel around to considering the agent as also a personal life – as the particular moral being, with a unique location in the world and a unique moral history, that those actions manifest as well as help to shape. Similarly, the moral consideration of a unique personal life can itself bring the mind to swivel around to considering certain of the person's actions in the light of moral rules or ideals that apply to anyone and everyone. But that is not the only way a two-fold process of moral thinking can proceed. Nor do we have to regard one kind of moral thinking as necessarily higher or more fundamental than the other, although as a matter of fact the need, the point, and the logic of conduct-morality have always been much more familiar, much more readily understood and invoked, than have the need, the point, and the logic of life-morality. That is why I want to concentrate on the latter. But if the experience of readers and critics of imaginative literature over the centuries testifies to anything, it is to the belief (which I also share) that all the so-called 'aesthetic' qualities of a literary work, all its formal and technical features, all its linguistic structures and powers, all its inter-connections with social, cultural, intellectual and historical contexts – in short, all the means by which it construes-and-constructs meanings in human experience and 'deconstructs' them – have abiding interest and value only in so far as they articulate such a two-fold process of moral thinking.

One of the most obvious examples of this internal relationship between the so-called 'aesthetic' features of a literary work and its two-fold moral thinking is James Joyce's *Portrait of the Artist as a Young Man*. Like a great many literary works, but far more self-consciously and openly than most – indeed, almost programmatically – it portrays both a series of voluntary intentional actions by its hero (Joyce's fictionalized surrogate, Stephen Dedalus), and also the various modes of life, personal and social, that those actions at different stages of his childhood and youth arise out of and help to shape. But as well as *portraying* Stephen as a young man gradually developing some understanding of the components both of his moral actions and his moral being – his inward self, his outward world, and the always tricky relationships between them – the selecting, re-shaping and presentational activity of the novel also *manifests* a mode of life: the fuller, more searching, more balanced, more securely objective, more productively active moral understand-ing of the artist as an older and wiser man. He looks back and sees 'that which I was' in 'that which I am and that which in possibility I may come to be'.[1] In other words, the subtle, complex organization of the novel, its densely-woven linguistic and metaphorical texture, the various styles and stylistic relationships of its parts or chapters, the temporal relationships it posits between its subject-matter and its own existence as this novel with this title written between these dates in these places, and having these 'aesthetic'-moral qualities – all exhibit and articulate the morally mature being that Stephen's life and actions are portrayed as groping towards.[2]

For as Joyce came to see when he tried to write an autobiographical novel showing why he had to free himself from the 'nets' of Ireland in order to become an 'artist', his first artistic problem was not simply to portray himself convincingly as a heroic superior spirit – though of course one large enough to see an occasional joke against himself – as in his first attempt, *Stephen Hero*. In scrapping that, he obviously recognized that his real artistic problem was a moral one: to portray and to show, as sharply and steadily as possible, what and how his life in Ireland had brought him to feel (if still only obscurely), and to understand (if still only partially), and to want to be (if still only in a romantically idealizing way). To capture all this, he needed to understand pretty thoroughly the limitations as well as the achievements of the earlier stages of his life; and with his now maturer insight and artistic power to define, explain, measure, and (by demonstration) justify the 'young man's' stumbling steps towards this very maturity.

This required something more than narrating his hero's activities in chronological sequence. It meant tracing the inner drama unfolding itself within those activities, tracing the 'slow and dark birth' of his 'soul' and the main developing forms of its life. It also meant realizing certain crucial voluntary actions by his hero as 'errors' – 'volitional' errors – which were nevertheless 'portals of discovery' for the developing life of his soul.[3] This is why the novel positively insists on the distinction between its hero's voluntary (or 'volitional') actions, his *conduct*, and the qualities and bent of his *life* as this manifests itself not only in conduct but also in non-volitional activities: in his gradually enlarging and clarifying consciousness and language, his desires and reactions, his perceptions and feelings, sensibilities, capacities, fantasies, hopes, judgments, self-images, as well as in the unfolding shape of all of these over time.

The crucial voluntary actions in the *Portrait* are of course those with which each of its parts or chapters culminates: (i) the little boy's protest to the Rector of his school about his 'unfair and cruel' beating by Father Dolan; (ii) the adolescent's taking of a prostitute; (iii) his religious repentance and confession; (iv) his rejecting a religious vocation, and finding instead that a (vaguely and romantically conceived) 'vocation' as an 'artist' is 'the end he had been born to serve'; and (v) his decision to free himself from Ireland and become a true 'artist' by going to Europe.

In each case, Stephen knows that he acts rightly or wrongly, he is clearly conscious of the rules or principles that determine the rightness or wrongness of his 'volition'. His first kind of 'error' is equally obvious: in each case, he supposes that the rightness or wrongness of his action establishes him and his consequent actions as definitively good or wicked. But he supposes this because (as we see and he does not) he acts as he does in each case partly because of the shaping pressures of his social and cultural environment, and partly because of a powerful but less than conscious impulse in himself towards a new, freer and more stable kind of life, a fuller and finer state of moral being. His second kind of 'error' is to suppose in each case that he has finally found 'life', finally reached maturity. Nevertheless, the genuine 'discovery' of which this 'error' is the 'portal' is indeed that of at least a somewhat larger, more mature mode of life – moral, social and cultural. The newly discovered possibilities of experience and understanding include those of earlier stages of his moral life, but (to us) they also point forward to its eventual supersession:

(i)   The cheers died away in the soft grey air. He was alone. He was happy and free: but he would not be anyway proud with Father Dolan. He would be very quiet and obedient...

  The air was soft and grey and mild and evening was coming. There was the smell of evening in the air, the smell of the fields in the country... the smell there was in the little wood beyond the pavilion...

  The fellows were practising long shies and bowling lobs and slow twisters. In the soft grey silence he could hear the bump of the balls: and... the sound of the cricket bats... like drops of water in a fountain falling softly in the brimming bowl.[4]

(ii) He wanted to sin with another of his kind... He felt some dark presence moving irresistibly upon him from the darkness... Its murmur besieged his ears like the murmur of some multitude in sleep; its subtle streams penetrated his being... In her arms he felt that he had suddenly become strong and fearless and sure of himself... He closed his eyes, surrendering himself to her, body and mind, conscious of nothing in the world but the dark pressure of her softly parting lips... and between them he felt an unknown and timid pressure, darker than the swoon of sin, softer than sound or odour.[5]

(iii) The boys were all there, kneeling in their places. He knelt among them, happy and shy. The altar was heaped with fragrant masses of white flowers: and in the morning light the pale flames of the candles among the white flowers were clean and silent as his own soul... Another life! A life of grace and virtue and happiness! It was true. It was not a dream from which he would wake. The past was past...[6]

(iv) Her image had passed into his soul for ever and no word had broken the holy silence of his ecstasy... To live, to err, to fall, to triumph, to recreate life out of life! A wild angel had appeared to him, the angel of mortal youth and beauty, an envoy from the fair courts of life, to throw open before him in an instant of ecstasy the gates of all the ways of error and glory. On and on and on and on!

  He halted suddenly and heard his heart in the silence... He ...lay down there that the peace and silence of the evening might still the riot of his blood.

  He felt above him the vast indifferent dome and the calm processes of the heavenly bodies; and the earth beneath him, the earth that had borne him, had taken him to her breast.

He closed his eyes in the languor of sleep...His soul was swooning into some new world, fantastic, dim...A world, a glimmer, or a flower?

Evening had fallen. A rim of the young moon cleft the pale waste of sky like the rim of a silver hoop embedded in grey sand; and the tide was flowing in fast to the land with a low whisper of her waves, islanding a few last figures in distant pools.[7]

(v)   The spell of arms and voices: the white arms of roads, their promise of close embraces and the black arms of tall ships that stand against the moon, their tale of distant nations. They are held out to say: We are alone. Come. And the voices say with them: We are your kinsmen. And the air is thick with their company as they call to me, their kinsman, making ready to go, shaking the wings of their exultant and terrible youth.

...Mother is putting my new secondhand clothes in order. She prays now, she says, that I may learn in my own life and away from home and friends what the heart is and what it feels. Amen. So be it. Welcome, O life! I go to encounter for the millionth time the reality of experience and to forge in the smithy of my soul the uncreated conscience of my race...[8]

In each case here, what is being represented is clearly Stephen's consciousness rather than Joyce's. Joyce's art is (to use his hero's own term in the *Portrait*) 'dramatic' in that the maturer artist's view of his hero, and of the world his hero inhabits, is completely embodied in what and how he has his hero see: 'the vitality' of the artist 'fills every person' – though especially Stephen – 'with such vital force that he or she assumes a proper and intangible esthetic life'.[9] The art of the *Portrait* makes the limitations of Stephen's various stages of moral life manifest themselves in the childishly simple consciousness, language, and conception of 'freedom' and 'happiness' in passage (i), for example; in the particular kinds of romantic sentiment and sentimentality in (ii) and (iv); in the still limited conceptions of freedom and happiness in (ii) to (v); in the facile religiosity of (iii); in the afflatus of (v). On the other hand, the art makes Stephen's positive growth also manifest itself in the increasing range, complexity and integration of Stephen's consciousness through the whole sequence; in his lessening dependence on the pathetic fallacy; in the kinds of increasing self-doubt and self-confidence in him and in his conceptions of himself; and so on.

As Joyce saw (and much more thoroughly than the hero of the *Portrait* does), this kind of objective 'showing' or self-manifesting is the basic principle of 'dramatic' literature, and it rests on a common enough fact about life-moral issues generally. It is a commonplace that such issues are extremely difficult to discuss objectively – though not, it must be said, quite as difficult as relativists make out. Even where arguments cannot be conclusive, there is still a difference between insight and cliché, between a rational judgment about something and the mere sum of some assorted facts about it plus an opinion or two – between a good argument, in short, and a bad one, or no argument at all. Nevertheless, the values engaged in life-moral issues are usually so deeply personal that they determine the very way one sees and describes the issue itself – its description indeed often being the most basic point at issue. William Blake put the matter very nicely in one of his letters:

Every body does not see alike. To the Eyes of a Miser a Guinea is more beautiful than the Sun, & a bag worn with the use of Money has more beautiful proportions than a Vine filled with Grapes. The tree which moves some to tears of joy is in the Eyes of others only a Green thing that stands in the way... *As a man is, so he sees*... [my italics][10]

'Sees' cannot be taken here in a wholly literal sense, of course; what Blake is referring to is a process that involves norms: to 'see' is to judge or evaluate, or notice or acknowledge as important. Taken in that way, Blake's point is one quite crucial both to literature and to traditional literary criticism, and always has been. Nor does it depend on holding Blake's particular views about the world. Dr Johnson makes the same point in the course of discussing Milton's 'L'Allegro' and 'Il Penseroso':

The author's design is not, what Theobald has remarked, merely to shew how objects derived their colours from the mind, by representing the operation of the same things upon the gay and the melancholy temper, or upon the same man as he is differently disposed; but rather how, among the successive variety of appearances, every disposition of mind takes hold on those by which it may be gratified.

The *chearful* man hears the lark in the morning; the *pensive* man hears the nightingale in the evening...[11]

Clearly, Johnson needed no Idealist philosophy, no lofty conception of the imagination as the access to visionary Truth, no theory of ideology, to grasp what ordinary observation, not to mention Shakespearean drama and literature generally, could have shown him. He puts it in rather eighteenth-century terms, of course; Joyce himself puts it in his own quasi-Aristotelian terms, but it is the same basic insight – this time applied to Shakespeare: 'He found in the world without as actual what was in his world within as possible.' Like Blake's remark and Johnson's, this not only points to a characteristic of life-moral judgments generally; as Joyce came to realize, it is just because it does so that it is also a key principle of 'dramatic' art in particular, his own as well as Shakespeare's.

Read in the light of this principle, the passages I have quoted from his *Portrait* exhibit some of the ways that literature, and especially 'dramatic' literature, is a form of moral thinking. In the first place, however, it is important to notice one way it is not. Although we certainly do evaluate the various modes of Stephen's life exhibited in the passages (and the parts or chapters the passages come from and lead into), we are not presented by the novel with modes of life we recognize objectively from the outset *as* modes of life, and which we can think about and evaluate as recognizable wholes by reference to some pre-existing moral ideal or model that the novel incites us to apply. The novel shows Stephen trying, and happily failing, to live according to such pre-existing ideals; but the limiting judgments of Stephen and of those ideals, judgments implicit in Joyce's selecting, shaping and stylistic activity, do not refer us to any pre-existing moral ideal or model. On the contrary – in practice, our evaluations are actually made, and consist, in a great many little responses to the representing and manifesting text. They are composed of countless inter-related, overlapping, mutually supporting or qualifying or even contradicting, acts of understanding-and-judgment: the acts in which we make moral sense (as best we can) of each linguistic component and structure, each social, cultural and personal detail represented by the novel, each voluntary and non-voluntary activity of Stephen and of the other characters – and so on. (I am supposing that we are able and willing to read the novel as representing and manifesting such things.) In short, our life-moral evaluations here are much more diverse, fluid, unpredictable, pluralistic, and difficult to put into words, than applying some pre-existing ideal or model of human life.

To make such evaluations is to think more open-endedly than that, and think in both conduct-moral and life-moral terms. In the quoted passages, for example, we have to think out what actually *is* represented and exhibited in the particular details of each passage and the particular words that do the representing and exhibiting – details like evening, grey light, darkness, a sense of inner and outer peace and so on – and also what is represented and exhibited in the recurrence of such details from one passage to another. The novel's 'dramatic' mode enjoins us to take such details as primarily realistic, details of Stephen's world as they are 'seen' by *him*, and which therefore manifest his moral life at each point of the sequence. But setting off in that direction, we then have to think out how far Stephen *chooses* to see things as he does, how far his 'seeing' is volitional, a voluntary intentional action, and what is the exact nature and quality of the action. How far do the details form the substance of his action, or an explanation of it, or perhaps its (good/bad) consequences? And can it be understood *entirely* in that way? How far does this or that detail also (or instead) manifest a non-conscious 'disposition' in Stephen taking hold on the appearances that would gratify it? And what disposition exactly? How far does this or that detail also (or instead) manifest one of Stephen's characteristic modes of consciousness, feeling and sensibility, a way of 'seeing' that is distinctively personal to him and perhaps biased in some important ways but which he cannot regulate? How far does this or that detail also (or instead) represent the effects on him of certain social or cultural conditions (Irish Catholicism, say, or romantic novels) or manifest the basic psychoanalytic structures of his (like anybody's) subjectivity? Or is the detail perhaps also (or instead) signalling – in a rather '*un*dramatic' but quite understandable

way – a meaning of the author's from outside anything his hero
sees and is? Similarly with other such details in the passages:
water, for example; silence; a desire for self-surrender or
rapturous self-transcendence; or the belief that the past is now
completely done with.

Along with all this, however, we have also to think out what
unites these passages both with their contexts and with one
another: which is to say that, right from the outset, we have to
think our way into the inner dramatic action of the novel. This
comprises at least two strands, two kinds of unity that wind
around each other. One is Stephen's maturation as a moral
agent – the unity comprising the contexts and the causes of his
volitional actions (seeking what he regards at each stage as
freedom and happiness, for example), the specific nature and
quality of those actions, and the consequences of those actions
– consequences in terms of which we may want morally to judge
the actions. The second kind of unity is that of his moral life –
its unity in width and depth, as it were, at each of its stages, and
its unity in length, as it were, over all of its stages.

As with most novels, the unity of the hero's moral life in the
Portrait is actually more prominent than that of his moral
agency. Stephen, we realize from the very first pages, has
distinctive personal inclinations, capacities, needs, habits, talents, as well as dispositions, in addition to universally human
ones (like sexuality, for example). These are elements of his
moral life that he is not necessarily conscious of at all, or
conscious of only as more or less vague impulses, desires,
longings, or just absences. In fact, as the maturer artist makes us
see, these elements not merely help to define Stephen's
consciousness and volitional actions, but also help to determine
them. They are part of his moral being, and they push his moral
life, in equally obscure ways, along this path or that. Thus the
second kind of unity we discern in Stephen's life is not the chain
linking causes, actions and consequences, but a temporal
pattern that includes all of these as its elements along with the
elements of his moral being. Seen in this way, for example, there
seems nothing of mere luck or contingency about Stephen's
aestheticism and his wish to become 'a priest of the eternal

imagination'. Given the moral being he is at successive stages, this is the only path his life could take as it moves through his volitional errors as a moral agent from one portal of discovery to the next.

This over-all pattern is connected with the very core of Stephen's moral life. Again like anybody else, the pattern manifests his particular 'nature', his 'soul', his 'essence', the 'principle' of his life, his deepest 'character', his 'moral being'. (There are reasons for and against using every one of such terms, but I shall generally use only the first and the last.) That nature is individual, indeed unique in some crucially important respects; but it can manifest itself *as* that only in time: not just in the sequence of his volitional actions but in the whole arc or span of his life, its particular unique history. Recognizing this familiar fact sometimes prompts us to think of a person's particular nature or moral being not just organically but also teleologically, and sometimes to think of our own in that way too. It helps us make sense of a moral life to think of it as a set of potentialities that thrust and grow themselves into being, that necessarily strive to actualize or realize themselves in time, and in the course of this perhaps become subject to consciousness and so to voluntary evaluation and deliberate choice. In Stephen's case, it obviously makes a very large difference to how we see and evaluate the successive modes of his moral life that he did in fact become an 'artist', and in particular the artist whose moral life knowingly realizes itself (for the moment) in this particular self-evaluative autobiographical novel. That difference has something to do with the value we attach to the consequences his actions happened, by 'luck' or 'fate', to have. But it has a great deal more to do with seeing the over-all pattern, the inner coherence, of his moral life as it is represented by the novel and manifests itself there.

In other words, we think of Stephen's various modes of life as modes of a moral *life* largely in finding at each stage how his distinctive non-volitional impulses and impulsions cohere with his feelings, sensibilities, desires, consciousness, as well as with his volitions and conduct. And we think of Stephen as the unique moral being he is largely in finding the specific pattern of growth, the distinctive over-all trajectory, that realizes itself in his non-volitional activities as well as his volitions and conduct. Thus the trajectory becomes something like a path as-it-were chosen by a sort of as-it-were unconscious volition, a quasi-volition: which is how Stephen puts it himself in *Ulysses* in speaking of the errors of a man of genius being 'volitional'. (It is important to notice, and to go on noticing, the 'as-it-were' and the 'quasi' here.) Or to put it another way, the trajectory comes to be something like a personal 'destiny', or a 'vocation', a path as-it-were sought out, but disclosing itself and actualizing itself only in Stephen's growth from one portal of discovery to the next. What is 'discovered' is the *right* because *necessary* path of his moral life. Thus in the passages quoted above, for example, we have to think out how and why one passage picks up the terms of an earlier one but incorporates them in a very different mode of 'seeing'. The sexuality and the need for 'sin' in (ii), for instance, become incorporated – along with the religious impulse, the need of 'grace and virtue and happiness' (iii) – into (iv), especially its romantically-excited 'ecstasy'. And these then become incorporated again, along with the now almost-conscious need in Stephen of some capacity answering to the 'vast' and 'calm' objectivity of nature in (iv), into the more balanced, and yet more complex consciousness and resolution of (v).

The reader has to think responsively, of course, answering to the thinking of the novel. He has to think through the sequence of Stephen's actions, not merely judging them as conduct, but deciding as well why the novel represents precisely those actions with those causes and those consequences. He also has to think out precisely what moral qualities are expressed at each point (sensitivity or sentimentality? religion or religiosity? detachment or indifference? – and so on) and to whom they are to be ascribed: to Stephen, another character, some aspect of the world represented in the novel, and/or the artist. There is no rule or model anyone can follow here – though it usually helps to have read a fair number of other novels, even if only to see what is different about this one. Yet to describe our thinking in this way still over-simplifies the matter in one crucial respect at least. For it suggests that these moral entities – hero, other characters, world, artist – all pre-exist our thinking and are already furnished with their moral qualities, so that all we do as readers is simply *recognize* those qualities as we notice examples of them. The fact is that these entities do not pre-exist our thinking in any substantial way. On the contrary, the process of moral thinking with which we answer to the novel is itself the process in which we *realize* Stephen as a character, as the moral agent and moral life he is; and so with the other characters, and with the Ireland of the novel, and with the artist. These may perhaps all be said to pre-exist as potential moral entities; but they take on moral substance only as we ascribe it to them in our thinking. Or to put it another way, the kind of moral thinking with which we answer to the novel is not merely analytic, critical and generalizing, not just *about* Stephen, for instance: defining inter-relating, explaining and judging all his activities, and their more general import, as objectively as possible. Our thinking is also constructive and particularizing: a process in which Stephen, or his world, say, or the artist, becomes 'real' to us (as we say) or takes on 'life' (or in the artist's case, what Stephen calls 'esthetic life'). It is a process in which we think *of* him – of this particular moral being with this particular 'destiny'.

II

For the traditional reader or critic of literature, the point and 'logic' of considering people as agents is likely to be more obvious than that of considering them as lives, since it is the usual way that practical and theoretical moralists have always considered them.[12] Naturally, anybody's account of the matter will be largely determined by the particular morality or moral theory he or she holds; but broadly speaking, conduct-moral thinking considers people in terms of universal concepts, universal reasons, and universal rules or principles. To consider anyone as a moral agent is to regard him or her as exhaustively described for the purposes of strictly *moral* consideration as a member of some class or sub-class of beings. The focus of moral attention are his volitions, his actions as voluntary and intentional; so he must be autonomous and (in a certain sense) authentic[13] – be capable, that is, of exercising a rational will in deciding how to act and in acting on his decision. His will faces a world external to it, a world largely (though not exclusively) composed of other agents (and patients) towards which the agent's desires and moral actions are directed. In literature, the moral agent (which may be a group considered as collective agents) is generally the subject of certain active transitive verbs – most especially, verbs of knowing, feeling, remembering, believing, reflecting, reasoning, choosing, preferring, deciding, intending, saying, promising, deceiving and doing. For the conduct-moralist, all these verbs refer to the performance of a determinate action or to the failure to perform it, or to habits of performance or failure. The agent either acts in a certain way, or he does not: otherwise, what is there to be morally judged? (It is important to remember that many of the relevant actions are mental ones.) What most interests most people about conduct-morality, of course, is its content: what it requires them to do or not to do – what, that is, are the direct objects of such transitive verbs – and the ideal standard or model by which an agent's performance or habit of performance is to be judged. The same interest applies to those who write about moral matters too. And what impels this interest is very largely the interest in judging, in determining responsibility, and assigning praise or blame, censure, and punishment. From the standpoint of life-morality, however, one very significant fact is the restricted range of such verbs; another is the restricted range of such ideals of performance; and a third is the restricted range of possible judgments: right or wrong (in various degrees), good or bad (in various degrees), worthy of praise or blame (in various degrees), virtue or vice (in various degrees), and so forth.

At this point it may be as well to make a couple of very broad but important distinctions. One is the difference between all the thousands of things a living person does, what we might call his or her *activity*, and those done voluntarily and intentionally, his or her *actions*. The difference is not always clear-cut and it is certainly not always clearly visible; but leaving aside questions about the possible 'intentionality' of all mental activity, and about the connections (if any) between that sense of 'intentionality' and those in common usage, we obviously can and do draw a line between a person's activity, for much of which we think we cannot properly hold him morally responsible or blame him (whoever else we might want to blame), and his actions, for which we think we can – even if it is not always certain just where the line is to be drawn. Knowing, for example, or feeling, or believing, or ignoring, or deceiving, can sometimes be regarded as the one, sometimes as the other. Very often, indeed, the most basic moral problem is a sort of legal one, about what, in a particular case, is to be regarded as some form of activity and what as action.

Traditionally, literature and literary criticism have tended to make sense of human lives in roughly three ways. A great deal of human activity is understood as mere *functioning* – of a physiological system, say, or a social one. Stephen Dedalus grows, willy-nilly; speaks and understands; he goes to school; he has sexual desires; and so on. We all age; we mate; maidens 'flower' and 'fade'. Hardy's Tess Durbeyfield 'rallies':

A particularly fine spring came round, and the stir of germination was almost audible in the buds; it moved her, as it moved the wild animals, and made her passionate to go...some spirit within her rose automatically as the sap in the twigs. It was unexpended youth, surging up anew after its temporary check, and bringing with it hope, and the invincible instinct towards self-delight.[14]

Much human activity is understood in another way: as what might be called *behaviour* – that is, activity determined by causal factors operating on individuals' minds: psychological factors say, or social, or cultural, or economic, or conceptual, or whatever. By 'growing up', for example, we sometimes mean functioning, sometimes behaviour. We understand Stephen's desire to 'sin' as he does, and then to repent as he does, in this way: as behaviour determined by the particular religion and society he has grown up in.

The third way that literature and literary criticism has understood human activity is, of course, as *action* or (more generally) as *conduct*: as activity of the will or as activities determined by the will. Naturally, every particular morality draws its own lines between conduct and other, non-moral kinds of activity; moreover, it grades different areas of conduct as more or less important, and concentrates on those it considers important enough to regulate. Then again, its grading usually implies, if it is not derived from, some universal normative conception of human nature or of the ideal human life, however sketchy that conception may be. Even so, the focus of attention is still the extent to which we can understand the agent's activity as voluntarily regulated in accordance with the rules or principles or ideals designed to realize that conception as far as possible, or as a more or less blameworthy failure to regulate it.

Needless to say, there are countless ways of understanding human activity, but even in these rough-and-ready terms it is clear that making sense of human lives can mean very different things. To claim that somebody's apparent conduct is really causally determined *behaviour*, for example, or that the subject of the actions in question is only a social or linguistic *function* (i.e. a fiction), is to reject the possibility of considering his activity morally – at least, in this sense of 'moral'. That, indeed, is very often the reason why people advance claims of this sort. For them, making sense of lives involves taking the term 'lives' to mean either people's behaviour or their functioning, and taking the term 'making sense' to mean only locating that within either a network of causal relationships or an impersonal dynamic system. And certainly, we all make sense of lives in both of these ways at times, even our own – indeed, we have to. There is a pervasive habit of using transitive verbs of action in a surreptitiously metaphorical sense to describe activities that on closer inspection are not just voluntary, intentional actions (Stephen 'sins', for example). And indeed, so readily do moralizers seize upon the opportunities this habit offers them that one can even feel some sympathy with thorough-going determinists or with those who want to get rid of the rational 'subject' altogether.

Nevertheless, most of us find that we cannot get rid of the subject altogether, if only because we sometimes *have* to understand ourselves and other people as moral agents; and in practice, most of us treat 'free will' and 'determinism' as merely different perspectives from which we can make different kinds of sense of people's activity. When we do regard them as agents, we take a person's 'life' to mean primarily the sequence of his voluntary or intentional activity, his actions, and their consequences as well perhaps; by 'making sense', we now mean something like understanding the *internal rationality* of those actions, grasping them in terms of the desires, beliefs, motives, feelings, practical thinking, norms and so on that regulate the will 'behind' the actions or are implicit in them. Considered in this way, the moral subject is not only real, but has a quite determinate identity given from the outset: the self or ego is unproblematically 'there'. It is definable in various ways – in terms of specific desires, preferences, motives or ends; specific passions or other psychological impulsions; specific beliefs, interests and social roles; specific capacities for feeling and rational thought; specific relationships with other objects in the world as well as with its own past and future existence; and so on. Different moralities and moral theories place different emphases on different elements of the moral self, and dispute endlessly about which are the most important. But out of some or all of these elements, and ideally under the regulative guidance of morality, the agent is seen as voluntarily forming the content of intentions, projects, deeds, and habits. 'Moral insight' or 'moral wisdom' is the term we use for the capacity to understand the elements and the moral bearings of actions or conduct – which is why such 'moral insight' involves the capacity to make acute moral judgments as well. And to judge anyone morally in this sense is to describe his actions or conduct (and perhaps especially that which affects other people) correctly in terms of the requirements of morality, and to measure them against those requirements – that is, against the yard-stick of specific norms, or ends, or ideals, or principles, or rules, or maxims, which provide criteria of good action. In relation to these specific, definable criteria, the performance of the will can be judged, whether in itself or in its consequences, to be more or less morally perfect – right or wrong, good or bad, good or evil, rational or irrational, or whatever.

This is no more than a quick, rough sketch of a familiar kind of moral thinking of course – or at least of some of the main features of it that are to be found in literature and literary criticism. But with an eye to literature that in some sense represents people – either real people (as in history) or fictional characters (as in 'dramatic' literature) – it is worth adding that this kind of moral thinking naturally regards certain features of anybody's nature – or personal 'character' – as salient. For obvious reasons, there is generally an intimate connection in any writer or critic between the fictional and the moral senses of 'character'. Considering people as moral agents, for instance, almost inevitably means focusing on those features of their natures that issue in conduct: what is most relevant about a person's 'character' – in fact, what is often meant by the very word 'character' – is the general way their activity is regulated by the criteria of good and bad action. Their 'character' is defined in terms of the specifically moral virtues and vices displayed by their habitual conduct. Their most important features are the particular qualities they have and those they lack among all those required for anybody's perfect perform-ance as a moral agent. Those they lack are a 'flaw' or deficiency in their moral being. And if one believes that people are to be defined primarily as moral agents, then any individual's moral 'character' as an agent comprises their most important features as a human being.

Of course this conduct-moral viewpoint recognizes other features as well. Everyone's 'character' includes some that can be made sense of only in causal terms: a person's particular psychological make-up, for example – his or her native 'dis-position' or 'temper' or 'bent of personality' – or those features determined by the individual's historical, social or personal circumstances. These issue in *behaviour*; and it has been one of the chief aims of the 'moral sciences' – from Plato and Aristotle onwards, through the character-writers of the seventeenth and eighteenth centuries, the moral educationists of the later eighteenth and nineteenth centuries, and the characterologies of modern psychology and sociology – to mark out the extent and operation of these determining circumstances. For the

conduct-moralist, however, they are relevant only as enabling
(or maybe disabling) circumstantial pressures on the agent's
will. For the conduct-moralist's purposes, that is, they need to
be specified, analysed, and tracked through time only in their
inter-relationships with the agent's conduct. His upbringing or
his economic activities may help or release his capacity to think
and feel and act in the right way. His 'disposition' may make
him attractive or unattractive, or it may cause his behaviour, or
his feelings, or his motives, or even his thinking, to incline in this
direction rather than that. But morally speaking, all this is only
part of the given circumstances in which he acts or upon which
he acts. What matters is *how well he conducts himself* in relation to
his disposition and other such circumstances: whether King
Lear *admits* his own 'folly', whether Emma Woodhouse *corrects*
hers, whether Maggie Tulliver's moral development helps her
overcome her 'natural longing' for Stephen Guest.

Considered in this way, therefore, any individual could be
said to have that favourite object of many nineteenth-century
writers, a 'true' self, alias a 'best' self, behind the ordinary,
empirical self. A point not often underlined by such writers (no
doubt because it might have made people baulk at its
implications) is that anybody's 'true' self or 'best' self is,
ideally, not essentially different from everybody else's. For it is
the subject of the verb in the phrase *how well he conducts himself*.
That is, the 'true self' is the will to achieve a perfect moral
performance by regulating the ordinary, empirical self, which is
the object of the verb. A person's moral 'integrity' consists in
the constant alignment of the self as object and the self as
subject, and both with the principles or criteria of good conduct.
His 'true life', the life of his 'true self', is therefore inward, and
perhaps obscure to other people: it consists in his will toward
morally good action at all times, given the enabling or resisting
circumstances of the world that the will confronts, which
include, of course, a man's particular psychological 'disposition'
and integration, his upbringing, his social place, his flaws of
'character', and the desires he is moved or tempted to satisfy.

In this conduct-moral kind of thinking, the term *fate* generally
means the sum total of those circumstances, especially those that

resist the good will: the good will confronts 'fate', battles against it. A man's *destiny* is the course and outcome of that battle, which begins with the birth of his moral autonomy and continues until the final defeat of the will by death, when the test is over – or at least when stumps are drawn, since the true result may not be known until later, when it will be announced by history or the great all-seeing umpire in the sky. A name often given to a will that refuses to act as the 'true' self is 'evil' (or nasty); a person who has no 'true self' is 'brutish'; a life that is not much of a 'true life' is (in the more edifying works of literature at least) generally short. From this point of view, *tragedy* is supposed to be a name for a person's failure completely to overcome fate – that is, to overcome the resistance of the world, or of his own flaws of character, or both. (What tragic poetry does, on this account of it, is to reveal the obscurer moral laws of the universe – which naturally are more likely to show up in plot than in character, since the latter is regarded from the outset as the determinate, clearly-visible moral self.) For a person's success in overcoming fate there are a number of possible terms: moral triumph, the good life, blessedness, felicity or true happiness, redemption, the life of reason, salvation, and so on. It is also possible to have a kind of Pyrrhic victory, which some literary critics are rather keen on, and which might be summed up in the formula, 'dead, but saved by learning that his own fatal flaw brought it on himself'. – Out by hitting his own wicket, as it were.

Clearly, then, considering people as agents does not preclude considering them as lives, at least in one sense; but it is a significantly – and sometimes a paradoxically – limited sense.

III

If we think of one prime example of an autobiographical moral history in English, Wordsworth's *Prelude*, we could describe its subject-matter as the 'pre-history' of the moral agent. It considers an exemplary life, an instance of the universal human case, and traces how it grows a 'best self' or 'true self': here, it says in effect, are the conditions and influences that foster the 'best self' or hinder its growth. In other words, it purports – like so many of the novels that followed it – to trace a single, unitary process from moral pre-history to moral history proper, from functioning to behaviour to conduct. *The Mill on the Floss* is another notable example of this, and perhaps more clearly than *The Prelude* it brings out some of the problems of making moral sense of lives in this limited, agent-centred way.

The most obvious problem is the indeterminacy of the line between the pre-history and the real history of the moral agent, and especially between that human activity which has to be considered as behaviour (that determined by causal factors operating on the mind) and that which has to be considered as conduct. *When* does a person become a moral agent? This is not much of a problem for Hardy, in *Tess of the D'Urbervilles*, say, since two of his main points there are the extent to which apparent conduct is really behaviour, and the extent to which conduct is at odds with life. Nor is it much of a problem for Joyce in *A Portrait of the Artist*, since one of his main points there is that Stephen's conduct is only one element of a total mode of life – both Stephen's and Ireland's, as it were – at each and every stage of his growth. Nor is it a problem for D. H. Lawrence, even in his quasi-autobiographical novel (almost synchronous with Joyce's), *Sons and Lovers*, since he is always concerned with people as lives, not just as 'stable egos' and moral agents. But it certainly is a problem for George Eliot in *The Mill on the Floss*.

The cause of the problem is not her beliefs about free will and determinism, but the same belief that made the moral history of Mankind a problem for many nineteenth-century writers. They took it that functioning, behaviour, moral life, and moral conduct formed (in that order) a single line of development in time – as if each was a more perfect version of its predecessors.[15] In other words, conceptual differences were translated into historical stages, and the history into a process that led (in a Whiggish conception of moral history) to the final emergence of the 'true', the 'highest' moral activity of humankind: conduct. The result is the sort of uncertainty we have in *The Mill on the Floss* about when exactly the young Maggie becomes a fully

responsible moral agent (or a 'truly' or 'fully' human being).
Her brother Tom regards her as that from a very early age, and
so at times does the novel itself. But it also suggests that her
activity is to be regarded only in causal terms as behaviour or
even as functioning – as a certain native disposition being
moulded and influenced in certain ways, but always tending to
revert to its own course – not merely in childhood but right up
to the point where she rejects Stephen Guest's last appeal. Yet
the novel may seem to treat that rejection too as only causally
determined behaviour in the same way, and not really a moral
action either, so that Maggie is destroyed just as she is about to
become a full, autonomous moral self. Various critics of the
book have argued for each one of these three views; and
although it may be tempting to talk about the novel's profound
complexity here, it seems to me more like a straightforward
muddle – a muddle which, like George Eliot's bother over free
will, and her revealingly crude conception of tragedy,[16] arises
from her trying here to make moral sense of people's lives with
a too exclusively conduct-moral conception both of morality
and of people.

Apart from problems about the line between moral pre-
history and moral history, however, such a conception gives rise
to problems about moral history itself. To the conduct-moral,
agent-centred historian, the *point* of making sense of a life is to
answer the question, 'how well has the person conducted
himself?' – or, to put it another way, 'how well has he
conducted his life?' Either way, however, the historian treats
the rules or norms of good action as the rules or norms of the
good (or the righteous, or the rational) life for men to lead: he
sees human life as, ideally, *led* or *conducted*. (For Aristotle, this
distinguished 'virtue in the strict sense' from mere 'natural
virtue'.[17]) The morally perfect life is identified with the perfectly
moral life; ideally, that is, all human activity of any note would
transcend the condition of functioning or behaviour and achieve
the condition of action. For the conduct-moralist, the moral will
should be universal emperor, for only its realm, that of moral
self-possession, volition and self-regulation, is really and truly
life in the normative sense of the word. The conduct-moralist

applies the point, we might notice, to a good deal of activity that we are usually content (in our normal non-ideal state) to value precisely because it is *not* within the scope of voluntary choice: activity that is idiosyncratic, for example, uniquely individual, or responsively spontaneous, or directly and unthinkingly warm-hearted, or engagingly vivacious. Ideally, the moral will would regulate much idiosyncrasy or individuality away; alternatively, it would take it as a regulative ideal of action – very much as many people do try to take it nowadays; or (most commonly) refuse to consider it a 'truly' moral quality at all. Similarly with spontaneity or warm-heartedness or vivacity: ideally, the moral will would either regulate the quality away, or dismiss it as morally irrelevant, or take an appropriately measured spontaneity or vivacity as a rule of conduct. One should strive to be spontaneous. At this point, we may well seem to have reached a *reductio ad absurdum*.

I think we have. Even though there are 'indirect strategies' for trying to achieve some highly valued qualities, there are still many such qualities – creativity, say, or 'moral' intelligence or warm-heartedness – where it is absurdly impossible 'to will what cannot be willed'.[18] In order to appreciate the absurdity fully, however, we need to remember how persistently the human race has wanted *not* to appreciate it. For what makes it absurd is the impossibility of giving certain qualities – not just those I have mentioned, but joy, or 'self-delight', or nobleness, or Blake's 'excess', for example – any content as a direct, conscious ideal of voluntary action without draining the idea of authenticity. For the ideal really applies to the way a person is alive – to his or her activity as a whole – not just to a specific idea in the mind directing the will to a specific set of actions or to a habit of such actions. The quality manifests itself in actions, of course, but manifests *itself*, as a supervenient quality – exactly as it manifests itself in functioning and behaviour. It is an ideal of life, not just of conduct. Arnold's 'perfection' is a case in point; and he merely travestied his own meaning when he suggested that there was a simple formula for achieving perfection: act, as we might say, so as to observe the rule three parts of righteousness plus one part of culture. To treat a life-moral ideal as if it were a conscious ideal of conduct means in effect substituting some pre-conceived *notion* of individuality, say, or nobleness, and some pre-known and readily-recognizable *signs* of it, for the quality itself – a quality that may well take a form we could not have expected or cannot easily recognize. There is an important difference, for example, between the real (and unpredictable) 'nobleness of life' that shines out of Shakespeare's Antony at times, and the pre-conceived (and rather conventional) idea of nobleness or of 'the noble Antony' by which he often tries to act. So with other life-moral ideals that have been translated into the goals sought by herd-like 'self-realizers', or into stereotyped 'individual life-styles', or self-congratulatory 'caring' and 'concern', or permissive self-indulgence.

The truth is, of course, that no one can ever be sure of achieving any life-moral ideal; but in so far as it can be deliberately sought, it is only *in*directly, by a subtle, experimental 'art of life', not just by following rules, or imitating models, of conduct. And as the term 'art' implies, its practice will necessarily produce different and unpredictable results: individual lives manifesting different and perhaps surprising versions and degrees of the ideal. There can be no single, universal, uniform model of it. Even so commonplace a moralist as Cicero recognized this about the ideal he called 'decorum', which seems to include something like a grace, and something like an integral congruence, in one's entire life. Men have such very different individual natures that what counts as a duty or a virtue is relative to the internal nature and needs, and the external circumstances and necessities, of each particular life – a point, we might notice, that Cicero has to make by reference to the particular lives of actual people. For him, therefore, 'decorum' lies partly in observing in one's conduct the general nature all men share, but partly too in co-operating with one's particular, distinctive nature, not fighting it.[19]

Nevertheless, it is worth noticing how persistently people have always sought the impossible: *rules* of life, whether for all human beings (including heretics, infidels, or lesser breeds) or for different sub-classes of them. Every moralist and moral philosopher should ponder a memorable line in Monty Python's *Life of Brian* just after the hero has been cornered by the crowd and has to pretend to be the Messiah they have been looking for:

CROWD: He is! He *is* the Messiah! (They all fall and worship him.)
BRIAN: Now *fuck off*!!! (Long pause.)
ARTHUR: [one of the mob]: How shall we fuck off O Lord?

The Arthurs of the world *want* rules for living; they *want* poetry to have a palpable design on us and tell us exactly how we ought to conduct our lives. Even Tolstoy became just such an Arthur. And it is partly this, of course, that led D. H. Lawrence to attack the whole idea of living by the will – though unfortunately he was then only too happy to tell Arthur how he might do it instead. But of course over the centuries there have been many attacks on the will and on trying to follow rules of life. One was the appeal from the letter of the law to the Spirit; another was the appeal from works to Faith. Indeed, this is the very point of concepts like the Spirit, or Faith, or the Inner Voice, or Grace, or virtù, or genius, or originality, or spontaneity, or imagination, or the life-force, or creativity – there are many others. They almost always originate as a way of specifying a crucial difference between 'conducting' our lives and living. And yet as the ineffable Arthur reminds us, they almost always end up being subverted into some new rule of life – into ends, or ideals, or criteria of conduct and of moral judgment. The same thing can happen with the very word 'life' itself. D. H. Lawrence, for example, sometimes (not always) talks as if it were a substantive idea, a very inclusive norm or criterion of judgment, instead of a term marking out what it is that some of our moral judgments are about.

As I have suggested above, one common way of dealing with such difficulties is that used by some philosophers: to push them aside by claiming that the scope of specifically *moral* values in human life is limited, and that living engages many other kinds of ideals and values than moral ones. There are spiritual or religious values, for example, or 'aesthetic' ones, or political ones, or psychological ones, or ideals that are purely personal.

Such philosophers might agree that, in a general sort of way, these values have some bearing on those voluntary intentional actions that are supposed to be the sole concern of morality; but, they imply or argue, each of these other kinds of value is really the concern of some other kind of specialist evaluation because *strictly* speaking it is not really moral. But of course there is no unwritten constitutional rule about what everyone should mean by 'moral'.

IV

To consider people as *lives* rather than as conductors of lives involves a different kind of moral thinking. It is harder to describe, partly because it includes regarding people as agents too, but regarding their conduct – even the conduct of their lives – as only one manifestation (though of course a very important one) of the real object of attention.

In the first place, this way of thinking involves the view, which Hume puts rather neatly in the fourth Appendix to his *Enquiry Concerning the Principles of Morals*, that morality and moral judgment are, and always have been, quite properly concerned with human qualities well beyond 'the dominion of will and choice'. As Hume quite rightly says, there is no conclusive reason why moral judgments have to distinguish voluntary qualities (or 'true' virtues) from non-voluntary ones, or 'moral' endowments from 'intellectual' ones, or qualities of the 'heart' from those of the 'head'.[20] Of course, to agree with him on this point is not necessarily to accept the particular moral theory he constructed around it; but he does at least recognize the existence of life-moral qualities as I call them, as well as conduct-moral ones. (Indeed, Section VII of the *Enquiry* is almost entirely devoted to qualities that 'animate', 'enliven', 'relish', 'excite', 'engage', 'strike', 'agitate', 'set in motion', 'seize', 'warm', 'melt', 'exalt' and so on.) Moreover, he also recognizes that the two kinds of moral judgment may well pull in different directions. For example, to 'cool reflection', heroism, military glory, has little to recommend it; yet considering the hero himself, 'the author of all this mischief', we may find 'something so dazzling in his character, the mere contemplation of [which] so elevates the mind, that we cannot refuse it our admiration'.[21]

Considering people as lives involves something else Hume recognizes, at least implicitly: that although 'many pages would not contain the catalogue' of moral 'virtues and accomplishments',[22] not all morally-relevant qualities can be named and analysed. Some can only be registered, as he puts it, by 'the blind, but sure testimony of taste and sentiment':

But besides all the *agreeable* qualities, the origin of whose beauty we can, in some degree, explain and account for, there still remains something mysterious and inexplicable, which conveys an immediate satisfaction to the spectator, but how, or why, or for what reason, he cannot pretend to determine. There is a manner, a grace, an ease, a genteelness, an I-know-not-what, which some men possess above others, which is very different from external beauty and comeliness, and which, however, catches our affection almost as suddenly and powerfully. And though this *manner* be chiefly talked of in the passion between the sexes, where the concealed magic is easily explained, yet surely much of it prevails in all our estimation of characters, and forms no inconsiderable part of personal merit. This class of accomplishments, therefore, must be trusted entirely to the blind, but sure testimony of taste and sentiment; and must be considered as a part of ethics, left by nature to baffle all the pride of philosophy, and make her sensible of her narrow boundaries and slender acquisitions.[23]

What this suggests, though Hume does not draw the conclusion, is that we are not able to predetermine a set of specific qualities that comprise *the* criteria of goodness, or *the* moral virtues; and therefore we must always expect that some of the most important moral qualities of a particular life – especially perhaps those that mark its uniqueness – may not be recognizable as examples of already-defined general qualities, but require of us an uncommon openness and subtlety of thought and a scrupulous, even imaginative, precision of language, in order to notice such qualities in the first place and to capture them in a way that enables others to notice them too.

This points to another kind of suggestiveness in this passage of Hume's. His own 'manner' in the last sentence actually exemplifies what he is talking about, I think; certainly its effect on my 'taste' and 'sentiment' is to catch my affection suddenly and powerfully. Equally significant, I think, is his word 'sensible'. It clearly means something different from just ordinary seeing or knowing or understanding – something more like noticing, with a shift in the *mode* of seeing or knowing or understanding: a deepened or a heightened awareness, a fuller realizing. This seems to me to suggest another way we can make sense of lives, just as Hume's own 'manner' in that sentence suggests what it is that we are then making sense of. For we cannot really regard that 'manner' as having been adopted by Hume's will or choice as a means to express his point. Neither can we regard it as a mere item of behaviour, causally determined by, say, his psychological disposition, or the culture of his day, much less a mere functioning of the 'structures' of his mind or of his language. It seems to have elements of action and behaviour and functioning about it, and yet to be none of them. Were we to call it 'expressive', this would raise a similar problem, for would 'express' be a verb of intentional, transitive action? Surely we would mean that in Hume's 'manner' something not about Hume, but something of him, is *as it were* expressed – not in the sense that it is (or was) Hume's intention to make this something visible to us, but rather in the sense that this something manifests *itself*.[24] (It would be a different something if we thought it the effect of Hume's intention to be expressive in some fashion or another.) But if this is right, *what* is manifesting itself?

Some of the things Hume does not seem to notice here are equally interesting. One is the way he shifts between speaking about this nameless 'I-know-not-what' as a kind of quality and speaking of it as a kind of 'accomplishment'. The difference here between the voluntary and the non-voluntary does not matter to Hume, of course, given his moral theory with its focus on the spectator rather than the agent. But it would matter to someone who wanted to catch others' affection – an Arthur, say, or a professor who felt he ought to develop some of those *endearing* eccentricities that the best professors are supposed to have – and who might think, indeed, that providing guidance to conduct is the only point of moral judgements. Yet what could we say to the professor? It is not necessarily a matter of his doing anything he does not do already, or of not doing something he does do; it may be a matter of his doing exactly the same things as he does already, but doing them in a different manner: laughing differently, or perceiving people differently, or being more intelligent, or being less moralistic, or having a different way of being spontaneous. We might have to say something like, 'Try to catch a manner beyond all the manners you can learn, a natural "ease" on the other side of conscious conduct and habit. Be *alive* in a different way. It would be good if you were a genius in the art of living, since a genius can snatch a grace beyond the reach of art; but at least change your whole self, be somebody else. Go and get transformed.'

That is quite often the sort of thing we do want to say to people – or to some people – and it is not wholly absurd. There *are* ways that people can become entirely re-fashioned, converted, transfigured, undergo a change of heart, learn an art of life. For the Arthurs who cannot, there are always Messiahs with rules for achieving it, from prayer and meditation, to psychoanalysis, to taking drugs or bringing about the Revolution; and as with all rules of life, the results are usually correlative with the method. Nevertheless, whatever we think of the results, whether they are brought about by eating organic food or by falling in love, our judgment of them is certainly, as Hume insists, a *moral* one. A case in point is Nicholas Rostóv's judgment of Princess Mary in *War and Peace*.

Had Princess Mary been capable of reflection at that moment, she would have been more surprised than Mademoiselle Bourienne at the change that had taken place in herself. From the moment she recognized that dear, loved face, a new life force took possession of her and compelled her to speak and act apart from her own will. From the time Rostóv entered, her face became suddenly transformed. It was as if a light had been kindled in a carved and painted lantern and the intricate, skillful, artistic work on its sides, that previously seemed dark, coarse, and meaningless, was suddenly shown up in unexpected and striking beauty. For the first time all that pure, spiritual, inward travail through which she had lived appeared on the surface. All her inward labour, her dissatisfaction with herself, her sufferings, her strivings after goodness, her meekness, love, and self-sacrifice – all this now shone in those radiant eyes, in her delicate smile, and in every trait of her gentle face.

Rostóv saw all this as clearly as if he had known her whole life. He felt that the being before him was quite different from, and better than, any one he had met before, and above all better than himself.[25]

This passage brings out something else that Hume does not notice. As with Hume's own manner in the sentence I mentioned earlier, so in another way here: the object and the nature of the moral judgment call out a special mode of judging. The judgment of Princess Mary, for example – and it is judgment as much as description – is not directed towards a particular new quality added to those she already possessed. It is directed to her whole way of being alive, and this calls for an answering wholeness of response and expression in order to characterize it. This is the point of the metaphorical language, for example – even 'life force', we would notice, is clearly metaphor. Another revealing index is Rostóv's sense that Mary is now 'the being before him' – a particular life, whose nature and value partly manifest themselves as the sheer *presence* to him now of a unique total way of being and doing. This kind of value in this kind of object is not reducible to any single abstract or general quality that anyone – Tolstoy or Rostóv – could point to, or even to any collection of such qualities; it also resides in qualities characteristic of this particular person and no other.

Hume's way of talking tends to short-circuit any adequate recognition of all this. For one thing, he takes his general terms to be less problematical than they are. A good example is his phrase, 'the passion between the sexes'. *The* passion, is it? What, we may wonder, is more real or more important in this context (let alone 'easily explained') about the features that Princess Mary shares with, say, the Wife of Bath, or Heathcliff with Mr Knightley ('passion'?), or Florizel with Tarquin, than the features they do not? It is not just that Hume's category seems to beg far too many questions; more than that, it is the cast or habit of mind here which is questionable. For Hume is still thinking of his nameless something as an abstract general quality which an individual may or may not instantiate; and he also seems to assume that we could in principle name and list all such qualities, that those instantiated by an individual comprise all the relevant moral features of the individual, and that the phenomena of a person present themselves to the mind only *as* instances of these general qualities.

In this, of course, he reveals how much he shares those eighteenth-century assumptions that make even subtle moralists like Dr Johnson and Jane Austen seem so distant from us in the clear, sharp (and ·ultimately comfortable) outlines of their moral categories and language. This applies to more than the actual *content* of their lists of morally-relevant general qualities; it applies to their implicit belief in the universal validity and applicability of such lists. Of course Hume is no Christian as Johnson and Jane Austen are, but for him as for them there seems no problem, at least in principle, about knowing what all the morally-relevant phenomena *are* with a person. Nor does he see any unresolvable doubts about the possibility of categorizing those phenomena or even about assigning them their correct names.

Another way of making the point here would be to ask what sense these eighteenth-century writers' moral categories would make of the lives of the Karamazovs, say, or of Stephen Dedalus, or (come to that) of William Blake. Johnson's inability to cope even with Falstaff is revealing:

The Prince, who is the hero both of the comick and tragick part, is a young man of great abilities and violent passions, whose sentiments are right, though his actions are wrong; whose virtues are obscured by negligence, and whose understanding is dissipated by levity. In his idle hours he is rather loose than wicked; and when the occasion forces out his latent qualities, he is great without effort, and brave without tumult. The trifler is roused into a hero, and the hero again reposes in the trifler. This character is great, original, and just.

Percy is a rugged soldier, cholerick, and quarrelsome, and has only the soldier's virtues, generosity and courage.

But Falstaff, unimitated, unimitable Falstaff, how shall I describe thee? Thou compound of sense and vice; of sense which may be admired but not esteemed, of vice which may be despised, but hardly detested. Falstaff is a character loaded with faults, and with those faults which naturally produce contempt. He is a thief, and a glutton, a coward, and a boaster, always ready to cheat the weak, and prey upon the poor; to terrify the timorous and insult the defenceless. At once obsequious and malignant, he satirises in their absence those whom he lives by flattering. He is familiar with the Prince only as an agent of vice, but of this familiarity he is so proud as not only to be supercilious and haughty with common men, but to think his interest of importance to the Duke of Lancaster. Yet the man thus corrupt, thus despicable, makes himself necessary to the prince that despises him, by the most pleasing of all qualities, perpetual gaiety, by an unfailing power of exciting laughter, which is the more freely indulged, as his wit is not of the splendid or ambitious kind, but consists in easy escapes and sallies of levity, which make sport but raise no envy. It must be observed that he is stained with no enormous or sanguinary crimes, so that his licentiousness is not so offensive but that it may be borne for his mirth.

The moral to be drawn from this representation is, that no man is more dangerous than he that with a will to corrupt, hath the power to please; and that neither wit nor honesty ought to think themselves safe with such a companion when they see Henry seduced by Falstaff.[26]

Johnson's sense of Falstaff, which embodies his evaluative response to Falstaff as a particular, indeed unique, total *life*, is clearly manifest in his first sentence about him – and all the more clearly by contrast with the third-person, analytic way he has just spoken about Hal and Hotspur. And yet this vital sense of the person as a life slips out of the grasp of Johnson's conceptualizing habits of mind as he goes on to make the necessary conduct-moral judgments about Falstaff. But in thinking *of* Falstaff as 'thee', as a living mental presence, he can catch only a general quality, 'perpetual gaiety', which Falstaff happens to instantiate, but which certainly does not make the same responsive kind of sense of his life as did the opening sentence. In fact, were we to ask what qualities, and qualities of what precisely, manifest themselves in Johnson's own moral sensibility, in *his* usage of his moral concepts and language, we could not give an adequate answer in terms of those concepts and judgment themselves, not even in Hume's variant of them.

The case of Johnson on Falstaff suggests something else about Hume's example of 'the passion between the sexes', though the point is not confined just to that. It is Juliet, we recall, and only Juliet, whom Romeo falls in love with, though at first he is captivated by the fair Rosaline; and it is only Juliet who falls in love with Romeo, not Rosaline or anybody else. Even in the rhyme about Dr Fell – 'I do not like thee, Dr Fell, / The reason why, I cannot tell...' – it is only one man who does not 'like' him and cannot tell why. The way Hume puts it, however, suggests that the 'concealed magic' is a quality or accomplishment that is objective in the sense that it could catch the affection (or repulsion) of any and every person of 'taste and sentiment': it is the same kind of thing as modesty, say, or cleanliness, or genteelness, or what we call 'charm'. But being in love may not be just the same as being attracted to a girl's 'charms', though lots of Restoration and eighteenth-century authors wrote as if it always were. Nor is the value of Juliet to Romeo, or of Romeo to Juliet, one that could possibly be universal – that is recognizable by any spectator with the requisite 'taste and sentiment'. One might say, I suppose, that it would be perceptible by anybody who loved Juliet as Romeo does; but who could that be? Saying this is only to use a speculative fantasy to go around a circle. Or one might say that it is not a truly 'moral' value Romeo sees in her; but, as Hume reminds us, why should we accept that particular view of what counts as a moral valuation? For Romeo, that value is a matter of life and death, after all.

But there are further difficulties for Hume here too, largely because the 'testimony' of taste and sentiment is not at all as 'sure' as he supposes. If a lover (like Romeo) or a hater (like Iago) sees a special 'beauty' in the life of Juliet or Cassio that other people do not see, the *value* of that 'beauty' is not, as Hume recognizes very well, a question of fact decidable by competent witnesses. But then neither is the presence or absence of the relevant quality or set of qualities in a person necessarily a matter of fact decidable by the testimony of others' taste and sentiment. In many cases, there are far more basic questions at stake than simply whether competent witnesses would agree that a certain general quality is instantiated here or not. Or to put it another way, we cannot always take it for granted that such 'beauty', say, is either a general quality really present which causes the appropriate feeling of love (or hate, or friendship, or whatever), or alternatively an illusion which is merely the effect of some more or less arbitrary feeling. It may be one or the other of these; but then again it may not. (This is why a good deal of Aesthetics is a sheer waste of time.) What is more, we cannot even take it for granted that some such quality is necessarily the object of the feeling of love or whatever, or the 'intentional object', if the word 'intentional' is anything more than an inconspicuous door through which questions of moral conduct can be smuggled into a matter that is notoriously not one of deliberate intention. There are other possibilities; indeed, the deepest evaluative-emotional relationships are precisely those that display them.

It may be, for example, that what is named as 'beauty' is a valuable potential mode or quality of being, and one which can realize itself more fully only if a particular person responds to it in a way that affirms its immanence and value. The princess who loves the toad in the fairy tale does not love him because, with *her* taste and sentiment, she recognizes a certain princely *je-ne-sais-quoi* about him; he becomes a prince because she loves him. Moreover, if her then kissing him is a voluntary intentional action, it is not necessarily the case that her loving is also an action, based (very sensibly) upon recognizing his potential qualities and appreciating their true worth. No doubt love sometimes does have that kind of internal rationality, but much less often than anxious parents or officious moralizers suppose. Nor again is the princess necessarily the victim of a curious sexual fantasy, or of a pathological tendency to be so infatuated by toads as to mistake them for princes. That sort of thing is common enough, of course, especially in adolescence – the advertising industry is largely devoted to exploiting it; but it is not always the case. Sometimes, as Thurber's cartoon reminds us, the improbable noise one hears actually *is* a seal barking in the bedroom. Nor again is the princess necessarily a girl who simply dotes on princes, or rather, on princely qualities – whether because she had been brought up that way or because she values them on rational grounds – and happening to find them instantiated in this unlikely guise, naturally loves them: unless or until, presumably, a more likely instantiation turns up.

Not everybody loves like Molly Bloom: 'I thought well as well him as another'. Many love the person, the particular, distinctive way *he* is alive, the particulars characteristic of him and him alone and not only the admirable general qualities he instantiates. In fact, we may quite reasonably want to restrict the term 'love' only to that sort of case. (Compare Lear's reaction to Cordelia in the first scene of the play: he wants her to declare her love of *him*, not just her love of his virtues. She, on the other hand, will speak only of the virtues of conduct.)

The case of the princess and the toad may quite well be of that sort too: this girl (and no other) loves this particular young man (and no other), whose inexplicable presence she (and no other) is sensible of in this particular creature (and no other). True, as with many such cases, all that we spectators can do is wonder what a nice girl like her can possibly see in the little toad; if we are well-disposed, we may even hope that, whatever it is, time proves her right. Nevertheless, we speak of 'seeing in', not 'seeing as'; and we do so because we know that although love sometimes is 'blind' in the sense that it is only the cause or the effect of delusion, it sometimes is 'blind' in another sense: that it involves a trust, a faith, not just in the existence and value and strength of certain potentialities in the other person, but also in one's own need, capacity and commitment to appreciate those potentialities and thereby perhaps help them realize themselves. This is why the blindness of love sometimes sees a person, and the course of time, far more deeply than the wisest spectator. (The same applies, *mutatis mutandis*, with hate, friendship, and so on.) In short, we may have to say that the princess's love (like many people's) *is* the seeing of this particular prince-in-potentia in this toad.

If so, then the princess's love is indeed partly an action, but not *only* the voluntary recognition of certain general qualities and an appropriate judgment of their value. It is partly behaviour too, but not *only* a psychologically or socially determined reaction. It is partly even functioning, but not *only* the working of a hormonal system, say, or of a system of courtship and mating. Nor is it only the sum total of these. It is rather something that cannot be entirely analysed in such terms: the moral activity of the whole self in relation to another, one life evaluatively responding to another – something, that is, which can manifest itself alike in physiological processes, consciousness, feeling and desire, sensibility, imagining, gesture and tone, as well as in choice, decision, intent and even indeed in the way the phenomena of the other life are categorized and represented.

A classic case of this is Cleopatra's 'dream' of Antony:

Cleo. His face was as the heav'ns, and therein stuck
    A sun and moon, which kept their course and lighted
    The little O o'th'earth.
Dol.   Most sovereign creature –,
Cleo. His legs bestrid the ocean; his rear'd arm
    Crested the world. His voice was propertied
    As all the tuned spheres, and that to friends;
    But when he meant to quail and shake the orb,
    He was as rattling thunder. For his bounty,
    There was no winter in't; an autumn 'twas
    That grew the more by reaping. His delights
    Were dolphin-like: they show'd his back above
    The element they liv'd in. In his livery
    Walk'd crowns and crownets; realms and islands were
    As plates dropp'd from his pocket.
Dol.   Cleopatra –
Cleo. Think you there was or might be such a man
    As this I dreamt of?
Dol.   Gentle madam, no.[27]

What Dolabella takes her to be asking him is whether this is a fair account of Antony's qualities, or more generally, whether a man might not have these qualities. To the shrewd, decent, but essentially power-orientated Dolabella, Cleopatra must seem to be either indulging her fancy (a voluntary action), or merely in the grip of a strong infatuation (exhibiting mere behaviour). Yet this is to miss the point, as becomes clear in her next speech; and as it happens – or rather, as Shakespeare makes it happen – Dolabella's inability to see the point has certain political consequences of a kind he is very interested in. For Cleopatra is asking a rather different question: What if one were to see *this* in a man – what then?

To see this in a man takes more than 'taste or sentiment'; it takes a love of the man. Or rather, it actually manifests a love of the man, since the manner of seeing is inseparable from the object seen, and these embrace *everything* the poetry expresses here – including something like an answering, life-enriching power, an answering delight and wonder, in the delight, wonder and powerful richness of the man's life. To 'see' this in him also takes a moral imagination large and deep enough to have just this 'dream' of the sense a man's life might make. It also takes a real belief, or trust, or faith, that one is not merely the victim of delusion or fantasy in this case, but responding as one must to what is really there in the man, however imperfectly realized. And it also takes a self capable of answering adequately to what is there with a 'seeing' that is inseparable from evaluation, an evaluation inseparable from emotional reaction, and an emotional reaction inseparable from voluntary actions. In short, it is to manifest one's own moral life. And that, as Cleopatra discovers, can mean that this sense of Antony is not just the only sense she can make retrospectively of *his* life; it is also the only sense she can make of her own past and future life. Her destiny is to be the person who had to see and answer to *this* as she has done. For her to recognize herself as also the same person who, now, has to 'see' a supreme value for her, as well as an inescapable personal necessity, 'in' that destiny – who has to identify what *had* to be as also what *ought* to be – is to make her destiny also her choice. (Thus one may see one's particular destiny as, at the very least, the only available set of conditions on which one could have been a human being and had a life at all.)

If one is lucky, of course, one's particular destiny may bring one to realize the nature and value of that destiny not only in a moral judgment, a mental action, but also in one's future activity as well – in everything one chooses to be and to do together with what one spontaneously or naturally is and does. If one is unlucky, it may happen that the only activity in which one can realize one's destiny is to be driven, and able and willing to die for the substance and value of that destiny. This is the case with Cleopatra, as she discovers. The external world, her previous activity in it, and her own nature combine to leave her no other way to realize the sense she finds-in-and-makes-of her life. Her 'dream' of Antony is at the heart of that sense; but the moral substance of that 'dream' is not something whose reality and value any competent person can witness. Like the limited kind of life manifested in mere philosophizing, which Hume realizes so sardonically, it is something that a person can only bear witness to in the whole way he or she actively responds to it – that is, at least as much in his spontaneous 'manner' as in practical reasoning and conduct.

I hope all this suggests why I think Hume is right about sexual love exemplifying a moral activity that appears in 'all' – or at least a good deal of – 'our estimation of characters', and right too about 'philosophy' being unable to get much grip on it – at least as he understands the term; but wrong about what that activity is. It may suggest too why I think he is also wrong if he supposes that, since 'philosophy' cannot deal with this kind of moral material, it cannot be thought about at all. Poetry certainly thinks about it.

The main difficulty in thinking about it lies in the distinctive particularity of *what* we have to think about, and the holistic *way* in which we have to think. The object of our attention is a particular person, but presenting himself or herself to us not simply as a member of a general class, with such and such objective general qualities, but also as a unique source of activity in the world we both inhabit – another unique way of being alive to that world. To make sense of his life is to make sense not simply of his actions and conduct, not simply of his psychology and behaviour, but of his entire activity; and to judge him morally is to evaluate the life manifest in all of that. This is presumably what Coleridge is driving at when he says that poetry 'brings the whole soul of man into activity'.[28] A poem manifests a unique way of being alive (a way never identical with the author's) in this holistic way. For it is a life that manifests itself as activity, not just as action or conduct. It emerges as a manner of perceiving and conceiving (conceiving 'characters', for example, or oneself) as well as in conscious thoughts and judgments; as implicit beliefs and assumptions as well as knowledge; as sensory and emotional activity as well as rational; as the form and style of consciousness as well as the contents; as spontaneous or involuntary responses as well as intentional actions; as sensibility as well as sense; as taste as well as reflective sentiments and preferences; as characteristic movement of the body as well as of the mind; – and so on. Of course, this is not to say, as Coleridge and many other Romantics wanted to, that there is an ideal moral norm of organic unity, in terms of which we must judge poetry because poetry ought to reflect or reveal the organic unity of nature and of the whole world. To consider people or poems holistically entails in itself no particular norm or ideal of human nature or of human life or of poetry.

V

Literature has always been concerned with making moral sense of lives, and in such a variety of ways that it is impossible to sum them up. Moreover, I doubt if there is much of interest to be said about what is common to all the diverse forms in which it has done so, from epitaphs, elegies and fairy tales to the dramatic action of epics, novels and dramas, from lyrics and epigrams to parables or biographies. The moral sense we make of a life may be a complex, dynamic image, for example, as in Cleopatra's speech about Antony, or a story, as in Cleopatra's own case. It may be an account of the special 'manner' of a person's ordinary, everyday appearance and activities, as with Princess Mary in *War and Peace*. It may be a distinctive pattern that emerges over time in a person's behaviour and actions and the unintended consequences of them, as in Pope's wry little 'Hymn Written in Windsor Forest' (1717):

> All hail! once pleasing, once inspiring Shade,
>   Scene of my youthful Loves, and happier hours!
> Where the kind Muses met me as I stray'd,
>   And gently press'd my hand, and said, Be Ours!
> Take all thou e're shalt have, a constant Muse:
>   At Court thou may'st be lik'd, but nothing gain;
> Stocks thou may'st buy and sell, but always lose;
>   And love the brightest eyes, but love in vain![29]

It may be a distinctive, unconscious 'project' or 'vocation' that a life acts out, such as Ortega y Gasset urges every biographer to look for in his subject:

> If 'vocation' is not taken to mean what it commonly does – merely a generic form of professional occupation, of the civil *curriculum* – but to mean an integral and individual program of existence, the simplest thing would be to say that our I is our vocation. Thus we can be true to our vocation to a greater or lesser degree, and consequently have a life that is authentic to a greater or lesser degree.
>
> If the structure of human life is viewed in this light, the most important problems for a biography will be the two following, which have not as yet been much considered by biographers. The first consists in determining what the subject's vital vocation was, though it is entirely possible that he was never aware of it. Every life is, more or less, a ruin among whose debris we have to discover what the person ought to have been. This obliges us to construct for ourselves – as the physicist constructs his 'models' – an imaginary life of the individual, the graph of his successful life, upon which we can then distribute the jags (they are sometimes enormous) which external destiny inflicted. We all feel our real life to be a deformation – sometimes greater, sometimes less – of our possible life. The second problem is to weigh the subject's fidelity to this unique destiny of his, to his possible life.[30]

It may be the path or trajectory along which a distinctive complex of individual needs finds fulfilment, as with Stephen Dedalus in *A Portrait of the Artist as a Young Man*. It may be a quasi-causal or quasi-psychological analysis, as with the sense Dryden makes of Buckingham in *Absalom and Achitophel*:

> Some of their Chiefs were Princes of the Land:
> In the first Rank of these did *Zimri* stand:
> A man so various, that he seem'd to be
> Not one, but all mankinds Epitome.
> Stiff in Opinions, always in the wrong;
> Was every thing by starts, and nothing long:
> But, in the course of one revolving Moon,
> Was Chymist, Fidler, States-Man, and Buffoon:
> Then all for Women, Painting, Rhiming, Drinking;
> Besides ten thousand freaks that dy'd in thinking.
> Blest Madman, who coud every hour employ,
> With something New to wish, or to enjoy!

Rayling and praising were his usual Theams;
And both (to shew his Judgment) in Extreams:
So over Violent, or over Civil,
That every man, with him, was God or Devil.
In squandring Wealth was his peculiar Art:
Nothing went unrewarded, but Desert.
Begger'd by Fools, whom still he found too late:
He had his Jest, and they had his Estate.
He laught himself from Court, then sought Relief
By forming Parties, but coud ne're be Chief:
For, spight of him, the weight of Business fell
On *Absalom* and *wise Achitophel*:
Thus, wicked but in will, of means bereft,
He left not Faction, but of that was left.[31]

Or it may be a kind of plot that a distinctive collection of qualities acts out within itself, as in the sense Pope makes of the same second Duke of Buckingham:

In the worst inn's worst room, with mat half-hung,
The floors of plaister, and the walls of dung,
On once a flock-bed, but repair'd with straw,
With tape-ty'd curtains, never meant to draw,
The George and Garter dangling from that bed
Where tawdry yellow strove with dirty red,
Great Villers lies – alas! how chang'd from him,
That life of pleasure, and that soul of whim!
Gallant and gay, in Cliveden's proud alcove,
The bow'r of wanton Shrewsbury and love;
Or just as gay, at Council, in a ring
Of mimick'd Statesmen, and their merry King.
No Wit to flatter, left of all his store!
No Fool to laugh at, which he valu'd more.
There, Victor of his health, of fortune, friends,
And fame; this lord of useless thousands ends.[32]

In every age, of course, people usually make sense of lives in terms of the moral stereotypes their culture offers them (and of which it largely consists): ideal patterns of life, like that of the hero, for instance, or the saint, or the true wayfaring Christian, or the man of reason, or the gentleman; or dynamic patterns of life, like that of growth and maturation, for example, or *hybris* and *nemesis*, or the wheel of Fortune, or the return of the repressed; social roles, like that of the prince, or the courtier, or the man of honour, or the humble poor, or the intellectual, or the bourgeois, or the rebel. We usually account for a particular life by fitting it, more or less comfortably, into one or more of such ready-made moulds; and we also tend to judge individual lives reductively as more or less satisfactory instantiations of the ideal type. Making moral sense of lives is, for most people for most of the time, no less a matter of short-hand formulae than is making moral sense of conduct and agents; but very often people try to apply to the life the logic of moral judgment appropriate to conduct, and do so by reducing the life to a mere instance of the type and taking the value of the type for granted. For some people, indeed, the very idea of 'virtue' seems to have meaning only in reference to some such socially-endorsed type.[33]

History and legend have provided our culture with scores of such moral stereotypes. So have myth and poetry, though these are generally not so much ideal types as something like descriptive or (in some sense) explanatory moral concepts: Oedipus, Narcissus, Odysseus, Job, Faust, Hamlet, Falstaff, Quixote, Satan, Pickwick, Bovary – to mention only a few that have added to the language useful terms for characterizing modes of life. Needless to say, the fresh moral insight and imagination that can discern and evaluate the distinctive qualitative shape *in* particular lives, rather than merely applying available stereotypes and judgments *to* them, is never very common; and even the freshest moral insight probably needs some basis, some conventional stereotypes, from which to begin. Yet in whatever way or at whatever level we make moral sense of a life, the process is one of seeking a specific, but not immediately obvious, *coherence* in the total phenomena of that life: a distinctive inner organization, a particular complex of inter-relationships, a specific entelechy.

In other words, we are seeking to understand the object not just functionally, or causally, or rationally, but all of these plus what we might call *formally*. We need to be careful with the word 'form' here, however. It does not refer to just any pattern that the eye might impose on the phenomena. Nor does it refer to an order imposed on a person's life by his will. It refers rather to a particular, dynamic, informing *principle* in the person's whole activity, including the actions of his will. To say that his activity is understood 'formally' means that it is now seen not as the effect, nor as a function, of such a principle, but rather as its self-manifesting realization. This is why all the phenomena of a life, understood in this way, will seem somehow necessitated by the inner principle, by what we see as the distinctive nature of the life. The necessity is not that of a complex of efficient causes, of determinism, but that of a formal cause, of inner structure.

This kind of principle is implicit, which means that it cannot be directly observed or directly described. It manifests itself in action and conduct among other things, which means on the one hand that it cannot be characterized in wholly objective, value-free terms, and on the other that it cannot be characterized in moral terms appropriate only to action, conduct, and conduct-moral·'character'. Moreover, such a principle manifests itself in a history, a personality, and a body that are unique to the individual, which means that it cannot be *fully* characterized in terms of ideal or descriptive stereotypes. Put together, all of this means that such a principle generally has to be 'caught' as it were, indirectly; and this normally involves (partly at least) 'rendering' it, characterizing the distinctive manner of the life in a way that *enacts* something of that manner and thereby helps the mind to grasp it, as it must, in its distinctiveness.[34]

A well-known and revealing example of this is a speech by Florizel to Perdita in *The Winter's Tale*:

> What you do
> Still betters what is done. When you speak, sweet,
> I'd have you do it ever. When you sing,
> I'd have you buy and sell so; so give alms;
> Pray so; and, for the ord'ring your affairs,
> To sing them too. When you do dance, I wish you
> A wave o' th' sea, that you might ever do
> Nothing but that; move still, still so,
> And own no other function. Each your doing,
> So singular in each particular,
> Crowns what you are doing in the present deeds,
> That all your acts are queens.[35]

This exhibits all the features of life-judgments I have already
tried to indicate. But as well as those, it brings out the need for
some kind of responsive 'rendering' of the life. Perdita's whole
way of being alive is characterized by the poetry enacting both
something of its distinctive manner and significance, and
Florizel's responsive, profoundly affirmative 'feel' for it. To
take an obvious example: in '...move still, still so, / And
own...', all the various senses of 'still' are essential; so is the
movement of the poetry – its poised yet fluid gracefulness, its
wondering pause on 'so' – which embodies the distinctive
nature, the value and beauty of Perdita's life as well as that of
Florizel answering to hers. And with the sort of insight that
makes Shakespeare one of the very greatest moral thinkers, he
gives Florizel those last four lines. Although they are about the
unique distinctiveness of Perdita's life, which makes the nature
and value of that life finally inexpressible in words, the lines also
apply – inevitably – to the poetry itself and the life *it* manifests.
Making sense of a life requires that it be 'sensible' to the mind
– in a meaning of that word closely related to Hume's: that it be
realized *as* a life, as the presence inhering in these distinctive
sensible or sensuous particulars and inconceivable without
them. This cannot be done by leaching those sensible particulars
away by regarding them as merely contingent circumstances in
which the really important object, the general category,
happens to be instantiated.

In moral thinking about lives, almost every term of agent-
centred, conduct-moral thinking takes on a rather different
meaning. 'Character' is the most obvious of these. The moral
subject now is not essentially a will confronting a world external
to it, but a life, which can be conceived only as a particular
physical being inhabiting a particular world in a particular
way. Again, there is now no limit to the range of morally
relevant verbs; moreover, adverbs now become as important as
verbs, for the manner or mode of actions is as relevant as their
being performed or not. There are many degrees and modes of
ignoring or deceiving, for example; many degrees and modes of
believing or feeling. 'Realizing' becomes a term more important
than just 'knowing', 'acknowledging' than just 'seeing', 'heart'

than just 'feeling', – and so on. Similarly, the difference becomes important between 'knowing' or even 'realizing' some possibility of the self mentally, and 'realizing' it in the sense of actualizing it in one's activity. The uncloseable gap between a person's consciousness and his activity, means that anyone's consciousness can now always be seen to be in one kind of 'bad faith'. And this applies no less to one's consciousness of oneself.

The 'self' now does not have determinate identity from the outset, but neither can it be reduced to a mere fiction. Its identity now has to be sought for; it is problematical; but it has the same kind of reality as does an informing principle. Similarly with the 'true self'. Even though we seek for the 'true self' as a *single* informing principle, it may not be that. It may be multiple, fragmented, its elements discontinuous with each other; but this does not mean that it is not real. A case in point is Dryden's account of Buckingham in the passage quoted above. If we put Dryden's lines beside Bishop Burnet's account of the same man, we can see the difference between making some moral sense of a life, however fragmented the 'true self' may show itself to be, and making no sense of it at all – or at least very little sense:

The first of these was a man of noble presence. He had a great liveliness of wit, and a peculiar faculty of turning all things into ridicule with bold figures and natural descriptions. He had no sort of literature: Only he was drawn into chymistry: And for some years he thought he was very near the finding the philosopher's stone; which had the effect that attends on all such men as he was, when they are drawn in, to lay out for it. He had no principles of religion, vertue, or friendship. Pleasure, frolick, or extravagant diversion was all that he laid to heart. He was true to nothing, for he was not true to himself. He had no steadiness nor conduct: He could keep no secret, nor execute any design without spoiling it. He could never fix his thoughts, nor govern his estate, tho' then the greatest in *England*. He was bred about the King: And for many years he had a great ascendent over him: But he spake of him to all persons with that contempt, that at last he drew a lasting disgrace upon himself. And he at length ruined both body and mind, fortune and reputation equally. The madness of vice appeared in his person in very eminent instances; since at last he became contemptible and poor, sickly, and sunk in his parts, as well as in all other respects, so that his conversation was as much avoided as ever it had been courted. He found the King, when he came from his travels in the year 45, newly come to *Paris*, sent over by his father when his affairs declined: And finding the King enough inclined to receive ill impressions, he, who was then got into all the impieties and vices of the age, set himself to corrupt the King, in which he was too successful, being seconded in that wicked design by the Lord *Percy*. And to compleat the matter, *Hobbs* was brought to him, under the pretence of instructing him in mathematicks: And he laid before him his schemes, both with relation to religion and politicks, which made deep and lasting impressions on the King's mind. So that the main blame of the King's ill principles, and bad morals, was owing to the Duke of *Buckingham*.[36]

The fact that Pope's account of Buckingham (also quoted above) – unlike Burnet's on the one hand and Dryden's on the other – does discern a very complex single form in Buckingham's life underlines the point I made earlier: that the moral subject may now be comprehensible only to a certain kind of responsive insight, one capable of *answering* to its life. Pope's sense of Buckingham manifests a deeper, more integrated imaginative life in the writer himself than Burnet's or Dryden's.

Certainly, lives cannot be characterized only in terms of the universal concepts applicable to agents – desires, interests, motives, and so on. These are now part of what has to be characterized. The question now is not just, which particular desire, or motive, or interest makes sense of a man's actions – Buckingham's, say, or Burnet's. That question now ramifies into others: why a man's mind forms this particular *conception* of 'desire', why he assumes that *this* is what having a 'desire' is, or what having an 'interest' is, or what a 'motive' for action is; why he 'sees' these aspects of the matter as more real or more relevant than those; why his eye picks out these rather than those as the salient features of the situation, or of another person, or of his own 'self'. In short, we try to understand why the activity even of his consciousness itself makes the world have the particular contours it does for *him*. And since each life has to be characterized in the particular terms that make sense of *it*, its salient features cannot be entirely determined in advance.

Very often, we do use terminology appropriate to behaviour or to conduct in making sense of lives in this way. The life seems to have been informed by a sort of 'impulse' or 'desire', or it seems to have 'grown', for instance. Or we speak of a sort of 'intentionality' about its direction, a kind of obscure 'purpose' it seems to have pursued. We might talk of 'existential choices', or an 'unconscious will', at the centre of the life. But if we do talk in this way, we need to remember that in this context these words carry an implicit 'as if'. They are being used in an extended or metaphorical way. An unconscious will to power, for example, is not the same as a conscious will to conscious power; and to make sense of lives in terms of the one is not to establish the other as an ideal of conduct. Existential 'choices' are not necessarily the same sort of choices we make in everyday actions; the sort of 'desires' that a particular life fulfils or frustrates are not necessarily of the sort that prompt all human beings to seek food and shelter. There are questions here, about the way that our sense of lives does enter into our conduct (which I shall have to leave aside for a separate discussion elsewhere); but to forget the metaphorical sense in which we use such terminology is the short way to conflate living with conducting our lives.

In thinking about lives, 'moral insight' clearly means something different too. It now refers to a capacity to make sense of people in the holistic way I have been trying to describe; and it involves a capacity to find terms appropriate to each particular life. Another phrase for it is 'moral imagination'. It still involves a capacity for judging, but this now means evaluating from within, as it were – a capacity to see the 'virtues' of a life in the older sense of that word, i.e. the distinctive powers, capacities, strengths it manifests, some of which may well be not virtues in the other sense, but vices. One of the virtues of Iago's life, for instance, is an indefatigable power to generate malice; in evaluating that life, it has to be seen as a power as well as a vice. Ortega was probably getting at a similar point (in the essay I have quoted from above) when he observed that a man's life may manifest a 'vocation' to be a thief. So was Keats, I think, when he remarked that 'what shocks the virtuous philosopher, delights the camelion Poet', who can have 'as much delight in conceiving an Iago as an

Imogen'[37] – and who, we might add, can enable us to see Iago's life with a similar insight too. In other words, moral insight here involves evaluating lives in terms that are necessarily multiple, complex, variable, and open-ended, rather than measuring them by reference to specific criteria or an ideal yardstick. Moral judgments of actions or conduct or conduct-moral 'character' can have, at least in theory, a conclusiveness that moral judgments of lives (in the sense I am getting at) cannot: which is probably why so many people try to turn every moral issue into one of conduct.

The accounts of Buckingham quoted above – Dryden's, Pope's and Burnet's – illustrate the difference between the two kinds of moral insight. Burnet shows a certain moral insight in considering his subject as an agent, but little or none in considering him as a life. Dryden shows more; he is certainly trying to understand Buckingham 'formally' and he does make some sense of his life as a fractured, discontinuous form. But it is a pretty shallow, conduct-coloured, yardstick-wielding sort of insight that can see nothing more precise or illuminating than 'variousness', 'madman', 'wicked but in Will' as the informing principles of the life. Pope's account mentions fewer facts, but it makes more sense of the life. Or to put it another way, Pope's imagination – in its energy, precision, and rhetorical and dramatic organization – is much more alive to its subject; and, as with other passages I have quoted, it is the life manifest in the poetry itself that provides the relevant terms for evaluating the life of its subject. Its sense of Buckingham crystallizes in the last couplet: it is a life that could and did triumphantly, fulfil itself, realize its virtues, only by becoming as it were the victim of its own out-flowing prodigality. The virtues of the life required vices of conduct; indeed, some of its main life-moral virtues were conduct-moral vices; but the delight in the one is as sharp as the condemnation of the other, and both judgments merge and qualify each other in the total sense of the life.

For most of the time, we notice no sharp discrepancies between our judgment of a person's life and our judgment of his conduct and conduct-moral character. If we judge a man's life to be narrow, mean and constricted, we are not surprised to find his actions habitually selfish or cruel. We generally feel a glow of metaphysical well-being when beauty, intelligence and warmth go hand in hand, not just with each other, but also with virtuous conduct. So we do when ugliness, stupidity and coldness go hand in hand with vice. The belief, or the hope, that all kinds of goodness are really one, dies hard; and a good deal of poetry, like a good deal of religion and moral discourse, panders to it. It gives us that glow, the assurance that both kinds of moral judgment always fit snugly together in metaphysical marriage, by claiming (or simply assuming) that in some ultimate way they do. If we want our heroes to be men who are both great and good, and our enemies to be thorough-going swine – contemptible as human beings and wicked in action – we also know that this is not always the case. We know too that it is a question about *lives* whether we are more conscious of a man's greatness or his goodness. In fact, some of the most profound literature turns on that very question. *War and Peace*, for example, explores it quite explicitly; and part of what makes it profound is its realization – which the greatest literature has always shared – that the issue is not at all simple and straight-forward. Admittedly, Tolstoy wanted to think it *is*, and he tries to show this with Napoleon for instance, by making it seem that he was not really a great man largely because he was not a good one – though, significantly, he manages this by concentrating on Napoleon as a moral agent rather than as a life. Like George Eliot, Tolstoy wants to believe that judgments of conduct form the most important element – indeed the decisive element – in judgments of lives, and occasionally he fudges things to make it seem as if they must. But like other great imaginative writers, he also realizes that it is often the other way round: that the sense we make of a person as a life may be different from our general assessment of his conduct, or it may actually be a decisive formative element in that assessment. To take just one tiny example of the point:

> Once she had a talk with her friend Natasha about Sonya and about her own injustice towards her.
> 'You know,' said Natasha, 'you have read the Gospels a great deal – there is a passage in them that just fits Sonya.'

'What?' asked Countess Mary, surprised.

'"To him that hath shall be given, and from him that hath not shall be taken away." You remember? She is one that hath not; why, I don't know. Perhaps she lacks egotism, I don't know, but from her is taken away, and everything has been taken away. Sometimes I am dreadfully sorry for her. Formerly I very much wanted Nicholas to marry her, but I always had a sort of presentiment that it would not come off. She is a *sterile flower*, you know – like some strawberry blossoms. Sometimes I am sorry for her, and sometimes I think she doesn't feel it as you or I would.'

Though Countess Mary told Natasha that those words in the Gospel must be understood differently, yet looking at Sonya she agreed with Natasha's explanation. It really seemed that Sonya did not feel her position trying, and had grown quite reconciled to her lot as a *sterile flower*. She seemed to be fond not so much of individuals as of the family as a whole. Like a cat, she had attached herself not to the people but to the home. She waited on the old countess, petted and spoiled the children, was always ready to render the small services for which she had a gift, and all this was unconsciously accepted from her with insufficient gratitude.[38]

Tolstoy's imagination recurs to this kind of issue again and again in the novel. More clear-sightedly than George Eliot, he faces the possible discrepancies between the two kinds of moral judgment – even if only as a fundamental problem for which he thinks he has the universal solution.

Along with the moral 'self', 'character', 'insight', 'judgment', there are other terms that take a different meaning in this kind of moral thinking: 'integrity', for example, or (closely related to that) 'destiny'. As with Shakespeare's Antony, such terms now cut below the realm of conscious motives, actions, and predictable consequences; the passage from Ortega quoted above points in the direction of the change, I think – though this does not require adopting his term 'authenticity', much less treating it (as he tends to) as an ideal or norm of conduct. But all of this has a bearing on the way we think of tragedy too – as a couple of sentences from A. C. Bradley may suggest:

The 'story' or 'action' of a Shakespearean tragedy does not consist, of course, solely of human actions or deeds; but the deeds are the predominant factor. And these deeds are, for the most part, actions in the full sense of the word; not things done 'tween asleep and wake', but acts or omissions thoroughly expressive of the doer, – characteristic deeds. The centre of the tragedy, therefore, may be said with equal truth to lie in action issuing from character, or in character issuing in action.[39]

What seems to me to limit Bradley's view of Shakespearean tragedy is not so much what it has been commonly said to be, a limited view of poetic drama, as (more basically) a persistent confusion – rather like George Eliot's – of the two different meanings we can attach to the key terms in this passage. In Shakespearean drama the two ways of thinking about people are generally wound around each other almost inseparably. Nevertheless, making the fullest moral sense of people depends on not confusing these two ways – not confusing, for example, the two possible meanings of terms like 'actions' here, or 'acts and deeds', which can refer either to voluntary intentional actions only, or to activity as a whole. So with the corresponding meanings of 'expressive', of 'issuing from', and above all of 'character'. At his most limited and Victorian, Bradley (like George Eliot) tends to conflate the two possible meanings into a predominantly conduct-centred one. At his best, he also recognizes the other sense, the life-centred sense, and with that, the possibility of harsh, terrifying, irreconcilable conflicts between the two. This is also an issue I shall leave for a fuller discussion elsewhere; but it may help to see first how such unacknowledged conflicts actually work to mask or muffle the drama in two of George Eliot's novels, and work to transform some of Pope's best work into a kind of personal drama, of which he himself is at once the author, the hero and the victim.

CHAPTER 4

'*Doing good to others*': *some reflections on* Daniel Deronda

I

How could a novelist as morally perceptive as George Eliot come to be so imperceptive, so earnestly soggy, with 'ideal' characters like Dorothea Brooke in the later sections of *Middlemarch* or the waxwork hero of *Daniel Deronda*? It does not explain much to say (as one of her most morally-sympathetic critics, F. R. Leavis, does, for example[1]) that there was always a streak of immaturity in her personality. Taken in one sense, this is not an explanation at all – it merely restates the problem in different terms. But even in a more substantial sense, it still does not make clear how she could have judged her flights of moral 'elevation', which strike any modern reader (as they struck some of her sharper contemporaries) as utterly at odds with the moral precision and specificity of other parts of the very same work, to be both proper and right: to be, that is, not only good (morally), but also supported by and completing (argumentatively) the moral insights and judgments realized elsewhere in the book.

To us, her moral 'elevation' is likely to seem merely Victorian – which is to say, neither proper nor right but only an example of tendencies characteristic of her time: the tendency to look for social 'community' in moral sentiment, for instance, or the tendency that Nietzsche noted,[2] to resort to an ardent credulity about conventional Christian morality in order to compensate for incredulity about conventional Christian doctrine. George Eliot's fondness for the word 'ardour' (or 'ardent') as a term of moral commendation seems revealing in itself: it does look as if she wanted, and trusted to, subjective moral enthusiasm to fill the absence of an objective moral order. Yet this is surely to oversimplify matters; for the truth is not that she merely wanted moral enthusiasm to fill this absence, and fell back on it with a sort of immature emotionalism; it is that she was intellectually convinced that moral enthusiasm could and should fill it. As Benjamin Jowett remarked in his notebook after talking with her in Oxford in 1873:

She talked charmingly, with a grace and beauty that I shall always remember. She gives the impression of great philosophical power. She wanted to have an ethical system founded upon altruism; and argued that there was no such thing as doing any action because it was right or reasonable, but only because it accorded with one's better feelings toward others... Her idea of existence seemed to be 'doing good to others'.[3]

That suggests how she herself might have seen her flights of moral elevation. Her conception of morality gave a decisive role to feelings, and altruistic ones particularly; and this went very readily with a view that the age found in Wordsworth: that the springs, the development and the expression of feeling are the springs, development and expression not only of moral consciousness and sensibility, but of moral action as well. The emotionality was built into the foundations of her moral outlook; and Jowett's description of that outlook underlines some of the difficulties about it – difficulties that, as a novelist, she sometimes saw and understood, sometimes not.

A very obvious one is the question Jowett evidently raised with her: is she not confusing the rationale of morality – the rightness or reasonableness of a choice, a decision, an intention, or an action – with moral psychology, with what causes someone to act, or to want to act, morally? Or is she not confusing a desirable, arguably perhaps even a necessary, condition of moral action – that the call of duty or goodness should be felt by the agent in his heart, not just be assented to in his head – with a sufficient condition? A third question is equally obvious, and even more important for a novelist as keen on self-sacrifice and as hostile to 'egoism' as she was: is morality a matter only of one's better feelings, or of one's actions, *towards others*? Is there not an important moral point (though of course one bearing on life-morality) in Natasha's remark in *War and Peace* about Sonya being 'one that hath not', a 'sterile flower', perhaps because she 'lacks egotism'? Is there not also an important moral point in Jane Austen's observation about Emma receiving Mr Knightley's proposal? She comments that

> as to any of that heroism of sentiment which might have prompted her to entreat him to transfer his affection from herself to Harriet, as infinitely the most worthy of the two ... Emma had it not ... [N]o flight of generosity run mad, opposing all that could be probable or reasonable, entered her brain.[4]

Is the same not true even in Sir Hugo Mallinger's advice in *Daniel Deronda* itself: '...my dear boy, it is good to be unselfish and generous; but don't carry that too far...you must know where to find yourself'.[5]

There are other difficulties too about George Eliot's moral outlook as reported by Jowett. Are we to refrain from actions affecting others, for example, if we have not (or not yet) acquired the better kind of feelings towards them? If not, how then should we regulate our actions? Then again, by what criteria are we to know which are our 'better' feelings? Is George Eliot perhaps only replacing a conventional code of action ('right' or 'reasonable') with a no less conventional code of feelings-towards-others (bad, good and better); and in doing so, making it seem as if one could always choose to do good to others by choosing to have, or to develop, better feelings towards them? And finally, and most basically, *is* doing good to others – or having certain 'better feelings' to act by – really the point of human existence? Are there not questions to be asked (as Jowett suggests, and as Nietzsche insisted) about the moral importance of altruistic morality itself?

All of these questions arise for us with George Eliot's novels, I believe, and they arise quite as much from her imaginative powers as from her imaginative limitations. This applies especially to the last question, which arises for us precisely because the novels do what literature can do at its best – explore the possible meanings and implications of such life-moral questions in the specificity, the particularity, they require, and with a self-scrutinizing honesty about their possible answers. And yet it must also be said that George Eliot's explorations are hampered by an unwitting tendency she shared with many of her contemporaries (and many people today, for that matter): to *conflate* the two different kinds of moral thinking I have called conduct-centred (or agent-centred) and life-centred.

The differences between them can be put in rather different terms from those I have used so far. Conduct-moral thinking focuses on certain crucial, but nonetheless limited, aspects of human experience and of human beings: on the self as a definite and analysable ego, on the will, on choice, responsibility, right understanding, right feeling, benevolence, social well-being, malice, self-delusion, harm, vice, blame, censure, punishment, retribution, 'nemesis', remorse, redemption, and so on. For this kind of thinking, the state of innocence is that which lies outside the reach of such terms as these; innocence is morally null, morally only pre-history, since the person is not, or not yet, a moral agent in the full sense. For life-moral thinking, on the other hand, the state of innocence may be anything but null. Life-morality focuses on the content to be given to such terms as soul, vitality, human well-being or happiness, heroism, noble-ness, perfection, grace, fullness of life, unity of being, fulfilment, energy, joy, mediocrity, meanness, alienation, narrowness, and so on. From this point of view, 'innocence' can be regarded (and often has been) as a state that manifests something like a natural perfection of being, a living image for us of how to *live* – how to live, that is, even with the elements that complicate our own lives, make us no longer 'innocent', and therefore tend to keep us out of Paradise (or Pastoral harmony): the consciousness of right and wrong, and the autonomous moral will. And of course an individual can hardly be *blamed* for lacking certain life-moral excellences, certain capacities of life, certain powers or 'virtues'. Somebody who actively prevented others from realizing their 'virtues', or who chose voluntarily not to try to realize his own, certainly could be blamed; but a person who merely lacked them could only be judged a limited, or mediocre, or narrow, or even deficient, human being.

A man like Grandcourt in *Daniel Deronda* is an interesting case here. He is obviously a nasty piece of work by any standard; and he illustrates how hard it would be to have any good feelings towards him, let alone better ones. But what George Eliot's stress on altruism and feelings tends to blur is the fact that there are actually two different kinds of standard we judge him by. He is selfish and cruel, which is morally wrong in anybody in any circumstances. But he is also arrogant, languid, cold, impassive and narrow; cankered with ennui; a self shrunken to little more than a need to dominate – a need all the more relentless for having no purpose or motive beyond maintaining a haughty but vacuous upper-class code of manners. This makes him (in George Eliot's own word) a pretty 'reptilian' specimen of humanity, of course, and makes the kind of social life he represents pretty deplorable too. But whereas we must regard him as choosing to act selfishly and cruelly, blame him, and even think he deserves punishment for it (drowning is almost too good for him), we can hardly do so with the other qualities. They belong to everything he is, even what is beyond his will or his consciousness itself; they also belong to everything he represents in that it has made him what he is. In his case, this latter kind of judgment is probably even more hostile than the former. We cannot blame him for his 'devitalized' nature or for the effects of social power on it; but our very being recoils with a mixture of moral fear and disgust at the kind of human being he is, and at a society that can produce, and even give respect to, such a mode of human life.

What George Eliot seems to want us to believe, however, is that both his selfishness and cruelty, and his cold, relentless impulsion to dominate, are equally manifestations of 'egoism' in him – that absence in him of better feelings towards others which for her is virtually the definition of immorality. Or to put it another way, she wants to conflate conduct and being. The difficulty about this is that 'egoism' has to mean two very different things. On the conduct-moral side, its meaning is obvious enough in Grandcourt's case: deliberately exploiting others, for instance, or acting maliciously, in the service of one's own interests, desires, or consciousness of power. On the life-moral side, however, its meaning is much less obvious, for the main criticism of Grandcourt here is surely not that he is self-centred, or proud, or conceited, or has an over-prominent and dominating ego. After all, Klesmer (say) is not less proud, conceited and self-centred in his own fashion, and he has an ego quite as prominent and dominating as Grandcourt's; but who thinks him a case of 'egoism'? The objection is surely to the brutally constricted and defensive ego Grandcourt has – the appallingly narrow, vapid interests, desire and conceptions of power that are all this ego can allow itself, and the impenetrable structure of indifference and disdain it has built itself into as a protection from conflicts within and frustrations without. It is these that make him something of a human monstrosity even if he did nothing positively wrong.[6] In fact, when we come down to it, what does he do *to Gwendolen* that is positively wrong? She comes to hate and fear him not for that, but for imprisoning all the potentialities of her moral being within the cramped and stony confines of his.

To regard him as a case of 'egoism' pure and simple would be possible, no doubt, if one thought that having any definite shape, any structure to the ego, were an *unnecessary* defence of the naked, feeling, 'true' self against the impact of the external world and of everything within one's human nature; or if one thought that just being a particular (and therefore limited) human being were a major and *correctable* deficiency in one's 'true' humanness. And it would be possible to think either of these in turn given two conditions.

The first is put very succinctly by P. F. Strawson in the article I referred to in chapter 2. After stressing the possibility that a moral obligation to act in a certain way may conflict with an 'ideal aspiration' of one's life, he continues:

On the other hand, it may be that a picture of the ideal life is precisely one in which the interests of morality are dominant, are given an ideal, overriding value. To one dominated temporarily or permanently by such a picture the 'consciousness of duty faithfully performed' will appear as the supremely satisfactory state, and being moral not merely as something that matters but as the thing that supremely matters. Or again the ideal picture may be...one in which the dominating idea operates powerfully to reinforce some, but not perhaps others, of a system of moral demands. So it is with that ideal picture in which obedience to the command to love one another appears as the supreme value.[7]

Sketching out some of 'the complex and various relations' between 'our conflicting visions of the ends of life and the systems of moral demand which make social living possible', Strawson notes the dream that has haunted various utopian writers: that of 'a self-enclosed ideal [community] in which the system of moral demands shall answer exactly, or as exactly as possible, to an ideal picture of life held in common by all [its] members'. And as he goes on to point out, this dream has haunted more than utopians. It has been the motor-power of many religions and religious revivals, of ideological movements, of certain social castes, and so on. What we also need to notice here, however, though Strawson does not, is the consequent tendency of such moral zealots to value individual lives only inasmuch as they instantiate *universal* moral rules or principles. This usually presents no problem to the religious reformer, say; he or she is very happy to conflate or telescope conduct and life; but it certainly does have problems for the novelist, especially one so liberal-minded as George Eliot, or for a liberal-minded critic like Arnold who still wanted to keep his 75/25 per cent formula, or for another liberal-minded critic like J. S. Mill in his criticism of Bentham. For Mill, we may recall, the older man's 'error' was (like that of other 'moralists by profession') to treat 'the *moral* view of actions and characters, which is *unquestionably the* first and *most important* mode of looking at them, as if it were the sole one (my italics).[8]

The second condition for George Eliot's view of 'egoism' is that, having conflated the 'true self' and the 'best self' (believing, that is, that right conduct is and should be 'the first and most important' element in every human life), one then identifies the 'best self' with the selfless performance of Duty, or alternatively with the practice of humility and self-sacrifice, on the grounds that we can find better feelings for others only if we become 'truly' alive and expose to the world *all* of our capacity for feeling. George Eliot does seem to have been inclined to believe something like this at times – though that does not mean that she always imagined dramatically in this way. In other words, her weakness was not just that she never quite left behind her the moral emotionality of a Maggie Tulliver, for example; more specifically, it was also that she never quite left behind her the belief in a kind of absolute nakedness and sacrificial abnegation of the self: the kind of belief in Thomas à Kempis that helped ruin the young Maggie Tulliver for life – in both senses of the phrase.

In *Daniel Deronda*, one effect of all this is the moral over-kill in the treatment of Grandcourt. He has to be made a proper object of Gwendolen's moral revulsion, so that her anger and hatred should seem the proper effect of her conduct-moral conscience – of genuine remorse and self-censure. Thus his 'egoism' and incapacity for 'better feelings' must be both worse and stronger than hers. But the most dubious effects of George Eliot's moral beliefs appear not in her treatment of Grandcourt, or even of Deronda, but of Gwendolen. Before touching on that, however, it is worth noticing one or two further differences between conduct-morality and life-morality.

Where the former, for example, tends to rest itself on the universal, *im*personal authority of God, or Reason, or Duty, or the Nature of Things, or whatever else, to win assent to a certain code of action (or perhaps of feeling-and-action), life-morality tends to rest on the authority of a particular *personal* mode of life (which is not necessarily individual, of course) to win respect, admiration, even a sort of love (or alternatively their opposite). To be brought to see a certain action (or feeling) as right or wrong, or as good or bad, we need to be, at least in some sense, rationally convinced; to be brought to see a certain mode of life, a distinctive way of being alive, as (say) noble or degraded, we need to be, at least in some sense, imaginatively converted. This is why culture-heroes, religious lives and writings, charisma, style – the power of personal utterance or example, or of personality itself – are so crucial in issues of life-morality. In fact, it is this difference between the two kinds of morality that, as we shall see, forms the tragi-comedy of those earnest conversations Deronda has with Gwendolen at various stages of the novel.

It is worth recalling an important difference between the two kinds of morality that I discussed in the last chapter: the way each tends to regard individuality itself. For conduct-morality, the individual's actions are simply instances, cases, of universal principles or rules. Circumstances alter cases, it is true, but only in so far as they call for qualifying rules, with a smaller mesh as it were. For life-morality on the other hand, individuality matters in itself. Not only does life-morality conceive a particular life or mode of life as a single, complexly structured whole; it also has to recognize from the start that its moral world is bound to be various. (Many life-moralists, of course, and well before Mill, have regarded such variety as not only necessary, but also as good: 'God's plenty'.) What this means in practice is that life-morality is concerned with the specific, unique particularity of the individual in a way that conduct-morality is not. Gwendolen, for instance, quite properly wants Deronda to regard her and judge her as a unique individual, whose life is hers and hers alone, not just as a member of a social or moral class, whose life consists in the performance of certain kinds of action. Only inasmuch as he does regard her as a distinctive life-moral being, it turns out, can she discern, by the reflection of his conception of her, what particular person she is.

This brings out something important about the way that George Eliot herself regards Gwendolen. In practice, one's own sense of being a particular, unique self, with sufficient substance to be worth something – even if only worthy to be judged *as* a self – largely depends on two things. One is the discovery of what, in the final analysis, we must do – not ought to do, or would like to do, but being what we are, must do. (This is the point Klesmer makes to Gwendolen: somebody whose moral being is really 'called upon' finds himself saying, 'I must know this exactly', 'I must understand this exactly', 'I must do this exactly – 'these three terrible *musts*', as George Eliot calls them.[9]) But our sense of being a particular self also partly depends (as in Gwendolen's case) on seeing what life-moral judgments others make of us. Conduct-moral judgments acknowledge our freedom to choose (and to change), our capacity to understand and feel rightly or wrongly, our inescapable responsibility for what we do; but they tend to reduce us to little more than that. All the thick, dense, vibrant texture of our experience; our awareness of all the particularities of the world; the ebbing and flowing of our 'sympathetic consciousness'; all the countless memories, sensations, feelings, desires, tastes, which we sense, or half-sense, in ourselves, or rather *as* ourselves: – these count as nothing to conduct-morality. And of course, it is right and proper that they do not. The judgments of conduct-morality treat us as being no more than any human being; they humble our tendency to think of ourselves not so much as always right, but as at least unique and somehow special: what George Eliot saw as the core of 'egoism' in everyone. And it is true that, to this kind of morality, we are not unique and somehow special. Nevertheless, to the other kind we are – and it is no less right and proper that this be acknowledged too, as indeed George Eliot does acknowledge it in the very way she gets 'inside' Gwendolen (or Grandcourt for that matter) and portrays the specific individual moral being she is. For Gwendolen herself, however, a sense of her moral being depends on what others acknowledge of it to *her*: which is why the ways she is treated by others, and especially by those to whom she is related by respect, admiration, or love, have a crucial moral significance in the novel. It is also why her 'egoism' is much more a question than the obvious fact George Eliot seems to think it is.

Another way of getting at the point is to consider what the saying *tout comprendre, c'est tout pardonner* is really getting at. Taken literally, it is not true, of course, and George Eliot can be praised (as Leavis praises her) for having the intelligence not to write as if it were true. But what *is* true is that shifting from a conduct-moral view of a person to a life-moral view may be to see things very differently. What had seemed to be voluntary action may now seem to be not voluntary at all, or not voluntary in the same sense. To take a well-known example from Dickens, Uriah Heep's 'detestable cant of false humility' looks rather different – more ironic, more aggressive, but also more pitiable – when he explains its origins and motive. It is, it emerges, a sign of life in him – a conscious means to achieve a

social status and a power that his upbringing had shown was out
of his reach except in that way; and it is interesting that after
giving David Copperfield this franker account of himself,
Uriah's 'spirits were elevated' and he becomes quite 'adventurous' in his aggression. But of course Dickens quickly
blocks off this possible other view of Heep by a characteristic
moral over-kill, making his character not only (life-morally)
'detestable', 'mean' and 'crafty', but also (conduct-morally)
'malicious' and 'revengeful', and to make trebly sure, (legally)
criminal as well.[10] But clearly, to shift our minds from one kind
of moral thinking to the other may well make a (conduct-moral)
vice come to look like a (life-moral) power or 'virtue', or a
virtue look like a weakness. What we had taken as conduct may
come to seem behaviour, and to have a quite different meaning
and significance. More specifically, what had seemed to be
'egoism' in one sense – the sense in which every moral agent is
a perfectly obvious ego, in relation to which we judge its actions
to be selfish or altruistic – may now seem not to be 'egoism' at all
in another sense, but rather perhaps the non-voluntary reaching
out of a particular human being, placed in these particular
circumstances, toward the realization of some vitally necessary
possibility in him or in her, even if it is only toward some sense
of actually *being* a self.

Consider Gwendolen's acceptance of Grandcourt's proposal.
How are we to see this? Is it to be seen as a voluntary action
(taken from a whole complex of motives) by a responsible moral
agent, which is to be judged in conduct-moral terms as wrong?
Or is it the behaviour of a particular moral being, recoiling from
the prospect of withering in dull, humiliating, hateful, ill-paid
drudgery, realizing an ignorant, foolish, even conceited, but
nevertheless positive impulse to live? The answer, of course, is
both. But really to accept this answer, we should notice, is to
accept that the two kinds of moral judgment may be (as I think
they are here) ultimately irreconcilable, and that we simply
have to live with this uncomfortable truth.

What we cannot do, I think, is to collapse one answer into the
other, as Leavis tries to do (and as George Eliot sometimes does
as well). For although Leavis sees how much Gwendolen's

acceptance is not a voluntary action, he seems to argue that because it does not come from a 'profound integrated self', she is to be 'judged as a moral agent' here in that her response to Grandcourt's proposal has really been 'established by habits of valuation and by essential choices lived'.[11]

To me, this last phrase, as applied to Gwendolen, seems almost absurd, and none the less so if it also expresses George Eliot's own view. For *what* 'choices lived' establish Gwendolen's response? In what sense has this twenty-year-old girl, with the natural ignorance and self-absorption of adolescence still about her, been a full moral agent all her life, choosing between right and wrong, living out these choices, and so forming the falsely valuing, self-ignorant, and therefore egoistic self that makes this wrong decision? This kind of judgment seems to me so much at odds with what George Eliot actually portrays as Gwendolen and her life (even if it is by no means at odds with what she keeps on saying about them), that it seems to issue from certain moral assumptions that are never properly tested. By these, I mean the assumptions that any *really* moral judgment must be in the terms of conduct-morality; that life-morality is not *really* morality unless it is somehow conflated with, telescoped into, conduct-morality; and that the ego posited by the latter is the *real* self, or the *really important* part of the self, posited by the former. A life-moral judgment on Gwendolen's acceptance, for example, would take as crucial moral facts both her perception of Grandcourt's horses as splendidly vital creatures (as well as a sign of wealth and social grandeur), and her perception of Grandcourt as a social power (as well as, or even partly because, a man capable of wronging others). A conduct-moral judgment regards these as merely part of a mistaken view of the world; its emphasis falls on the 'really' moral facts: the choices and habits of choice that produce the mistake, and for which Gwendolen must be held responsible. In short, by accepting the above assumptions, it reconciles any life-moral considerations with itself by translating or reducing them into its own ('really' moral) terms. The belief that life-moral considerations not only can but should be so reduced was very common in the nineteenth century, as indeed it still is; but that does not validate the particular life-moral assumptions that the belief expresses.

II

In its intentions, *Daniel Deronda* is something like an analytic study both of 'egoism' in a wide variety of forms – some pathological, some pathetic, some merely limiting 'spots of commonness' – and of the opposites of 'egoism', ranging from spots of goodness, as it were, to habitual selflessness, to the loftiest altruism. The only areas in which George Eliot allows egoism to be both necessary and good are two, I think: in love (as with Catherine Arrowpoint, Mirah and Deronda himself), and in art (as with Klesmer and, up to a point, Deronda's mother). Here, as she sees, there is obviously no alternative to living out the particular life that is in one; and inasmuch as the ends to which the self is directed are impersonal and good in themselves (true love, great art, a salvationist political creed) then her general moral principle could be saved by regarding this kind of egoism as not really 'real' egoism.

The basic problem with all this is that, while one may regard altruism, a person's better feelings towards others, as the only principle of *moral* action, the most immediate, perhaps the central, principle of *all* action in and upon the world is generally some form of egoism. The problem here is not the merely verbal one – that every form of 'altruism' can be redescribed as a form of 'self-interestedness'; it is the substantive problem of how far it is people's better feelings towards others, pure and simple, that actually do make them 'strong in will/To strive, to seek, to find, and not to yield'. Simply to conflate life-morality with conduct-morality by equating a person's 'true' self with his 'best' self is to run into difficulties about this. One is the kind exemplified by Savonarola in *Romola*, whose religious zeal finally brings him to actions that can be seen as both quite genuinely altruistic and quite genuinely egoistic. Having got to this interesting paradox, however, George Eliot simply wonders at it and then drops it; she certainly does not give it the kind of tough, probing analysis she is prepared to give conficts *within* either kind of moral thinking.

The figure of Deronda illustrates a related difficulty. He stands in obvious contrast to Grandcourt; he is very conspicuously the non-egoist. What this means is that his life-moral qualities – his wide sympathies and understanding, the health and integrity of his self, his manly beauty, his social assurance and freedom, his perfect manners, his splendid whiskers, and so forth – have to include (on George Eliot's assumptions) a sort of natural, spontaneous altruism. So included it is. In him, the 'true self' is unmistakably the 'best self'. But the effect of this is to leave him without any particular principle of action. To Deronda himself, as to George Eliot, it seems that all he lacks is a particular direction for action; the principle is there, but it needs to be pointed to some good end and triggered off. So a good end is provided: good both in life-moral terms (hence the gaseous mixture of historicism, nationalism and religiosity about Jewishness), and in conduct-moral terms (hence the absence of any hint of self, or of feelings towards himself in particular, on Deronda's part). The cost of all this is a sort of radical inauthenticity in Deronda, which George Eliot does not notice; his wax-work quality as a character perhaps owes as much to her moral beliefs as to anything else.

Two tiny examples may illustrate the point. The first is a passage where depiction and commentary are inseparable:

A too reflective and diffusive sympathy was in danger of paralysing in him that indignation against wrong and that selectedness of fellowship which are the conditions of moral force; and...he had become so keenly aware of this that what he most longed for was either some external event, or some inward light, that would urge him into a definite line of action, and compress his wandering energy...But how and whence was the needed event to come? – the influence that would justify partiality, and make him what he longed to be yet was unable to make himself – an organic part of social life... [12]

One can see the important point this is trying to make; but 'the influence that would justify partiality'? It is as if his subsequent Zionism were only a 'partiality', but was nevertheless 'justified' by the combination of Mordecai's view of history ('inward light') and the discovery of actually being a Jew himself ('external event') – though it would presumably not be 'justi-

fied' without their 'influence' upon him. It is a revealing move:
the justifying influence saves his 'partiality' towards the Jews
(even perhaps towards Mirah?) from appearing egoistical. His
willingness to be influenced, his unconscious will to surrender
his conscious will to this sort of influence (rather like the
intellectual's will to submit to an ideology), the life-moral
vacuity left by the lack of any positive vital impulse of the self,
not to mention the kind of moral being that could prefer Mirah
to, say, Gwendolen: all this is quietly glossed over.

The other example underlines the same point: Deronda's
claim, which he makes more than once, about his Zionist
activity – is that he is 'taking it as a duty'. It is a very Victorian
turn of phrase, of course; but how far is the selfless altruism
claimed in the word 'duty' not designed to obscure, even from
the speaker's own consciousness, the (supposedly immoral)
egoism implicit in the 'taking'? It is as if, outside the privileged
areas of love and art, anything a person finds that his or her
particular self must do to realize its potentialities could be really
moral only if it were described in the language of objective,
impersonal 'duty'. Life-moral considerations, we may well
think, would require a morally critical novelist like George Eliot
to explore the strengths and limitations of the particular self's
vitality in order to assess it. But the life-moral claim is once
again collapsed into that of conduct-morality, which judges it
immoral to act from any impulse of the self whatever. The touch
of something like an unwitting 'bad faith' in Deronda here is
only partly seen in the novel, and then only late and with a
rather unfocused irony, as Deronda listens to his mother's
account of how she had to abandon the moral claims of the
social life she was an organic part of, in order 'to live out the life
that was in me' – the nature, the genius, of her particular life –
while he is preparing, in fact, to live out his.[13]

The treatment of Gwendolen is so much deeper, more
detailed and complex than this that I can only suggest in a very
general way how it too is affected by the same tendency. What
happens here, I think, is that George Eliot's persistently
conduct-moral viewpoint and commentary seem to miss, or at

least to blur, the far more interesting (and moving) life-moral story she depicts.

The conduct-moral story in the book is perfectly in focus: the core of 'egoism' in Gwendolen (as in most people); her self-regarding consciousness, feelings and conduct; her desire to charm and predominate (without earning the right to do so by her moral conduct and her conduct-moral virtues); the ignorance and folly these produce; the 'nemesis' these all bring upon her; the return of the repressed sense of right and wrong in her hysterical guilt about Mrs Glasher, and her desperate murderous hatred of Grandcourt (really a desperate hatred of herself); and so on. In this story, Gwendolen is never in a state of innocence; she is a moral agent from start to finish; so that although she has certain virtues, the vices of her character bring about her tragedy. ('So much pride and courage and sensitiveness and intelligence fixed in a destructive deadlock through false valuation and self-ignorance – this is what makes Gwendolen a tragic figure': to quote again from Leavis, who nevertheless goes on to insist that this is all the conduct of a 'responsible moral agent', as if her native pride, courage, sensitiveness and intelligence were not also part of what brought her to the 'destructive deadlock'.)[14] The conduct-moral emphasis falls upon the correctable, that is 'true' self; which in her case is so spoiled, so indulged, so unregulated by any teaching about good and evil, so shallow, so uncaring for anyone but herself and (to some extent) her mother, so undeveloped in right feelings and right understanding, that only the violent collisions with reality all this causes – reality both external and internal – can make her into a fully reflective and unegoistic moral agent.

But the life-moral story about Gwendolen in the book is a different one, with a more uncertain ending, and perhaps amounting to a tragedy of another kind. This centres on the distinctive, native 'pride and spirit' that attract Grandcourt to her in the first place, the force of independent life in her. Along with her beauty and her latent capacity for love, this is what makes her real charm. But it goes not with 'confidence in herself and her destiny' (as George Eliot puts it[15]) but with something more like the opposite of that: with a radical insecurity, a wavering and unstable sense of herself, the *lack* of a necessary kind of 'egoism' in her. It is this lack that prompts those partly false but at least definite 'selves' she presents to the world. It is the same lack that threatens her consciousness with indefinite fears and a dread of uncontrollable 'evil' forces within her. And it is this same lack again that exposes her to the effect, not just of Grandcourt's apparent self-possession and mastery of his life, but of her uncle's self-possession and assurance, of Klesmer's, and (first, last and most deeply) what she sees – or is supposed by George Eliot to see – as Deronda's. Right from the beginning, it is not simple 'egoism' that causes her to find (and to accept) a judgment on herself in Deronda's gaze, and that always brings her to men in whom she feels a life-moral superiority, a capacity to judge her, to which she is unstably ambivalent precisely because she both wants it and fears it very deeply – wants so that it might define and endorse her, and fears because it may annihilate her instead. George Eliot certainly sees the relevance of Gwendolen's undeveloped sense of awe at the mystery and authority of natural processes – the awe that for George Eliot, as for Wordsworth, was the fount of moral consciousness, feeling and conduct. But in *this* story, other facts are no less relevant. An obvious one is the absence of a father in Gwendolen's psyche. She has never had a father, or even a step-father, from whom she received any combination of moral authority and personal love that might have provided her with an object of psychic aggression and yet also a source of reassuring forgiveness, creating some definite and adequate sense of her self and preventing a tendency to self-directed, self-destructive guilt. Another relevant fact is that the only marriage her consciousness has lived with, her mother's second marriage, was a disastrous failure; yet another is her position as the eldest daughter in an entirely female family, and therefore the one most called upon, not only by circumstances but also by her mother, for responsibility and emotional support.

This life-moral story is more ambiguous than the conduct-moral one. It depicts Gwendolen's dependence on – in fact, need of – the acknowledging love (or even respect, or even mere attention) that could assure her of actually being a particular self with valuable possibilities of growth and achievement as well as of error, let alone a self conscious of the value or even the reality of its pride, courage, sensitivity and intelligence; and it traces her failure ever to find that kind of love. The force of life in her issues in toughness and resilience as well as in the distorted forms of self-mistrust and self-assertion, guilt and murderous frustration; but we do not know whether it finally remains still unextinguished, assertive, strong, unhumbled by defeated love, the acceptance of a humdrum social routine, and submission to Duty. When she writes to Deronda at the end, ' It is better – it shall be better with me because I have known you', we can only wonder if she, or George Eliot, means by ' better' everything we hope she does.

All of this is part of yet a third story in the book, of course, though it is there only in a rather notional way, being far less fully imagined than the other two. This is about moral luck, chance, gambling and taking the risk that even a moral gain (whether gain in conduct-moral terms or in life-moral ones, whether on the personal level or on the social one) may involve an unacceptable moral loss, which must nevertheless be accepted. This story has no single hero or heroine. It includes, for example, the devastating change in Gwendolen's life initiated at the outset by Deronda's morally critical glance at the gambling table and the conduct-moral self-consciousness it induces in her, so that she comes to seem doomed to (life-moral) loss by the very capacity to distinguish (conduct-moral) loss from gain. Thus this story includes that of Gwendolen's two necklaces, the history of Deronda's mother as well as the ironies of Deronda's response to and reliving of it, the story of the stolen ring, which obviously reverses another story about a ring stolen by a daughter, Jessica, from her father, Shylock and so on. But although this story does partly raise the possible irreconcilability of conduct-morality and life-morality, what is more immediately relevant is George Eliot's reluctance to face that possibility directly and explicitly in her view of Gwendolen's moral history.

One small example is indicative of the general habit, I think – the treatment of Gwendolen's relationship with her mother,

Mrs Davilow. To return for a moment to Gwendolen's acceptance of Grandcourt, we need to be quite clear what her real mistake is. It is not, surely, doing wrong to Mrs Glasher. This is how Gwendolen sees it, of course, but she exaggerates it so wildly that we are forced to wonder what her guilt about it is masking. It is interesting that Maggie Tulliver, when confronted with Stephen Guest's proposal, also develops some powerful (not to say hysterical) feelings about 'wronging' others, which mask from her consciousness her life-moral incapacity to face the risks of love once again. In Gwendolen's case, she is certainly wrong not to have challenged Grandcourt with her knowledge of his false position; in that respect, she has also evaded a risk she should have taken, and could have taken, had she been strong and assured enough in herself to do so. But if her mistake in accepting Grandcourt was not really that, neither was it to have acted from selfish or merely 'social' motives, or from merely superficially altruistic ones, or from a mixture of all these. The decision was wrong irrespective of motives; and what was wrong about it was surely to marry without love, on the mistaken (and rather pathetic) decision that conventional social respect and attention were enough for her own needs. To speak of this last decision as 'established by habits of valuation and essential choices lived' would certainly make sense; but it would not be Gwendolen's habits and choices we would mean. Similarly with the phrase used of her throughout the first part of the novel, 'the spoiled child'. That too makes a good deal of sense – so long, that is, as 'spoiled' is also taken to mean 'maimed'. Gwendolen's relationship with her mother is even more important than George Eliot suggests, I believe, and also rather different from what George Eliot seems to think it is.

What sense of herself, we might ask, does Gwendolen get from the most influential person in her life? The answer starts to emerge very early in the book. In chapter 3, for example, we are given an episode that took place when Gwendolen was twelve years old – an age that George Eliot evidently supposes makes Gwendolen a full moral agent. (The sort of moral toughness this exhibits in George Eliot, I should perhaps say, does not strike

me as it seems to strike some readers – as a mark of her maturity
and greatness. It seems to me merely another example of her
Victorian assumption that the only really 'moral' point of view
is that of conduct-morality.) Gwendolen asks her mother why,
after the death of her first husband, she married the man who
became Gwendolen's 'unlovable' step-father: '"Why did you
marry again, mamma? It would have been nicer if you had
not."' It would indeed, as Mrs Davilow knows only too well;
and what emerges from her is an outburst revealing in a number
of ways. She colours deeply, a slight convulsive movement
passes over her face, and she replies with an unusual 'violence':
'"You have no feeling, child!"' Gwendolen, who was fond of her
mamma, felt hurt and ashamed, and ... never since dared to ask
a question about her father.'[16]

What mamma expects of Gwendolen, in fact, becomes clear
on the very next page, and it remains clear all through: not
merely to *feel* for mamma, but to fill the place that mamma's
husbands have abandoned. She is to provide the emotional
support that mamma needs, and (more importantly) to provide
the household with a somewhat wayward, but firm and
authoritative will. Mrs Davilow is not merely foolish and over-
indulgent towards Gwendolen; in her weakness and dependence, she exacts a crippling price for that indulgence. A young
girl like Gwendolen, no matter how forceful a personality, does
not get to make the crucial decisions in such a family as this, set
its tone, control its attention, and generally rule the roost, unless
mamma really wants her to, at whatever moral cost to the girl.
In effect, mamma will love and indulge her little girl if she is
good and loves mamma and supports her in playing her role as
mamma; like any 'double-bind' relationship, the process has
to work in silence and on mamma's terms. If one wants to talk
about 'egoism' in all this, it would be as well to be clear about
what it consists in and what causes it. To some critics, Mrs
Davilow actually seems 'charming'. To me, I must say, she
seems rather one of those (life-morally) inadequate women who
transmit unhappiness from generation to generation like a
disease.

An episode at the end of chapter 9 is especially telling. When

Mrs Davilow remarks, '"I declare when your aunt and I were your age we knew nothing about wickedness. I think it was better so"', Gwendolen, in a flight of high spirits and forgetting that she is not talking to an equal, replies: '"Why did you not bring me up in that way, mamma?"' This touch of moral intelligence produces in mamma a 'crushed look' and violent sobbing: she has been judged! Unlike her mamma in chapter 3, however, Gwendolen sees that she 'had given a deep wound'; and (again unlike dear mamma) she rushes to soothe it: '"Dear mamma, I don't find fault with you – I love you…How can you help what I am? Besides, I am very charming. Come, now…Really – I am contented with myself…"' 'How can you help what I am?' – the implications and ironies not just of Gwendolen's question, but also of her asking it, go to the very heart of her condition. 'Contented' with herself – how much so? And how much of her selfishness and egoistical conduct (which are real enough), how much of her confident, high spirited manner (which is superficial enough), how much of her willingness to accept Grandcourt, of her self-punishing guilt and self-murderous hatred, of her baffled and confused need of loving, of her sense of her own self, are not the struggle of a life trying to realize itself in a social world where it finds (as in another way, Deronda finds) no image, no form, adequately answering to its needs and potentialities?

George Eliot's explicit view of this little episode in chapter 9 is essentially a conduct-moral one:

> Gwendolen dreaded the unpleasant sense of compunction towards her mother, which was the nearest approach to self-condemnation and self-distrust that she had known; and Mrs Davilow's timid maternal conscience dreaded whatever had brought on the slightest hint of reproach. Hence, after this little scene, the two concurred in excluding Mr Grandcourt from their conversation.[17]

Another deathly silence, of course: father *and* suitor. Mrs Davilow's timid maternal conscience might well fear reproach, just as Gwendolen might well dread having to feel compunction towards it. Nor is the kind of self-condemnation and self-distrust that Gwendolen consciously 'knows' the most important kind that she suffers from.

III

In considering people as moral agents, we might well find such ideas as *hybris* and *nemesis* useful or even necessary quite often, but it is less likely that this would apply to such ideas as moral luck, or fate, or destiny. On the other hand, considering people as moral lives, we might well find these latter ideas indispensable – mainly, perhaps, to emphasize some important pattern in the life that seems, whether to the subject or to an observer, at once to demand and yet to baffle explanation. Gwendolen, for example, is morally 'luckless'[18] from the moment Deronda's gaze pushes her decisively into a double consciousness (not unlike that of Deronda's mother), which then seems to make her lose all of her gambles with life along with her vivacity and moral innocence. Deronda himself is quite incredibly lucky, always winning his moral gambles along with a highly suitable wife who is as susceptible to Duty as he is himself. His only major setback is with his mother; the Princess turns out to have as little use for his incipient love as he has for Gwendolen's. But otherwise, he gets from life not only what he wants, but what he most wants to want. His personal wishes (which, being personal, could perhaps be thought 'egoistic') emerge as the content of his very loftiest wish: for some duty, to which he ought to 'devote his life', to be laid upon him from outside. To 'devote his life' to it makes his wishes self-evidently *non*-egoistic, morally unimpeachable; his life seems at once morally (even, in some way, religiously) right – as well as interesting and entirely fulfilling. His moral luck is not that he can make his destiny his choice; it is that his choice, his nature, his talents and virtues, his spontaneous interests and preferences, his love, his ideals, his personal and racial origins, his grandfather's ideals, his opportunities on the world-historical stage to do good to others, his accidents, decisions and possible destiny, all fall harmoniously together. What is more, they enable him both to do and to be something morally nobler – or at least grander – than any Englishman could do or be in England. He is so lucky, in fact, that he comes to suspect some cunning, communal historical *Geist* is behind it all – which, coming from George Eliot, who actually did organize it all, seems rather like a bit of intellectual hocus-pocus.

Given all this, however, it is no wonder that Gwendolen should increasingly look to Deronda for moral understanding, support and direction; and no wonder either that Deronda should advise her (as so many moral advisers do) in effect to behave and become something rather like himself. Indeed, there is nothing about him so truly egoistic (though George Eliot never pushes that term at us in relation to him) as the way he preaches to Gwendolen. The 'refuge' she needs from her 'personal trouble', for example, is 'the higher, the religious life, which holds an enthusiasm for something more than our own appetites and vanities. The few may find themselves in it simply by an elevation of feeling; but for us who have to struggle for our wisdom, the higher life must be a region in which the affections are clad with knowledge.'[19]

George Eliot explains that Deronda's 'half-indignant re-monstrance', as she calls it, arises from thoughts about himself rather than from any 'severity towards Gwendolen'; but the term that arises in a reader's mind is less likely to be 'severity' than 'priggishness'.[20] Deronda is even unheedingly insulting to Gwendolen. It is not any enthusiasm for her 'appetites and vanities' that troubles her, nor is 'refuge' in 'the higher life' relevant to her problems. As she points out, if 'affection' is indeed 'the best thing', her problem is that she has no affection around her, not even from the one person she really cares for, mamma. If her moral suffering is, as he claims, 'a painful letting in of light', then why, as she objects, is its 'cruelty' out of all proportion to the gain? And in any case, 'there are some feelings – hatred and anger – how can I be good when they keep rising?' In fact, Deronda is so useless about any of this, that (as George Eliot does see, at least dramatically) Gwendolen has to end up reassuring *him*: he has done her some good, even though she does not say what good precisely.

This scene is typical of many in the book, and not least in the way the drama itself becomes a mode of moral thinking – thinking which largely consists in seeking out and imagining the particulars of the drama, and which may or may not coincide with such general moral ideas as George Eliot might have thought she was expressing here. As Deronda goes on preaching, for example, what are we to imagine Gwendolen making of his lofty sentiments? The novelist tells us that, at Deronda's insistence about seeking a 'larger *home*' for one's personal '*passion*' (my italics), Gwendolen looked 'startled and thrilled as by an electric shock', not just 'surprised' and 'struck', say. Again, what are we to make of the remark that 'for the moment she felt like a shaken child – shaken out of its wailings into awe, and she said humbly – "I will try. I will think"'? What is the force here of 'awe', 'wailings', 'child'? And what is Deronda's feeling in all this? How far is it perhaps a defensive retreat from her particular problems into generalities about other people, including himself? Then again, how indeed can she be good, or even do good, to Grandcourt, when she has no better feelings towards him than hatred and anger? Ought she try to cultivate better ones, even if we ourselves cannot imagine what better ones he deserves? Or are we being 'egoistic'? But then what good is Deronda doing her here except in having 'better feelings' towards her – feelings of at least wanting to help her and to listen to her (even if he is not able to hear her very well), and of caring about her life? (Who else in her world gives her as much as that? But then why does George Eliot make her so morally isolated?) Is it simply that Deronda does do her some good just by having better feelings to act out of, despite the very limited relevance of his actions? But if so, it seems not so much 'good' in a conduct-moral sense, helping Gwendolen to conduct herself more virtuously, as in a life-moral sense, helping her realize the potential virtues, the positive powers or capacities, of 'the life that is in her'?

What I called the tragi-comedy of this scene, as of the other conversations between Gwendolen and Deronda, lies in what might be called the moral cross-purposes of the two characters. What causes the tangle are the differences between, on the one hand, the rules of life he gives her so liberally (read books, broaden your horizons, think of other people, take up some objective interests and so forth), which are not quite what she wants and not at all what she really needs; and on the other

hand, the vital sympathy and inner self-confidence with which
he bestows such precepts on her and which produce precisely
the admiration and attraction towards him her life-moral crisis
does need. George Eliot sees some of the ironies very clearly, of
course: the force on Gwendolen of Deronda's 'better feelings'
for her in the scene I have just been discussing, for instance.
Similarly with Deronda's physical touch as Gwendolen tells him
of Grandcourt's drowning:

> That grasp was an entirely new experience to Gwendolen: she had
> never before had from any man a sign of tenderness which her own
> being had needed, and she interpreted its powerful effect on her into
> a promise of inexhaustible patience and constancy. The stream of
> renewed strength made it possible for her to go on...[21]

But is George Eliot clear about the importance of such an
appalling absence of physically expressed tenderness in Gwendolen's life, and the degree of pity it must draw from us? Does
George Eliot think that Gwendolen is just being 'egoistic'
again, for example, or does she see Gwendolen's pathetic need
of the kind of firm conduct-moral judgment and loving life-
moral reassurance she has never had from a father?

> 'Don't be impatient with me.' The tremor, the childlike beseeching in
> these words compelled Deronda to turn his head and look at her face.[22]
> '...even the stillness – everything held a punishment for me –
> everything but you. I always thought that you would not want me to
> be punished – you would have tried and helped me to be better. And
> only thinking of that helped me. You will not change – you will not
> want to punish me now?'[23]

What Maggie Tulliver might have said to *her* father can be
heard somewhere behind these words – and it is hard not to
wonder if George Eliot herself heard it too.

So again with Gwendolen's 'childlike sentences' later on: 'I
will do what you tell me; ...but what else shall I do?' Part of
Deronda's reply is the perfectly sound advice,

> 'think that a severe angel, seeing you along the road of error, grasped
> you by the wrist, and showed you the horror of the life you must avoid.
> And it has come to you in your spring-time. Think of it as a
> preparation. You can, you will, be among the best of women, such as
> make others glad that they were born.'

The words were like the touch of a miraculous hand to Gwendolen. Mingled emotions streamed through her frame with a strength that seemed the beginning of a new existence, having some new *powers* or other which stirred her vaguely. So pregnant is the divine hope of moral *recovery* with the *energy* that fulfils it. So potent in us is *the infused action* of another soul, before which we bow in complete *love*... (my italics).[24]

George Eliot is certainly clear about the life-moral process in Gwendolen at this point, and about what empowers it. Who else has praised Gwendolen even as much as Deronda does here: as potentially among the best of women, as having a life that can be precious and enlivening to others, as a life still only in its spring-time?[25] But George Eliot is up to something else too:

But the new existence seemed inseparable from Deronda: the hope seemed to make his presence permanent. It was not her thought, that he loved her and would cling to her – a thought would have tottered with improbability: it was her spiritual breath...[26]

Gwendolen is once again not *thinking*; once again she is just breathing and assuming; but this time, it seems, her fault is a more common kind of egoism:

we are all apt to fall into this passionate egoism of imagination, not only towards our fellow-men, but towards God. And the future which she turned her face to with a willing step was one where she would be *continually assimilating herself to some type that he would hold before her.* Had he not first risen on her vision as a corrective presence which she had recognised in the beginning with resentment, and at last with entire love and trust? She could not spontaneously think of an end to that reliance, which had become to her imagination like the firmness of the earth, the only condition of her walking.[27] (my italics)

And George Eliot has prepared a final snub for this ultimate form of 'egoism' in Gwendolen too: not merely in Deronda's engagement to somebody else, but even more in his engagement with the 'vast mysterious movement' of world-historical forces. In the latter (as in the American Civil War), 'life looks out... with the awful face of duty, and a religion shows itself... something else than a private consolation'. It is therefore 'something spiritual and vaguely tremendous' to Gwendolen that simply overwhelms her residual egoistic assumption that 'whatever surrounded her was somehow specially for her', and does so with a shock which is 'deeper than personal jealousy' and which 'quelled all anger into self-humiliation'. We are presumably meant to see Gwendolen's *self*-humiliation as the last step of her moral maturation – though it might have been better suggested, I think, that Gwendolen's conception of her 'self' could seem constricted, stunted, when she glimpses the possibility that such great and testing events might be no less 'specially for *her*' than for Deronda.

I have quoted these various passages because I think they represent pretty fairly the nature and extent of George Eliot's conscious life-moral understanding of Gwendolen after her marriage – indeed one might almost say the extent of the good she does her heroine out of 'better feelings' towards her, since there are not many 'better feelings' visible towards Gwendolen before her marriage. But this life-moral attention to Gwendolen, both before and after her marriage, seems to me entirely over-matched in the novel by George Eliot's conduct-moral attention to her, by the extent to which she thinks of her heroine as a moral agent rather than an unfolding life. There is no doubt (to recall Strawson's phrases) about 'the interests of morality', in the conduct sense, being given 'an ideal overriding value'. 'Being moral', in the conduct sense, is indeed 'not merely... something that matters but... the thing that supremely matters'. And 'being moral' essentially *is* a matter of 'duty faithfully performed' or some 'duty' sought out and undertaken, of avoiding 'egoism' by 'devoting one's life' to 'doing good to others' out of one's 'better feelings towards them'. The moral weight of the novel unmistakably lies in this kind of thing:

[Gwendolen:] 'I want to be kind to them all [her family] – they can be happier than I can. Is that the best I can do?'

'I think so. It is a duty that cannot be doubtful,' said Deronda. He paused a little between his sentences, feeling a weight of anxiety on all his words. 'Other duties will spring from it. Looking at your life as a debt may seem the dreariest view of things at a distance; but it cannot really be so. What makes life dreary is the want of motive; but once beginning to act with that penitential, loving purpose you have in your mind, there will be unexpected satisfactions – there will be newly-opening needs – continually coming to carry you on from day to day. You will find your life growing like a plant.'

Gwendolen turned her eyes on him with the look of one athirst towards the sound of unseen waters...[28]

This kind of thing seems to me to mark a limit in George Eliot, both as a moralist and as a novelist – if the two can be separated. Her criticism of Gwendolen's 'egoistic' expectation that she would continually be 'assimilating herself to some type that he [Deronda] would hold before her', seems to be directed at Gwendolen's assumption that Deronda would always be available to do this for her. It is not directed at her more basic mistake, the assumption that moral life is a matter of consciously and conscientiously assimilating oneself to some pre-conceived ideal. Similarly here: George Eliot does not seem to recognize that Gwendolen's conscience has been so over-excited already that what her moral life really needs of Deronda now is not what she obviously wants – namely, precepts on how to conduct it. Rather, she needs help to begin freeing her life from a paralysing over-load of conduct-morality. But for George Eliot, issues of moral conduct are always liable to dominate issues of moral life; and there is no sign of authorial dissent from the advice she puts into Deronda's mouth here. All that the advice does, of course, is lumber Gwendolen's mind with yet more heavy Victorian moral furniture: performing one's duties; penitential loving purposes (how much of each, one wonders?); and satisfying her moral needs by satisfying those of others. To regard one's life as a debt may not strike Deronda as dreary, but as the remark about 'want of motive' betrays, there are reasons for that in the particular nature and circumstances of his own life: for example, in the fact that he is free to take or not to take his particular line of altruistic action as a 'debt' or a 'duty', and in the self-enlarging, self-fulfilling content of that 'duty'. There are some important differences between devoting one's life to a world-historical mission like Deronda's, and devoting it to the penitential love of Gwendolen's mamma. Indeed, Deronda's advice, which is priggish enough in any case, almost seems designed by his author to blur the differences between a 'duty' fulfilling the needs of one's particular nature, personal and social, and a duty to sacrifice the needs of one's particular nature to ministering to the needs of one's family – and of anyone else who turns up.

Deronda's claim that Gwendolen's 'life' under these conditions will grow like a plant must therefore strike the reader as wildly implausible, even if it does not seem to strike George Eliot that way. The claim might seem more plausible if Gwendolen's life consisted only of such thoughts and feelings and actions as might put her into the general conduct-moral class of 'the best of women' who make others glad – and also, of course, if 'the best of women' meant what Deronda means by it. But Gwendolen's life consists not just of voluntary intentional actions, but of the whole bent and range of her activity as a moral being. And as we see that life manifesting itself in countless details, it consists in positive powers or 'virtues' as well as in conduct-moral flaws: in an out-ranging spirit and vivacity, a capacity for gaiety and laughter as well as for conceit and showing off, a nature not just superficial and thoughtlessly selfish and self-centred but also large and genuine enough to attract the goodwill of a Catherine Arrowpoint, a mind quick and witty (and informed) enough to outmatch a Mrs Arrowpoint and to interest a Klesmer, a capacity for love that is not merely penitential but (sometimes) free and patient, a good deal of bossiness but also a resilient courage to lead others and also to venture herself into unknown waters, a will often merely wilful and egoistic but also directed to mastering life – in addition to a capacity for hatred and rage and wickedness, and for equally destructive self-doubt and self-punishment, as well as some deep, tangled needs and fears about men. It would be more to the point, in fact, if Deronda advised her to remember that her life grows like a plant willy-nilly, and to trust to it: to allow the great rage in her to die, and not to forsake all that she was, but rather to feel and live with the whole of her moral being as it now is. But then what does George Eliot allow Deronda to know of Gwendolen's whole moral being? Or to put the question another way, how else could he, as the moral being George Eliot has made him, see Gwendolen's moral life except as a case, an instance, of the familiar universals of conduct-morality? Perhaps the really odd thing about the novel here is that George Eliot seems not to notice the narrow limits of her hero's moral experience, wisdom and nature.

Thus in allowing Deronda to assume that a conduct-moral view of Gwendolen's life is sufficient, or that it is (in Mill's phrase) 'unquestionably the first and most important' view of it, George Eliot seems to join him in conflating 'duty' as it would apply (repressively) to Gwendolen's case, and 'duty' as it would apply (fulfillingly) to his own. There is no equivalence between the two kinds of 'duty', of course; but to push the matter further, there is no good reason why Gwendolen does not deserve a destiny able to fulfil her whole moral being too: it is no less fine and masterful than Deronda's and in some ways more so.

But if George Eliot's view of Gwendolen here seems pretty much the same as her hero's, there are other things in the novel that do question or qualify it – most especially, the case of Deronda's mother. The Princess is a much more substantial and important element in the novel than is often thought. It is she, for example, who insists – and Deronda has to agree with her – that *her* life, which was 'growing like a tree',[29] had to break free of an orthodox, universal conduct-morality that would have stifled her genius, and stifled it precisely by making her one of the best of (Jewish) women. And of course George Eliot sees the irony of her son, as a result of hearing her story, actually coming to reverse *her* argument and *her* liberation for a similar end for himself. Moreover, the Princess makes two other points that, although they do not influence Deronda's advice to Gwendolen in the passage above, do perhaps bear on how George Eliot sees that situation, and certainly bear on how we do.

The first is that his mother's action in virtually giving him over for adoption, which might have seemed egoistic and unloving in her (and which in conduct-moral terms it obviously was), did do him at least some good: it enabled him to grow up with the inner security and self-assurance of an English gentleman. (It also makes Sir Hugo's feelings and actions towards the boy shine out as perhaps the finest example of moral conduct in the book. Indeed, were it only moral conduct that mattered, Sir Hugo would surely have to be the book's true hero.) And the Princess is right in this. Deronda's life has been spared in his most impressionable years an insecuring double-consciousness, which semitism and anti-semitism must other-wise have forced on him, and which has been forced in a number of ways on the Princess herself, and in yet another way, on Gwendolen. In short, the Deronda who advises Gwendolen is, as we have been given to see, both morally simpler and morally luckier than she is.

The Princess's second point is that a man cannot, as Deronda claims he does, really understand the moral conflict she experienced:

'No', said the Princess... 'You are not a woman. You may try – but you can never imagine what it is to have a man's force of genius in you, and yet to suffer the slavery of being a girl. To have a pattern cut out – "this is the Jewish woman; this is what you must be; this is what you are wanted for..."'[30]

This too bears on the later passage. Deronda can see little or nothing of a truth that George Eliot does partly and sometimes see: that Gwendolen cannot be wholly defined as her conduct self, as an agent who could assimilate herself to some pre-determined ideal type or pattern of womanhood. She is still open, still an unfolding life as well as a bewildered woman – bewildered largely because, as the Princess rightly insists, the world makes it very difficult, if not impossible, for a woman to live out the whole of the life in her. In fact, the world makes it especially difficult for a Jewish woman, and (for a different reason) an English woman too. In the one case, she has to contend with the patriarchal character of her morality; in the other, with a long-settled social order that offers a woman far less chance of getting free of ideal types and patterns than does, say, an historically awakening society. And the world makes it more difficult still for a woman like Gwendolen, not lucky enough to have a socially acceptable kind of genius – such as the Princess's, for instance, or George Eliot's.

And yet even here, in dealing with genius, George Eliot seems reluctant to compromise the supremacy of conduct-morality.

For her, the appropriate result of the Princess's having had to deny the ordained duties ('bonds') of motherhood, family, community and religion is a kind of emotional sterility. The Princess has nothing to give her son any more; she is, as she puts it, a 'shattered woman'.

I will confess it all, now that I have come up to it. Often when I am at ease it all fades away; my whole self comes quite back; but I know it will sink away again, and the other will come – the poor, solitary, forsaken remains of self, that can resist nothing. It was my nature to resist, and say, 'I have a right to resist.' Well, I say so still when I have any strength in me. You have heard me say it, and I don't withdraw it. But when my strength goes, some other right forces itself upon me like iron in an inexorable hand; and even when I am at ease, it is beginning to make ghosts upon the daylight...[31]

And just as her denial of Deronda's feelings for her is later echoed by his own denial of Gwendolen's at their last meeting so this speech of the Princess's is echoed in Gwendolen's cry of pain: 'I said I should be forsaken. I have been a cruel woman. And I am forsaken.'[32]

If Deronda's advice to Gwendolen represents a limitation in George Eliot, these two speeches seem to me to represent in miniature her genius as a moral novelist. Her finest gift is the capacity to imagine her fictions – to think *of* her stories and her characters – more deeply and more fully than she could always think *about* them. Her genius, that is to say, is dramatic, not discursive, even if it sometimes seems the other way round. As we shall see in *The Mill on the Floss*, she can think imaginatively of a fictional reality that actually stands against what she thinks she thinks about it, and also against what she thinks she is presenting by way of ideas elsewhere in the novel – as, to take an obvious example, in the Jewish sections of this one. And the two little speeches above, and the relationships between them, can perhaps best suggest the kind of moral-dramatic genius I mean.

What George Eliot thought about these speeches, or thought she did, is left implicit of course, but it is not hard to see. The Princess is an example of how necessary it may be for a genius to assert her own 'egoistic' needs against the ordained duties and ideals of conduct-morality; but her present state shows how the impersonal force of morality returns irresistibly, like a nemesis, asserting its supremacy over the self as the self inevitably ages, weakens and disintegrates. Gwendolen is an example of something similar: the supremacy of conduct-morality asserts itself in the pain and desolate loneliness that are the nemesis of *her* egoism – her assertion of self in knowingly doing wrong, and in her still petty, self-absorbed unawareness of 'the larger destinies of mankind'.

But if this or something like it represents how George Eliot might have thought about the two speeches intellectually as it were, what the speeches help to create dramatically, along with all the other manifestations in the novel of Gwendolen as a moral life, is something rather different. Nor is it only the powerful word 'forsaken' that links these two speeches; the word also serves to focus other parallels. Each speech, for example, expresses a variant of the *other* woman's state of soul, so that when Gwendolen's cry comes near the end of the book it brings us to think of both women in the one thought: the one who had all too much father, and the other who had all too little. (Mirah is yet another daughter, of course.) What the women share is not just an uneasy conscience, however; in both speeches, the whole moral being seems *haunted* by its past deeds, no matter how defensible or not the deeds may have been. It is the moral transgression, the harm done to others, the lack of better feelings towards them, that makes the thought of moral retribution so painful and yet so irresistible. One woman has resisted and denied her father and (with far more cruelty) her son; the other has denied the forsaken Mrs Glasher and her children and (with no less cruelty) her own moral and emotional integrity.

And yet each woman's moral life is visibly deepened, enlarged, intensified, more fully realized, made finer *as* a life, in that haunting. What seemed to be the resurgent supremacy of conduct-morality over each self is really the fear of being morally overwhelmed, negated, of having no self at all. At bottom, it is the fear of death; and it naturally takes a different shape in each woman's mind. In the Princess, it is obviously the fear of utter forcelessness, of no longer being the strong, 'whole' self that 'resisted' and affirmed its own powers or 'virtues' against her father's code and ideals of conduct. In Gwendolen, it is a double fear she has shown all along. Its first element is obvious in this little speech: the fear of always being as unloved, because unworthy of being loved, as she has always been (cousin Rex notwithstanding), of having once again no tenderness, no warm understanding and absolving 'better feelings' *from* others – the insecurity and emptiness which she has tried to remedy with such admiration as she could force from others, and which Deronda alone seemed able to help with. The second element also goes back to her childhood: the suppressed but paralysing fear of solitude and of some awesome supernatural judgment and destruction – which, as the translator of Feuerbach would certainly see, projects a fear of something unforgivably worthless and even lethal in herself.[33] But the fact that it *is* a fear of blankness and death exhibits a crucial sense in which conduct-morality cannot be supreme, cannot be 'unquestionably the first and most important' way of seeing people – especially for a novelist. For first and most importantly, people are living moral beings, which is to say that these two women are firstly these two particular, unique moral lives or selves; and the way that anyone sees the nature and claims of conduct-morality, and sees and fears negation or destruction, manifests his or her moral life at least as clearly as does any other activity. Thus in each woman the flash of naked fear shows her more vividly alive than ever: it shows her, that is, not merely a properly self-punished and therefore pathetic moral example, but also as a stronger, more distinct, but more vulnerable, and therefore potentially tragic, individual life.

To get at the point another way, we might notice that while the whole novel has obvious affinities with Henry James and the 'great tradition' of moral fiction generally, it also has affinities with Ibsen. Either of these two speeches about being 'forsaken' could come straight out of an Ibsen play, for example – not to mention the Princess's phrase about past rejections beginning to make 'ghosts upon the daylight'. And what underlies this affinity is something that George Eliot could perhaps only think imaginatively, dramatically, where Ibsen could also think about

it intellectually: the possibility that the transgressions and flaws
of the conduct self may (as appears here for a moment in these
two speeches) be 'portals of discovery'. They may be the
activity of a life finding what it most finely has it in it to be.

The point here is not the one Deronda is given to make earlier
in the book, that (as he puts it to Gwendolen with tactless but
effortless superiority)

> I meant that those who would be comparatively uninteresting
> beforehand [namely Gwendolen] may become worthier of sympathy
> when they do something that awakens in them a keen remorse. Lives
> are enlarged in different ways. I daresay some would never get their
> eyes opened if it were not for a violent shock from the consequences of
> their own actions. And when they are suffering in that way one must
> care for them more than for the comfortably self-satisfied.[34]

Nor is the dramatic point simply that suffering does one good
– a moral belief still curiously persistent, especially about other
people's suffering. It is closer to that made in one of Deronda's
silent (but still gratingly superior) reflections about how much
more 'interesting' Gwendolen had become:

> Mrs Grandcourt was handsomer than Gwendolen Harleth: her grace
> and expression were informed by a greater variety of inward
> experience, giving new play to the facial muscles, new attitudes in
> movement and repose; her whole person and air had the nameless
> something which often makes a woman more interesting after
> marriage than before, less confident that all things are according to
> her opinion, and yet with less of deer-like shyness – more fully a
> human being.[35]

We do not have to share Deronda's pretty offensive patronizing
attitude in order to see Gwendolen becoming 'more fully a
human being'. The point made dramatically by so much in the
novel is that conduct-moral considerations are *not* always
supreme over life-moral ones; that each woman's kind of
'egoism', along with its consequences, may be a vice of conduct
and yet be a virtue, even a necessity, of the life – one of the forms
in which her moral being realizes its possibilities. The fear of
being 'forsaken' reveals how frail the egoism really is in each
woman, how hard for them to hold on to. But then 'egoism' is
probably the wrong word for what is threatened by their

haunting fear of weakness, loneliness, dissolution, lovelessness, and for the courage to keep that fear at bay. Whatever we call it, however, it is an attribute that would make Deronda a much more impressive figure if he had it.

As I see it, the 'impression of great philosophical power' that Jowett spoke of in George Eliot lies in her power to realize dramatically, and with a different kind of moral judgment, more than her Victorian cast of mind often allowed her to realize intellectually. The life-moral thinking of *Daniel Deronda* is still largely implicit but it is much more prominent and much more thorough than that of any of her earlier novels – which is why the book points, not just backwards to the complicated tangles of those earlier novels, but forwards to the more direct and explicit concern with life-moral issues that distinguishes 'modern' literature (from, say, Nietzsche and Ibsen onwards), just as it had distinguished Shakespearean drama.

CHAPTER 5

Moral thinking in The Mill on the Floss

I

Who but a philosopher would think it was *praising* poetry to call it more philosophical than history?

Poetry... tends to express the universal, history the particular. By the universal I mean how a person of a certain type will on occasion speak or act, according to the law of probability or necessity; and it is this universality at which poetry aims... The particular is – for example – what Alcibiades did or suffered... (*Poetics*, translated by Butcher, 145 1b)

Aristotle's observation is true enough, no doubt, as far as it goes. But what *it* expresses, surely, is how a person of a certain type will probably or necessarily speak about poetry. The philosophical type of man will tend to see poetry as exemplifying recognizable universals – for example, those of moral psychology; and he will naturally value it for this because he is the type of man for whom the recognizably universal – types, categories, principles, universally valid reasons, rules, ideals and laws – is always more basic, more important, than the particular, the contingent, the distinctively individual, the unique: even in matters of moral insight and wisdom. That indeed is one of the reasons we would call him a philosophical type of man.

Of course, to say this is to express just such a moral-psychological judgment oneself. Nor can we avoid making such judgments. Being occasionally reflective and partly rational, all human beings may be partly or occasionally philosophers. We constantly need to make this kind of judgment about human beings and human life, even if we do not share the philosopher's faith that it is the only really important kind. And of course this is true with poets, even if it is not the only important truth about poetry. The 'serious' poets almost by definition are ones who have, and know they have, important general truths about human life to express in their work. The nineteenth-century novelists, for example, took it virtually for granted that they would and should be valued for their moral seriousness – none more so than George Eliot, who positively insisted on it. In a novel like *The Mill on the Floss* she might use a good deal of autobiographical, i.e. 'particular', material, but there is no mistaking her persistent aim in the work, which is to show the particulars as *cases*, *examples*, *instances*, of universal principles. Being up with the Higher Thought of her time, she sometimes wants to show these particulars as 'concrete universals' in a Hegelian sort of way – instances of the historical development of humanity and reason; but her chief aim is to show them as instances of universal moral principles. Yet the more seriously we take the book, the harder it is to be sure exactly *what* universal principles it expresses, and the reasons why this is so are worth pondering, if only because they make the moral thinking in the novel so difficult to untangle.

One reason is a formal quality of this novel: its untroubled Victorian fusion of quasi-dramatic presentation, narrative report and description, and direct, essay-like commentaries by the 'author'. As various critics have noted, this makes it hard to account for some significant discrepancies of moral attitude in the novel, since the formal narrator comes to seem an 'unreliable' authority on the action and yet to have an indeterminate position in relation to it. We might take a tiny example early in the novel, where the narrator or the author comments on the way people's 'unmodifiable characters' only reveal themselves in time, and how 'the dark-eyed, demonstrative, rebellious girl' may eventually show herself to be quite a 'passive' being.[1] Are we to suppose that George Eliot thinks 'demonstrative' and 'rebellious' not just the most accurate, but (more importantly) the most relevant, terms in which to characterize the young Maggie Tulliver? What should we conclude from the pretty obvious fact that they are not?

The simple solution might seem to be not to trust the author, but to trust the tale. But the trouble is that we often find it impossible to tell which is which; and as the novel progresses, the effect of this is compounded by a larger source of difficulty: the novel's insistent aim at recognizably universal moral principles.

The result is visible in an episode like that in Book 5, chapter 3, for example, where the adolescent Maggie talks with Philip Wakem. The particulars of the scene draw our attention to the state of mind Maggie is in; to the quite sensible arguments Philip directs against her cult of 'resignation', and her virtual ignoring of them; to her feelings towards Philip and their relation to her feelings for her brother, Tom; to the revealingly non-sexual meaning she gives the word 'love'; to her significantly limited conception of her own nature; to Philip's baffled wish to fill more of her life than he does, and the little stratagem he offers her to square her conscience about seeing him; and so on. Yet the authorial commentary that follows the scene immediately fastens upon the universal moral categories, principles, and rules which it supposes have just been illustrated and which it supposes must be foremost in the reader's mind: the principles of right and wrong conduct, the nature of selfishness, the reasons for such 'morbidity' as is exemplified in Philip's bad conduct, and so on.

This disjunction between the moral significance of the particulars and the universal moral principles they are supposed to show becomes most visible and most troubling in the novel's crisis – Maggie's relationship with Stephen Guest. Whose, for example, is the moral consciousness in the following passage, which is no more than a representative example of the writing in this part of the book?

Maggie, all this time, moved about with a quiescence and even torpor of manner ... But under this torpor there was a fierce battle of emotions, such as Maggie in all her life of struggle had never known or foreboded: it seemed to her as if all the worst evil in her had lain in ambush till now, and had suddenly started up full-armed, with hideous, overpowering strength! There were moments in which a cruel selfishness seemed to be getting possession of her: why should not

Lucy – why should not Philip suffer? *She* had had to suffer through many years of her life; and who had renounced anything for her? And when something like that fulness of existence – love, wealth, ease, refinement, all that her nature craved – was brought within her reach, why was she to forego it, that another might have it – another, who perhaps needed it less? But amidst all this new passionate tumult there were the old voices making themselves heard with rising power, till, from time to time, the tumult seemed quelled. *Was* that existence which tempted her the full existence she dreamed? Where, then, would be all the memories of early striving – all the deep pity for another's pain, which had been nurtured in her through years of affection and hardship – all the divine presentiment of something higher than mere personal enjoyment, which had made the sacredness of life? She might as well hope to enjoy walking by maiming her feet, as hope to enjoy an existence in which she set out by maiming the faith and sympathy that were the best organs of her soul. And then, if pain were so hard to *her*, what was it to others? – 'Ah, God! preserve me from inflicting – give me strength to bear it.' – How had she sunk into this struggle with a temptation that she would once have thought herself as secure from, as from deliberate crime? When was that first hateful moment in which she had been conscious of a feeling that clashed with her truth, affection, and gratitude, and had not shaken it from her with horror, as if it had been a loathsome thing? – And yet, since this strange, sweet, subduing influence did not, should not, conquer her – since it was to remain simply her own suffering... She refused it less and less, till at last the evening for them both was sometimes made of a moment's mutual gaze: they thought of it till it came, and when it had come, they thought of nothing else. One other thing Stephen seemed now and then to care for, and that was, to sing: it was a way of speaking to Maggie. Perhaps he was not distinctly conscious that he was impelled to it by a secret longing – running counter to all his self-confessed resolves – to deepen the hold he had on her. Watch your own speech, and notice how it is guided by your less conscious purposes, and you will understand that contradiction in Stephen.[2]

As we might suspect from the swelling *vox humana* invoking those 'old voices', this sort of writing involves some pretty dubious moral thinking about moral thinking. Not only does George Eliot treat Maggie too self-identifyingly and too much from within; an even more fundamental weakness is that Maggie provides her creator with an all-too-convenient 'within' in which to instantiate some of her universal moral principles.

If we ask, for example, why the 'fierce battle of emotions' is described with so marked an absence of 'fierceness' and 'battle' in the writing, we discover that the closer we look, the less it seems a *moral* battle at all. It is hard to believe that Maggie (of all people) could be experiencing this particular 'fierce battle' and yet be capable of thinking of its content as 'emotions' in this objective way. What can be meant by 'emotions' here, when all the good motives, ends, ideals and virtues present themselves to her mind clearly *as* good, and all the evil, selfish ones present themselves clearly as bad? In a genuine moral conflict, 'emotions' are not so readily separable from valuations, nor both from judgment and will, as Maggie's seem to be here. The ambiguously-used third-person ('Maggie', 'she', and so on) reinforces the persistent assumption that Maggie's ultimate 'self' stands somewhere outside this battle, assaulted there by tempting thoughts of selfishness, but able to know and name them for what they are, and able to know and name all the deepest and best 'organs of her soul', all her virtues, her 'divine presentiments', the 'sacredness of life', her 'truth, affections, and gratitude'. If she can know all this, she is a very lucky girl; any really fundamental moral conflict is not for her. What makes such a conflict for most people is that questions of what is most valuable, good or right, and questions of what one most deeply feels, and needs, and is, have to be answered together, and from within conflicting states of the self. And this means that, as in many (if not most) real predicaments about how to act or how to live, the crucial question is how the situation should be described, in what universal moral terms it should be thought about. This is a point that literary critics and even moral philosophers very often ignore; and yet one's decision about this is a decision about what, among all the countless circumstances of the situation and all the countless ways they can be described, are its morally salient features.

This is why, in a predicament like Maggie's, the question about other people is not likely to be 'Why should they not suffer?' In the midst of such perplexities we do not already have the solution – the clear unchallengeable knowledge that our supreme duty is to avoid any suffering to others, no matter what the circumstances. But in this passage, the moral values are all given from the start; they are all universal; and Maggie can simply recognize them *because* they are values for anybody. What is more, they carry categorical imperatives to Maggie, with no 'ifs' or 'buts', because (and this is the unexpressed but central point for George Eliot) we are to infer that they carry such imperatives for everybody. In short, Maggie provides George Eliot with a consciousness that seems to respond to, and determine itself by, the relevance and authority of certain values; and this because those values are assumed to have a clear, unquestionable status as universal and categorical.

This is why the passage lacks much dramatic force. The only dramatic issues are, firstly, Maggie's feelings about acting upon these values – which would be to break off all relations with Stephen – and secondly, the curious way she drifts away from actually doing so: a drift that seems a wilfully indulged moral 'passivity', a mere evasion by the will of clear and categorical reason – precisely the kind of semi-deliberate withdrawal of moral vigilance she allows a little later to carry her drifting in the fateful boat-trip with Stephen. In short, the writing focuses upon the feelings and the moral effect of feelings. Moral action is conceived as essentially a matter of feelings moving the will – feelings for oneself (selfishness) against feelings for values and feelings for others' wishes, interests and claims. And morality itself is conceived as essentially a matter of moral action – of deciding and acting.

Even in this passage, however, it is interesting to notice that Maggie cannot be reduced to merely the sum total of a moral consciousness, feelings and a (somewhat recalcitrant) will. To put it another way, George Eliot's imagination begins to move out of the control of the universal moral principles she is aiming to express. The last two sentences are a striking signal for this. For what are we to see as the 'secret longing' beneath *Maggie's* 'conscious purposes'? Is it merely her 'selfish' wish to have Stephen and, with him, everything she thinks she means by 'fulness of existence'? Or does George Eliot realize that the 'fulness' Maggie's nature really *needs* is not reducible to such suburban dreams as 'love, wealth, ease, refinement, all that her nature *craved*'? If we pursue this line of thought, the attention we have been pressing on Maggie's moral consciousness swivels round to the other side of the matter – to her consciousness not as the *scene* of the moral battle, but as the *prize* of the battle. Viewed from this angle, the conflict is clearly not a matter of one emotion versus another, not of 'personal enjoyment' (a selfishness that ought to be renounced virtually by definition) versus everything she conceives as making for 'the sacredness of life'. The conflict is between all these recognizable and acknowledged moral considerations on the one hand, and on the other hand whatever it is that her particular individual nature needs and is vainly trying to force into her consciousness *as* need rather than mere craving – something that makes for a life full enough to answer to reality, and in being that, to be even more sacred than she can now conceive.

Seen in this perspective, her question, 'Why should not Lucy – why should not Philip suffer?', now appears, not as a rather vacuous example of selfishness, but as the manifestation – in the distorted form of resentment – of needs of her nature that she has previously denied on moral grounds. One is her natural, 'unmodifiable' unease with the universal canons of good looks, good character and good conduct of which Lucy has always been such a shining example (Lucy by name, and Lucy by nature). Another is her natural hostility to Philip's claim not just to her pity and affection, but to her love, her whole self, on the grounds of universal 'spiritual' and moral values. More importantly, her lack of moral decision and action here also takes on a different significance. Her real need finds its satisfaction not in action but in a state of being – in the 'mutual gaze' that gives shape and point to existence, and in 'singing' or 'speaking'. Clearly, the need of Maggie's nature this satisfies is not one *she* thinks moral; but neither can we see it as merely a 'craving' for the kind of love that can just be added to wealth, ease and refinement, to make up a conventional middle-class 'fulness of existence'.

Yet here is one of the central problems Maggie unwittingly

faces. For by what familiar general moral term could she name either the need or its satisfaction except 'fulness of existence'? And how could she specify the content of that, except in terms necessarily personal, particular and open – which is to say, *metaphorical*? She had tried to express it to Philip earlier:

'What a dear, good brother you would have been, Philip... I think you would have made as much fuss about me, and been as pleased for me to love you, as would have satisfied even me. You would have loved me well enough to bear with me, and forgive me everything. That was what I always longed that Tom should do. I was never satisfied with a *little* of anything. That is why it is better for me to do without earthly happiness altogether... I never felt that I had enough music – I wanted more instruments playing together – I wanted voices to be fuller and deeper.'[3]

For Maggie (or anybody else) to regard the vital needs this makes manifest as merely selfish, or merely a matter of 'feeling' or 'emotion', would obviously beg far too many questions about their nature and value. This applies even more to the re-lationship with Stephen; and it also matters more there because the needs of her nature that Stephen answers to have to be placed *morally* against Lucy's claims on Stephen, who is Lucy's fiancé, and Philip's claims on her, Maggie, who feels she has become Philip's fiancée (even if largely because of dear Lucy's unselfish 'goodness'). But if 'feeling' or 'emotion' will not do, neither will 'sexual passion' or 'sexual love', and for the same reasons. Even 'personal love', which is probably the best general moral term Maggie could find, begs some important moral questions as soon as it is used in relation to others like 'self-sacrifice' and 'duty'. For what moral imperative could 'personal love' finally carry against those? The obvious solution, one might think, is for Maggie to see the issue as one of 'self-fulfilment' or 'self-realization'. This, which is a recog-nizable general moral value, seems to be what is at stake. And yet *could* Maggie see it as that, or indeed *should* she? For one thing, such a term cannot withstand much moral pressure (which she would be the first to apply) on the 'self' bit of it – except by stipulating that it is only the morally-endorsable 'best self' or 'true self' which deserves to be realized or fulfilled;

and that gets nowhere. But more importantly, *is* it 'self-fulfilment' or 'self-realization' that is really at stake here? I should want to argue that it is not, that the problem goes deeper.

II

It arises, I believe, from the very way that morality is conceived – and not only by Maggie and George Eliot – and from two assumptions especially. The first is that morality is essentially concerned with conduct, with voluntary intentional actions, which includes making choices and decisions, and also involves certain dispositions and habits – that is, conduct-moral 'character' and 'virtues'. The second is that morality is essentially concerned with such action in relation to others – to other people or indeed to God conceived as 'other'.

The first assumption is very deep-rooted, of course. Morality has always tended to become assimilated to law; and while there are obvious historical reasons for this, it has some far-reaching consequences. Maggie's brother Tom illustrates some of them very clearly. He is one of those

minds strongly marked by the positive and negative qualities that create severity – strength of will, conscious rectitude of purpose, narrowness of imagination and intellect, great power of self-control, and a disposition to exert control over others … with the authority of conscious right … For Tom's part, he held himself bound by his duty to his father's memory, and by every manly feeling …[4]

There is no doubt that Tom expresses a recognizable conception of morality as consisting of universal rational principles, ideals, duties, imperatives or rules. In relation to these, as he is always pointing out to Maggie, no one is exempt – though sisters are probably less exempt than others. In other words, human nature is relevant to morality only in its universal characteristics. As a Tom Tulliver sees it, not just actions, decisions and purposes, but the whole of consciousness – intellect, imagination, fantasy and feelings too (perhaps especially feelings) – are only functions or effects of the conduct-self, and if they are not, they should be. That is, they are controllable by the conscious will, which is the centre, the very core, of the self; and the will directs the self towards the good or the right, or towards the bad or the wrong. For him, self-control, self-mastery *is* morality in operation – which is why he values his own self-mastery, demands the same of others, and despises Maggie's lack of it.

A major objection to this, as George Eliot sees quite clearly in Tom's case, is the narrowing and dulling of life it entails, and she makes the point by showing us particulars that can *only* be characterized in general terms like 'narrowness'. For this is what Tom's 'great power of self-control' exhibits. But what is equally clear to us if not to George Eliot is that the most basic, most important self-control in Tom is not the one he is conscious of. It is rather the control exercised by the 'less conscious purposes' of his nature over his consciousness itself and hence over his conscious will. It is the unconscious control exercised over what he can allow the 'true self' to need or to be, either in his own case or in those of others; control over what he can allow his (or any other) self to recognize it is 'bound by'; control over what he can see as important or valuable – or even, on some important occasions, real. The kind of visible self that is delimited and fixed by this kind of control answers to the nature, the 'less conscious' self, that is doing the controlling. It is its objective correlative, as we might say.

Thus to conceive morality as Tom Tulliver does is to think of people only as he needs to think of himself: simply as determinate, or determinable, human agents. The 'self' is seen as consisting of those recognizable interests, projects, thoughts, feelings and qualities that the conscious will has already determined or may determine in the future – plus, of course, the will itself. Personal responsibility therefore occupies a central position in this kind of moral thinking. To the Tom Tullivers of the world, the only alternatives to strength of will, rectitude, worthiness, approval, or reward, are culpable weakness or fault, guilt, blame, disapproval, or punishment – with forgiveness as perhaps an optional extra. Terms like 'virtue', or 'passions', or 'integrity', or 'measure', all seem straightforward, at least in principle: their content is regarded as the same for all human agents; and all human actions can be *wholly characterized*, morally speaking, as instances of them. And not the least powerful form of control on one's own self or on others is the insistence that this is what morality really is, that whatever falls outside the scope of these general terms and principles is not really a moral matter at all. It may be a 'personal' one, or a 'social' one, or a 'cultural' one, or 'religious', or 'spiritual', or 'psychological', or 'aesthetic', or a matter of 'taste', or even one 'ethical in the broad sense'; but it is not, in the true, strict sense of the word, really *moral*. Poor Maggie. What really *moral* claim could there be in a mutual gaze with Stephen Guest, or even in her wanting more instruments playing together and voices to be fuller and deeper?

Her plight is made worse by the second assumption, which usually accompanies the first: that morality is essentially concerned with acting well towards others. The most limiting effects of this are to be seen not in Tom, but in Maggie, and in George Eliot herself.

One effect is that 'egoism' becomes an almost obsessive problem, as it does in *Daniel Deronda*, for example, which only reveals in more subtle ways what is very evident in *The Mill on the Floss*: that a concentration on 'egoism' can easily obscure more fundamental questions about the moral 'self'. But it is enough at the moment to notice once again that 'egoism' as a *psychological* term refers to a necessary, universal, but morally neutral human characteristic, while as a *moral* term, it is supposed to distinguish bad from good: the one is selfishness, the other altruism. Moral psychology can thus become a bewildering maze of both senses of the term; and moral judgment, of others or oneself, can become fraught with anxiety about which sense applies in the particular case. Any action, any motive for action, any trait of character, may have to be traced back to its original springs in order to decide: a task for which the novel seems the ideal instrument, of course.

But as *Daniel Deronda* again shows, this problem leads to even greater anxiety if (like George Eliot) one also regards *feelings* as what move the will into positive action. Good becomes not just feeling for others, especially for their pain and suffering, but feeling *more* for them than for one's own identifiable wishes or interests. Bad becomes not just failing to feel for others as 'equivalent centres of self', but failing to feel for them as more-than-equivalent centres of self. Altruism has to be a 'feeling' for others like some (non-sexual) kind of love in order to be capable of moving the will to good action; everyone always ought to try to have these better feelings, and the best people are those who actually do. Of course, by its very nature any kind of love is partial; it does tend to grant one law for the lion and another for the ox; but so long as one always tempers mercy with justice, or treats oneself as the ox and the other as the lion, then it is morally sound. It is assumed that, since all action springs out of (psychological) 'egoism' anyway, nobody need or ought to try to feel self-love. Self-sacrifice, self-abnegation is the thing. The trouble with this, however, as *Daniel Deronda* makes clear, is that moral thinking becomes only a matter of assessing the nature and object of one's feelings. What gets left out is the possibility that it might be more accurate to speak of a state of the self – a state of which consciousness and feelings are only two mani-festations – than of the self having, and being conscious of having, certain feelings.

But as Maggie's case makes clear, this whole line of thought is open to other objections too. One is that it makes it all too easy to take the outsider's, the third-person view, as always the truly *moral* view. Being in love sexually, for example, can easily seem to be morally assessable only in the way that other people might analyse it: as a case of choosing to have feelings of (say) the wrong kind (for example 'desire' or 'infatuation' or 'ex-citement'), or of the wrong quantity (for example 'passionate'), or directed to the wrong object (for example an 'unworthy' one), or serving the interests of the wrong person (for example oneself, or those without the 'natural claim' to your affections that brothers or cousins or fiancés have), or some or all of these. But what if being in love is not capable of being dissected and described in this way? What if it is less like a special kind of volition or feeling, which in principle is open to anyone and essentially the same for everyone, and more like, say, a direct experience of the divine: a transformation of one's whole way of being alive, a radical reorientation of the particular person one happens to be? What if being in love with this particular person happens to be for you a re-experiencing of the world in a way that reveals and releases and indeed newly *creates* value and interest in it for you?

A second objection is that this line of thought makes feelings morally important in much too simple a way. Real feelings cannot be switched on or off at will, nor voluntarily made to fit some standard outside themselves, no matter what morality says. In some respects, of course, George Eliot understands this perfectly well. This is what makes Maggie's renunciation of Stephen call for real resignation, and makes her suffering 'tragic' in George Eliot's eyes. As the novel shows, what one can consciously do with one's feelings is disregard them. But what George Eliot sees less clearly in Maggie's case is that unconsciously, or at least unwittingly, one can also manipulate one's feelings, or displace them, or puff them up – in short, falsify them – and do so from the best of conscious motives. And in Maggie's predicament over Stephen, this is just what happens to her feelings towards Lucy and Philip. She believes she ought to feel more strongly and sympathetically for them, and for the 'duty' she owes them, than for any 'interest' of her own; it would be selfish and therefore immoral not to. That comes perilously close to believing she ought to feel for them and feel 'duty' towards them more strongly than she does for Stephen. But while that seems impossible, what other measure – on her assumptions – should she use? Morally speaking, it seems, there is no limit to what she ought to feel for their suffering if she lets Stephen court her. The effect of all this is her over-wrought moral fantasizing about pity and gratitude and so on: she *has* to feel the suffering of others, just because it is that of others, in a way that makes it affect her actions more than any suffering of her own (or Stephen's). The resulting falsity emerges in the muddles I have already mentioned. It emerges too in the blank opacity of the other 'selves' she fantasizes about – the 'Lucy' and the 'Philip' she supposes she is feeling for. Not only do her fantasies conceive them as presenting her with moral claims more uncompromising than decent people like Lucy or Philip would present, or even feel; Maggie's fantasies even pre-empt the capacity of others – indeed their right – to feel anything *except* pain, or to act towards her and Stephen as generously as they might well choose to. What is really fighting against her love for Stephen, we begin to realize, is not her 'higher' nature (i.e. her feelings for others), nor even her conscience (her feelings for goodness and 'duty'). It is rather a wish to feel morally good, to feel unselfish, in order to satisfy her need to feel assured of her own value. And that way of satisfying that need is by no means a self-evident 'good', much less a supreme 'good'. Her wish to be morally perfect seems more like a wish to placate the moral judgment of others, a fearful shrinking from any risk of guilt, a profound lack of confidence in her self and in any moral imperatives that issue from her own nature. But if we realize this, how clearly does the novel do so?

It does partly, I think, because it also partly recognizes a third objection. Given the stress on feelings and actions toward others, it can seem somehow morally right, if your love for somebody you ought to love is so strong and so unselfish that its strength is transferred to *all* his moral claims on you, making them seem as strong and limitless as the love you willingly give. Desdemona's love for Othello makes this kind of slide, to the eventual destruction of both of them. Cordelia's love for Lear does not, to the eventual destruction of both of them too. Maggie's childhood love for Tom does; and this, of course, is the double-bind into which he fastens her – for good, as we might say.

Maggie's love for Tom always prompts her to assent to his view of morality and to his view of her 'self'. Thus she always feels morally inadequate and blameworthy when she fails to live up to what he requires her to do or to be. If she rebels at times, it is only against his unfeelingness, his unwillingness to understand her feelings and good intentions, or to forgive her, or to indulge her a little; it is never against his view of what is morally right, or his view of what morality is. She takes his moral correction as what he believes it to be: a manifestation of his 'truly' loving her. And so it is, in a way, for he certainly loves her, even if not so intensely as she loves him. But her nature's need and capacity to love him are so intense, so unguarded and un-self-controlled, that their effects produce yet another need in her. She needs to find, in his love and regard, a definition and a ratification of a self whose life seems all too outflowing, intense and troublesome. As we see it, therefore, her childhood love for Tom is more than the deepest 'feeling' of her life. It is the form which first evokes, and satisfies, some of her nature's most basic needs and capacities; but in doing so, it also moulds her sense of them for ever after. There is nothing of herself she is not willing to devote to Tom – though unfortunately, it seems, there are some things in herself that her will cannot always control; and that 'unfortunately' is the trap by which her love becomes both the cause and the instrument of her bondage. For Tom *wants* her to love him as completely as she does – and partly because he loves her. But partly too because she will grant to his wishes and attitudes the special partiality that love does grant. And partly too because she morally ought to and, for that reason, has to accept his moral rectitude in return: as when he insists, for example, that she can claim no special status before the universal rules of morality, which he obeys with exemplary self-mastery. Her love has to ratify *his* existence and value too.

In short, Maggie's deepest bond to the past is one she never comes to see objectively: that her very conception of herself as a moral being, and her conception of morality as well, have been most powerfully formed in her relationship with Tom. Only her father embodies a different conception of morality and endorses a different conception of her moral being – as a self whose nature, as we see, is also quick, bold, adventurous, passionately eager, vividly dramatic, uncensorious, unfearful and prodigal of itself, and being more than a little alive, needing more than a little *from* life. This is the Maggie who 'hated blame: she had been blamed all her life, and nothing had come of it but evil tempers. Her father had always defended and excused her, and her loving remembrance of his tenderness was a force within her that would enable her to do or bear anything for his sake.'[5] But, alas, her father is a man whose own nature seems to prove him only a fool, and the world to be more than he could hope to understand or master; while her love for Tom makes her so fear the effects of loving with her whole unfortunate self that she seems only too ready to abort any possibility of doing so again.

On top of all this, then, the universal moral ideals of self-sacrifice and resignation she imbibes from Brother Thomas à Kempis only complete the work of the family bankruptcy and brother Thomas Tulliver. Maggie becomes a 'passive being' in relation to others, and at the most fundamental level. She comes to master herself, control her life, by a kind of mental dissection of it: by dividing it up between 'feelings' and 'self'; between 'craving' or 'passion' and the recognizably 'moral' emotions of her 'better self'; between 'egoism' and the duty of self-abnegation. By this kind of moral dissociation she does become at long last reconciled with Tom, though reconciled – it seems by mere ill-chance – only in the complete passivity of death. Or *is* it mere ill-chance we are supposed to see here? For in the light of Maggie's unwitting, but morally suicidal, self-dividing, we may well wonder what the novel means by its epigraph, which is also the epitaph on their graves: 'In their death they were not divided.'

III

If there are difficulties about conceiving Maggie's (or any other individual's) moral psychology and morality itself entirely in terms of universal principles applying to everybody's voluntary intentional actions, especially in relation to others, this is certainly not because such conceptions are wrong or because we could somehow dispense with them. The difficulties arise only because this is not all that morality is concerned with, nor this the only kind of moral thinking; and to suppose it is, I would argue, is to head for trouble – trouble, for example, of the kind Maggie has in thinking about herself or her life. The novel itself seems to get into much the same kind of trouble too – but here, I think, the book's ambiguity derives from the strength of George Eliot's 'dramatic' imagination and the way *it* thinks morally, as against the limitations of her explicit conception of morality and the way she thinks she thinks morally.

Those limitations appear most clearly in the novel's crisis: a part of the book that, unlike the rendering of Maggie's childhood, has bothered a great many readers. Something seems to go amiss, though there is no general agreement about what it is. To some readers, Maggie's rejection of Stephen seems so obviously right that it hardly prompts them to scrutinize her reasons for thinking it so; to others, this rightness is much less obvious and yet oddly enough few of them examine Maggie's thinking any more critically. In fact, many readers' troubles in thinking about the novel seem to be rather like Maggie's troubles in thinking about herself; certainly, many seem to share the same kind of assumptions about the nature of morality.

To see these assumptions as inadequate does not depend on our judgment of the rightness or wrongness of Maggie's rejection of Stephen. For my part, I do not think we are shown enough of Maggie and of Stephen to judge with much assurance; but in any case, Maggie's way of thinking in terms of universal moral ideals and prescriptions begs the basic questions. So does George Eliot's moral thinking too, and for the same reason in each case: because it recognizes no ground on which Maggie's love for Stephen could count as a *moral* consideration at all. This is why one of the most revealing passages in the book is Maggie's argument with Stephen at Mudport after the compromising boat-trip.[6] The description of the trip itself engages George Eliot's own universal moral categories and principles in their most dangerous form – at once insistent and yet disguised as 'symbolic' details. But the subsequent argument raises most of the important questions about Maggie's.

In the first place, we might notice, the couple's earlier decision to part is now described by Maggie as 'what we both felt – that we owed ourselves to others, and must conquer every inclination which could make us false to that debt'. Moral obligation is conceived as an identifiable 'debt'; but more important, their love is seen as mere 'inclination', a mere part, or function, of the 'selves' that 'we' owe to others. Those 'selves' and that 'we' are conceived as essentially *wills*.

Stephen claims that 'the feeling which draws us towards each other is too strong to be overcome:... natural law surmounts every other'. He too conceives their love as a mere 'feeling', against which their wills have struggled; but this is less important than the empty, indeed self-destructive conception of 'natural law' he invokes. If this is all 'nature' can say for itself, what moral content *could* it have? Maggie's reply sees this, and goes on to assert a 'truly' moral principle against it.

...but I see, if we judged in that way [by 'natural law'], there would be a warrant for all treachery and cruelty – we should justify breaking the most sacred ties that can ever be formed on earth. If the past is not to bind us, where can duty lie? We should have no law but the inclination of the moment.

This sub-Wordsworthian argument may dispose of Stephen's 'natural law', but in Maggie's mouth in this context it must prompt some questions of its own. It is certainly true that we are bound *by* the past; if we were not, we would have no stable moral self – and no conception of what morality is or why it matters. But this is not the same as being bound *to* the past, as if that were the only source of duty. It clearly applies to contracts and promises, for instance, but it seems to rule out any moral status for, say, wanting a greater 'fulness of existence' than the past has allowed one. For *how* do natural 'ties' (affection for one's family and friends, for example) become positively binding in a moral sense? With an eye to the bonds that the past (in the shape of Tom) has fixed on Maggie, we might well think the real question is which *bits* of the past are to be seen as morally binding, as distinct from the rest. Is one of them Maggie's love of Tom, and everything that implies, but not the bold adventurousness? Or the other way round?

In other words, the real moral question concerns the adequacy of our entire consciousness – of the world, of ourselves, and of the past. For the past may be causatively binding on us in ways we do not notice. It may determine how we conceive of value and morality, for instance, and our conception may be an inadequate one. Moreover, in determining other things, the past may determine the way we tend to conceive the past itself, determine what we tend to see as the bits of it that really matter, and the extent to which they should bind us. In short, it is precisely what we take the past to be and the ways we think it binds us morally that require scrutiny – and unfortunately, Stephen cannot know enough about Maggie's past to ask the relevant questions. As it is, Maggie virtually identifies 'duty' as consisting in voluntarily conceiving oneself as bound to the past. Hence the readiness with which morality can be conceived as 'law' – moral law to 'bind' us, because causal law 'binds' us – and the ease with which she can take anything but obedience to the law as merely fortuitous, irrational, 'the inclination of the moment'. On these terms – at once Wordsworth-like and Kant-like – it is all too easy for her love of Stephen to get defined out of moral existence. For what these terms most fundamentally exclude is the possibility of moral creativity: the capacity, which love can have – as can poetry too, for example – to accept and yet transform 'the past' as part of its transforming and re-binding of the self.

But Stephen tries another tack: 'there are ties that can't be kept by mere resolution'; all that their wills can provide now is an empty form; and would Philip and Lucy really thank them for 'anything so hollow as constancy without love'? Maggie's reply is two-fold: firstly, that virtues like 'faithfulness and constancy mean something else besides doing what is easiest and pleasantest to ourselves' – a truism, but one that allows the key assumptions to slip surreptitiously into place. *Is* it a question of doing merely what is easiest and pleasantest to themselves? And even if Stephen has an 'egoistic' motive in making the point, does that really affect its validity? Secondly, Maggie invokes a universal ideal of right 'feeling': had she been 'better, nobler', and not 'weak, selfish, and hard', the claims of Lucy and Philip, and sympathy for their 'misery', would have been 'so pressing on my heart… that the opposite feeling would never have grown in me'; or at least they would have 'destroyed all temptation'. This is familiar ground in Maggie, but its sheer irrelevance to Stephen's point is very striking. For Maggie, it seems, what anybody *wants* has no moral weight. Moral ideals are imperatives, and categorical imperatives at that, even if the beneficiary of your good will chokes to death as you push it down his throat. But at the same time you must avoid his suffering, at whatever cost to yourself. With her mind floundering around in this kind of mess, it is no wonder that she can only blurt out a pious (Kant-like) hope that 'O, *some* good will come by clinging to the right.'

Stephen drives home none of the points to be made against all this. But George Eliot gives him one that does go, however obliquely, to the heart of the matter – as Maggie's response makes plain: '"…it would be hateful – horrible, to think of your…ever being the wife of a man you didn't love." A deep flush came over Maggie's face, and she couldn't speak.' It does not seem much, but we need to see what the point is and why it matters. Maggie's flush indicates its nature, just as her silence (one of George Eliot's finest dramatic touches) indicates its cogency. What Stephen finds 'horrible' are the sexual implications of such an alternative, and it is these he forces on her attention. It is a way of asking her if there is no moral significance for her in their love being a sexual love – which is necessarily particular, exclusive, even 'egoistic' if you like, but which is not to be reduced to anything simpler than it really is. Inasmuch as it is both sexual *and* love, it involves the whole of the self, the body as well as the mind, desires as well as thoughts and feelings; and it involves all this in relation to, and only in relation to, a particular person. The sexual dimension matters because it is inseparable from every other, and also because here the self *has* to be spontaneous. The sexuality of love can be a medium in which the self declares the inclinations, not of a moment, but of its true nature, and commits itself to them. In the sexuality of love, therefore, the self manifests (even to its own view) how fully it really 'owes' its own being, not to 'others', nor even to any one 'other', but to this particular, unique other.

And that raises a quite fundamental question about the whole issue. Given that the sexual love of two people is like this, then there is not very much that the 'philosopher' in Aristotle's sense can usefully say about it, nor much it can usefully say to the philosopher, since it is essentially, and specifically, not a matter of the recognizably 'universal'. Its very point, and its value, are inseparable from the particular selves it involves. It not only flows out of these particular lives, but flows into them – in deep ways, actually re-constituting them. In other words, the philosopher's 'universal' cannot encompass the whole reality of sexual love because such love only exists within what Aristotle calls the particulars of a 'history'. It has shape, meaning, and value only in terms of the whole unique life or 'history' which each self (by 'nature', or 'fate', or a set of specific causes) embodies and which it must continue to live out. To insist on the body's necessary involvement is to underline this essential particularity of love, and its essential difference from any set of actions or intentions directable by the will according to any rule, for the will is in love too. This is why Maggie and Stephen are discussing something that cannot be valued only in terms of its external relations with the morally universal. It is also why sexual love cannot be given value by a 'gratuitous' existential act of choice, as if it were somehow free of everything that manifests *itself* in the body's imperatives and prohibitions.

To say this to Maggie, let alone make it stick, is beyond Stephen's capacity, of course. When he tries to, it comes out wrong: 'it is the first time', he insists, 'we have either of us loved with our whole heart and soul' – as if it were a question of whether their love met this universal rule about how to love. And to that Maggie does have a reply: it does not meet that rule.

'No – not with my whole heart and soul ... I have never consented to it with my whole mind. There are memories, and affections, and longings after perfect goodness, that have such a strong hold on me ... I couldn't live in peace if I put the shadow of a wilful sin between myself and God.'

This tardy appearance of God on the scene is not very relevant, I think: certainly, Maggie has not been arguing on that basis. But Maggie's point about herself, that she has never consented to it with her whole mind, is true and valid enough – as far as it goes. What it does not go to, however, is the crucial and more radical question of who or what is the 'I' that has never consented. Just because we know so much about Maggie, we cannot help asking, as Stephen does not, whether what she takes as her 'whole mind' is the same as the whole of Maggie, and whether her rejection of Stephen is a decision merely of her will or a resolution of her whole moral being.

IV

What George Eliot sees as morally 'universal' is not exactly the same as Maggie does, of course, but it is no less question-begging. One sign of this is Stephen's main limitation as a dramatic character, which is that he lacks enough intelligence to see how Maggie avoids or begs the key questions, and enough knowledge of her life to use the insight if he had it. The real trouble with him is not so much that he is unworthy of Maggie (for who can decide that for somebody in love?) as that he is unworthy of George Eliot. Conceived as he is, he does not force his creator to think much harder than she does about her own moral thinking.

The Mill on the Floss would no doubt be a more impressive novel if George Eliot clearly understood how jumbled are the moral attitudes that bind and finally destroy Maggie, and we could therefore read the book as a sympathetic but critical exploration of the jumble. As it is, however, George Eliot's stress falls rather on the 'tragic' inner divisions and conflicts that are 'the individual lot' of certain (finer) people. There is a good deal of characteristic Victorian pathos about this in the novel; the poignancy is supposed to lie in the need for a tough endurance of misery and pain, a real resignation to stand firm against the counter-currents of 'love' and of regressive yearn-ings for 'home', harmony, and the golden, Edenic unity-of-being of childhood. The kind of moral thinking implicit in all this emerges explicitly in the 'commentary' at the end of Book 7, chapter 2. The difficult complexities of 'the individual lot' call for a kind of 'casuistry'; they should make us 'check' and 'enlighten' our moral maxims and general moral rules with 'patience, discrimination, impartiality', and with 'the insight that comes from a hardly-earned estimate of temptation, or from a life vivid and intense enough to have created a wide fellow-feeling with all that is human'. ('Be like my novel.')

The question whether the moment has come in which a man has fallen below the possibility of a renunciation that will carry any efficacy, and must accept the sway of a passion against which he has struggled as a trespass, is one for which we have no master-key that will fit all cases.[7]

This conception of Maggie and her predicament may well prompt reflections about Victorian attitudes to sexual love and sexual renunciation, but its claim to a finer conception of morality than that of the 'man of maxims' is not as impressive as it thinks. For as the word 'case' reveals, it offers no more than maxims with, as it were, special adjustments for exceptional or qualifying circumstances (and for 'feeling'). A 'life vivid and intense' seems to be definable and valuable only as a vehicle for universal moral imperatives, vague though they may be: 'do not expect perfection to be easy in this world, always resist temptation and weakness, endure life with grim resignation, but also be patient, discriminating and impartial toward others, and cultivate a wide fellow-feeling for all that is human'. Excellent morality, of course; but as we can see, conducting ourselves in that way requires no radical questioning of the universal categories and imperatives in which we conceive 'all that is human' and, with it, the 'self' which either 'rises above' or is 'mastered' by a 'passion'.

Yet there are things in the novel (and elsewhere in George Eliot) that do call those categories and imperatives into question, showing them to be less than comprehensive, less than adequate to the whole range of moral thinking. For it is not just sexual love that cannot be wholly encompassed in such terms; neither can our entire sense of the 'human' or the 'self'. To think about these requires something more than what George Eliot calls 'casuistry'.

One way of getting at this is to consider the similarity between thinking about these moral issues and thinking about works of literature. In both areas, we have to be alive to the possibility that the particular 'case' may not be a case – a recognizable instance of 'bad poetry' or a 'bad self', for example – but something that challenges the whole way we conceive poetry or the moral self. We may find that we cannot quite classify this something, or fully explain it, or even adequately describe its nature, and yet we may well find it valuable precisely because of what cannot be encompassed by general terms and reasoning. We have to think about it, therefore, in a way that cannot be taught or judged entirely by rules, because we have to consider the object not just as particular, but also as unique: not just *a* poem, or *a* self, but as *this* 'poem' or *this* 'self'. To do that is to regard its distinctive qualities as not merely fortuitous or contingent – accidents that only distinguish one case or instance from others – but as of the essence, necessary to its very nature as the thing it is.

And as sexual love may remind us, there are times when we have to think of people in this way – including ourselves. This is why the philosopher's or casuist's moral examples generally seem to beg the most fundamental and intractable questions we may find in real moral predicaments, where the problem is often how to see the situation, how to think about it. In examples, the essential features of a situation are pre-selected for us; these are taken to be fully described for all relevant purposes by a certain set of general terms; and everything else is brushed away with a *ceteris paribus*. But there are at least two difficulties about this. One is the assumption that it is always possible, theoretically at least, to treat moral predicaments in this way without their losing some of the essential features that make them predicaments at all. The other is the related assumption, that it would always be morally sufficient to treat them in this way. And these assumptions have their analogue in imaginative literature. They underlie a good deal of allegory, for instance, and other preconceptualized kinds of art – which is no doubt why many people find these so attractive.

'Dramatic' art can work differently; and, as I argued in chapter 3, when it does, it thinks morally in a way that philosophy cannot. It provides a form in which moral issues can be thought about more adequately because they can be thought about not only in general terms, but also concretely, in the given particulars. As well as conceiving, analysing, and judging human beings in terms of 'the universal', literature can also take their uniqueness as part of their essential nature as human beings. It does not merely tell us about them as complex cases or examples, even though the philosophic mind finds it difficult to see literature or talk about it in any other terms. But such literature does something else besides: it presents human beings immediately in the very activity and flow of life, 'renders' them dynamically, as specific moral lives. Its thinking about them therefore has to consist in particulars – particulars that make moral sense, not inasmuch as they merely instantiate 'the universal' by 'representing' it, as Aristotle supposed, but inasmuch as they *manifest*, in a unique 'history', a human life. To see the particulars as manifesting a human life involves grasping their internal coherence, which means the range over which, and the depth at which, they cohere – it involves 'making sense' of them, that is, in relation to other possible ways of being alive. Doing that, I argued, is necessarily a process both of moral understanding and moral evaluation.

I think this helps explain why the presentation of Maggie's childhood does not seem to go amiss as her crisis over Stephen does. That earlier part of the novel does make this kind of moral sense; and its rendering of Maggie's life is clear, integral and strong enough for descriptive judgments in terms of recognizable general qualities to be seen as necessary (or not), relevant (or not), carrying decisive implications (or not), in relation to it. In other words, the novel achieves here what only 'dramatic' literature can attempt (and enable in its readers): it thinks in terms both of a moral psychology centred on the self as a moral agent like any other, as an instance of human volition; and a moral psychology centred on the self as a specific, organic nature like any other precisely in being unique, an individual dynamic 'economy' of particular human needs, desires, capacities, and so on. The one places attention on the universal terms and rules that should regulate motives, intentions and choices; on the self that controls and conducts its life; on the conscious will and all that issues from it as moral purpose, moral virtue, moral character. The other places attention on the distinctive pattern of the self's whole activity, both conscious and (in George Eliot's phrase) 'less conscious', issuing from needs – the area between drives and motives; on the particular native disposition or inclination or 'unmodifiable character' of the self; on its 'virtues' in the older sense of powers, and the specific conditions of their growth and decay. It focuses on the implicit shape or trajectory of a life as a whole, on the *un*conscious will (if 'will' is the right word) that constitutes a human being's distinctive 'law of life', to use George Eliot's own phrase once again.[8]

What goes amiss with *The Mill on the Floss*, I think, is a failure to combine these two ways of thinking once Maggie becomes old enough to be considered a full moral agent – a failure caused by the belief that only the first, which is concerned with *conduct*, is really and truly moral. It is a failure fully to recognize and reckon with the differences between the two kinds of moral consideration, even their incompatibility at times, and the weight each has to be given nevertheless. In effect, this obliterates the differences between the two by collapsing one into the other – as when 'the fulness of existence' Maggie's nature needs is collapsed into universal 'goods' that she 'craves', for example, or when the entire moral significance of Maggie's love for Stephen is reduced to that of a 'case' of personal 'passion', or when the 'tragic' divisions in Maggie's life are supposed to be those between passion and conscience, personal feelings and the demands of morality, the unity or reconciliation of 'home' and the bitter struggles of the world, egoism and resignation, sister and brother.

Another way of seeing what gets blurred or left out in this latter part of the novel is to ask what it means to say (as many readers would, including myself) that Maggie's rejection of Stephen – no matter whether or not it is right or good in relation to universal criteria of moral conduct – is nevertheless an evasion of 'life'. This cannot refer to any failure of Maggie's conscious will, for she does choose what she and George Eliot see as making for 'true' life – i.e. the 'moral' life. To say that she evades 'life' nevertheless, is not to say that there is some other universal ideal she should have chosen in preference to the one she did choose: 'romantic' love or 'Promethean' energy, say, or some kind of unorthodox or unconventional vitalism. And to speak of her 'evading' life is not to forget the ways she differs from, say, Anna Brangwen in *The Rainbow*, who is at least conscious that she wants something other than 'being good, and doing one's best', something that could 'rouse' or 'implicate' her entire soul.[9] In this respect, Maggie is only a forerunner to Anna and, beyond her, to Ursula Brangwen: her real need has not yet formed into a conscious 'want', and even if it had, the 'fulness of existence' for anybody can present itself to his or her mind only as fragmentary, hypothetical intimations and metaphors anyway.

With Maggie, we can use the word 'life' meaningfully in this context only in relation to her specific nature and the specific conditions of its existence and growth; and we could only point to whatever manifests itself *as* her life in the particulars of her 'history'. Those particulars include, for example, all the ways that her life thrusts forth and grows in childhood, both above and below the sight of others, with eager, adventurous spontaneity; everything that evinces the 'passionate sensibility which belonged to her whole nature, and made her faults and virtues all merge in each other';[10] the Maggie who always really hated blame, of others as well as of herself; the Maggie who, well before she meets Stephen, imagines herself (in 'nonsense') avenging the unhappy dark women in novels, by carrying off the love the 'blond-haired women' always seem to win;[11] the Maggie who does not and *cannot* love Philip, except with her 'better self'; above all, the Maggie whose distinctiveness lies in being open, potential, responsive to new and fuller experience of the world.

This Maggie's moral life is only partly definable as a developing consciousness of universal rules and ideals, along with a developing will to serve them, which conflicts with 'egoistic' feelings and inclinations. If George Eliot had followed out the promptings of her own imaginative nature, she would have seen that the promptings of Maggie's were toward a 'fulness of existence' that, as it so happened, Stephen seemed to answer to, though in a different way from the way that recognizably universal moral goods can. He does so in the way that, as it so happened, Rousseau did for George Eliot herself in 1849. A passage in one of her letters is very pertinent to the issues here:

I wish you thoroughly to understand that the writers who have most profoundly influenced me … are not in the least oracles to me. It is just possible that I may not embrace one of their opinions, that I may wish my life to be shaped quite differently from theirs. For instance it would signify nothing to me if a very wise person were to stun me with proofs that Rousseau's views of life, religion, and government are miserably erroneous – that he was guilty of some of the worst bassesses [*sic*, basenesses?] that have degraded civilized man. I might admit all this – and it would be not the less true that Rousseau's genius has sent that electric thrill through my intellectual and moral frame which has awakened me to new perceptions, which has made man and nature a fresh world of thought and feeling to me – and this not by teaching me any new belief. It is simply that the rushing mighty wind of his inspiration has so quickened my faculties that I have been able to shape more definitely for myself ideas which had previously dwelt as dim 'ahnungen' in my soul – the fire of his genius has so fused together old thoughts and prejudices that I have been ready to make new combinations.[12]

In *The Mill on the Floss*, George Eliot seems to forget or blur this kind of moral significance – the place of Rousseau (of all people!) in and upon the whole of her life, like the place of Stephen (of all people!) in and upon Maggie's. But it is important to notice exactly what that significance is. Stephen's value to Maggie exists only because she has come to be the self that loves him; he answers to what her life now needs. But the value is realizable only in the loving. That loving awakens her to new perceptions, which make man and nature a fresh world of thought and feeling, and gives shape to dim *Ahnungen* in her soul; yet this is only one sign, one manifestation, of Stephen's value, not its whole content. Thus his value cannot simply be described as an instance of what, in her case, 'enhances' life. It lies rather in his being the irreplaceable *focus* of her life, re-shaping the significance of all her experience by also re-vivifying the reality of what she experiences.

There is a great deal more that might be said about the passage quoted from George Eliot's letter. In words and phrases like 'quickened my faculties', 'genius', 'my intellectual and moral frame', 'make new combinations', the 'mighty wind of his inspiration' (inspiration, we may notice, not example), as well as its talk about being enabled to 'shape more definitely' dim *Ahnungen* in her 'soul', it suggests some pretty far-reaching considerations about imaginative literature as moral thinking, only some of which apply directly to *The Mill on the Floss*. But it may help us to see how and why these do apply if we ask what moral value Stephen *could* have appealed to in his argument with Maggie – had he been conceived in a more scrupulously testing way.

Clearly, he could not effectively appeal to any duty Maggie has in respect of herself: to a universal good like self-fulfilment, self-realization, the flourishing of her life, or whatever. It is precisely Maggie's conception of her self – the fixed, 'stable ego' she knows – along with her (perfectly valid) disapproval of selfishness, that is the problem. Nor can his appeal for Maggie to pity his own pain carry much weight with her if (like her creator) she tends to see any 'egoistic' motive as invalidating the moral status of a claim. Stephen's moral appeal would have to be to something impersonal if it were to carry real weight with her, and avoid any objection to its 'egoism' as against clear-cut, recognizable ideals like altruism and self-sacrifice. But it might well have been to something impersonal, not in the sense that the interests of other people are, nor in the sense that impartiality is, nor in the sense that universal moral rules are, but rather in the sense that a person's own distinctive talent or genius or vocation is.

Some of the episodes in the novel by an older (and wiser) George Eliot, *Daniel Deronda*, are interestingly related to the issues here. One is the relationship of Catherine Arrowpoint and Klesmer; another is Mirah's with her father; but most relevant, I think, is the history of Deronda's mother, a woman who did deny the moral duties she found in her past and denied them for the sake of her genius: 'I wanted to live out the life that was in me', she says to her son; 'my nature gave me a charter'.[13] The novel acknowledges that as a great singer, Deronda's mother did have such a charter; and it also suggests what Stephen might have appealed to in Maggie: to 'the life that is in her' – but 'life' in the sense I have tried to suggest above. For it is the life of a self she does *not* know – partly because it cannot be fully known except by living it out, but also partly because her moral conceptions and fantasies have filtered the signs of its existence out of her consciousness, or made her unable to acknowledge its pressures and needs for what they are.

All the same, the existence and needs of that unknown self are discernible, even if Maggie does not see them and there is nobody else to help her do so. And they are perhaps most discernible just where Maggie would not or could not look for them. They are the emergent shape, the necessarily implicit coherence, of all the particulars of 'the life that is in her' – the being who is alive in a way that nobody else in her world is. And when this life comes to find Stephen, it issues not into moral 'nobleness' of conduct, or a willingness to accept suffering and resignation as her lot, or even 'tragic' self-division, but into a distinctive, *un*divided 'fulness of existence'. There is just enough in the novel to render the outlines of this –

Her eyes and cheeks were still brightened with her childlike enthusiasm in the dance; her whole frame was set to joy and tenderness; even the coming pain [of separating from Stephen] could not seem bitter – she was ready to welcome it as a part of life, for life at this moment seemed a keen vibrating consciousness poised above pleasure or pain... Something strangely powerful there was in the light of Stephen's long gaze, for it made Maggie's face turn towards it and look upward at it – slowly, like a flower at the ascending brightness.[14]

True, the 'hovering thought that they must and would renounce each other' intensifies the 'rapture' of this moment for her. But that has little to do with the way 'her whole frame' is awakened and quickened by Stephen, as George Eliot's was by Rousseau's 'inspiration'. Maggie's distinctive 'nature' – her whole being, including her body – issues into flower. This, and the past *it* has grown out of and embodies, are what Stephen might have appealed to in his later argument with her, if he could have appreciated what his gaze had made manifest – in fact, what his own being had simultaneously created, found and answered to in Maggie's. But his creator does not endow him with the relevant insight, and denies it to Maggie. Instead, George Eliot slips in that word 'seemed' – 'life...seemed a keen vibrating consciousness': she feels impelled to posit something false about Maggie's consciousness here, or to make Maggie feel some falsity in her consciousness, rather than allow that Maggie's love *is* a life newly 'vivid and intense' – *is* a sharper, fuller, vivified sense of reality. There is nothing false about that here. On the contrary, it is George Eliot's retractive impulse here that is false. But it is a sad and rather depressing fact about all her novels that, while she can portray a love that is morally corrective or morally destructive, she never portrays with anything like the same conviction a love that transforms the self creatively, opening its life to a world newly alive with interest and significance.

V

It is probably worth stating bluntly what I am *not* trying to say. My point is not that internalized social attitudes, whether Maggie's or George Eliot's, effectively suppress Maggie's real, 'alternative' self. The issue is not one of a real self versus a false one. Despite the elements of fear that tend to falsify Maggie's consciousness – fear mainly of Tom's and Lucy's view of her, but also fear of herself – there is nothing unreal or false about her conception of her moral self, as far as it goes. She *is* facing a choice, and she is quite properly trying to act according to universal moral principles. Nor am I saying merely that the principles to which she looks constitute a false morality: one that is merely conventional, or narrow, or formal. It is false, I believe, and probably in all of these ways, and more so than George Eliot recognized; and this belief, for anyone who shares it, must affect one's view of the book. But I want to suggest a more basic problem about the adequacy of Maggie's – but more importantly, George Eliot's – way of *thinking* about the moral issues involved.

Any universal morality, I have claimed, has to present itself to the individual's mind (or be capable of presenting itself) in the form of specific rules, or ends, or norms, or ideals by which to regulate action or conduct; and part of the authority of their claim on the mind and will of any self lies in their being universal, in applying to anybody and everybody relevant, no matter whether the morality expresses a conception of right and wrong, or good and bad, or virtues and faults, and no matter what conception of human nature or of human reason or of the 'human', or humanity's place in the scheme of things, it implies or depends on. On these terms, though, what happens to the self as distinctive, as a unique, dynamic 'economy' of capacities, needs and possibilities? It is virtually impossible for them to get any moral purchase at all. After all, is morality not a matter of what is right or good, not what is right or good 'for me'? Indeed, on these terms, 'individuality' comes to seem just another universal moral value, to take more or less importance on grounds no different in principle from any other value. On these terms, therefore, the actual choice Maggie makes is undeniably a moral one, in the sense that, no matter whether we agree with the particular content of her morality or not, it is a choice of a recognizably moral value, even a choice of the 'moral life' as such, as against... well, as against what? What is 'exemplified' in her love of Stephen and what that consists in: her 'keen vibrating consciousness... above pleasure or pain', being 'like a flower' turning to an 'ascending brightness'? How could we characterize this fully and exactly in a way that enabled it to present itself, or to become part of anything else that could present itself, to Maggie's mind as a universal rule or ideal to regulate action?

I cannot think of any such description that would be specific enough to be both accurate and relevant. Even 'personal love' does not seem right, since the value lies in the distinctive qualities of this way of being alive here – which is Maggie's whole frame flowering, slowly, towards this brightness, and not Maggie instantiating sexual love as Lucy, say, or some other character, or anybody at all, might also instantiate it. To think of Maggie's way of being alive here as a 'good' that she could recognize whenever it turned up, towards which she could choose to direct her actions, or as an instance of some norm or ideal she could recognize and choose to act by, seems to me as impossible as trying to think of it as a state she could achieve by merely choosing to be in it. The root of the problem is that Maggie could not be conscious of herself or of her history or life in the relevant way. Despite George Eliot's word 'seemed', Maggie does not and could not think of 'life' here as a 'keen vibrating consciousness poised above pleasure and pain', just because at this moment she *is* just such a consciousness without any awareness left over, as it were, to think reflectively about 'life'. Nor could she think of herself as gazing, slowly, like a flower, nor even of Stephen as the ascending brightness, just because, once again, her 'whole frame' *is* that. A novel or a drama can make us realize how we understand and value people in ways they themselves cannot – and cannot because the understanding and the valuation are not capable of being expressed entirely in general terms: as when, for example, it is the whole, distinctive, unique thing the person is that we are valuing, or when it is the whole, distinctive, unique way that he, being himself, is alive to the world. And if this means that there are some things of moral value, and some moral considerations that those things involve, which can never be formulated so as to provide specific directives to the will – then what of it? It may be inconvenient, but it is surely one of the difficulties about moral thinking we have to live with.

But how then could the relevant value and the relevant considerations present themselves to Maggie in the relevant way, without distortion or falsification and yet with the full force they must bear? I say 'full', not 'decisive'; for I am not arguing that any such value or consideration must be absolute or supreme. In fact, it is moral precisely because it is not. Nor am I suggesting that it is a special kind of value, for superior souls or *Übermenschen*, which is always higher or better than the usual kind; nor that there is any escape from conscious choice. But one possible way the relevant value could present itself to the mind, I think, is as it does to Klesmer or to Stephen Dedalus, or as it did to Pope, or as it should have but did not quite to Deronda: as the sense, the *Ahnung*, of an inner personal necessity – as the value of a personal genius or a personal vocation, say, presses on the mind with a claim at once personal and yet beyond anything nameable merely as 'self'. Similarly, the value of one's own and only particular, unique life might present itself as the pressure of some inward 'fate' or 'destiny' which calls as if from outside the ordinary conscious self, rather in the way Hamlet, for example, heard it in the Ghost: 'My fate cries out... Still am I called!' This kind of felt pressure has nothing to do with determinism, nor with the power of 'natural law', nor with the intractable reality of external circumstances. To suppose it has is only to try to translate the real thing into morally universal terms, and to falsify it in the attempt.

And it is precisely this failure in moral thinking that Maggie – and George Eliot – fall victim to. They are so anxious about being moral, about living 'the moral life', that they forget it needs both feet – both conduct-moral and life-moral considerations – to stand on and get anywhere. Or to put it another way, they are so anxious that one's life should serve impersonal values, which transcend self, selfishness and egoism, that they forget that one's life may also be the vessel of certain values which can exist only as modes of personal life, which enter one's 'history' without direction by the will, and which can transform both the self and its consciousness of the world by giving-and-finding a new, keener reality in both.

I am not saying that if Maggie had realized this it would or should have led her to accept Stephen instead of rejecting him, or that it would or should have led her to reject him nevertheless. But it certainly would, I think, have brought her to a keen and vibrant consciousness of what is not acknowledged in the novel – the real nature, the real difficulty, and the real cost of her decision, whatever it was. It might even have brought Maggie to a keen and vibrant consciousness that her very capacity to realize the nature, difficulty and cost of her decision was itself a manifestation of Stephen's real (and irreplaceable) value to her. Yet if Maggie could perhaps not reach to this last, almost paradoxical realization, George Eliot certainly could. Indeed, it is in precisely this kind of realization, this kind of moral thinking, that the life and the irreplaceable value of imaginative literature manifest themselves: which is why it is important for the philosopher not to treat the particulars of literature as merely instantiating moral universals, and for the literary critic not to be so fascinated by the particulars that he neglects the moral thinking in them.

Nobody has ever thought the last Book of *The Mill on the Floss* successful, not even George Eliot herself. But she thought that the failure was merely accidental and formal: it just happened that she had not been able to 'develop as fully as I wished the concluding "Book" in which the tragedy occurs' because 'my

love of the childhood scenes made me linger over them'.[15] The
reader, however, may well conclude that there were reasons
why she should have 'loved' and 'lingered' in that way; and
that they are connected with the reasons why there is *no* tragedy
in the concluding Book, not even the outlines of one. For what
made her 'linger' seems to have been a real and searching, if not
wholly recognized, process of moral thinking, which *was* her
'love'; and what precludes any tragedy is the failure of that
process to continue.

A necessary condition for any real tragedy, I would suggest,
is real moral thinking. And what that means in this novel is,
firstly, depicting some realization on Maggie's part of the
inward pressure of the 'life that is in her', or at least some
realization of the flowering of that life, of the keen and vibrant
consciousness of reality which is her love for Stephen; and
secondly, a real reckoning with it *as* that – either on Maggie's
part or, failing this, on George Eliot's. George Eliot tries to
provide some such realization all right – but with a totally
inadequate grasp of what is involved and with what scrupulous
honesty she therefore has to treat it, both in itself and in its
implications for the whole structure and moral import of the
novel. The attempt comes in the final chapter ('The Last
Conflict'), when Maggie receives Stephen's letter begging her
to call him back from 'pain' to 'life and goodness'. George
Eliot's rendering of Maggie's response is too long to quote in
full, but with no evident touch of irony, the narrative reduces it
to terms like 'the leap of *natural longing*' in her, the temptation to
her of a future 'in which hard endurance and effort were to be
exchanged for *easy delicious leaning* on another's loving strength',
the contradiction between that possibility and her 'past self in
her moments of *strength and clearness*' coming upon her 'like a
pang of conscious degradation', and the '*light*' that eventually
comes to her with the

memories that no passion could long quench: the long past came back
to her, and with it the fountains of self-renouncing pity and affection,
of faithfulness and resolve. The words that were marked by the quiet
hand in the little old book that she had long ago learned by heart,
rushed even to her lips, and found a vent for themselves in a low

murmur that was quite lost in the loud driving of the rain against the window and the loud moan and roar of the wind: 'I have received the Cross, I have received it from Thy hand; I will bear it, and bear it till death, as Thou hast laid it upon me.'

For George Eliot, the tragedy is presumably that at the very moment all this reflection and decision brings Maggie to her knees to pray,

'O God, if my life is to be long, let me live to bless and comfort – '
    At that moment Maggie felt a startling sensation of sudden cold about her knees and feet...[16]

It is tempting to think this represents a fuller, deeper, more ironic, or really tragic view of Maggie's 'history'; but even if it is meant to, I must confess I cannot see that it succeeds in doing so. The kind of moral thinking required here needs to manifest more imaginative life than a sense of cold about the heroine's feet.

CHAPTER 6

Finding congenial matter: Pope and the art of life

> Yet by some object ev'ry brain is stirr'd;
> The dull may waken to a Humming-bird;
> The most recluse, discreetly open'd find
> Congenial matter in the Cockle-kind;
>
> (*The Dunciad*, IV, 445-8)

I

Pope uses the term 'moral' surprisingly little, but when he does, his belief in a total divine, natural and moral order leads him to use it mainly in its narrow, conduct-prescriptive sense, as in the first quotation below, though occasionally in its wide, life-exploratory sense, as in the second quotation:

> What makes all physical or moral ill?
> There deviates Nature, and here wanders Will.[1]

> not in Fancy's Maze he wander'd long,
> But stoop'd to Truth, and moraliz'd his song:[2]

> Who now reads Cowley? if he pleases yet,
> His moral pleases, not his pointed wit;
> Forgot his Epic, nay Pindaric Art,
> But still I love the language of his Heart.[3]

In this third passage, I take it that 'moral' means something like Cowley's sense of and observations on human life: how he 'sees' it.

But if Pope's beliefs make his use of the word 'moral' itself not very interesting, there is an interesting doubleness in his conception of 'integrity',[4] and also, I think, a developing complexity in his conception of what we might call (though not

186

in J. S. Mill's restricted sense) poetic 'arts of life'. By this I mean those ways of being alive that poems exhibit but which they also offer their readers, less as examples or ideal models of how to live, than as something rather like moral 'touchstones' (to borrow Arnold's term) : necessarily particular, individual modes of life by which readers might better discern the nature and value of others' lives and especially of their own.

To get at this complexity, however, we need to avoid a very common tendency with Pope's poetry: to read it too much as discourse, as one or another form of speaking about life, and not enough as drama, as presenting modes of human life that exhibit themselves in activity. True, most of Pope's poetry is formally spoken in his own voice; his self (in some guise or other) is always at the centre of the stage; yet even so, his praise of Homer applies to his own finest work as well: it is 'of the most animated nature imaginable; everything moves, everything lives and is put in action'. At his best, he is like the other great poet he admired, Shakespeare, 'not so much an imitator as an instrument of Nature' – an embodiment, that is, of the creatively moral nature of humanity: ''tis not so just to say that he speaks from her, as that she speaks through him'.[5]

It is not hard to see why the emphasis with Pope himself has very often been put the other way round. Pope started it, in defending his work for the truth and the skill with which he 'imitated' the nature of the world around him, and for his sincere attachment to the moral principles and ideals to which that world was (or should be) committed. These were the terms in which he could most readily (and modestly) defend his work, and the terms his age could most readily understand; and it is true that they do fit some aspects of his work quite well. Nevertheless, they were hardly adequate terms even then to describe his deepest impulses as a poet or his finest poetry. On the contrary, it is just his tendency to a simple 'imitative', instrumentally rhetorical conception of his art, and a correspondingly simple view of his own sincerity (and that of others), that, as we see it now, most limit his work. All too often, his ideals presented themselves to him, as they did to his age generally, as a system of impersonal objective 'truths' and impersonal prescriptive 'laws' and 'rules' – religious, moral, social, psychological and artistic; and he took care (and pride) that, just as his 'true' self lay in consciously acknowledging and observing these, so his poetry only spoke, with conscious honesty, from his 'true' self to the 'true' self of others. And indeed it does, or at least seems to. It is properly orthodox in form and diction, as in belief; it is always conscious of decorum, social and moral as well as artistic; it is 'correct'. It constantly reaches toward comprehensive, epigrammatic generalization – the Augustan way of trying to master life by seizing the whole of it and objectifying it in the form of impersonal knowledge, ideas, laws and rules. Yet Pope's poetry is far more complex than this, just as his self – as he came to appreciate – was more complex than the mere combination of an intellect consciously observant of 'truth', plus a will consciously observant of the precepts of 'virtue', plus a talent consciously observant of the 'rules' of art.

In some ways, Pope could hardly help realizing that his moral consciousness was not essentially passive, a matter simply of recognizing known moral 'truths' and 'laws' external to the self as one might recognize a table, and that his moral being, his moral life, was not reducible to such correct perceptions issuing in correct voluntary conduct. As he obviously understood, the 'dramatic' poet – the poet who seeks to catch the inmost moral nature of people, things, actions and institutions in his world so as to make them 'speak through him' – has to have both a certain detachment from them, and also an imaginative sympathy, a potentiality somewhere in himself, answerable to the outward facts. This applies to the 'tragick' poet, whose business (as Pope put it in an early poem, a Prologue to Addison's *Cato*) is

> To wake the soul by tender strokes of art
> To raise the genius, and to mend the heart;
> To make mankind, in conscious virtue bold,
> Live o'er each scene, and be what they behold ...[6]

But the same applies to the social and moral satirist too, which means that he has to be, in some degree at least, rather like Pope's 'character' of Atossa – a kind of moral chaos:

Scarce once herself, by turns all Womankind!
Who, with herself, or others, from her birth
Finds all her life one warfare upon earth:
Shines, in exposing Knaves, and painting Fools,
Yet is, whate'er she hates and ridicules.[7]

It is significant that these lines from 1732–4 echo a wry joke
Pope had made long before, in the Preface to his 1717 volume,
primarily about himself: 'The life of a Wit is a warfare upon
earth.' Put like that, the remark applies to *any* human wit –
'wit' in the full seventeenth and eighteenth-century sense of the
word; and a 'warfare' of the active, articulate human spirit not
only outward against the resistant world, but also inward,
between opposing elements and potentialities and needs in its
own 'earthly' self. And joke or not, this proved all too true for
a wit that also shone in exposing knaves and painting fools, and
that understood from within everything it hated and ridiculed.
What Pope also came to understand, however, was a crucial
moral question this brought with it. (It is Atossa's uncon-
sciousness of the question that makes her the *victim* of her own
nature.) For what kind of moral being is a creature who is as
various, chameleon-like, as an Atossa, and even more, a poet
capable of being by turns all mankind? If everyone ought to be
integer vitae – a 'true' self centred on, unified by and fixed in
consistent obedience to the prescriptions of religion, morality,
taste and civilized society – what could this mean for a poet,
whose 'genius', whose unique life, also consisted in perpetually
answering to the world, responding to the various forms of its
life, with a wit correspondingly labile, outgoing, multiform?
And for a poet like Pope, whose embattled life required him to
present and defend his poetic self morally, the problem was
doubly difficult, since behind it lay two deeper issues he was less
perfectly conscious of: one socio-cultural, the other personal.

The first is too complex to be more than mentioned here.
Obviously, to speak of Pope as a 'dramatic' poet is not to mean
a poet who wrote for the stage. Pope's age offered a great poet
no adequate theatre like Shakespeare's, on which he could
present and explore in an objectified form the substance of all
serious drama – the most serious, *un*resolvable conflicts in the

moral life of his time. The established social, political, religious and moral order did not encourage that sort of exploration. Moreover, its ideology enshrined the belief that all fundamental moral conflicts can and should be actually resolved, by people aligning their consciousness and conduct with the objective *discordia concors*, the 'order in variety', the 'reconcil'd extremes', of the Creation itself: the natural and moral scheme of things observable and recognizable by anyone except fools, who cannot see it, and knaves, who do not want to. The requisite alignment was inward as well as outward – more so, in fact. Once the conflicting elements, perspectives, potentialities, interests, and attitudes of the self were properly aligned, then outward observance in professed belief, action and manners, in all that conduct consists in, would follow. But if this outlook tended to choke theatrical drama with ultimate harmonies, preconceived characters, and foregone conclusions, the real substance of drama remained, though with some rather complicating conditions attached.

If the heart of drama is always conflict, 'warfare', the territory it seeks to win is what (in any age) lies beyond the reach of the categorizing, generalizing, rationalizing consciousness of the time. It lies in what the available knowledge, beliefs, ideas, suppositions, rules and other intellectual machinery can only point to silently, and only the deepest, subtlest, most responsive imaginative thinking can render to the mind. The substance of the drama lies only partly in the human life 'imitated' – in the human world outside the mind. It also lies in the way that world is brought into the theatre of the mind in the immediate here and now. Ideally, of course, that imitation and presentment are not just entertaining; they are informed by a quest for significance – a significance that (ideally, as in Homer or Shakespeare) discloses itself not as the discourse of the dramatist, but as the informing 'action', the inner shape, of the drama. Thus drama, or 'dramatic' literature, lives in the most direct, immediate exhibition possible at the time (by whatever artistic means, in whatever artistic genre) of modes of moral being, life-moral 'selves'. Such 'selves' are not necessarily formal characters; the *dramatis personae* of a work may be different states of soul, for example, or different attitudes (as in a great deal of poetry). But the drama consists in the direct, absorbing, struggling embrace of each 'self' with its objective world – a struggle in which both the 'self' and the world come to disclose something of their nature and significance.

On this kind of drama, the effect of the Augustan poet's reflexive consciousness could be pretty deadening, especially his belief that men ought to be 'in *conscious virtue* bold'. It hardly makes for 'dramatic' poetry to believe that every virtue is already known and needs only to be depicted and recognized for what it is, and that consciousness is, or can be, unproblematically transparent. Indeed, the common moral psychology of the time assumed that not only all the virtues, but also all the passions and all the elements of human nature were similarly recognizable. And the age further assumed that drama simply depicted, in language conceived of largely in referential and instrumental terms, the various separate, already-defined, and virtually self-identifying human elements in their (already well-charted) collisions with each other and with the moral scheme of things. In fact, the real substance of drama lay beyond or below the separate, recognizable 'passions' and other human elements of the moral philosopher. It lay rather in the difficulties and struggles of internal alignment, in the effort to make the language of conscious reference and rhetorical effect a medium in which a mode of *life* could express itself adequately. In short, it lay in the wholly-absorbing, passionate 'warfare' of the self with its own consciousness and moral will.

That warfare had a history ranging back through some key examples of Renaissance 'self-fashioning'[8] and multiform self-exploring – Petrarch, More, Montaigne and Shakespeare, to name no others; and increasingly during the seventeenth century, and certainly by Pope's time, the 'self' had become a much more problematic entity than the intellectual equipment of the age could readily describe or explain. Some of the most basic and yet most intractable conflicts were clearly those within men and women, between their actual being and activity on the one hand, and their consciousness of the world and of themselves on the other. What was difficult to capture in the

available intellectual terms was where and how such internal
conflicts really occurred: at the point, that is, where simple
dichotomies between subjective and objective broke down,
where the individual's perception of reality and his or her own
distinctive nature (or 'genius') – where what a person 'sees'
and what he or she is – are virtually inseparable. For this is also
the point where what people believe, what they value, and what
they have the capacity to be and to do, are virtually inseparable
from what they feel and desire. It is also the point where all of
these various activities of the self shape and are shaped by the
pressure of a social and political world to decide, to judge, to
choose, and to make specific commitments. A number of things
mark a basic shift in outlook during the seventeenth century
which inevitably affected a 'dramatic' poet as intelligent as
Pope: the economic, political and social pressures forcing on
people a heightened sense of their individuality; the contro-
versies of the time between warring conceptions of the world, of
politics, and of the 'true life' and salvation of the soul; spiritual
journeys and meditative exercises seeking the 'true self' in the
religious scrutiny of its various actions and possibilities; formal
'character' portraits trying to define and even classify moral
'selves'; a hardening intellectual conviction that the individual
consciousness is the focus, or condition, or even ground, both of
the 'self' and of social and political order; poetry reflecting on
how its own kind of life and consciousness relates to those of 'the
busie Companies of Men' in the world.

It was here that the second, the personal, issue arose; and it
helped to ensure that for Pope any such exploration would also
be an internal drama – a drama of warring elements, attitudes
and perspectives within a self struggling to relate them in a
coherent sense both of the external world and of its own nature
and place in the world.

The personal issue originated in Pope's tendency, right from
the start, to identify himself as a 'Poet'. His sense of his own
being was largely comprehended in that idea – an idea with an
established, clear and perfectly honourable content. A 'Poet'
was what his nature and circumstances destined him to be; and
his moral life, he saw, consisted in making that destiny his

choice, rather like a 'calling' or a vocation. The only problem
was that he also sensed the nobler 'power' and 'fire' of poetic
genius in himself – a wit, a spirit, beyond the ordinary, 'called'
and willing to snatch a 'grace' beyond the reach of mere rules,
whether social, moral, or artistic. 'Genius', like 'wit' and the
'sublime', were key life-moral terms in Pope's time;[9] and Pope
himself was much more drawn to 'genius' and 'fire' in literature
than to 'rules'. Even in his early poems it is not hard to see,
behind the carefully modest, respectful, socially complaisant
manner in which he essays himself in one acceptable genre after
another, a 'genius', a mind 'active, ambitious, and adventurous' (as Johnson well describes it), 'always investigating,
always aspiring'[10] – more ardent, less 'correct' and accom-
modating, than the conventional ideal of a Poet allowed. He
came to realize that both his public fame and his moral (not to
say religious) justification depended not simply on being
'correct', not simply on the *conduct* of his 'true' self, but on the
total activity and qualities of his 'genius'.

To follow the development of his poetry is to see how, at every
stage, the way he understands this last point corresponds with
the way he understands himself. So does his understanding of
how other lives are also morally shaped by capacity, need and
circumstance as well as by choice.

At first, for example, his understanding was relatively simple:
he thought his moral justification lay in the way he *used* his
poetic genius. He tended to think of his genius, that is, merely as
a kind of skill, a mere instrument of his 'true', his conduct-
morally 'correct' self, rather than as the articulate life of his wit;
and he tended to think of his wit as the instrument of his
understanding and will rather than as his whole being in
activity as physical and moral sensibility. To have understood
himself better would have been to see that his genius necessarily
engaged certain elements in himself (answering to those in the
world) which his 'correct' understanding and will, his consciously 'true' self, would prefer to deny or suppress: doubt,
fear, negation, hate, desire, fantasy, aggressive violence and the
like. The closest he could get to admitting these into his sense of
his own life or other people's lives was as yet only theoretical: as

in the kind of opposition he saw in *The Temple of Fame*, for
instance – between seeking a conscious moral integrity, which
might well require the 'true' self to become cockle-like and
reclusive, to retreat from the world; and a conscious claim to
public recognition, which might well require the whole of the
self to engage with the world as the only way it could *master* it.
Similarly with his youthful sense of 'Dulness' as the 'safe Opiate
of the Mind' –

> Fit for all Stations, and in each content
> Is satisfy'd, secure, and innocent:
> No Pains it takes, and no Offence it gives,
> Un-fear'd, un-hated, un-disturb'd it lives.[11]

The *un*realized implications here about his contrasting sense of
wit are striking. So is the difference from his later capacity to
take, and give, plenty of offence with Dulness.

Even more significant were his difficulties in aligning the
authentic life of his wit with his conscious (and obviously
sincere) moral beliefs and ideals. The 'order in variety' we are
supposed to 'see' in *Windsor Forest*, for example, is no doubt
visible by a morally 'true' self restricting its life to 'home-felt
Quiet' and 'observing a Mean' in 'soft retreats'. On the other
hand, when Pope is more fully alive to other things it is possible
to 'see' in Windsor Forest, and the poetry is correspondingly
more substantial, his wit answers to a world much harsher and
more violent, where life may aspire to order and peace but
seems unable to reach towards them except by bloody conflict,
and where all things differ but do *not* altogether agree. In
'Eloisa to Abelard' and the 'Elegy to the Memory of an
Unfortunate Lady', he does at least recognize in others, and in
himself as their sympathetic Poet, the value of a passionate life
that will not or cannot compromise with 'correct' conduct and
'conscious virtue', and from which there is no place, no retreat,
on earth; though here again the recognition is still largely
unrealized, still rather notional and rhetorical – still tethered,
we might say, to a merely stock ideal of the Poet.

The *Essay on Man* is a later (and notorious) example of the
difference between the life of his wit on the one hand, and his
moral beliefs and ideals of conduct on the other. There has

never been much doubt that as 'discourse' the poem's claims
are not very impressive. Philosophically (or epistemically)
speaking, it is hard to take the poem seriously at all.[12] But the
central literary-critical objections go not to the poem's doctrines, but to its 'dramatic' weaknesses. Dramatically speaking,
the poem works as poems generally do: it presents a mode of
human life – a mode which, in this case, is offered to the reader
as Pope's – in which these doctrines, these observations and
propositions, seem true and important. What often happens in
the *Essay*, however, is that this mode of life shows itself too
sharply at odds with itself, or too drastically truncated as a
mode of human life, to evoke much respect. As a man sees, so he
is; and as many readers and critics have noted, there are
persistent gaps between the all-embracing divine and natural
Order that Pope's understanding sees (or wills itself to see) and
the world as his sensibility and imagination see it.

But there are equally striking gaps here between Pope's
'conscious virtue' and his moral sensibility and imagination.
Indeed, some of the moral 'truths' he claims to demonstrate
virtually deconstruct themselves. The first eighteen lines of
Epistle II form a good example ('Know then thyself, presume
not God to scan...'), where verbs like '*Plac'd* on this isthmus of
a middle state...', '*Created*...half to fall', 'in endless Error
hurl'd', do scan God (for who did the placing and creating?) in
the very process of affirming Man as 'the glory' of the world as
well the 'jest' (jest to whom?), and yet finding the requisite self-
knowledge of Man is nothing but the recognition of a 'riddle'.
A similar case is the 'truth' Pope claims to see in Epistle IV, that
'an honest Man's the noblest work of God'.[13] Even when we
understand 'honest' as meaning true and virtuous, we might
still think that Pope knew better than this; in fact, the passage
betrays a kind of doubleness, a tension, that appears in a good
deal of his work.

On the one hand, Pope locates the highest moral value in
conscious 'honesty', in *conducting* one's life in accordance with
the universal precepts and principles of morality. It is this kind
of value that he always claims for his own poetry: his art always
seeks ('in conscious virtue bold') to recommend and exemplify

what every 'honest Man' must think and do. On the other
hand, he also locates the highest moral value in the genuine
'nobleness', the truly great 'wit', the authentically sublime
'genius', manifested in certain lives (Aurelius and Socrates, for
example) and in the work of certain poets (Homer and
Shakespeare, for example). What he does in the passage about
'the noblest work of God' is simply conflate moral agents and
moral lives, universal conduct-moral virtue (acting honestly,
rationally, wisely, rightly) and the capacities, needs and shape
of a particular life (Pope's genius and his aspiration to poetic
greatness, for example, or the Unfortunate Lady's aspiration
beyond 'the vulgar flight of low desire'). Thus he argues that
''tis phrase absurd to call a Villain Great' – which it usually is,
of course; and that it is the man 'who noble ends by noble
means obtains' (or at least tries to obtain them thus) who is
'great indeed' – which he is, of course. But is there nothing that
might mark a man (a non-villain) as great, as distinct from
'honest'? After all, something must mark an end or a means as
noble, as distinct from 'honest'. When Pope claims here that 'A
Wit's [only] a feather, and a Chief a rod', his own wit or genius
must know very well what makes this reduction, like the
conflation, fallacious – just as it also knows, and actually
exhibits, 'in Parts superior what Advantage lies', even while it
is discursively insisting that the only advantage is a painful
moral sensitivity and wisdom and a merely 'painful prehemi-
nence! yourself to view / Above life's weakness; and its comforts
too'. (Poor Pope!) In fact, his whole grand objective moral
Scheme of Things seems to require a good deal of Dulness to see
and accept it – a capacity for being content, satisfied, secure
and innocent, *not* presuming, *not* being proud and aspiring,
repressing precisely the adventurous, investigating, aspiring wit
that can *make* man the 'glory' as well as the 'jest and riddle of
the world'. 'Cease', 'submit', be 'secure' and 'safe', the rest is
unreal: this is not renunciation, but self-amputation. Indeed for
a conscious dramatic-poetic genius, it is something not far from
bad faith.

Even the mature Pope was always inclined in his 'philosophical' moments to believe that moral life can be conflated

with moral conduct, and treated as really consisting in voluntary, intentional, 'correctly' regulated actions. His *non-*philosophical poems actively question this belief, but in his philosophical discourses it does not seem to occur to him to ask himself the obvious question: by following what precepts or rules or ideals *could* one be most fully authentically alive both as a human being like any other and as the particular unique being it is one's destiny (and perhaps choice) to be? It is his self-deluding belief that there is an answer to this question which underlies the extraordinary passage in the *Essay on Man* explicitly on the art of life:

> Love, Hope, and Joy, fair pleasure's smiling train,
> Hate, Fear and Grief, the family of pain;
> These mix'd with art, and to due bounds confin'd,
> Make and maintain the balance of the mind:
> The lights and shades, whose well accorded strife
> Gives all the strength and colour of our life.[14]

It is the conception of 'art' that is most revealing here. This art of life seems only a matter of mixing and confining, making and maintaining – that is, a matter of acting in accordance with certain known, objective rules or principles in order to achieve a specific, objective, pre-determined result. In other words, it is a craft, or at most an applied art, working on material external to the agency itself and directed to an end that is similarly external: a conception of 'art' so strikingly limited that it is hard to understand how Pope failed to be struck. As he knew as well as anybody – indeed, more sharply than most – love, joy, hope, hate, fear and grief are not simply feelings or 'passions' detached from the moral will. The poetry he had already written (not to mention the poetry he had translated, especially *The Iliad*) actually insists that they are states of soul, modes of life, that typically include the moral will as well as every other activity of the self. Then again, there is the sheer psychological absurdity of Pope's art of life here. Who ever said to himself in the morning that he really must acquire a little grief during the course of the day so as to keep his mind properly balanced? Indeed, anyone able to practise the art Pope describes here already has more 'balance of the mind' than he or she needs. Of course, most of us want our lives to be strong and colourful, and Pope is right to see these as moral qualities; but we will hardly achieve them by treating strength and colour as qualities external to actual living (as they can be treated as external to right conduct), and qualities that we can add to our life by the same sort of actions as comprise right conduct. As Pope must have known, the art of life is no more at our command than the art of poetry. He seems to have fallen victim here to the same desire for simple formulas as he does in the fatuous theory he propounds in the first *Moral Essay*, that the moral 'consistency' of an individual's life is objectively determined by, and objectively discernible in, a single 'passion' ruling it from birth to death. Once again, he is right to consider such 'consistency' as a moral matter; but as his own poetry demonstrates once again, the consistency or coherence or integrity of a *life* (the Unfortunate Lady's, for instance, or Eloisa's, or Pope's for that matter) does not consist in anything as simple as a single 'ruling passion'. Pope is trying to make a highly implausible efficient cause (to borrow Aristotelian terminology for the moment) do the work of a formal one, which is why he seemed to some contemporaries (Johnson was one of them) to be propounding some kind of determinism or fatalism. But he was not the first or the last to want to fix moral life down with apparently objective 'natural' laws, and personal and social rules and ideals derived from them.

II

To turn to the *Epistle to Arbuthnot*, which was published not much later than the *Essay on Man*, is to see how yet another, more complex sense of himself went with a much greater dramatic power, and both with a different art of life.

Like many of Pope's poems, *Arbuthnot* is rather uneven – mainly, I think, because of its attempt simply to identify the well-known talented Poet (who is depicted as speaking the poem), the sincere and 'honest' Private Man (who is depicted as simply a dutiful and virtuous agent) and the plain-speaking Public Figure (who is depicted as simply a combination of the other two). The poet who actually writes and shapes the poem implicitly claims these figures not as fictions, but as aspects of himself, Alexander Pope, and himself as therefore aligned with the 'correct' artistic, social and conduct-moral principles and ideals professed by one or other of these aspects. And it is in these terms that the poem performs its main discursive function: to vindicate the moral integrity and *bona fides* of Pope's conduct as a man and a poet.

As a defence of Pope's moral conduct, the poem is brilliantly adept in its rhetorical emphases and structure; but of course it also has to be tactfully silent about the basic reason why such a defence came to be needed at all. The Poet-speaker cannot decently explain, for example, *why* 'All fly to *Twit'nam*, and in humble strain / Apply to me...' (ll. 21–2): we have to understand the reason for ourselves, and our doing so helps to put us inside the Poet's door from the outset. So too with the reason all the poetasters seek Pope's literary judgment or patronage or help, or try to flatter him, or attack and vilify him; he has not just *happened* to become a literary celebrity. Similarly, with the Poet's perfectly reasonable wishes to have a private life, to 'maintain a Poet's Dignity and Ease' (l. 263), to cultivate his friendships and his soul; and similarly again with his claims never, as a Poet, to have lied, or attacked honesty and innocence, or to have been proud or servile, and to have withstood every kind of hostility, solely 'for thee, fair Virtue!' (l. 359). Why should all this *need* saying? Why all the excitement and hostility? After all, what has Pope done? As far as conduct is concerned, he has only written 'many an *idle Song*' (l. 28, my italics); he has served the Muse only to lighten the painful burden of his life; and in any case he took to writing only because it came so easily and *naturally*, because it prevented him from no duty and because the best critics encouraged him. Later, he (very correctly) 'moraliz'd his song' (l. 341); wrote 'modest Satire' (l. 189); and spoke his mind without fear or favour, since he regarded a knave a knave no matter how high or low. But of course all of this clearly leaves out certain other, quite crucial aspects of his poetry, which are only hinted at in brief occasional remarks: 'A *Lash* like mine no honest man shall *dread'* (l. 303, my italics); *'insult* the Poor, *affront* the Great' (l. 360, my italics); 'I cough like *Horace ... Ovid's* nose ... immortal *Maro* ... great *Homer'* (ll. 116–24): even to flatterers, it seems, Pope is not known for the modesty of his poetic aspirations. In short, what does not get into the Poet-speaker's discourse is precisely what the poem presents dramatically: Pope's genius, his 'power' and 'fire', the exceptional *life* of his wit, which is by no means merely civil and 'correct'.

Who but Pope, for example, could have created the Poet-speaker and his circumstances and household pests in the brilliantly funny opening of the poem? Or the unforgettable 'characters' of Atticus and Sporus? Or the subtly changing and developing *tones* of the speaker? Unless we see and respond to the life that manifests itself dramatically in the first twenty-six lines, for example, we miss the good humour, the sanity, in the absurd exaggerations, the self-confidence in the critical characterizations of others (and of himself), the exasperation of spirit in the endless distractions, and – most of all – the extent to which this life of the wit depends, and tacitly acknowledges it depends, on the chaotic Dulness it wages 'warfare' on. As a dramatic manifestation of Pope's life (rather than just his conduct) the poem treats his poetry very seriously indeed, and his poetic genius as both unique and the most important and valuable aspect of his life. Seen in this light, his works are certainly not just 'idle Songs', or his case that of any 'honest' man, or his virtues only the 'fair', pacific and dutiful virtues of conduct. The life of his wit also includes capacities that are warlike: a power that is willing to wound and not afraid to strike, for instance, a comic fantasy that can hate as well as ridicule, a delight in 'exposing Knaves, and painting Fools' even while acknowledging that he understands what he attacks because he can find something of it even within himself.

A tiny example is the dramatic way his wit presents us simultaneously with both Codrus and the Poet-speaker Pope:

> You think this cruel? take it for a rule,
> No creature smarts so little as a Fool.
> Let Peals of Laughter, *Codrus*! round thee break,
> Thou unconcern'd canst hear the mighty Crack.

Pit, Box and Gall'ry in convulsions hurl'd,
Thou stand'st unshook amidst a bursting World.[15]

This shows in Pope the Poet-speaker a self-possession, a composure, not entirely unlike that of Codrus, but it also shows in him the sensitivity (sensitive to a possible objection, for example), the capacity to hurt and to be hurt, and the intelligence, that he sees Codrus as lacking. But 'through' these (to recall Pope's phrase about Nature speaking through Shakespeare), and through other things here too (the placing of the passage in the whole structure of considerations developed through the poem, for example), the dramatizing wit manifests much else: a wry self-awareness, for instance – a capacity to realize both the similarity and the difference, and to accept the joke against itself. This capacity is unstated, of course – it may be the sort of self-awareness that its possessor is quite un-conscious of exhibiting – but it is dramatically there, exhibiting what we see as a sanity, a perceptive honesty, that are clearly integral to the life of the wit even though Pope's conduct did not always exemplify them.

Similarly with the figure of Atticus a hundred lines or so later. The wit that sees-and-presents him in *this* context (even though much of the passage dates from much earlier) exhibits the same 'genius' and 'fire' and desire of 'fair Fame' as inspired its object; it also exhibits the candour, the generosity of judgment, and the disinterestedness that Atticus lacks; and again it realizes in these a life large, courageous and aspiring enough to venture itself in total, frank, *unguarded* engagement with the world, even if this might put its self-esteem, its 'conscious virtue', at risk. (The opposite of Atticus, we might say, is the Unfortunate Lady, along with the Poet who identified with her.) The almost unbridled disgust with which Sporus is 'flapped' later in the poem actually illustrates the point. It exhibits the opposite of a morally-correct moderation; but the wit can implicitly admit that its activity is the antithesis of strict conduct-virtue, as I think it does, just because it realizes its own life is not what it sees its object's life as: a *'vile* antithesis'.[16]

In other words, the *Epistle to Arbuthnot* suggests an art of life very different from the kind described and embodied in the

Essay on Man. If *Arbuthnot* exhibits any 'balance of the mind', for
instance, the balance does not consist in organizing the
'passions' so as to observe known, objective moral norms, but in
the way Pope's mind (or wit) presents, as accurately as its
nature now and here allows, the various particulars it now and
here 'sees' as the world and as its own moral history in that
world. Nor is the strife in which the wit finds the strength and
colour of its life in *The Epistle to Arbuthnot* a 'well accorded'
mixing of the 'passions'. It is the 'warfare upon earth' in which
the wit manifests its nature as it engages, in its whole activity,
with the world and with language in seeking to *realize* what it
'sees' – especially as what it 'sees' as valuable and important.
Moreover, the openly dramatic form of the poem tacitly
acknowledges – indeed, insists – that the unity, the coherence of
the wit's life through time is too complex to be encompassed in
any one discourse, any one description or narrative, much less in
any one predetermined principle or ideal. The poem includes
such discourses, of course, but in being allocated to the Poet-
speaker they become part of the drama, not of the dramatizing.

In *The Epistle to Arbuthnot*, Pope's real nature is never simply
declared in any discourse of his rationalizing, 'correctly'
regulated, and defensively prudent conduct-self. In fact, some of
that nature 'speaks through' discrepancies, gaps and silences
that are unnoticed by the Poet-speaker quite as much as
through the connections and consistencies he does notice. What
does it show of Pope's wit, for example, that it ends the poem
with the sunset glow of his parents' simplicity and the simple
'honesty' of his dutiful conduct towards them? Why is it
important to Pope as well as to the Poet-speaker that his father
'walk'd *innoxious* thro' his Age' and 'held it for a rule / It was a
Sin to call our Neighbour Fool'; and that the son wants simply
to 'rock the Cradle of reposing Age' and with '*lenient* Arts
extend a Mother's breath' (ll. 382 ff; my italics)? Is this not a
reappearance of that defensive impulse of his now quite noxious
and unlenient art (in the first *Dunciad* for example) to secure
itself in a willed simplicity of conduct that amounts in effect to
a curtailment of its life? The Poet-speaker does not ask that
question; it is a question the drama of the poem implicitly asks

about the Poet-speaker and about itself, even though Pope was probably never conscious of any such question as he wrote the poem. And it underlines how much the life of his wit lies in its dramatizing – in its ranging responsive energy, its masterful, self-delighting pounce on significant particulars of the world within and without, its evident prowess, even its power to question and 'deconstruct' moral conduct – rather than in the observance of predetermined moral principles and ideals.

Nevertheless, both moral life and moral conduct are necessary objects of the poem's thinking and of our own. It is just because of the unique life of Pope's wit or genius, for example, that we *care* whether it includes genuine 'honesty' of conduct or merely an evasive simplicity. By the same token we do not care *so* much that his right conduct comes to seem to us the supremely important element of his life as it sometimes seems to Pope in his ideas about people, including himself. On the other side, it is just because this unique genius does care, as everybody should, about his conduct and moral 'character', and tries to make them integral, even central, in the life of his wit, that we feel free to delight in the other elements of that life – in its fantastic play, for instance, or in its variety, in what Dryden might have called the comprehensiveness of Pope's soul. For Pope's concern with moral conduct anchors the fantastic play and dramatic life of his wit in particular facts of personal, social, cultural and political history, in the world where a genius counts for no more than any honest man: the world not just of Grub Street, but of inescapable choices, actions and responsibilities. The *Epistle to Arbuthnot*, for example, constantly reminds us that the writing, publishing and discourse of the poem itself are public actions in a public world at a particular time, and that the dramatic depiction of the exasperated Poet shutting his door on the world at the beginning of the poem is a means by which the dramatizing wit begins by actually opening *its* door to the world.

III

Almost from the start of his writing career, Pope seems to have had some double conception of his poems as both works of art and moral actions. Or to put it another way, he always thought of his poems as exhibiting an art of life – a particular, 'touchstone' form of moral life, which involved of course voluntary, intentional, correctly regulated moral actions.

For the young poet (up to and including his 1717 volume), there was a certain pathos in the limits that poetic consciousness placed on moral action in the world. The one was open and responsive to incompatible values; the other ineluctably committed to choosing between them. (This was Andrew Marvell territory, of course.) In particular, the pathos lay in the necessary cost that moral action and sympathetic imaginative understanding of such action imposed on each other. The more the Poet had to feel or suffer in order to understand certain kinds of action the less he could be an agent, and vice versa. Thus Pope ends Eloisa's lament, like the 'Elegy to the Memory of an Unfortunate Lady', with a reference to himself:

> And sure if fate some future Bard shall join
> In sad similitude of griefs to mine,
> Condemn'd whole years in absence to deplore,
> And image charms he must behold no more,
> Such if there be, who lives so long, so well;
> Let him our sad, our tender story tell;
> The well-sung woes will soothe my pensive ghost;
> He best can paint 'em, who shall feel 'em most.[17]

Nevertheless, it is still true that the younger Pope saw his poetic wit as a form of action as well as a form of suffering – action in the ordinary outward world of moral conduct, that is, as well as in the inner world of poetic or 'dramatic' consciousness. In fact, the best of his early poems are those that avoid any 'pathetick' exploitation either of the differences between art and action, or of their overlap. The tone and expository wit of the *Essay on Criticism*, for example, consciously exhibit the 'common pursuit of true judgment' which is its subject and to which it deliberately submits itself: a kind of

activity in which (as the poem suggests) a common social, moral
and cultural life realizes itself, which is *truly* judgment (not
arbitrary subjective reaction, or mechanical rule, or fashionable
cant), and which is *true* both to its particular object and to the
qualities embodied in the relevant achievements of earlier wits.
The 'Epistle to Miss Blount... after the Coronation' is a still
more perfect instance – indeed, in its way, it is virtually a little
paradigm of Pope's self-conscious wit and the conflicting moral
ideals and actions comprehended by and in its dramatic
'warfare upon earth'. But of course *The Rape of the Lock* is the
finest of these early poems, the most substantial and the most
'dramatic'. The gap between the 'mock' and the 'heroic'
aspects of its form is part of the drama, and it produces a
constant current of moral ironies; but the ironies are clearly
more than a vehicle of satirical criticism of fashionable London
society. They are also a way of pointing to what is immediately
exhibited to us: a social world, whose very variety and confusion
prompt the mind to try to grasp it all in intellectual or artistic
formulas, but which constantly slips between the fingers of the
mind – partly because the reality is too complex and too fluid,
but partly because the mind itself is also part of the same reality
and, if it is intelligent enough, realizes that it is. Pope's mind
certainly is intelligent enough. The continually mobile, in-
ventive, delighting wit of the poem clearly knows that its own
life – its brilliant, delicate sensibility, the gaiety and 'good
Humour' of its ironies, the unfaltering ease and lightness of its
address, the elegant precision of its insight – is a more perfect
(because morally more perceptive, comprehensive and coherent) form of the easy, glittering, 'polite' and vibrant life the
fashionable belles and beaux reach towards, but only partly
achieve. The life of the wit celebrates and partakes of their life
– including all of its warring impulses, those creative of order
and beauty and those destructive of them – quite as much as it
criticizes the false consciousness their life produces and feeds
upon. And of course Pope knows this. The poem realizes that its
own life consists not only in the play of '*quick* Poetic Eyes'
comprehending 'all the *Murders* of your [Belinda's] Eye', but
also in returning that comprehension back to 'you', offering its

own finer moral consciousness as an enriching and reconciling addition to the life of the real world, offering itself, in fact, as the relevant 'art of life'.

The fact that it did not quite work out that way, that the poem did not actually resolve the real quarrel it started from, could hardly have surprised Pope, however. The Muse knows that the lock remains forever lost to Belinda – a loss that no poem can realize in its full actuality precisely because the civilized consciousness the Muse embodies requires that the loss be forgiven, if not forgotten. Similarly, the Muse knows that it cannot fully realize the far greater losses exacted by the elegant society it addresses and inhabits, the truly lethal brutality normally shut out of social consciousness: 'at ev'ry Word a Reputation dies'; 'Wretches hang that Jury-men may Dine'. Yet at the same time the Muse also knows that, by understanding the 'rape' and the loss far better than Belinda's world can, it consecrates her lock to an ever green life in the artistic-moral world it creates. It is a world where anything and everything can be fully known for what it is and be fixed in its proper place and value, but only because the Muse lifts its objects out of the stresses and contingencies of real life, annihilates them to a green thought, and so renders them dead – mere figures:

> There Heroes' Wits are kept in pondrous Vases,
> And Beaus' in *Snuff-Boxes* and *Tweezer-Cases*.
> There broken Vows, and Death-bed Alms are found,
> And Lovers' Hearts with Ends of Riband bound;
> The Courtier's Promises, and Sick Man's Pray'rs,
> The Smiles of Harlots, and the Tears of Heirs,
> Cages for Gnats, and Chains to Yoak a Flea;
> Dry'd Butterflies, and Tomes of Casuistry.[18]

In some ways, these lines look forward to *The Dunciad* more than a decade later, where Pope is even more alive to the paradoxical relationships between his wit and its material. *The Dunciad* has an 'Elasticity and Fire' that feed on a world much more densely peopled, gross, lively, various and particularized, than that of the *Rape*. Correspondingly, the wit has a denser, less delicate life, reaching into the chaotic, sprawling density of

Dulness, in order to exhibit the 'wild, dancing light', the ceaselessly swarming energies, of its object as a kind of non-life by contrast with its own concentration of mind, its own ordered dancing light, and its own moral and artistic fixing into place. But the wit not only does this; it also draws attention to the verve with which it does it, and to the enormous joke of its knowing that it does it:

> 'Twas on the day, when Thorold, rich and grave,
> Like Cimon triumph'd, both on land and wave:
> (Pomps without guilt, of bloodless swords and maces,
> Glad chains, warm furs, broad banners, and broad faces)
> Now Night descending, the proud scene was o'er,
> But liv'd, in Settle's numbers, one day more.
> Now May'rs and Shrieves all hush'd and satiate lay,
> Yet eat in dreams the custard of the day;
> While pensive Poets painful vigils keep,
> Sleepless themselves to give their readers sleep.[19]

Who could resist a wit as funny and as vividly dramatic as this? Clearly, not Pope himself: along with everything else such poetry exhibits, it exhibits an obvious delight in its own creativity, its capacity to make exquisite beauty out of deprivation and ugliness – a delight so large and so confident that it can even flow out to hug its very material. And once again, this poetic self-awareness makes the poem a social and a moral act, which exhibits another, more adequate art of life. For it binds the poet and the reader into an alliance of wit – very much as the opening lines of the *Epistle to Arbuthnot* do, or the pleasure in the *Imitations* of finding Horace alive again in London but with Pope's face on him. It is an alliance for 'warfare': there is aggression with the delight. But it is also an alliance for fellowship and mutual respect. Nor does it ever become mere in-group knowingness: the alliance is both more difficult to enter than that and also more open. Its point, indeed its substance, is a mode of personal and social life that includes anyone with the wit to realize, as the poem does, the inescapable paradoxes in which such a life is enmeshed. In fact, its enemies are precisely those without the wit to see the ultimate paradox, the supreme joke – that the life of wit is dependent on *them* for its material, as

the spirit is on the flesh, as consciousness is on being, so that (as
the young Pope had put it) 'Wit, which most to scorn it does
pretend, / With Dulness first began, in Dulness last must end.'
The last phrase is the other side of the supreme joke, of course:
wit's warfare is never wholly victorious, never establishes a
lasting peace, and is always fatal to itself – a truth Pope came
fully to realize only in the last book of the final version of *The
Dunciad*, his last major work in fact:

> Ye Pow'rs! whose Mysteries restor'd I sing,
> To whom Time bears me on his rapid wing,
> Suspend a while your Force inertly strong,
> Then take at once the Poet and the Song.[20]

But before that, his art and his sense of it developed yet further.

I V

Although the *Essay on Man* and the four Moral Essays associated
with it are not very impressive as philosophy, they do show a
clear bent in Pope towards a more impersonal kind of art than
most of the early poems (with the significant exception of the
Essay on Criticism) or even the first versions of *The Dunciad*. In the
most obvious sense, they aim at the impersonality of abstract
argument; in a slightly different sense, they also aim at tracing
out impersonal psychological and social causes and effects (the
'ruling passion', gender, money, conspicuous consumption,
and so on); and the art of life they exhibit in these respects
comes to little more than Mill's: a body of rules or precepts
concerning Morality, Prudence and Aesthetics ('the Beautiful
or Noble'), based on the principles of Moral Science and
regulated by a doctrine of Ends.[21] Formally, of course, these
poems are personal 'epistles', and the Moral Essays certainly
exploit the looser, more casually structured possibilities of the
form. They tend to wander from one consideration to another,
one attitude to another. Nevertheless, their aim is clearly to
make 'Nature', properly understood, 'speak through' the poet.
At least, that is how Pope might have put it to himself. To us,
however, who have no such unified, moralized conception of

'Nature', these abstracting kinds of impersonality seem a less impressive aim or achievement in these poems. We still read them, especially the Moral Essays, and with present interest; they are certainly not just historical documents; but we read them, I think, rather as Pope still read Cowley: for their 'moral', for the 'language' of Pope's 'heart', for the *dramatic* impersonality that makes passages in them break through the general (and implausible) abstract texture and intentions.

The passages I mean are obvious enough: passages like the one I quoted in chapter 3 – the account of the life of Buckingham, 'great Villers', in the third Moral Essay, for example; or the account of life at Timon's Villa in the fourth; or of Atossa's life or that of those 'Ghosts of Beauty' and 'Veterans of the World' who 'haunt the places where their honour died' in the second; or the life of Sir Balaam at the end of the third.

With such passages as these, it is not (as Pope suggests of Shakespeare) that the poet becomes morally transparent, as it were, but rather that he seems to comprehend and judge each mode of life out of a deeper and fuller self than is called out to comprehend and judge abstract arguments, for instance, or even an agent's conduct. In fact, Pope's avoidance of straight-out conduct judgments on most of these modes of life is so conspicuous that it highlights his apparently more fatalistic, but actually more holistic, sense of the life in question. Seeing it as he does usually generates a pretty steely tone – something like that of black comedy, for example, or even of tragedy – precisely because the life is seen as ineluctably shaping and shaped by the particular psychological, social or cultural circumstances in which it is lived out. It is seen, that is, not by a simply firm, fixed, 'honest' self pressing towards a clear, definitive judgment on conduct, but by a self that includes the 'honest' one and yet is clearly different, larger, in at least two important respects.

In the first place, it is also *un*firm, *un*fixed, in the way that Pope claims in the second Moral Essay that the moral character of women is. As Pope came to see, the 'dramatic' poet's self needs a chameleon-like fluidity in order to 'see' and catch the metamorphic, chameleon-like qualities of nature, people, social manners and so on – something like the positive power that Keats called 'negative capability', or the elusive, contradictory, many-faced person that Pope depicts himself as in his *Imitations of Horace* during the last decade of his life. In the second place, however, the 'dramatic' poet needs a kind of moral impersonality: a large, sympathetic, but disinterested interest in different modes of life and the light they cast on one another, an objectivity capable of seeing a life whole and seeing it steadily, and a holding back from impatient conduct judgments. It is the kind of moral objectivity that some people mistake for a quite *non*-moral, merely 'aesthetic', point of view.

It is true that (to quote Johnson again) 'among the successive variety of appearances, every disposition of mind takes hold on those by which it may be gratified'. Every wit seeks what its own life – its capacities, needs, desire – impel it to; as it 'sees' other modes of life, so it manifests its own. Or in Pope's version of the point, 'by some object ev'ry brain is stirr'd', so that even those most shy of engaging with the world,

> The most recluse, discreetly open'd find
> Congenial matter in the Cockle-kind... [22]

Only Pope could have seen it as wittily as that – or rather, could have imagined the Goddess of Dulness saying something so discreetly to the point. For 'congenial' here obviously means more than agreeable; it also means answering to the particular 'genius', the distinctive moral being of the individual, and the answering may be negative just as well as positive. What a wit finds it must *attack* is also 'congenial' in this sense:

> Not write? but then I *think*,
> And for my Soul I cannot sleep a wink.
> I nod in Company, I wake at Night,
> Fools rush into my Head, and so I write. [23]

Similarly, 'matter' means more than an object of attention; it also means the material with which a particular wit actively engages, for or against, and in which it therefore manifests the nature and qualities of its own life. In this sense, 'matter' may be the moral conduct of others, for example, or their moral lives – or indeed, one's own.

As the sociable but yet rather reclusive Pope obviously appreciated, all of this applies to him as well as to the most recluse. What he now, in the last decade or so of his life, finds 'congenial matter' answers to what and how his 'genius' sees at this stage: his deepening realization of how much every mode of human life, even his own, is determined not just by choices and conduct, but also by the native dispositions, weaknesses and talents of the individual, and by the structures, forces and inertia of Nature, social institutions and social practices, politics, history, cultural forms, and so on – not to mention plain, ordinary stupidity. To realize this more thoroughly was to realize more fully the 'matter' with which his wit had always been engaged – indeed, had *had* to be engaged in its 'warfare upon earth'.

In other words, Pope came to appreciate in the 1730s (though perhaps not fully to understand intellectually) that his long-standing poetic self-consciousness was an element of his moral life which he could neither marginalize nor transcend, and which was therefore an essential part of his 'matter'. To see in a new and deeper way the inter-connections between the life of his wit and the life his wit found as matter to work on, was to find a new aspect of the matter and a new dimension of the wit. His essays in philosophizing brought no understanding of this; quite the contrary. But his increasing sense of an enveloping social and political corruption, and the need to withdraw from it, did lead him in these years to a new sense of the moral function and value of his 'genius', and to poetic forms at once more personal and more impersonal, more completely 'dramatic', than before.

What his matter now required was more than the rather 'pathetick' references to the Poet or the Muse that recur in his early poems, more than drawing attention to his own 'Elasticity and Fire' as in *The Dunciad*, more even than the traditionally-sanctioned *personae* available to the Poet. In the poems of the 1730s – the Moral Essays, the *Imitations of Horace*, and the *Epilogue to the Satires* especially – he certainly used many such traditional *personae*: not just the talented Poet, the dignified Recluse, the sober Moralist, the Sage, the amiable Friend, and so on, as earlier; but now were added the plain, domestic Citizen removed from the corruption of the age; the protesting Man of Principle; the 'honest' Poet who is not a slave to words, a vassal to a Name, or a dupe to Party, but who tells the truth and goes his own moderate way; the outspoken Satirist, not afraid to name names; the sublime moral Prophet; even the inconsistent, chameleon-like Portraitist. He exploited these brilliantly; but (as in *Arbuthnot*) the point of doing so was a double one: not just to express what he had to say in each guise, but also to let speak for itself what was manifested in his finding such guises congenial and necessary. Although his guises are all dramatized figures – 'Pope' as a particular character, as it were – the significance of the poem is not simply what that character says and does, even if he is always the hero of the piece. It also includes the significance of the dramatizing itself. In other words, the poetry is inevitably dramatic, and the drama inevitably reflexive – reflexive not just in the obvious sense that (as in *Arbuthnot*) his subject is his own career or attitudes, but in the deeper and more interesting sense that he evidently finds he can adequately project and explore the world he inhabits only through projecting and exploring his own congenial, manifold sense of it. Given how he is now able to 'see' the world, himself, his wit, his circumstances, and the relationships between them, he can realize all of this only by dividing himself into a rather put-upon object *in* the social world and a critical, protesting subject *outside* it.

In all of the major poems of the 1730s, though somewhat differently in each case, the poet pretty obviously comprises both 'Pope' and Pope. The drama lies in the 'warfare' of each with the world, and also in the subtle interplay between 'Pope' and Pope. Each 'Pope' is a willed, carefully constructed mode of life; each 'Pope', that is, embodies, not an *art* of life, but merely a set of *rules* of life – a craft of life. As well as 'Pope', some of the poems include a few other lightly-sketched characters, who represent other, more limited, kinds of sense that Pope could make of the world (including his own place in it) – were he, that is, less virtuous in conduct or less responsively and creatively alive as a wit. Thus the implicit dramatic action in these poems – the inner, unfolding structure of meaning – is the impossible fate of a social and personal life free of corruption, 'warfare' and self-division: a moral state that could incorporate and compose all the warring elements within and without, and reconcile the fullest life of wit and an unswerving virtue of personal and social conduct.

Thus the poems positively require the reader to notice that each 'Poet', each of Pope's guises, is at once sincere and 'honest' (it is the poet who '*will* not lie'), necessary and authentic (it is the guise of the poet who '*can't* be silent'), limited (it is never the poet's *whole* being), and fictional (it is never simply *identical* with the dramatizing wit of the poem). The pressures of the world Pope inhabits, as he experiences them (which is to say, as his particular 'genius' finds them congenial matter), are such that they can be answered to only in this way or that – a way always seen in each poem as different from that of the supposedly *true* Pope, who is appropriately simpler, more peaceful, more innocent, more moderate, more harmoniously self-possessed in conscious Virtue. The pressures of the world visibly force Pope to choose to be 'Pope' the protesting Man of Principle, for instance, rather than the simple domestic Citizen or the quiet poetic Recluse he 'truly' is. In order to respond to the world's corruptions adequately, he is forced to be 'Pope' the free, honest Satirist, or the Prophet armed with his 'sacred weapon', attacking and shaming people who lack moral 'honesty'.

Only as this or that figure can he be morally true to himself; only in this guise or that can he express Truth – that is, what morality, reason, good taste, or even mere decency, constrain a free man to want to say. Conversely, his own history, circumstances, his commitments, his whole moral nature – including his very susceptibility to fools and knaves – force him to answer to the world in this way or that. They visibly force him, that is, to attempt the visibly impossible: to try to concentrate his whole complex moral being in a single, straightforward moral action – in speaking out as the honest Satirist, or protesting as the Man of Principle, and so on. All he *can* do, as we are meant to see, is disperse his moral being into different 'selves' – in sharp contrast to those occasions when the whole life of his wit does find congenial matter in the particular coherence, the necessary inner economy, the whole fate, of such modes of life as Buckingham's, or the Veterans' of the World, or Sir Balaam's.

Naturally enough, what Pope's various *personae* say about the world has received most critical attention, and quite properly so. That is part of what Pope means, even if it is always a fictionalized 'Pope' who says it. But there is also what the poems depict and manifest dramatically. Thus they depict what it is in the world that makes 'Pope's' moral life its victim: 'Shut, shut the door...' 'Fools rush into my Head...', and so on. They depict what enables 'Pope's' wit to stand over against the world as its moral victor: 'Welcome for thee, fair Virtue! all the past:... welcome ev'n the last...', 'Yes, I am proud; I must be proud to see / Men not afraid of God, afraid of me...'. And they depict what robs every such moral victory of its fruit – nature's infinite capacity to outdo fancy:

> Feign what I will, and paint [vice] e'er so strong,
> Some rising Genius sins up to my Song.[24]

What the poetry also manifests, however, is Pope, the comprehensive being whose wit is (and knows it is) both victim and victor: the poetic genius who also lives in another dimension, creating his song for some rising poetic genius to *sing* up to it. Thus the poetry exhibits a relationship that Pope's beliefs often obscured from his understanding, though by the time he wrote the final *Dunciad* he was obviously pretty clear about it. For it is the pressures, the resentments, the follies, the knavery, the discord, the Dulness of the world which positively 'stir' and liberate the life of his wit. They are a very large part of the matter his genius finds congenial. They invite as well as irritate him to realize his moral being as something other than simple, undivided, fixed, 'true' and 'honest': to discover and exercise the freedom and vivacity with which his wit can play creatively and critically in and upon the world, including himself.

This symbiotic relationship between the matter and the critical-creative wit of *The Dunciad*, especially of the final version of it in four Books, has become by now something of a critical commonplace. As with most of Pope's later work, *The Dunciad* exhibits an art of life that could be summed up as 'finding' what really 'stirs the brain', finding really 'congenial matter'. Put like that, it is a formula that carries less of a prescriptive rule than a warning. For it is a reminder that *any* 'genius' – even that of Sporus, for instance, or Cibber – is compelled to manifest the qualities of its life in answering to whatever matter is fated to be congenial to it: 'Puns, or Politicks, or Tales, or Lyes, / Or Spite, or Smut, or Rymes, or Blasphemies'.[25] Only a higher kind of 'genius' can be stirred enough to realize what it is fated to find congenial, and to make whatever sense it can of the matter. And it is a still higher kind of 'genius' that finds its congenial matter in the noblest human passions, fire and energies. The lower kinds of 'genius' are precisely those that cannot be stirred enough even to know that they are Dunces:

> Swearing and supperless the Hero sate,
> Blasphem'd his Gods, the Dice, and damn'd his Fate.
> Then gnaw'd his pen, then dash'd it on the ground,
> Sinking from thought to thought, a vast profound!
> Plung'd for his sense, but found no bottom there,
> Yet wrote and flounder'd on, in mere despair.
> Round him much Embryo, much Abortion lay,
> Much future Ode, and abdicated Play;
> Nonsense precipitate, like running Lead,
> That slip'd thro' Cracks and Zig-zags of the Head;
> All that on Folly Frenzy could beget,
> Fruits of dull Heat, and Sooterkins of Wit.
> Next, o'er his Books his eyes began to roll,
> In pleasing memory of all he stole,
> How here he sipp'd, how there he plunder'd snug
> And suck'd all o'er, like an industrious Bug.
> Here lay poor Fletcher's half-eat scenes, and here
> The Frippery of crucify'd Molière;
> There hapless Shakespear, yet of Tibbald sore,
> Wish'd he had blotted for himself before.[26]

Of course, just as a dunce's genius seeks and finds whatever matter is congenial, so does Dulness or Wit await its happy meeting with the genius who is congenial enough to make any

sense of *it*. The Cockle-kind has to await the Dunces fated to
study it; Theobald's 'Shakespear' has to await Cibber as the
reader fated to admire and plunder it. This I take it, is the
matter Pope was congenially making sense of in his witticism
that *The Dunciad* 'was not made for these Authors, but these
Authors for the Poem'.[27]

The art of life exhibited in the epistles and satires of the 1730s
is no less complex than that in *The Dunciad*, and certainly more
complex than Pope himself sometimes seems to suggest. Rather
as he conflated 'honesty' with nobleness, he occasionally seems
to conflate conscious Virtue (and Truth to Virtue) with the life
of wit, or to treat them as if they were the self-evidently supreme
value in life. Thus, to take the best-known example, he claims in
the second dialogue of the *Epilogue to the Satires*, that Truth and
Virtue give 'Immortal' life to 'Verse as mean as mine'; indeed,
he even claims that his 'sacred Weapon', ridicule, is 'to all but
Heav'n-directed hands deny'd'. The weapon is 'given' by the
Muse, but 'the Gods' must 'guide' it:[28] the 'Gods' presumably
because the weapon calls for reverence as it is used for 'Virtue's
Work'. In other words, Pope is once again regarding his
satirical 'genius' as a talent to be used and directed instrumentally, from outside it as it were, by a will directed by and to
established moral values and ideals.

This view of his satire is not negligible or a mistake. In any
society, especially in any society that is corrupt or oppressive,
the writer can and should be the spokesman of moral consciousness and conscience; and Pope was not wrong to suppose
that Truth and Virtue do help make verse 'Immortal'.
Nevertheless, they only help, and they cannot give immortality
to verse that is really 'mean'. As Pope knew very well, the life of
his own wit required him to be many other 'selves' than the
virtuous truth-teller and namer of names with a gift for ridicule
in verse. To find his congenial matter in the world he also had
to be, somehow, the object of his own moral self-scrutiny, self-
knowledge, self-control and self-fashioning, while at the same
time being the unavoidably self-projecting, fictively-'constructive' subject that performs all these actions; while still also
being the victim and the victor (bearing his 'sacred Weapon')

of his society. Then there is the art of negotiation that is
exhibited in his work. His wit has to negotiate between, on the
one hand, a vital consciousness that is quick, spontaneous and
wide-ranging, that involves sensibility and feelings of any kind,
that is able to entertain different, even irreconcilable thoughts
and values, and that is capable of 'finding' (or creating) various
modes of life dramatically; and on the other hand, a moral
consciousness that reflects and deliberates, that draws limits to
speculative plurality, that holds to established, recognizable
ideals of life and rules of conduct, that resolves conflicts of
thoughts and values, and that is regulated by the will so that

> What right, what true, what fit, we justly call,
> ... be all my care – for this is All...[29]

What is more, the elusive, always unfolding, undefinable, and
yet fated, life of wit is often the master as well as sometimes the
servant, the instrument, of the established, recognizable, regu-
latable, and yet autonomous, self of moral conduct. Conduct-
morality asks, 'to what is any person's "genius" directed?' (a
question expecting the answer, 'to Truth, Virtue, the Gods'
and so on), or 'by what is it provoked?' (a question expecting
the answer, 'vice, folly, corruption, "the strong Antipathy of
Good to Bad",[30]' and so on). Life-morality asks those questions
and others as well: 'what mode of life manifests itself "in" this
impulse to Virtue and Truth, and in the wish to wield the
"sacred Weapon"?' 'What mode of life manifests itself in other
impulses too?', for the impulse to Virtue and Truth is always
bound up with others. In Pope's case, there is, for instance, the
impulse to give up poetry for prose, and

> ... smooth and harmonize my Mind,
> Teach ev'ry Thought within its bounds to roll,
> And keep the equal Measure of the Soul[31]

since 'Vertue's self may too much Zeal be had; / The worst of
Madmen is a Saint run mad'.[32] There is also the impulse to be
'fix'd, and our own Masters still';[33] the impulse to personal
disorder and intellectual incoherence, with 'each Opinion with
the next at strife, / One ebb and flow of follies all my Life';[34] the

impulse to '[heal] with Morals what [satire] hurts with Wit';[35] the impulse to be a poet (rather than a prose-writer or a mere 'Man of Rymes') – one who can give the breast 'a thousand pains', make people 'feel each Passion that he feigns', 'inrage' as well as 'compose' with 'more than magic Art', and even 'tear [the] heart' with pity and terror.[36] Then again, there is the impulse to 'match the Bards whom none e'er match'd before';[37] the impulse to emulate 'Giant Handel's' power 'To stir, to rouze, to shake the Soul'.[38]

V

The life of Pope's particular wit is certainly a warfare upon earth, but the main contestants are not, as he sometimes supposed, Good and Bad or Right and Wrong. Nor are they the Passions or Self-love on the one side, and on the other the Reason that should guide or rectify them and the 'art' of life that should mix and confine them. The most basic conflict seems to me to cut across these others, and to lie rather in the opposition of two different modes of moral life in his 'genius', of energies pressing in conflicting directions. And being a conflict of modes of life, each includes, as a necessary part of it, values and ideals of conduct. The life of Pope's wit over time, the unfolding of his particular 'genius', might almost be described as a deeper and fuller realization of this warfare: a realization that shaped itself in shaping the matter that his wit at various stages found congenial.

On the one side was an out-going, centrifugal mode of life, its energies exploratory, aspiring, aggressive, as well as responsive and sympathetic. These energies form the impulse to instruct, to judge morally, to correct, to make the world a better place; they also form the unceasing metamorphic strivings of nature and of man, which manifest themselves in folly, Dulness, knavery and corruption, as well as in effort and daring. Seen in this light, *wit* for Pope seems to embody something like the vital desire of a moral being – the out-reaching desire, perhaps not conscious, perhaps 'o'erflowing the measure' (as Philo says of Shakespeare's Antony) – to master and transcend the conditions of its

life, and in doing so, to realize as fully as possible the
potentialities of its life. Wit manifests the distinctive, particular
desires, powers and plenitude (such as they may be) of a life:
every individual's need and capacity to 'live o'er each scene,
and be what they behold', to find and to grow upon congenial
matter, even if only by a deeper sensitivity of feeling towards
others or by 'exposing' fools and knaves. Thus a wit cannot ever
be wholly self-composed like Codrus, ever be 'fix'd', ever be its
'own Master still', while it is capable of being 'stirred' by the
world to engage with and master *it*. Nor can it ever wholly
realize its life in any single action (or line of conduct) or in any
single conception of itself as this or that particular 'genius'. It
cannot wholly realize itself in a life of action, as distinct (in the
old classical and Renaissance distinction) from a life of
contemplation, nor even as an inconsistent chameleon.

A multitude of possible fates await human wits, but for Pope
they are always 'fates': in some form or other, defeat is
inevitable. Part of the pathos of any 'genius', as Pope sees it, is
that the capacity of human wit to realize the whole of its
potential life never matches its desire or need to do so. Its
capacity may be too slight to do more than Dulness ever can do
– fritter itself away in trivia like the cockle-kind, or just dribble
away through cracks and zig-zags of the head. It may be baffled
by the incoherence or incompatibility of the various forms it has
to take in the world. The world may contain nothing to answer
to the needs of a particular life except empty victories, derisory
prizes, shrivelled and shrivelling fruit, as it does for its female
'veterans'. Even at best, the capacity of any human wit is
limited, both in itself and by the resistance of its matter,
however congenial; every realization of its life is a way of
diffusing and exhausting it; anyone's particular individuality is
like 'the lurking principle of death' that one receives with one's
very breath;[39] its 'restless fire' (to use Johnson's phrase from
'The Vanity of Human Wishes') always, by its very restlessness,
by its very capacity to be 'stirred', 'precipitates on death'. The
only triumph finally available to one poet's 'genius', for
example, is that at the end of *The Dunciad*: his wit realizes its
fullest life, the very sea-mark of its utmost sail, by realizing as

fully as it can in thought and in relation to everything else, the inevitability of its own exhaustion, defeat and death in the congenial matter with which it first began.

But against this centrifugal mode of life (with its norms and ideals of conduct) there is in Pope's 'genius' an opposing centripetal one: the pull of his wit towards a centre, a home, a secure point of rest for its 'fire'. This is the life that the self needs for sheer stability, consistency, an abiding structure, a sense of continuous identity. All of these needs and capacities 'stir' wit to define itself – to locate its 'fit' place, to regulate and perhaps harmonize its consciousness and its desires, to know and so to possess itself – in relation to a larger, objective, impersonal moral Order in which it can see itself as part. To discern the 'ought' in the 'is' of the world, to observe the Laws of Nature in thought and then to observe them in conduct, would be (so Pope and many others supposed) to realize and so help fulfil that impersonal Order, one's true 'human' nature, and the character and value of one's particular 'genius'. Yet whatever intellectual muddles this may involve, the impulse of any wit inwards towards peace with itself, towards a central integrity of moral understanding and will, is for Pope clearly also a mode of life he finds necessary to human beings as he finds it congenial to himself.

The problem with this mode of life is not so much the intellectual confusion it produces, since that is heavily out-weighed by the life-moral reassurance it can obviously provide, as the cost in the possibilities of life it precludes. The *Essay on Man* makes crystal clear how every realization of the objective moral Order requires wit to repress or abandon some parts of itself, especially any inquiring, challenging or aspiring consciousness, as 'false' or 'unreal'. The more firm the pacifying Order, the more brittle it may prove. Thus in the life of Pope's own wit, the perfect but very limiting Order of *The Rape of the Lock* gives way to the much less perfectly ordered but much denser life of the first *Dunciad*; that, in turn, to the attempts at a more comprehensive, more fully conceived Order of the *Essay on Man* and the 'philosophical' parts of the Moral Essays; and that in turn to the freer, more 'dramatic' sense of life of these

and the other poems of the 1730s. For what gradually emerges
in his work, though most clearly only in the last *Dunciad*, is the
realization that every total moral Order wit can conceive
involves it in some kind of self-negation – reducing its 'warfare'
in some kind of peace, and thereby reducing its life in some kind
of death. If Dulness is the death of wit in frittering meta-
morphosis, dissipation and exhaustion, the only 'all-composing
Hour' wit can envisage is that of yawning sleep, the loss of all
the strength and colour wit gives and takes in the world, the
Empire of Chaos: '*Wit* shoots in vain its momentary fires'.[40]

All through Pope's work but especially in these poems, his wit
seems to respond to, project, and exhibit both the 'centripetal'
and the 'centrifugal' modes of life. They are also modes of
death, of course, and involve different kinds of personal 'fate'.
Both also include ideals and rules of conduct, which are not
necessarily very different in each case: honesty, for example, is
honesty in both. What does differ here are priorities. Each mode
finds different ideals more and less congenial: the honesty that
ideally extends and even expends the self in action, for instance,
as compared with the honesty that ideally confirms and
preserves the self in action. The two modes of life are not moral
'extremes', however, which can and should be reconciled or
balanced, nor is there any ideal 'mean' between them. Their
conflict within the one wit is real and total, with no refuge from
it 'upon earth'. And which mode predominates in Pope's wit at
any point – which 'disposition' seeks to gratify itself in what it
'sees', which finds more congenial matter in the world – is not
a matter of voluntary, rational moral choice on his part. There
is nowhere for him to stand in order to make such a 'choice of
life' (a point central to Johnson's *Rasselas*). As Pope knew very
well,

> The merchant's toil, the sage's indolence,
> The monk's humility, the hero's pride,
> All, all alike, find Reason on their side.[41]

But if rationality, or what counts as 'rational', is itself part of
a mode of life, the distinctive 'fire' and seriousness of these later
poems exhibit a notable art of life. In one way, that art is very
obvious, but the power and complexity of the poetry show how

difficult, perhaps impossible, it might be to learn a similarly congenial art for oneself. For the art might be described quite simply as always, for however brief a time, living fully in either mode – a fullness that, in the case of Pope's wit here, includes remembering that it also lives, and no less fully, in the other.

CHAPTER 7

Literary judgment: making moral sense of poems

I

In the traditional institution of literature and literary criticism, the practice of judgment has always been central and always been seen as central, even though the preferred kind of judgment has varied from age to age, critic to critic. However, it has been, and still is, commonly supposed that judging a poem (by which I mean a novel, or play, or any work of imaginative literature) must consist in ascribing certain evaluative aesthetic predicates to the poem: unity, complexity, originality, emotional force, realism, formal perfection and the like. A judgment is supposed to be a reasoned *verdict* on the poem: the poem is good or bad inasmuch as it has these or those qualities. Criticism is taken to be an account of the poem's good-making and its bad-making qualities; so that critical judgment is distinguished from interpretation, which is taken to be only an account of the poem's meaning, and from description, which is taken to be a value-free account of all its qualities, and from history, which is taken to be only an account of its objective temporal contexts. Furthermore, the purpose of criticism is supposedly to express approval (or censure) of the poem and to recommend it to the approval (or censure) of others, and in doing so to rank it within the canon of poems that have been approved and recommended by most competent judges over a long period – poems that have stood the test of time and can therefore be regarded as classics.

This is not quite what I mean by critical judgment. It is obviously one sort of judgment; but I mean something which can take a wide variety of forms, and which may well be very unlike a verdict – something that may not even look as if it were, or should be, the application of a single set of specifiable, 'objective' and authoritative criteria. In this, I rather agree with F. R. Leavis's well-known reply to René Wellek, 'Literary Criticism and Philosophy', and especially with Leavis's theory there about the place of theory in critical judgment. It is a common mistake, Leavis argues, but a mistake nonetheless, to think of the good critic 'as measuring with a norm which he brings up to the object and applies from the outside', since what is required is 'a kind of responsiveness that is incompatible with the judicial, one-eye-on-the-standard approach':

The critic's aim is, first, to realize as sensitively and completely as possible this or that which claims his attention; and a certain valuing is implicit in the realizing. As he matures in experience of the new thing he asks, explicitly and implicitly: 'Where does this come? How does it stand in relation to…? How relatively important does it seem?' And the organization into which it settles as a constituent in becoming 'placed' is an organization of similarly 'placed' things, things that have found their bearings with regard to one another, and not a theoretical system or a system determined by abstract consider-ations… [The critic] aims to make fully conscious and articulate the immediate sense of value that 'places' the poem.[1]

As one commentator on this essay of Leavis's points out, Leavis does give here a pretty fair account of much good critical procedure, but hardly, as the essay stands, an adequate account of the logic of critical judgment.[2] In fact, I would add, Leavis's account hardly covers all of his own procedures as a literary critic, an academic teacher, and a socio-cultural critic and activist. Even in his own terms, it is clear that 'things' could not have simply '*found* their bearings with regard to one another' for him, any more than they can for anybody, without a good many presuppositions and a good deal of subtle, wide-ranging and difficult thinking; though I think he is right to claim that such thinking needs to be in terms of specific poems and situations, and not be of the kind that is bound to 'a theoretical system or determined by abstract considerations'. But Leavis's account is at least sharp and cogent enough to suggest why I take a critical judgment to be traditionally something like the moral (or 'human') sense one finds one has to make of a poem as a 'dramatically' present utterance – has to, that is, under the pressure of what the poem is and of one's own fullest and most considered response to it. In other words, I mean the kind of evaluation in which 'objective' understanding and 'subjective' personal response form an inseparable compound, and which issues as a view of what are the poem's actually salient meanings and of its actually salient formal qualities, quite as much as (indeed, in practice, rather more than) a set of explicitly evaluative predicates. The crucial valuing (to adapt Leavis's phrasing) is perhaps always 'implicit in the realizing' of what the poem 'is' – that 'is', of course, being a matter necessarily open to critical dispute.

It is also quite common for philosophers theorizing about Art to suppose that there are certain evaluative predicates which are applicable only to Art and which comprise something called 'aesthetic value', or a certain sub-group of these which are applicable only to poems and which comprise something called 'literary excellence'. Both suppositions seem to me on a par with the belief that there is a special 'poetic' mode of language, or that there is a special, 'poetic' kind of truth: mistaken not only in themselves, but in their fundamental intention as well. For they all try to assert some conclusive theoretical reason why readers and critics should not do what they always have done: that is, ascribe to poems precisely the *same* kind of evaluative predicates, and perhaps even the same range of them, as they ascribe to human actions, human beings or modes of human life. Such theories assume that poems (being a form of Art) are not only different from human actions, beings or modes of life – which is obviously true – but *so* different that they have to be evaluated in essentially different ways and in essentially different terms. To a literary critic in the traditional sense, this is likely to seem very odd. Whatever may be the case with painting or music or pottery, it is hard to think of any quality of a poem that a traditional critic would regard as 'aesthetically' valuable which could not equally be said to be 'morally' valuable. What is more, it is hard to think of any good, independently evaluative literary criticism which positively requires this assumption about the special, non-moral nature of 'aesthetic' judgment. When a traditional critic is about his or her proper business, he does not confuse poems with people, of course, but neither does he apply an essentially different set of evaluative terms to them.

To speak of the 'morally' valuable qualities of poems here is to use the word 'moral' in the more inclusive sense I have been trying to explain, not merely in the common but restricted sense that refers only to a religious-legal code of conduct and the particular ideal conception of human nature that underpins that code: in short, its conduct-moral sense. I also mean something like: engaging any of the evaluative norms applicable to human beings or to human 'states of soul' or to modes of human life or to the patterns or shapes of human lives over time; in short, its larger, life-moral sense. For it is important to notice that, while traditional literary criticism along with the study of literature based on it *is* both 'moral' and 'humanist', it is so in a deeper sense than that it simply looks to the content, the discourse, of a poem for what it says or exemplifies about human agency, human conduct and human nature.

Admittedly, many critics in the past have understood both terms in just this limited sense, and many people still do. They suppose that the value of a poem is simply that of the conduct-moral meanings to be found in it: of the metaphysical-moral 'truths' it expresses, or the general 'vision of life' it gives readers to 'see', or the 'higher moral order' or 'deeper moral reality' it shows them behind the appearances of things. To this rather simple-minded belief, philosophers and theorists (starting with Plato) have naturally objected that poetry cannot be treated as the same thing as philosophy. A poem's specifically 'poetic' (or 'aesthetic') value must be that of the 'art' or the 'inspiration' with which it expresses, or represents, or embodies, or reveals such truths or realities – it being philosophy's business, or theology's, or science's, to check up on the truths or realities. This has sounded plausible enough to make many people conclude that the value of a poem must then be some sort of combination of the two: it must equal the value of its ideas or 'vision' plus the value of its 'art'. But that, as our own age has come to realize, will hardly do either, no matter in how sophisticated a way it is put. To eyes disenchanted with all the 'ideological' certainties of the past (though perhaps less sensitive to their own beams), it appears little more than a formula for privileging certain ideas or beliefs or attitudes as 'truths' or 'realism' or 'vision of life' or whatever, and certain genres or forms of writing as 'inspired' or 'serious' or 'great' or 'poetic' or whatever, and then using these as if they constituted unproblematical, objective criteria by which to measure poems. Indeed, for some disenchanted minds, this is all that 'humanism' seems to amount to anyway, and all that traditional literary judgment – making moral sense of poems – amounts to as well.

I do not think it does in either case, but we need to be clear what the particular issue is here. It is not what we think of past ideologies – 'systems of thought and belief which have had their day' – nor what our own 'system' should be. It is what kind of thing a traditional literary critic takes a poem to be *most* like when it comes to deciding what he *ultimately* values it for: and it is the two words in italics that mark what is basically at stake.

To discuss these questions at all, I think we need to put aside what traditional critics have said in general, theoretical terms about poetry, morality and value. Much of that (not all) does seem pretty dubious, I would agree. But the issue is about the critics' actual, 'practical' judgments; and it relates to critics as diverse as Ben Jonson and D. H. Lawrence, Blake and Arnold, George Eliot and T. S. Eliot, Dryden and Henry James, together with a host of others. What seems to me to be implicit in their practice (no matter what theories they hold) is that for them a poem is *not*, in the final analysis, most like any of the various things that have been suggested at various times, and in terms of which they have, in the first analysis, understood poems: a verbal artefact, for example, made according to the rules and conventions of the craft; or a message from a master-mind; or a form of instruction in wisdom; or a personal 'ideal'; or a fantasy; or affective rhetoric; or an image or picture of the real nature or order of things; or homily, or parable, or allegory; or religious celebration or prophetic revelation; or personal confession; or a source of 'pleasure' and an object of 'taste'; or a revealing social product, or a historical document; or a symbol of a deeper or higher Reality; or a sort of magic; or a quasi-theatrical performance; or an acting out of deep psychological patterns, individual or collective; or a code-determined or language-determined construct; or a self-reflexive play of signifiers, an instance of 'writing' (or 'reading'). For traditional critics, a poem *is*, in some important respects, like some or all of these things (to mention nothing else), and one has to examine it under those aspects in order to understand something of its nature. But in the end, when it comes to considering all of its various aspects in relation, and embracing them all in an evaluative judgment – at that point, they have traditionally treated it, I think, as *most* like the many-faceted, complex activity of a human being, in which a particular mode of human life manifests itself.

It is in this deeper sense, I would argue, that such criticism is both 'moral' and 'humanist'. It has valued a poem, ultimately, for the particular quality of the life that manifests itself in all of the poem's aspects – for the poem's whole distinctive and (as it were) instinctive way of being alive in, and to, our common world.

Needless to say, no one can consider literally all of a poem's aspects, and different people (and different ages) have inevitably disagreed about the nature, significance and importance of such aspects as they noticed and did consider. Moreover, a poem's 'insights' about human conduct, its grasp of moral 'realities', the 'truth' of its 'vision of life', are no less relevant to the traditional critic's evaluative sense of a poem than they are to anybody's evaluative sense of a person or a mode of life. Nevertheless, as the best critics have seen, it would be a too moralistic, or ideological, sense of people or of poems that stopped there, and took this necessary conduct-moral consideration as sufficient in itself. There are other modes of activity, as well as style, manners, sympathies, emotions, sensibility, deeper impersonal forces and structures, and a host of other matters (conscious and non-conscious), that need to be considered as well.

To put the point another way, I am suggesting that the most
basic model or paradigm in terms of which critics have
traditionally evaluated poetry is that of a human being in
activity: that they have made moral sense of poems in exactly
the same way as they have made moral sense of people,
including fictitious people in poems (dramatic characters,
personae, implied narrators and readers and so on). What this
implies, of course, is that the history of evaluative criticism can
be fully understood only in relation to the complex and
changing content of that paradigm: in relation, that is, to the
history of the prevailing moral psychologies and moral values –
the prevailing moral languages, in fact – in terms of which
people at various times have made moral sense of their fellows
and themselves. Our socio-cultural tradition includes many
over-lapping but partly competing moral languages: Homer's,
Plato's, Aristotle's, the Old Testament's and the New Testament's, Augustine's, Aquinas's, Kant's, Mill's, Marx's, Freud's,
etc., etc. That tradition has never been single or systematic even
in the most morally homogeneous ages. But I think that the use
of this basic paradigm forms the thread of continuity in at least
the English literary-critical tradition, and that it underpins the
complex practice we enter upon in the critical study of English
literature. I also think that this is why it is largely in poems, and
in the criticism of poems, that our sense of people is (and
continually has been) formed, tested and re-formed – even, I
might add, the sense of them as being in some ways rather like
texts.

II

Just to say this is not to demonstrate it, of course; I am only
suggesting an hypothesis that itself needs to be critically
explored in a history of literary criticism. But it was partly with
traditional literary criticism in mind that I distinguished in
chapter 3 at least four ways in which we make moral sense of the
manifold activities of people – ways in which readers and critics
have also, I think, traditionally made moral sense of poems: as
(i) the functioning of an impersonal system; or as (ii) causally-
determined behaviour; or as (iii) voluntary action; or as (iv) a

total life, a particular mode of human vitality. All four, I would
suggest, have their counterparts in literary criticism.

The first two, in fact, are currently very popular in literary
criticism – or rather, in 'literary science' – just as they are in the
'human sciences'. Poems can be regarded as (*most* importantly)
the functioning of a social system, for example, or a linguistic
system, or a system of psychological forces, or a semiotic
system, or a system of formal devices, or a system of cultural
inter-textuality, or whatever. And because such functioning
requires no reference to concepts like intention, will, responsibility, value, or judgment, it seems to provide a basis for a kind
of literary study that appears (at a first glance) not only
'scientific' and 'value-free', but free too from what many
people disapprove of very deeply: the individual subject. Yet if
this procedure seems a way of making anything *but* moral sense
of poems, or of people, it is certainly not free of moral values, at
least in this respect: that it requires a judgment about what kind
of things poems (or people) are ultimately most like, about what
kind of sense of poems (or of people) is most fundamental and
therefore more important. For all its 'scientific' pretensions, it
necessarily competes with making other kinds of sense of poems
or people, and it privileges that understanding and its application. Hence, of course, its struggles for academic prestige
and influence. Quite apart from which is any further tendency
on the practitioner's part to assume some general political
judgment about the system he or she has in view.

Much the same goes for making sense of poems as behaviour:
that is, as determined by causal factors operating on the minds
of poets and readers. If this calls for any reference to an
individual subject, it certainly places no explanatory weight on
individual moral agency, on the subject's intentions, will,
values, judgments or responsibility. Poems are understood as
determined by language, ideologies, world-pictures, 'epi-
stemes', social conditions, relations of production, sexual
stereotypes, cultural or literary habits or conventions, the
prevailing methods of literary production and consumption –
or whatever else. It is not a new way of making moral sense of
poems. Seventeenth and eighteenth-century critics were very

conscious of the effects of 'polite civilization' and its history – of primitive social conditions on heroic poetry, for example, or of popular audiences and the English love of individual liberty on Shakespeare, or of social and poetic traditions on 'frigid caution' in the theatre, and so on. It is no accident, as the determinist would say, that literary history and historical sociology were born together. And as these early versions also show, this is (despite appearances) also a way of making *moral* sense of poems as of people, for it implies that, when value or the lack of it is in question, it should be ascribed less to any individual than to the general conditions that produce or inhibit certain kinds of human behaviour or of poetry.

But of course the most common way of making moral sense of poems as of people is by reference to agency; and with poems, the most common way of doing this has always been by regarding them as the acts of responsible agents. A poem is conceived in the way that Pope often regarded his poems, for example – that is, as something said, or written, or made, or published, or depicted, or represented, or expressed, or ima-gined (or some or all of these) by an author acting in a specific personal, social and historical context. It is judged like any other complex act – that is, in terms of its internal moral rationality: of the agent's true or false consciousness, beliefs, intentions, motives, and will to further the good or the right. (Many feminist and political judgments of poems are of this kind.) Evaluative qualities are ascribed to the author, or to his or her skill or talent or 'vision' or whatever else is regarded as the operative agency if not his ordinary person. There is no need to elaborate on this way of making moral sense of poems just because it is probably still the way most people do so most of the time; and this will probably continue to be the case, I think, no matter which contexts and aspects of a poem people will come to believe it important to consider in forming this kind of judgment.

However, as Romantic and post-Romantic critics began to see, it is also possible to regard a poem as itself an agent, especially if the 'poetic imagination' is conceived as different in essential ways from the ordinary person of the author. It is possible to think of a poem (that is, of the 'imagination' manifesting itself as the poem) as seeing, or saying, or representing, or expressing, or rendering, or exploring and ordering, or realizing, and so on. (But not, of course, writing, or making, or publishing, or amending, or a number of other things that only a person can be said to do.) This is the point of Lawrence's advice not to trust the author, but trust the tale, for example, or of a term like 'enactment'. The latter is sometimes used as if it referred only to something like onomatopoeia, the sound echoing the sense. More properly, it refers rather to the way a poem itself acts, to the moral values and qualities it manifests in how it (in some sense) *chooses* to see the world, to feel, to think, to speak, to imagine, to represent, to express, or whatever. The poem is regarded as the subject of whatever verbs of voluntary action the critic takes as relevant. He ascribes to it 'serious' intentions, for example, or 'self-critical' motives, 'fuller' understanding, or a 'sincere' will directed to truth. Any failure in its self-conduct, however, is likely to prompt the critic to explain it causally, by switching back to regarding the poem as the product either of circumstances or of the author-as-agent. Moreover, in so far as the critic has rules or criteria or norms or principles or ideals for a poem's 'conduct', he will measure it (as he measures a poet's conduct or that of any other agent) by that yardstick, and find it more or less good or valuable.

This is where I think Leavis's reply to Wellek needs qualification, for it is not entirely true that critics do not apply any such yardsticks. In previous centuries, they notoriously did. They tended to believe that there was a single, complete set of rules or norms or criteria for each 'natural kind' of poem, which was to be applied to individual examples of the kind, and the poem (or usually the author) praised or censured accordingly. Even so, of course, intelligent critics saw that these rules or norms or criteria had to be applied, as judges apply laws, with a certain amount of 'practical wisdom', not just mechanically. The critic still had to decide which requirements were relevant, how much weight was to be attached to each, how far they were to be disregarded or even amended in view of the poem's 'genius' or sublimity or originality or simply its 'grace beyond the reach of art', and how much its imperfections mattered in view of the poem's distinctive virtues and 'spirit'. But critics did not doubt that there were universal norms and criteria to apply. Pope's *Essay on Criticism* expresses such a view in the early eighteenth century, just as Wordsworth's *Preface* and Coleridge's *Biographia Literaria* adumbrate another such view, though with different norms and criteria, nearly a century later. It is perhaps less easy to see that we today also have our own norms or criteria of poetic conduct, which we also apply – either to authors or to poems – with a similar amount of 'practical wisdom'. We require a poem to have a purposiveness, for example, an *internal* intention, and to acknowledge any conditions or qualifications that affect that intention: we require it not to be sentimental, say, or indulgently un-self-critical or incoherent, or over-controlled and merely diagrammatic. We require it to be linguistically and formally 'well made' in relevant ways. We require it to realize, with the relevant degree of specificity, exactly what it is saying and doing. We require it to express perceptions, feelings and thoughts that are more than superficial or commonplace, to be more than a merely conventional or empty exercise. Then again, while we may not use such words as 'intelligent' or 'mature', probably every critical reader applies the *sort* of criterion they name, whatever he or she may accept in satisfaction of it. Psychological depth is another: we require a poem to have more and less conscious levels of meaning, related to each other in a significant, not a merely artificial or totally incomprehensible, way.

This is not to say that we need to believe (as many earlier critics did) that there is a single, exhaustive set of criteria for a good or perfect poem, or that we need any such conception as that of the ideally good or perfect poem. (How many of us nowadays would think it possible to list all the criteria of good or perfect conduct, or to hold a single, universal conception of the ideally good or perfect man?) At most, these are regulative rather than substantive ideals. Nevertheless, we can and do regard a poem as we regard a human act or agent: as an instance of certain universal norms or ideals of conduct – for example coherence, self-awareness, depth of insight, or whatever – in terms of which we describe and judge it. We judge it to exemplify coherent feeling, say, or self-critical thinking, or deep expressiveness. Indeed, our moral language largely consists of such descriptive-and-normative terms, and of examples of them, which practical wisdom draws upon in order to describe-and-judge acts or agents, and criticism in order to describe-and-judge poems or poets.

It is important not to underestimate the extent to which poetry and criticism not only use these moral languages, but also preserve them and keep them current. Since they comprise the staple medium of our 'intercourse with intellectual nature', in Johnson's phrase, and our converse about 'the reasonableness of opinions', learning them – learning how to recognize different kinds of moral qualities and respond to them, and how to apply (and if necessary to reform) their names and descriptions – is largely what moral education consists in. And in our culture over the centuries, that moral education has largely depended on reading and responding to poetry, and learning from it how to recognize, discriminate, and name human qualities and actions. When, for example, we look back at the enormous weight that sixteenth-century humanists gave to this elementary, didactic function of poetry (a function they unfortunately confused with a deliberate over-all purpose or end), we might remember how much we still need that function ourselves – for instance, in helping to develop moral awareness and habits of moral action in children. And any critic inclined to dismiss this moral function of poetry as too elementary to take seriously might find it instructive to talk to people who live under regimes that not merely abuse, but deliberately and systematically pervert, all the language of moral discourse.

But our culture includes yet another way of making moral sense of people and of poems: seeing and evaluating them not just as voluntary acts or agents, but more broadly, as manifesting lives, distinctive, individual modes of human vitality, human being.

Making this kind of moral sense of poems is not at all a 'bourgeois' invention nor even a recent one. It goes back at least as far as Plato – in fact, it is what underlay his fear of the moral power of poetry,[3] just as it was the conception of poetry as human action that underlay Aristotle's defence of its moral value. The difference reflects two rather different conceptions of people as moral beings, both of which we have inherited and use, and both of which affected English literary criticism quite early. Thus even in the sixteenth century, we find Sidney talking in 'Platonic' terms as well as Aristotelian ones – not about what a poet should 'imitate' so as to enlighten and instruct, but about the kind of spiritual life a poem can embody in itself and thereby enkindle in its readers, almost despite themselves. The poet's power lovingly to re-create the ordinary world is a morally creative power to *make* us 'know what perfection is' and *make* 'the too much loved earth more lovely'. In creating the figure of a Cyrus, say, he can *make* 'many Cyruses', to the extent that readers catch something of the same loving, attentive, aspiring moral creativity as the figure embodies. It is rather vague and high-flown, but the basic critical point of this 'Platonic' element in Sidney's *Apologie* (and in other sixteenth and seventeenth-century writers), like the similar critical point of the Longinian element a century later, deserves more attention than it usually gets. Clearly, Sidney was only too correct in his wry observation that 'these arguments will by few be understood, and by fewer granted'.[4] But I suspect they were understood and granted by the greatest literary mind of the age, and through Shakespeare then had a much wider influence on English criticism. But Shakespeare's thinking about poetry, which seems to me deeper, subtler and more far-reaching than that of most writers then or since, calls for a separate study in itself, not least because his thinking is dramatic, embodied in his plays themselves.

Sidney's reference to the conduct-ideals exemplified in a Cyrus is obviously an attempt to defuse the 'life-moral' power that Plato feared in poetry – its capacity to affect the whole human being: perceptions, sensibilities and feelings as well as reason and will – by enlisting that power into the service of orthodox sixteenth-century Christian-humanist ideals and virtues and rules of conduct. For there *is* something to fear about poetry by those who believe they have the correct recipe for human perfection – especially given most people's itch to take some mode of life as an exemplary ideal from which to draw rules and regulations of conduct. Substitute for a Cyrus, a Werther, say, or a Childe Harold, or a Courtly lover, or a Restoration 'wit', or a Man of Feeling, or an Aesthete, or a Rebel, or any of the other figures that have prompted nature to imitate art at various times, and one can begin to appreciate both the ceaseless moral curiosity and creativity of poetry, and people's constant tendency to confuse the distinctive forms of life they find in poems with models of conduct – treating the poem's moral life as if it embodied a set of universal precepts of voluntary action.

It is a mark of Dryden's good sense that he avoids this confusion in his famous remarks about Shakespeare and Jonson in his essay *Of Dramatic Poesie* – a passage that is a simple, almost paradigmatic, case of this life-moral kind of judgment:

[Shakespeare] was the man who of all Modern, and perhaps Ancient Poets, had the largest and most comprehensive soul... If I would compare... [Jonson] with *Shakespeare*, I must acknowledge him [Jonson] as the more correct Poet, but *Shakespeare* the greater wit... I admire him [Jonson], but I love *Shakespeare*.[5]

Once again, as in Sidney, we find the revealing stress on 'love': on the vital response of the whole person, awakened by and directed towards a particular individual's whole way of being alive (the kind of response that has often been confused by critics and philosophers of art with mere 'delight' or 'pleasure'). Moreover, this 'love' is pointedly distinguished by Dryden from 'admiration', the response of the rational moral self approving and taking pleasure in *any* person's voluntary conduct that is 'correct' according to universally-applicable rules or criteria. The source of the love, like its object, is clearly not just Shakespeare's voluntary acts as a poet, but his unique, incomparably large and comprehensive 'soul' or 'wit'; and Dryden is content to characterize it (very broadly), praise it, even love it, as a special gift, and to think of it as a touchstone in assessing other poets. What he quite rightly does not do is take it as exemplary, as a model according to which everyone ought to regulate his conduct. For what could be the result if they tried to do so? The touchstone would become transformed into a set of abstract ideas, and the ideas put into practice as conscious Shakespeareanizing – or with non-poets, perhaps as a sort of broad, bland, eclectic aestheticism, which calls itself 'generous', 'appreciative' and 'non-judgmental', and grows complacently self-righteous in the face of sharp and definite critical rejections: in short, a mode of being less likely to remind us of Shakespeare than of a familiar kind of plush-lined complacency.

The relevant point here is that made by George Eliot when she distinguishes sharply between the life-moral value of Rousseau's works, and their very different conduct-moral value (see pages 176–7 above). What sends an 'electric thrill' through one's 'intellectual and moral frame', enkindling and vitalizing it with the 'fire of genius', may – but may not – be what would best inform and regulate one's moral understanding and conduct. But if making moral sense of poems as 'lives' is not to take them didactically – not, that is, to evaluate them in terms appropriate merely to acts and agents – what does such a judgment involve?

It involves, I think, something much closer now to Leavis's description – and to Sidney's, come to that. First of all, it involves reading a poem so as to discover how to respond to it 'with the same Spirit that its Author writ' – to quote Pope's dictum in his *Essay on Criticism*; and Pope himself provides an example of what he meant by this in the Preface to his *Iliad*.

It is to the Strength of this amazing Invention we are to attribute that unequal'd Fire and Rapture, which is so forcible in *Homer*, that no Man of a true Poetical Spirit is Master of himself while he reads him. What he writes is of the most animated Nature imaginable; every thing moves, every thing lives, and is put in Action. If a Council be call'd, or a Battle fought, you are not coldly inform'd of what was said or done as from a third Person; the Reader is hurry'd out of himself by the Force of the Poet's Imagination, and turns in one place to a Hearer, in another to a Spectator. The Course of his Verses resembles that of the Army he describes … *They pour along like a Fire that sweeps the whole Earth before it.* 'Tis however remarkable that his fancy, which is every where vigorous, is not discover'd immediately at the beginning of his Poem in its fullest Splendor: It grows in the Progress both upon himself and others, and becomes on Fire like a Chariot-Wheel, by its own Rapidity. Exact Disposition, just Thought, correct Elocution, polish'd Numbers, may have been found in a thousand; but this Poetical *Fire*, this *Vivida vis animi*, in a very few. Even in Works where all those are imperfect or neglected, this can over-power Criticism, and make us admire even while we disapprove. Nay, where this appears, tho' attended with Absurdities, it brightens all the Rubbish about it, till we see nothing but its own Splendor.[6]

Here, to use Blake's phrase, life is clearly delighting in life. The key critical terms are not those relating to particular poetic elements or techniques and to how correctly Homer handles them, but those relating to what manifests itself *as* those particulars: energy, power and splendour. Much of that in turn is conveyed by Pope's metaphors, and they suggest not only speed, growth and light, for example, but over-powering force, consuming energy, and a light that transforms even 'rubbish'. The similarities are obvious with Sidney's emphasis on the morally creative power of poetry, but it is characteristic of Pope – whose insight in this area is deeper than anything Sidney reached – that his phrases ('no man ... is master of himself', 'the reader is hurried out of himself') also suggest that one's ordinary moral state, in which voluntary action and self-control are paramount, is destroyed or at least transcended in the creation of another and fuller one. No doubt it was Longinus who influenced Pope's language here most directly, but perhaps Dryden had an effect too. For although Pope's distinction is between 'admiring' and 'approving' rather than between 'loving' and 'admiring', the point of the distinction is much the same: the response of the whole being to a particular mode of life is set against the response of the moral reason to any of 'a thousand' poetic agents whose actions are 'exact', 'just', 'correct', and so on.

But even here, it is obvious that a life-moral judgment involves more than just reading with the same spirit that the author writ. It involves answering to the spirit of the author with one's own – loving it perhaps, or not, but in any case understanding and 'placing' it in relation to others. It involves, that is, the engagement – and often the extension – of one's deepest normative sense of human possibilities.

That sense does not arise only out of one's own individual self, of course. For some people, it is still, as it was for centuries, primarily founded in and regulated by religion. (God is not quite as dead as Nietzsche claimed.) For other people it is founded primarily in politics. For others again, primarily in 'gender'. (In some, to whom ways of being alive are merely 'life-styles' adaptable and changeable at will, it seems to be founded primarily in the advertising business.) For the modern 'humanist', however, a normative sense of human possibilities needs to be more various, more liberal, less fixed and formu-larized, than any of these allows. For him or her, it is *primarily* founded in, and regulated by, nothing more restrictive than 'culture' – culture understood in this context as a highly complex (not to say tangled), yet creatively open and ever-changing, range of moral 'lives' and life-moral evaluations. For the 'humanist' critic making this kind of moral sense of a poem, culture is not a static collection of 'the best which has been thought and said in the world', as Arnold put it, but rather (as Arnold should have meant) a living tissue of defeasible, decayable, but yet rational and renewable, *judgments* – judg-ments, for example, of what *is* 'the best which has been thought and said'. Some of the attacks on Arnold, by T. S. Eliot on the one hand and Leftist critics on the other, turn on this question of primacy; other attacks turn on the limited and 'bourgeois' selection of possibilities and evaluations that Arnold identified as culture. Nevertheless, I think he was right in principle. Even if traditional criticism has sometimes brought modes of life to be judged at the bar of religion or politics, it has always been able and willing (at least since the Renaissance) to bring religion or politics to be judged at the bar of a wider sense of human variety and possibilities; and Arnold also seems to me to have been right in claiming that this wider sense largely derives from, and is regulated by, reading and responding to literature, poems. (Reading them as poems, I mean, not as Holy Scriptures.) It is true, of course, that the substantial content of culture (or tradition) – *which* poems, for instance – must always be a particular selection from the whole; but precisely because it is laden with explicit and implicit values, it is always open to criticism and revision. It is true that some of the values it bears can be illegitimately privileged by being enshrined in a fixed canon, or by being identified with the whole of an open and many-stranded culture, or by being treated as beyond dispute in some other way. On the other hand, it is in that culture, in the other strands and traditions it includes, that we generally find the moral possibilities, and the moral language, with which to contest these values, or this privilege, or even this concern with origins and history.

For this kind of evaluation, however, moral language does not consist only of general and abstract terms and examples of them. Its key terms are now particular – unique individual modes of life. And here again I think Arnold was right, at least in principle, and Leavis after him – though I do not much like Leavis's phrase (in the passage quoted above) about an 'organization' of 'similarly "placed" things', which – as he would be the first to point out if he had noticed it – makes poems seem too like pots and the critic's mind too like a well-arranged museum. But it is true, I think, that a sense of human possibilities is thinkable, specifiable, only in concrete terms – not as a set of abstract ideas, but as particular modes of life, which serve, not as examples of universal rules and criteria, but as something like 'touchstones'.

Whatever we think of the 'touchstones' Arnold himself offered, or his naive belief that their character and value would be self-evident, he does seem to have half-seen this quite crucial point. In making sense of poems as 'lives', one is responding to, and also bringing to bear, conceptions, thoughts, intuitions, that are impossible to name, or to analyse, or even to characterize, entirely in ordinary, categorial language. What one is trying to capture and evaluate is an individual, dynamically-informing 'spirit' or 'principle of life' – something that manifests itself not just in these particulars, as if it were somehow extractable from them, nor 'through' them, as Pope puts it, for that may suggest they can be left behind. It manifests itself rather *as* these particulars. This is why first-hand acquaintance with the poem is necessary for any life-moral judgment, in a way that it is not, I think, for a conduct-moral one: in the latter case, a poem – like an act or an agent – *can* be fully characterized for the purpose in hand in ordinary categorial language. One can think *about* a life in such language, of course; but thinking *of* it, having it available for 'placing' in relation to other possibilities, requires capturing its specificity and also that of the other possibilities: by demonstrative quotation, for example, or (as I suggested in chapter 3) by using metaphor, or story, or a sort of mimicking, or one of the other means of poetry itself, as part of the characterizing-evaluating process. A descriptive list of the poem's qualities will not do, nor even an account of the causal or structural interconnections between its qualities, though this is getting nearer. What is required is a vital sense and 'sense' here reaches toward 'sensory' and also 'sensibility' of its distinctive vitality.

In as much as the particulars of a life include not just voluntary acts, or what can be thought of as such, but the whole range of active being – perceptions, capacities, dispositions, susceptibilities, fantasies, feelings, passions, tastes, and so on – terms applicable to conduct may change their meanings somewhat. In making sense of a mode of life, one will have to use terms like 'intention', for example, or 'desire', or 'will', but often in an extended, metaphorical, 'as-if' sense – though this is presumably one of the reasons why some American critics grew uneasy about the so-called 'intentionalist fallacy'. If one is rather literal-minded, and also supposes that any value-judgment can derive only from an agent-centred, legal-religious moral code of conduct, then any critical talk about 'intention' will seem like an ominous prelude to censuring poets, or 'dismissing' poems, for failing to measure up to the relevant criteria. But in life-moral judgments one is not applying such a code or such criteria in that way – not, that is, unless one is fortunate enough already to know the universal, ideal pattern of human life. Without that, one has to treat every particular life as new, unprecedented, essentially (not just contingently) individual, and capable of disclosing some unchartered aspect of reality; and the terms in which one characterizes-and-evaluates it will have to be correspondingly complex, multiple, often metaphorical, open-ended, and not even looking much like a set of specifiable criteria.

III

Although life-moral and conduct-moral judgments imply different, and perhaps irreconcilable, conceptions of poetry (as of people), it seems to me one of the great strengths of the English critical tradition that it has not only combined both kinds of concern, but has always been ready to have one kind lead the mind over into the other. Indeed, it is often the friction between the two that gives interest and depth to the criticism, as it does to the work it is discussing – and as it generally does to human experience as well. On the other hand, it is sometimes hard to distinguish between the two kinds of judgment. What looks at first sight like one can turn out to be the other; the difference may lie not so much in the explicit terms of the judgment as in its implicit 'spirit' and point. Here are two examples, one from Johnson, the other from Leavis. The first is a passage from the 'Life of Pope':

About this time Warburton began to make his appearance in the first ranks of learning. He was a man of vigorous faculties, a mind fervid and vehement, supplied by incessant and unlimited enquiry, with wonderful extent and variety of knowledge; which yet had not oppressed his imagination nor clouded his perspicacity. To every work he brought a memory full fraught, together with a fancy fertile of original combinations, and at once exerted the powers of the scholar, the reasoner, and the wit. But his knowledge was too multifarious to be always exact, and his pursuits were too eager to be always cautious. His abilities gave him a haughty confidence, which he disdained to conceal or mollify; and his impatience of opposition disposed him to treat his adversaries with such contemptuous superiority as made his readers commonly his enemies, and excited against the advocate the wishes of some who favoured the cause. He seems to have adopted the Roman Emperor's determination, 'oderint dum metuant'; he used no allurements of gentle language, but wished to compel rather than persuade.

His style is copious without selection, and forcible without neatness; he took the words that presented themselves; his diction is coarse and impure, and his sentences are unmeasured.[7]

At first glance, this looks like a straightforwardly conduct-moral judgment. The verbs in the second paragraph all refer to voluntary acts on Warburton's part: selecting the coarse and impure instead of the decent, not making means neatly appropriate to ends, not measuring by the yardstick of the pleasing or the effective. The implication is clearly, and quite rightly, that the man could and should have acted (as a writer) better, more correctly, than he did.

Yet in the context created by the first paragraph, the qualities that Johnson picks out in the second seem to apply not just to Warburton's acts as a writer, but to his whole consciousness and sensibility, indeed his whole way of being alive, including the form of his life in time. His voluntary acts are obviously an important and integral part of that way of being alive, but only a part; so that when it comes, the last word, 'unmeasured', seems to focus not only the 'spirit' in which Warburton wrote, but the 'spirit' in which he lived.

It is here that the 'spirit' of Johnson's own prose is important. All the terms of energy and power, plenitude and pride, in which he catches Warburton's spirit, are themselves visibly 'measured' by contrast: given full weight, yet nicely and neatly discriminated. The syntax of the second sentence gathers pace; the word 'yet' heralds both a logical and temporal reversal; 'oppression' and 'cloud' are no more than possibilities that slow down, but do not as yet arrest, the forward movement of the prose and of the life: 'oppression', we may notice, foreshadowing the devastating legal and political metaphors to come, 'cloud' foreshadowing the eventual self-negating of the mind's light, its 'knowledge' and 'pursuits'. The arrest takes place with the opening of the fourth sentence: it is as if Warburton's life, like the energy of Johnson's prose, slams into the 'but' of two hard moral truths: that even knowledge can be too plentiful; and that pursuits can be too eager. What Johnson now fastens on is the way that Warburton's very force entangles itself with strength. Johnson analyses the process, but he also captures a sense of it in the rhythms and analogies. The result is that, beyond the conduct-moral judgments ('haughty', 'disdained', 'impatience' and so on), there gradually emerges another, holistic one, of the kind that *Rasselas* and 'The Vanity of Human Wishes', for example, are full of. For Warburton's life begins to show something like an inward shape or form, which embraces all of its outward manifestations, both the voluntary and the non-voluntary ones, and makes them all appear as the working out of a deeper necessity. It is the necessity of a formal principle, however, not just of causal consequences. For Warburton's life is seen as having carried in its central principle of vehement energy the principle of its own eventual distortions and limits. Being what he was, for instance, the qualities of his style, diction and sentences evince the kind of being he was. Thus he is seen as a voluntary agent, morally responsible for his acts and faults, for the way he chose to use his natural talents and capacities. But yet he is also seen as, in some obscure way, the victim of the particular kind of life he was born with, given by no choice of his own – a life vehement, fervid, disposed to realize and exercise its inherent power. In the end, there-fore, the conduct-moral judgment – that Warburton would have been a better man, more virtuous, more admirable, more successful even, had he acted more 'correctly', swivels around to an alternative, equally valid, life-moral judgment: that Warburton's 'spirit' – which includes both the agent *and* the victim – would have been less distinctively, less power-fully, indeed less splendidly and imperiously alive, had he been more like his critic (and the critic's readers too perhaps), able to ponder, to select, to discriminate, to be decorous and to measure.

Altogether, the passage is a miniature but wholly charac-teristic example of Johnson's own 'spirit', and also of his deeper critical procedures in the *Lives*. Nor could the passage have a more telling point than within a critical account of the life and works and 'genius' of Pope.

By contrast, the passage from Leavis looks at first sight like a straightforwardly life-moral judgment. It is obviously directed at Milton's capacities, dispositions and states of mind, at the 'spirit' in which he 'writ', the quality of the 'life' that manifests itself in the poem, rather than with measuring his voluntary acts as a poet by specifiable criteria or yardsticks:

[Milton's] strength is of the kind that we indicate when, distinguishing between intelligence and character, we lay the stress on the latter; it is a strength, that is, involving sad disabilities. He has 'character', moral grandeur, moral force; but he is, for the purposes of his undertaking, disastrously single-minded and simple-minded. He reveals everywhere a dominating sense of righteousness and a complete incapacity to question or explore its significance and conditions. This defect of intelligence is a defect of imagination. He offers as ultimate for our worship mere brute assertive will, though he condemns it unwittingly by his argument and by glimpses of his own finer human standard. His volume of moral passion owes its strength too much to innocence – a guileless unawareness of the subtleties of egotism – to be an apt agent for projecting an 'ordered whole of experience.'[8]

But, as with Johnson, it is the 'spirit' of the judgment that may give us pause about what it is really directed at. Even if one agrees with its general reservations about *Paradise Lost*, it is hard to miss the polemical edge in its tone, the tendency to push a case: '*sad* disabilities', '*disastrously* single-minded', 'a *complete* incapacity', '*mere* brute assertive will', '*guileless* innocence'. The 'spirit' of the passage begins to seem rather like that of counsel for the prosecution.

That impression is confirmed, I think, by the apparent concessions, especially 'his *strength*' and 'moral *grandeur*, *moral* force'. In what, one wonders, does Leavis see this 'strength' in *Paradise Lost*? What does 'moral grandeur' mean, if it can be so glaringly deficient? More particularly, what evinces 'moral grandeur' and 'moral force'? It is hard to believe that one would want to use such terms at all if they can go along with such moral stupidity as this. In other words, one begins to wonder about the correctness of the categorial terms Leavis chooses in order to describe the poetry. Another consideration tugs in the same direction. When we come to examine the account, nothing that Leavis says really relates the 'moral grandeur' and 'force' to the accompanying incapacities in any *internal* way. The 'but' in the second sentence is (like Johnson's) a pivot in the judgment; unlike Johnson's, though, it captures nothing in the nature of the 'life'. It marks only Leavis's switch from one list (strengths) to another (disabilities), and this precisely because the strengths are not specified, not examined, and therefore cannot be seen as in any way integral to the whole. In fact, the more we look the more the talk about strengths seems to be a mere gesture, a nominal, tactical concession to the defence, to the standard view of Milton. Either that, or it simply refers to the ambitious size and scope of the moral enterprise Milton decided to undertake in *Paradise Lost*.

The effect of all this is to underline two implicit points in the judgment. What may make Milton's strengths and weaknesses seem, at first glance, to go naturally together is the implicit reference to a familiar Victorian type, which descends from a familiar Puritan type, and to our knowledge of the sharply critical analyses of the type in Jacobean drama and the Victorian novel. Milton is seen as a sort of combination of, say, Arnold of Rugby, the young Dorothea Brooke, and Zeal-of-the-Land Busy. The idealistic ambitions and the actual disabilities are therefore pretty much what we would expect; indeed, the disabilities are so large that we wonder how even Milton could have missed them. This goes with the other implicit reference: to Milton's choosing to write *Paradise Lost* and to continue with it as he did. It is only in relation to *that* that these are 'disabilities'; it can only be to this extended voluntary act that the prosecuting counsel's tone is directed; and the case he is putting to us is that Milton's moral disabilities for the task were so great, so glaring, and of so familiar a kind, that even a touch of ordinary human 'guile' would have seen them. In other words, that Milton did not show the moral awareness that one would expect of any 'reasonable man' in the circumstances, so that, although he was clearly too innocent to think of defrauding anybody, his actions do show a significant degree of negligence, of what might be called culpable stupidity. Proceeding as he did is clearly not the way his critic (or his critic's reader) would have acted – even if he were of no more than average, reasonable, moral intelligence. In short, the life-moral judgment – that the 'life' that manifests itself in *Paradise Lost* has these strengths and limitations – swivels around to a conduct-moral one: that Milton has to be held blameworthy, culpably responsible, not of course for having the moral nature he had, but for not mistrusting and scrutinizing it. There is this yardstick, after all:

the modicum of critical self-awareness that is required of any moral agent, let alone one who decides to write a grand poem justifying the ways of God to man.

What neither Johnson nor Leavis do, however, is what Victorian critics were rather prone to: simply confuse the two kinds of moral judgment, or conflate them, or collapse one into the other, as if the highest mode of life were self-evidently that which treated moral conduct as the highest good. In criticism, this comes out as a blank disjunction, a non-sequitur, where there is a swivel in Johnson or Leavis. John Stuart Mill is a case in point. In his Inaugural Address in 1867 at St Andrews, for example, he seems at one point to want to talk about the life-moral value of poetry – the way that 'the arts of expression tend to keep alive and active the feelings they express'. What he actually comes out with, however, is this sort of thing:

It would be difficult for anybody to imagine that 'Rule Britannia,' for example, or 'Scots wha hae,' had no permanent influence on the higher region of human character...

[Poetry] brings home to us all those aspects of life which take hold of our nature on its unselfish side, and lead us to identify our joy and grief with the good or ill of the system of which we form a part; and all those solemn or pensive feelings, which, without having any direct application to conduct, incline us to take life seriously, and predispose us to the reception of anything which comes before us in the shape of duty. Who does not feel a better man after a course of Dante, or of Wordsworth, or, I will add, of Lucretius or the *Georgics*, or after brooding over Gray's *Elegy*, or Shelley's 'Hymn to Intellectual Beauty'?[9]

Mill's own response to Wordsworth was not what he says here, of course; but neither was it what he says it was in this later passage in the *Autobiography*:

What made Wordsworth's poems a medicine for my state of mind, was that they expressed, not mere outward beauty, but states of feeling, and of thought coloured by feeling, under the excitement of beauty. They seemed to be the very culture of the feelings, which I was in quest of. In them I seemed to draw from a source of inward joy, of sympathetic and imaginative pleasure, which could be shared in by all human beings; which had no connexion with struggle or imperfection, but would be made richer by every improvement in the physical or social condition of mankind. From them I seemed to learn what would be the perennial sources of happiness, when all the greater evils of life shall have been removed. And I felt myself at once better and happier as I came under their influence.[10]

In fact, Mill's response to Wordsworth was far more radical, far wider, and much less readily specifiable in its nature and effects than this suggests. Indeed, on this account of it, Wordsworth seems to have merely confirmed Mill in his unhappy disjunctive conception of 'feeling' on the one side and 'thought' on the other. Shakespeare, I believe, would have made much better medicine for his underlying state of mind, if only that state of mind had not prevented him from seeing how and why. But in any case, Wordsworth's full effect on Mill actually required the *whole* of the *Autobiography* to define it. For even Wordsworth altered not just Mill's capacity to feel, but also the whole way he saw the world (and himself), the way he thought about it, the direction of his interests, the friendships he made – indeed, the texture and shape of his entire life. If it made him a 'better man', it was not just because it enabled him to understand his moral purposes and to act better as a moral agent. In short, the moral sense he actually made of Wordsworth was not at all like the effects of 'Rule Britannia' on 'the higher region of human character'.

Similarly with Arnold's response to Wordsworth. His essay on him (1873) obviously owes a debt or two to Mill's account, but for him too Wordsworth had had a profound effect on his moral life. As he put it in 'Memorial Verses', written nearly thirty years before the essay, Wordsworth (like himself)

> upon a wintry clime
> Had fallen – on this iron time
> Of doubts, disputes, distractions, fears.
> He found us when the age had bound
> Our souls in its benumbing round;
> He spoke, and loosed our heart in tears.
> He laid us as we lay at birth
> On the cool flowery lap of earth,
> Smiles broke from us and we had ease;
> The hills were round us, and the breeze
> Went o'er the sun-lit fields again;

Our foreheads felt the wind and rain.
Our youth return'd; for there was shed
On spirits that had long been dead,
Spirits dried up and closely furl'd,
The freshness of the early world.[11]

It is true, of course, that Arnold also thought Wordsworth limited, less 'comprehensive', beside Goethe; Wordsworth's eyes, he acknowledged, had 'averted their ken from half of human fate'. Nevertheless, for all its sentimental vagueness, his judgment in 'Memorial Verses' is directed to the mode of life realized in Wordsworth's best poetry. The moral value of that poetry is located in its vital, and hence re-vitalizing, powers, or (what is the same thing) its giving a sharper and fuller reality to the world: 'our foreheads *felt* the wind and rain'.

Arnold's essay on Wordsworth fortunately leaves the 'tears' and the 'smiles' out of it, but it too says something about the moral vitality of Wordsworth's poetry: it speaks, for example, of the 'joy' that, with 'extraordinary power', the poetry 'makes' us 'share', and of its 'new and sacred energy'.[12] And yet the way Arnold put it, though less reductive than Mill's, sometimes makes it look as if the 'extraordinary power' of the poetry is a separate rhetorical quality that is somehow merely super-added to its *real* moral substance: to the right moral feeling and action it exhibits and encourages. The 'joy' it makes us share, for example, is 'the joy offered us in nature, the joy offered to us in the simple primary affections and duties'. Admittedly, it is one of Arnold's points that Wordsworth's greatness lies largely in his 'feeling' the connection between a re-vitalized sense of the world and the primary affections and duties, between moral life and moral conduct. But by simply telescoping one into the other (rather as Wordsworth himself often did), he ends up not having much to say about the nature and quality of Wordsworth's poetic vitality, and making it seem basically a matter of effective edification.

The truth is that the moral life of a poem may well not be edifying, nor even instructively unedifying either. The value of encountering it may be simply that of encountering another mode of life than our own. But it is probably the belief on the part of some Christian humanists (and other worthies) that a poem's moral life ought to be edifying or instructive, and only counts if it is – the moralistic outlook that conflates the two kinds of moral valuation – which has persuaded many people that *any* moral evaluation of poetry nowadays represents only a 'system of thought and belief that has had its day'. This seems to me to mistake a part of the English critical tradition for the whole, and to miss in how wide a sense it is 'moral' and 'humanist'. Neither term is necessarily bound up with a particular, fixed moral code or a particular, fixed ideal conception of Man – much less with the telescoped code and conception of 'bourgeois' or 'Victorian' moralism or of more recent variants of the same thing. Equally important, neither term is necessarily bound up with a solely 'mimetic', or realistic, or symbolic, or indeed any other single conception of poetry – much less a didactic or edifying one. What they *are* bound up with is no more nor less than a serious concern, on the part of poets and readers alike, with making moral sense of human experience and modes of human experience in the ways I have been trying to indicate.

This is why I do not believe that evaluative criticism is any more dispensable or out-dated that it has ever been. It may be out of fashion in the academic study of literature, though it was never much *in* fashion there – and given the quite common academic misunderstanding of what critical judgment consists in, it is perhaps not much of a loss if it is. But one need look no further than the nearest weekly review to find evaluative literary criticism still alive and flourishing, and still for the same good reason – that poetry and the criticism of poetry comprise an irreplaceable form of moral thinking.

Here, to take an example that happens to be at hand, is a recent reviewer on a book of Henry Miller's:

Such prescience on Miller's part is worth attention:

'Joyce, who employs a dead language, is, by the irony of things, being hailed as a life-bringer. This remarkable man, whose activity can be likened only to that of a powerful, unisolated microbe, has done more than any man of our time to hasten the process of dissolution. The astounding luxuriance of his language is not a sign of new life, not the exuberance of vitality, but rather the manifestation of a cancer which is ravaging our souls. He proliferates with such virulence that the body of our literature offers not a single point of resistance. There is not even the sign of an antitoxin making its appearance'.

Like all the intelligent spirits of his time, Joyce knew that the way forward was down, down to the forgotten fragments of mythic memory, the original springs of human narrative; and yet, as Miller sees, such descent is dangerous: 'So much has been said about the revival of a mantic personality, about a possible renascence of art through tapping the unconscious leaven of the mind – in all of which there is a ring of truth were it not also unfortunately the death knell which is sounding.' For archaeologists of the unconscious the danger is twofold: first is the temptation to stay down there, paddling about in pools of verbal narcissism. The second danger, more important, is the temptation to shine the torch of science on this dark stuff instead of reverently planting it in new soil: to know it rather than be known through it.[13]

It may be rather ludicrous for one critic, myself, to be quoting another quoting yet another about a writer, no matter how important the writer is; but I do so for two reasons. The first is that, in its minuscule way, it illustrates something of how the 'conversation' of a culture works; and the second is that both Miller and the reviewer touch on yet another reason why many people fear judgments, especially life-moral ones.

It is often very hard to make moral sense of a poem, and sometimes even harder to put into words exactly the moral sense one does make of it – and the more complexly disturbing the poem, the harder it is. With Joyce, for example, it is amazing how little genuinely evaluative criticism one can find of *Ulysses* and (more especially) of *Finnegans Wake*. Both books seem to have leaped straight from being no more than a scandal to conventional orthodox academics, to being unquestionable academic classics; and I say 'unquestionable' advisedly, since I know how scandalous it now seems to conventional orthodox academics (particularly in America) to judge the vitality of either work, as I would judge that of both, to be sometimes dubious and limited in important ways. In fact, *Finnegans Wake* has become the very ideal, the acme, of contemporary 'textu- ality' – the replacement for Homer and Shakespeare – without, as far as I know, any generally convincing answer having been given to the sort of critical challenge that Miller expresses; and it is hard to avoid the suspicion that one of the main reasons for this is simply that *Finnegans Wake* fits so snugly with the sort of thing that academic study often does with poetry – that being one of the book's chief limitations. For if no one can read the book – as one might read the *Iliad*, say, or *King Lear*, in a way that engages, extends and challenges one's moral understanding and imagination and one's capacities for practical judgment – anyone can study and 'theorize' under its aegis, in a way that engages, extends and challenges only one's ingenuity and capacity for intellectual and verbal free-association.

Nor is the spirit in which its author writ *Finnegans Wake* likely to disturb anyone studying it. Open oneself to the spirit in which the author writ the *Iliad* or *King Lear*, and try to judge *it* in relation to one's deepest sense of human possibilities, and who can tell what disquieting moral capacities or incapacities might reveal themselves within? If Plato's fear of poetry was not misplaced, neither is the common fear of life-moral judgments. But there are academic ways of studying poetry that maintain an insulating detachment from the raw, difficult-to-handle stuff itself – ways that keep it essentially external to the self, and prevent the difficulties of trying to judge its life from bothering one. This can be achieved by a prior and total commitment to some 'ism', since that can very readily obviate the need for the moral thinking and exploration, including self-exploration, of a poem. Clearly it is much easier to avoid any engagement that involves putting one's own familiar moral self at risk. Or at least temporarily avoid the risk – for in the long run there is no morally neutral space in which we can be agents or lives.

CHAPTER 8

Afterword : some limits of philosophy?

It must be obvious that my argument all through this book owes a great deal to Iris Murdoch's *The Sovereignty of Good* – a book which so deepened my understanding of the moral aspects of literature that my debts to it are now much too basic and too pervasive to be spelt out in detail. But it must also be obvious that some of the particular points in my argument are very like views expressed by other recent English and American moral philosophers: Cora Diamond, Mary Mothersill, Richard Rorty, Stuart Hampshire, Bernard Williams, Alasdair MacIntyre and Martha Nussbaum, to mention only a few. Most of these also give literature an important place in ethics – so important, in fact, that taken together they provide a 'humanist' critic with a body of theory sufficient to explain and support a focus on the moral dimensions of literature.[1] But while the critic is right to look to them, they supply explanation and support only up to a point. If literature is a distinctive and irreplaceable kind of moral thinking, as I have argued, it is because there *is* (to recall Hume's observation) 'a part of ethics left by nature to baffle all the pride of philosophy'. It seems to me significant that, however widely a philosopher conceives the scope of the 'moral', he or she tends to think primarily of the conduct-moral, when it comes to discussing specific works of literature. This happens in various ways, but even philosophers who want ethics centred on lives rather than just on actions – generally 'Aristotelians' of one kind or another – often seem in the end not really to mean it; not, at any rate, in a strong enough sense of *lives*.

It may be useful therefore to discuss very briefly a few

examples of such philosophical arguments to suggest where and why I think a 'humanist' literary critic might well have reservations about them: firstly, one or two arguments that do seem to be based on a suitably wide conception of the moral; and then two or three in an 'Aristotelian' vein about ethics and the relationship this is supposed to have with literature.

I

To begin with, I hope it is clear enough by now why I would agree with Cora Diamond, that most moral philosophers confine the sphere of the 'moral' too narrowly to *actions*. In their view, it is 'our actions, our choices, which give a particular shape to the life we lead; to be able to lead whatever the good life for a human being is *is* to be able to make such choices well'. Against this, Diamond points to the very different conception of the moral sphere expressed, for example, in two phrases of Iris Murdoch's: 'the texture of man's being' and 'the nature of his personal vision'; and as Diamond says, it is this larger conception that is especially relevant to literature.

We cannot see the moral interest of literature unless we recognize gestures, manners, habits, turns of speech, turns of thought, styles of face as morally expressive – of an individual or of a people. The intelligent description of such things is part of the intelligent, the sharp-eyed, description of life, of what matters, makes differences, in human lives.

To this, a literary critic would have to agree – but also have to add (what Diamond does not mention) the diachronic rhythm(s) and pattern(s) of a man's being as well as its texture – something that also cannot be adequately expressed in conceptual terms. But Diamond is right about the effect of our conception of the 'moral' on such matters as *where* we find moral significance in a literary work; the *kind* of moral thought and imagination a work expresses and invites; and the power of literature to remind us constantly that one of our deepest moral difficulties is understanding and *describing* facts – something for which we need (as she says) such qualities as 'moral energy, discipline, imagination, creativity, wit, care, patience, tact, and delicacy'.[2]

Conversely, I hope it is also clear why I would disagree with any new attempt (like those of John Stuart Mill and R. M. Hare discussed in chapter 1) to restrict the term 'moral' only to judgments of people's conduct, while judgments about their 'emotional' states are shunted off as 'aesthetic' on the grounds that, as one recent philosophical paper explains, this 'allows us to preserve our intuition that morality implies choice'. Thus 'moral' judgments are supposed to be those that 'lead us to blame, and even punish'; 'aesthetic' ones, on the other hand, those that only 'justify avoiding the person, warning friends against the person, and hoping our children do not turn out like him or her'.

We like the generous spirit... because a generous spirit is beautiful, the sort of thing that is a pleasure to behold, and misanthropy is ugly... We blame, reproach, and punish someone who has committed a moral delict; we withdraw from, feel revulsion toward, someone with an ugly soul. We shun the misanthrope and embrace the big hearted not because we blame the misanthrope for becoming such, but simply for being such. In this way judgments of character based on the emotions a person feels, the impulses she or he displays, are like aesthetic judgments.[3]

As a matter of fact, there are better reasons than a recognition of people's emotions for the temptation to call life-moral judgments 'aesthetic'. Our judgments of human lives, for example, are holistic, and so of course are judgments of the life manifested in a literary work; what is more, a great many works of literature are concerned specifically with depicting and judging different human 'souls', different modes of human life, in relation to one another. Even so, nothing seems to be gained and a good deal is lost by labelling as 'aesthetic' our judgments of emotional states and so finding a place for supposedly 'romantic virtues' such as 'integrity, sincerity, and spontaneity, in...judging a life'. Why 'romantic'? Why not simply 'moral virtues'?

This is related to the reasons I think a literary critic would

disagree with one of the sharpest and liveliest recent aesthe-
ticians, Mary Mothersill, when she concludes that

> all attempts to force aesthetics into the mold of ethical theory must end
> in paradox and confusion. The two have, as it were, different centers
> of gravity. The pre-theoretical intuitions for ethics are themselves
> lawlike: they are the elementary rules of right conduct that one ought
> to keep one's promises, alleviate suffering, tell the truth, work to
> preserve standards of equity and fairness, treat others with respect,
> and so forth. These rules serve as controls both for casuistry and for
> speculative theory...Reasons for acting, reasons for judging a par-
> ticular act or policy of action right or wrong, reasons for accepting or
> rejecting an ethical theory are all linked directly or indirectly to
> elementary rules of right conduct.
>
> In the domain of taste there are no interesting laws or 'good-making
> characteristics' and no principles or 'critical features'. Given even a
> sketchy description of Brutus's act, one can say: 'He may have had
> reasons but nonetheless he was Caesar's *friend*!' No description, no
> matter how detailed, of a work of art entitles an analogous weighing of
> merit and demerit.[4]

Applied to works of art, this seems wholly persuasive – if, that is,
one thinks of ethics, as Mothersill does here (and as American
philosophers generally do) only in terms of conduct-morality. If
one thinks of it in life-moral terms, however, Mothersill's
conclusion is much less persuasive, and unpersuasive for a
reason implicit in her own point later in her book about
knowing or understanding works of art as individuals:

> the understanding or knowledge that is focused on an individual, that
> is, has as grammatical object not a propositional clause but a name or
> a description, is difficult to characterize coherently...[It] admits of
> degree...[It] is related (somehow or other) to what one knows *about*
> [the object]...and also to various appropriate skills such as knowing
> how to present, describe, perform [the object]...But I do not know of
> any serious attempt to characterize the relationship between 'know-
> ing', 'knowing that', and 'knowing how' which can be brought to
> bear on the situation in aesthetics.[5]

That is true, and although Mothersill is concerned here only
with the individuality of serious works of art, exactly the same
applies to the individuality of human lives or modes of life. As I

have argued, even if a mode of life is shared by a group (Pericles' Athens, to recall Mill's examples, or Calvin's Geneva) it is still knowable in the relevant sense, and capable of being evaluated as a mode of life, only as an individual – if for no other reason than its necessarily specific time and place, its defining contingencies. To grasp such a mode of life, or the life of some of Shakespeare's characters (of Macbeth, say, or Cleopatra), or the life or 'spirit' of the play itself, or of any novel or poem, is in every important respect like grasping people as moral beings: it is to think *of* them as well as *about* them, and so to reach towards a fuller, intensified sense of the individual – a sense of its distinctive reality as well as of its (or his or her) distinctive make-up and qualities. As Mothersill says, 'What Hume is describing [in his essay, 'Of the Standard of Taste'] ... is both more familiar and harder to describe: it is the process of getting to know a particular work of art as one might get to know a person.'[6]

The expressive character of an individual is a function of its aesthetic properties, grasped as a unity; it is a *Gestalt* property. It is the individual's *anima* or soul. If we choose to speak this way, and I can see nothing against it, then, contrary to Kant's usage, every individual will have a soul, but, in keeping with Kant's distinction, some beautiful individuals will have souls that deserve devotion and demand attention and respect; others will not. Some things, like a pebble or a clear and cloudless sky, have simple souls. They please in virtue of their aesthetic properties, but those properties once noted and appreciated, do not invite prolonged critical analysis. Decorative formal designs ... may be elegant, intricate, admirable, and yet, once understood, easily forgotten. All persons and some works of art – those to which we pay homage – have souls that are complex, multi-layered, and partly hidden. They are not to be taken in at a glance, and long study leaves room for fresh discoveries.[7]

This last passage seems to me right in its main direction, but curiously awry in its main assumption. The 'expressive character' of an individual is indeed grasped as a unity; it can indeed be called the individual's '*anima*' or 'soul'; and all persons, and some works of art, do have 'souls' that are complex and multi-layered and require attention and respect. But to return to the first sentence of this quotation, are the properties that produce the expressive character of an individual *person* really 'aesthetic'? Is 'aesthetic' the right word for the critical attention and understanding required by individual persons (as by serious works of art)? In both cases, the obvious term for the properties expressive of the individual *person's* 'soul', for those properties we point to in describing-and-judging someone as a (mode of) life, is surely 'moral' – nor is it any abuse of the term to apply it to the 'soul' of a serious work of art too, though not to pebbles or cloudless skies. The trouble with Mothersill's argument here seems to come from her general philosophical belief that 'beauty' is common to works of art and natural objects, and is the proper object of 'taste' or criticism and of 'aesthetic' inquiry.

Even so, Mothersill's main point here does reinforce the general argument that 'taste' or criticism is a matter of understanding and evaluating a work *as* an individual (in the same sense that a person is an individual), and that it is therefore a form of 'practical wisdom' rather than the application of pre-determined ideal models of life, or pre-determined criteria or rules or theory. As Mothersill sees, literary criticism cannot be codified; on the contrary, it is necessarily 'continuous both in aim and in methods with the most informal procedures of everyday life'. As a kind of teaching, it 'aims to modify feeling and redirect attention rather than to impart information or show students how to do complicated things'. And with her eye on such critics as Lionel Trilling, John Bayley, Susan Sontag, Edmund Wilson and Harold Rosenberg, she quite rightly insists on the mixture in their work of 'appreciation, technical lore, sociological speculation, *Geistesgeschichte*, critical theory, polemics, and expressions of personal preference'[8] – as well as the relative critical evaluations grounded in the informal practical wisdom that brings such different considerations together and weighs them in relation to each other. And of course this also applies to our own evaluative judgments, including our judgments of such critics.

One philosopher who does see why the 'moral' and the 'aesthetic' cannot be sharply distinguished, and who therefore seems at first sight not restricted to a merely conduct-moral view of literature and literary criticism but concerned precisely with their life-moral nature, is Richard Rorty in his book *Contingency, Irony and Solidarity* (1989). Rorty puts his points about literature in terms of his general attack on 'metaphysics' – the belief in a (chimerical) ultimate truth, which he sees as characteristic of religion, science and philosophy in the past – in favour of what he calls 'irony', the belief, which he sees as characteristic of literary criticism in the present age, only in different 'final vocabularies' for describing and re-describing the world in the light of what we want to do with it.

On the face of it, Rorty's argument might seem highly congenial to the literary critic. Literary criticism, he thinks, has now risen to 'pre-eminence' over the old 'metaphysical' disciplines in 'the high culture of the democracies'. Speaking as a literary critic, I must confess that I have not experienced this change myself, but according to Rorty, it has also 'widened the gap between the intellectuals and the public'. For the 'public rhetoric of modern liberal societies' (in contrast, presumably, with the rhetoric of professional 'intellectuals' with one another) is shot through not only with 'metaphysics', but also with the distinction between the moral and the 'merely' aesthetic. For the function of that distinction is indeed, as Rorty says, often to 'relegate "literature" to a subordinate position within culture and to suggest that novels and poems are irrelevant to moral reflection'. (Or – Rorty might have added – vice versa.) Indeed, for the contemporary critic, 'literature' includes 'just about every sort of book which might conceivably have moral relevance – might conceivably alter one's sense of what is possible and important'.[9]

For Rorty in this vein, it clearly seems to be the 'moral' in a large sense, the life-moral, to which literature has special relevance. It seems to be the very diverse life-moral possibilities that literature manifests which are the business of literary criticism to understand and evaluate in relation to one another. But Rorty the philosopher begins to show himself in the way he conceives what this involves. Rather like Strawson, for example (discussed in chapter 2), Rorty sees writers as representing

competing personal ideals, or as he puts it, 'self-images', as well
as distinctive 'vocabularies'. And as modern 'ironists', what we
want to know, he thinks, is which images we should adopt in
order to pattern ourselves on them, and when we should
redescribe ourselves in this or that 'vocabulary', so as 'to make
the best selves for ourselves that we can'. To advise us on these
matters, Rorty claims, is the central function of literary criticism
at the present time: 'the critic is now expected to facilitate
moral reflection by suggesting revisions in the canon of moral
exemplars and advisers, and suggesting ways in which the
tensions within this canon may be eased – or, where necessary,
sharpened.'[9]

Such comparison, such playing off of figures against each other, is
the principal activity now covered by the term 'literary criticism.'
Influential critics, the sort of critics who propose new canons – people
like Arnold, Pater, Leavis, Eliot, Edmund Wilson, Lionel Trilling,
Frank Kermode, Harold Bloom – are not in the business of explaining
the real meaning of books, nor of evaluating something called their
'literary merit.' Rather, they spend their time placing books in the
context of other books, figures in the context of other figures. This
placing is done in the same way as we place a new friend or enemy in
the context of old friends and enemies. In the course of doing so, we
revise our opinions of both the old and the new. Simultaneously, we
revise our own moral identity by revising our own final vocabulary.
Literary criticism does for ironists what the search for universal moral
principles is supposed to do for metaphysicians.[10]

What makes literary critics 'moral advisers' is not, as Rorty
quite rightly says, that they have 'special access to moral truth'.
But he thinks it is 'because they have been around'; they are, to
use an older cliché, not so much wise as wised up about books,
and therefore unlikely to get 'trapped in the vocabulary of any
single book'. (This is evidently a pretty bad situation for
'ironists' to get into.) Rather, 'ironists'

hope critics will help them continue to admire books which are prima
facie antithetical by performing some sort of synthesis. We would like
to be able to admire both Blake and Arnold, both Nietzsche and Mill,
both Marx and Baudelaire, both Trotsky and Eliot, both Nabokov
and Orwell. So we hope some critic will show how these men's books

can be put together to form a beautiful mosaic. We hope that critics can redescribe these people in ways which will enlarge the canon, and will give us a set of classical texts as rich and diverse as possible.[11]

This brings out the point of the word 'placing' for the nature and structure of life-moral critical judgments, though not its limitations: its suggestion of a certain fixity, as if all the activity involved were that of the critic 'placing' an inert object. But of course the process Rorty is describing is far from being distinctive only of our own age. From classical times, in fact, that process has been the justification of 'imitation', literary as well as religious: *imitatio Ciceronis* as well as *imitatio Christi*. By adopting the 'vocabulary' and 'image' of the model, the moral agent was supposed to achieve a similar perfection of life or a personal 'place' in the relevant authoritative tradition. But Rorty's way of putting it misses both the point and the difficulty of any such imitation: it makes it seem a process anyone can simply learn from his preferred guru – a way of voluntarily conducting oneself so as to bring about a change in one's moral being, one's very life. In other words, what Rorty's own 'vocabulary' fails to catch is precisely what Mothersill means by '*anima*' or 'soul': the *spirit* of the model, the value of which is the reason for 'imitation' and which is the real but elusive object of their imitation – all the more elusive perhaps to those concerned only with imitable 'vocabularies' and 'images'.

In other words, to talk as Rorty does about 'moral exemplars and advisers', and 'revising our moral identity' by 'revising our final vocabulary', and 'adopting self-images', is actually to revert to a merely conduct-moral conception of literature – one that any conventional Renaissance humanist would have recognized at once. It is this same conception that underlies the old belief, which Rorty evidently shares, that books can be divided into those which 'supply moral stimuli to action' and those which 'simply offer relaxation' (the verbs here are revealing), and the former group sub-divided according to the particular moral 'purpose' or 'function' they 'serve', the kind of formulable moral insights they help us to 'see' or to 'notice', or the kinds of new 'final vocabulary' they try to 'work out'.[12] In this vein, Rorty sounds positively mid-Victorian. And yet, as we shall see, even a philosopher as responsive to literature as Martha Nussbaum can lapse into talking of literature giving us 'correct' moral insights, or precepts to 'see' or to 'notice', as if these were not always in literature manifestations of an individual moral being, a particular 'vision' whether of a character in a work or of the work itself, and always limited by that fact.

So external and instrumental a conception of literature and literary criticism as Rorty's raises other problems as well. For example, to emphasize 'vocabularies' as he does seems to overlook what it is that makes any 'final vocabulary' interesting to us and seem worth adopting in the first place: I mean the writer's manifest belief that it is not just a disposable 'vocabulary', but a necessary way of capturing truths about what he most deeply and fully sees the world really to be. Rorty's own 'vocabulary' is a case in point; and whether or not we want to 'adopt' it depends, as always, on how we judge its truth-bearing power. But emphasizing 'vocabularies' raises another problem too. It makes it seem right, and indeed unproblematical, to read all kinds of books, and to evaluate them all, solely as 'discourse'. The widespread contemporary use of this term shows that the problem here is not just Rorty's, but he certainly illustrates it; and it arises from a typical philosophers' assumption (at least as old as Aristotle) that literature thinks and talks about the world in essentially the same way as philosophy (what other way is there?) and differs only in talking about different subjects, different bits of the world:

> novels are usually about people – things which are, unlike general ideas and final vocabularies, quite evidently time-bound, embedded in a web of contingencies. Since the characters in novels age and die – since they obviously share the finitude of the books in which they occur – we are not tempted to think that by adopting an attitude toward them we have adopted an attitude toward every *possible* sort of person. By contrast, books which are about ideas, even when written by historicists like Hegel and Nietzsche, look like descriptions of eternal relations between eternal objects...[13]

If literature is 'about people', it is in a much deeper and fuller sense than Rorty recognizes: what he says here seems little more than truistic. Of course, it does have an obvious bearing on the critic's use of the term 'universality'. Moreover, the exemplary and advisory aspects of literature (and I am not in the least denying their importance), which most philosophers are responsive to, do prompt readers to think about a work in terms of 'discourse': to consider what it is saying consciously and unconsciously about classes of actions and agents, the rationality of its attitudes, its politics, its 'final vocabulary' – in short, what it asserts or implies in general terms about general objects. The 'dramatic' and presentational aspects of literature, on the other hand, inevitably prompt the reader to think more searchingly and intensively both of the work as an individual, and of the particular life it (consciously and unconsciously) manifests – a life which is 'time-bound, embedded in a web of contingencies', as Rorty sees, but which, as he only partly sees, is not only irreducibly individual but for that very reason also central to reading literature and to its critical evaluation.

Some such consideration as this probably underlies Rorty's attempt to counter-balance his term 'vocabulary' with his other term, 'image'. It is not hard to understand why he, like Strawson and others, uses it; as Mothersill would put it, 'image' points to a crucial '*Gestalt* property' of literary works. But the term seems no less limiting than 'vocabulary' or 'discourse', and certainly not an adequate complement to them; indeed, it underlines one reason why it is better to speak, not of 'self-images' to be 'seen' in literary works, but of modes of life manifesting themselves in literary works in the process of being grasped, made sense of, *as* that. For one thing, 'image' suggests something entirely objective to a perceiver, something with a clear, specific shape, something already defined, which one needs only to look at carefully to see for what it is. The term is altogether too flat and too definite for the complex, indeterminate moral being we make sense of as an Iago or an Imogen, or as a Hegel or a Nietzsche – or as one's wife or as one's close friend. In other words, as I have argued, 'image' implies a too meagre content for what a serious literary work presents us with, and even so, a content of the wrong sort. We have to discover and rediscover such sense as we can make of a moral being. Similarly with our connection with the work. We discover what possibilities this or that 'life' represents in ourselves, not in the process of adopting it as a 'vocabulary' or as an 'image' or as both, but as we do with people, in the process of getting to know it and making such moral sense of it as we can. That process includes, of course, making sense of it as an individual whole and also of its characteristic 'vocabulary' or 'discourse'; but to speak of 'making moral sense of a life' does not suggest a process that can be completed, fully and finally achieved, as 'seeing an image' does. In a literary work, as we have seen, the process involves making sense of a moral being in terms of dispositions and potentialities and the dynamic inter-actions and inter-relations of such dispositions and potentialities with all the particulars that manifest an individual life, whether that of a dramatic character, or that of the work as a whole. 'Discourse' is too misleading a term for this, and 'image' too undramatic – even in the simple sense that it is too static. It catches nothing of the way a life unfolds itself progressively, and nothing either of the ways in which the dynamic action of a literary work is a process of realizing – 'realizing' both in the sense of thinking with new intensity, and in the sense of a potential mode of life coming into existence.

In short, neither 'vocabulary' nor 'image', nor a combination of the two, seems to me to catch what basically interests us in 'dramatic' literature, or in any form of writing (or miming, or dancing and so on) that we treat as 'dramatic' – even, to use Rorty's examples, Hegel's writing, say, or Nietzsche's, in so far as we read it so as to grasp the individual mode of life it manifests or (in Mothersill's vocabulary) its individual '*anima*' or soul. Such 'dramatic' literature generally exhibits a special kind of moral thinking, and what marks the good literary critic is the developed capacity to understand and evaluate it sensitively and intelligently. True, a vagueness about evaluation, or a positive (and self-refuting) hostility to it, is all too common among literary theorists nowadays, but it is especially puzzling in Rorty's account of literature and criticism. When he says that 'we ironists hope, by this continual redescription, to make the best selves for ourselves that we can', for example, he possibly means something like an 'art of life' in the sense I have used of Pope; but if so, it is not at all clear what his word *best* means here, or *selves*, or *make*, and how these meanings are related to those of such terms as *images* we *want* to *know* whether to *adopt*. Then again, what distinguishes one ironist's redescriptions from another's: our own, say, from that of any repressive political regime or that of such ironists as Richard Nixon or other 'doublespeakers'? Or when Rorty speaks of the vocabulary 'concocted' by an author, is 'concocted' quite the word for Blake and Arnold, Nietzsche and Mill, Marx and Baudelaire, Trotsky and Eliot, Nabokov and Orwell? Maybe, we might decide, it is the appropriate word for some of the work of most of them and for all of the work of some of them. But the different critical judgments possible – indeed necessary – here only underline the fact that Rorty seems not to notice or not to care about such differences along with everything they imply about his 'irony'. For that 'irony' seems to depend on regarding as of equal validity and equal value every 'image' and every 'vocabulary' that some critic or other admires. Nor does Rorty's appeal later in the book to an essentially conduct-moral 'solidarity' much improve the matter. As for the reader thus 'putting together' ('concocting'?) a 'beautiful mosaic', it is hard to tell whether this sounds more like Yeats in one of his off-moments or Gilbert Osmond in one of his better ones: *this* is surely not the point of attacking the distinction between the moral and the aesthetic.

So too with evaluating literary critics. One can see why Rorty praises some critics for having proposed new 'canons' (a term that, with its religious and authoritarian associations, we would all be better without): critics such as Arnold, Pater, Leavis, Eliot, Edmund Wilson, Lionel Trilling, Frank Kermode, Harold Bloom. On the other hand, it implies no disrespect towards any of these to observe that they represent pretty different orders of critical depth and cogency. Surely we need to make some evaluative critical discriminations among these critics and their 'canons' – some 'placings' of their work of exactly the same life-moral kind as led each critic to propose his 'canon'. Similarly, when Rorty speaks of our acquiring 'a set of classical texts as rich and diverse as possible', he seems not to notice a crucial difference between 'as *rich* as possible' and 'as *diverse* as possible'. In fact, it is hard to see in his account what we could call richness as distinct from diversity. And with the critics he lists, it seems to me a travesty of their work to locate its interest and value in their just having 'been around', as Rorty puts it, and therefore been 'in a better position not to get trapped in the vocabulary of any single book'. The truth is that these critics have been far less concerned with keeping readers out of that trap, or with enlarging the 'canon', than with discriminating more important books from less important ones. What is more, they have given reasons for those discriminations – reasons that need to be understood and (where we think it necessary) answered or qualified with better reasons. 'Canons', or what many contemporary American academics call 'canons', do not get changed arbitrarily, because of fashion or boredom or the Higher Agitprop, for that matter, nor do they always need to expand. Of course one can see what Rorty means by saying that we 'revise our own moral identity by revising our own final vocabulary', but as the practice of these critics makes very clear, this is not just a conduct-moral but a life-moral matter, and it involves a good deal more of our moral being – a good deal, like our relationships with the past, that we cannot *choose* to revise – than adopting an 'image' or 'vocabulary' that happens to attract us. Literature and literary criticism are relevant to answering Socrates' question in more complex, more difficult, less voluntary and less 'ironic' ways than Rorty describes.

II

To any moral philosopher of an Aristotelian bent – and there has been a notable increase in their number over the last two decades – my general argument may well seem deficient in one of two ways at least. The first is that I ignore the possibility of conduct-morality being actually derived from life-morality, thereby closing any gap between them: a possibility of which Aristotle is often supposed to be the classic exemplar.[14] The second is that I am merely insisting on a commonplace of moral philosophy: the differences between a broadly 'Kantian' ethic, focused on rationally required duties of action and conduct, and a broadly 'Aristotelian' ethic, focused on the virtues that comprise or underpin human well-being or flourishing, or 'the good life for man'. After all, what is my 'conduct-morality' but the former, and my 'life-morality' but the latter?

To this, I can only reply that I do not mean to be 'Aristotelian' in either of these ways. I certainly do not think that conduct-morality is dispensable, but neither do I think that, for us here and now, there is any single, complete account of 'the good life for man' that we can realize by voluntary intentional actions. For example, I find it impossible to believe that, as Stuart Hampshire puts it, Aristotle gives us an account of 'the perfect life for a man'.[15] Not all possible virtues have established names; nor does Aristotle's list encompass all the virtues (not even all there were for Johnson in the eighteenth century); nor do Aristotle's virtues encompass the whole substance of morality itself. As moralists, we always have to reckon with the innumerably different lives that people actually live, and the morally complex and changing culture they actually inhabit; a 'quality which is a moral excellence or vice in one man would not [necessarily] be a moral excellence or vice in another'.[16] Not only do judgments about the relative importance of different human excellences and defects – judgments which have been called 'ultimate' and which I call life-moral – occupy an area where we have nothing to rely on except what Johnson called 'the reasonableness of opinions'; we have constantly to avoid the temptation simply to conflate conduct-morality and life-morality. To quote Hampshire again,

It must remain an arguable [ultimate] question whether those human excellences that can normally be attained intentionally, by effort and by practical reason, are to be considered of supreme value, just because they are so attained: whether the exercise of will, and whether good intentions, are the most noble potentialities of men, as they have often been thought to be. As the moral excellences are often taken to be the only important excellences that can normally be attained directly by those who are persuaded to try to attain them, there is a natural tendency to represent them as the most important of all human excellences, if only as a device of persuasion.[17]

The point is well taken, and is highly relevant, as we shall see, to defining the moral significance of a novel by Jane Austen, for example, or Henry James.

As for Aristotle, he may seem to be a life-moralist in the *Nicomachean Ethics* – explaining how to *live*, and what *eudaimonia* or the ideal happiness or well-being of Man's life consists in – but he actually devotes more of his attention to conduct-morality, to *how* to live. For Aristotle, of course, the two questions are so closely related that he does tend to conflate them, and he does so by the usual means of essentialist and teleological arguments about human nature and human activities – arguments, it must be said, that earlier ages have found more cogent than our own is likely to. As Hampshire is only one to point out, for us a concern for individuality is essential to any morality that we would find acceptable; but such a concern is very different from Aristotle's, whose interest is directed to 'the ideal specimen of humanity, having all or most of the excellences that are peculiar to the species', and different too from that of Christian, or utilitarian, or Kantian moralists, who also seek to 'legislate for humanity'. For Hampshire, what he calls 'impressionistic predicates' – his examples include clumsy, delicate, tense, rough, deft, stately, cringing, languid – may well name *moral* qualities: it depends on whether such a quality is significant in 'some conception of the good'; and diverse conceptions of the good are 'associated with diverse ways of life'. And in his discussion of imagination as a mode of moral thinking, of love, and of art, as all irreducibly concerned with the concrete and the individual, Hampshire here comes much closer than Aristotle ever does to a conception of moral life as including, but extending well beyond, the area of action and conduct.[18]

Of course, Aristotle does not wholly conflate the conduct-moral with the life-moral. The good life for man, human flourishing, depends on certain external and contingent factors as well as on potentialities within everyone's power to realize in himself. Moreover, these potentialities include the virtues of the rational mind, the 'intellectual' virtues by which we come to possess Truth, as well as the virtues of human 'character', the specifically 'moral' virtues: virtues which we can make into our second nature, as it were, in the form of good dispositions, correct moral perceptions, well-disciplined feelings and desires, cogent deliberations, right choices, and hence just and noble actions. Nevertheless, Aristotle gives the central, dominating place to deliberation, choice and voluntary action: which is why, from my point of view here, there is no great divide between him and Kant: both are basically conduct-moralists. This is not at all to deny the marked and important differences between an Aristotelian (or quasi-Aristotelian) and a Kantian (or a quasi-Kantian) view of moral conduct, as between other forms of conduct-morality. Aristotle conceives conduct in terms of the finest, noblest and the most stable states of human character; and he conceives those states of character in terms of the distinctive nature of Man, the completest well-being of human Life, and the kind of moral goods that can generally be directly achieved by deliberation, choice and action. Moreover, for Aristotle moral conduct is mediated by an 'intellectual' virtue, practical wisdom, which (in so far as one possesses it) discerns what particular virtuous action is required in each particular set of circumstances. For Aristotle, that is, morality does not present itself to the agent as a set of universal precepts or rules, which God or Reason requires all men to follow at all times in all of their actions. He thinks of it rather as presenting the agent with choices between conduct that is noble or base, worthy of praise or of blame, constitutive of a happy or an unhappy life. His moral virtues (leaving practical wisdom aside, that is) are justice, courage, temperance, liberality, magnificence, magnanimity, good temper, friendliness, truthfulness, ready wit and tact; and for Aristotle these form an interconnected and sufficient set of action-guiding ideals or norms of character – norms that people should be educated into appreciating and incorporating in their inward as well as outward conduct.

Not surprisingly, however, Aristotle's tendency to conflate the conduct-moral with the life-moral produces some revealing strains in his argument: the very restricted moral importance he allows to non-voluntary qualities, for example; or his wobble in Book III, chapter 5 of the *Ethics* between taking 'responsibility' in a conduct-moral sense (which justifies praise and blame) and in a life-moral sense (which requires us to own to everything we are, including what was or is not in our power to change); or his very truncated view (compared to Plato's, for instance) of the effect that music can have on the soul.[19]

His account of the moral virtue of 'magnanimity' (*megalo-psychia*) in Book IV, chapter 3 is especially interesting in this context. Difficulties arise from the very beginning of the account: 'It makes no difference whether we consider the state of character or the man characterized by it', he says. But surely it makes a very big difference? It makes sense, for instance, to explain a virtue or a virtuous state of character so that all moral agents might learn to practise it; on the other hand, it makes no such sense to suggest that a man deliberately conducting himself in certain ways will eventually achieve such a virtue as *this* and make his spirit greater than it is. Even Aristotle sees the fallacy of imitating a magnanimous man: performing the same actions is not to capture the same spirit. In other words, a man 'characterized' by magnanimity is (although Aristotle does not say so) a being with more *moral* capacities than those required for virtuous conduct. What Aristotle does say is that a man's magnanimity manifests itself even in the very way, the style, in which he performs such undeliberated activities as walking or talking or retreating in battle. Moreover, the magnanimous man is distinguished as much by what he does not do as by what he does. Indeed, had Aristotle developed his description of the magnanimous man fully, it would have been the description of a whole way of being alive – one whose central quality and value is magnanimity. Seen in that light, magnanimity is not a single virtue in itself, but (as Aristotle himself says) something like a crown or adornment of all the other virtues, without which (he says) it cannot exist but which makes them greater than they are in other men. In fact, it is a *life-moral* state, just as that of philosophic contemplation is for Aristotle. And yet having got almost to the point of seeing this, Aristotle backs away, noting how hard it is to be truly magnanimous, and proceeding to offer some tips to those who aspire to greatness of spirit.

To a critical modern reader, therefore, Aristotle's conception of the good life for man is likely to seem only an historically-bound version of such an ideal, one necessarily limited by the history, the society, the culture, the class, the gender and the individual '*anima*' of its author – just like any other version, in fact. The role he gives to the non-voluntary aspects of a life seems too restricted; on the other hand, the overwhelming importance he gives to acting rightly from the right moral understanding, the right motives, and the right exercise of practical reason, seems to give too large and unqualified a role to rationality and even to a transparently clear moral consciousness. On his account, a life of moral virtue seems, not necessarily self-centred, but somehow too narrowly directed and too deliberately calculated and controlled. Similarly with his over-emphasis on the same set of known potentialities in every life; it obscures the informing presence in every life of individual and unknown possibilities – possibilities intrinsic to each particular 'soul' but discoverable only in that soul's often spontaneous, undeliberated answering to the call of what it finds 'congenial' in the world. As James Joyce put it in his own sub-Aristotelian terms, Shakespeare '*found* in the world without as actual what was in *his* world within as possible' (my italics); this con-geniality is a process that does not apply only to a great 'genius', but to every person's 'genius'. Then again there is too little in Aristotle about the moral circumstances within which and on which a person finds he has to live and act; too little about the dispositions formed in a person by social institutions and practices, or just by other people, especially but not exclusively in the pre-conduct years of life; too little about the way a mode of life sometimes seems to an individual to choose him or her, rather than the other way round. What matters here, I think, is not Aristotle's too meagre recognition of moral luck, so much as his blankness about the moral importance in every life of such matters as moral discovery, moral destiny, even moral helplessness: for example, the fact that underlies our conscious choices and actions, and subtly affects them, of our *having* to be (not just happening to be) the only particular, individual 'soul' we ever can be; or of having to live out the only life there is in us; or of *having* only this particular life in us to live out. (But perhaps this is the idea of moral luck in another guise?)

To acknowledge the enormous variety of lives that manifest themselves in literature, and the enormous variety of judgments we make about them, is to find it simply incredible that the most important qualities of human beings, including greatness of soul, are those that they realize in their inner and outer conduct as agents. No less incredible is the belief that all good lives follow Aristotle's few simple patterns: the life of moral virtue, the life of philosophic contemplation, and the (largely political) life of the *megalopsychos*. Every life has its own moral needs and pressures, its own moral economy, its own trade-offs between more of one good and less of another – every gain perhaps inevitably entailing a loss, if not necessarily vice versa. Each life has its own strengths and limitations, which are not always easy to distinguish from one another – if, indeed, they are distinguishable. Each has its own development and decay (which are also often hard to distinguish), its own outgoings and adventures and returns, its own form unfolding in time. Yet even the virtuous, the philosophic and the magnanimous men Aristotle describes are not individual lives or 'souls' in anything like this sense; they are only specific *types* of 'character'. They are abstractions characteristic of that generalizing, 'philosophical' cast of mind of which Aristotle is typical and which I touched on in chapter 5 above: that type of mind which cannot apprehend and value human lives except as examples or instances of types or universals. This is why, for all his supposed concern with the life-moral, Aristotle seems to me not to have much to say about it – compared, that is, with writers of rather less unmitigated 'discourse': Montaigne, for instance.

III

Considering how much Aristotle is a conduct-moralist, there-fore, I do not see him, as Bernard Williams does in *Ethics and the Limits of Philosophy*, as representing 'ethics', a radical alternative to what Williams calls 'morality' or 'the morality system'. Williams takes Kant to be the best philosophical representative of 'the morality system', but he also regards it as 'the outlook, or, incoherently, part of the outlook, of almost all of us';[20] and since it incorporates fundamental mistakes, he claims, we would be best rid of it altogether.

At first glance, it is true, what I have called 'conduct-morality' does seem to be pretty much what Williams means by 'the morality system'; what I have called 'life-morality', pretty much Williams's 'ethics' – focused on 'considerations of well-being and of a life worth living' and on 'internalized dispositions of action, desire and feeling';[21] and what I see as the gap, often the conflict, between them may be what for Williams is rational 'incoherence'. (Perhaps not being a philosopher makes one more tolerant of that sort of 'incoherence'.) Certainly, both his 'morality' and my 'conduct-morality' are focused on voluntary intentional actions, and require corresponding notions of responsibility and blame; both ignore the extent to which actions are determined by moral 'character', and moral 'character' by forces beyond the will, beyond even the consciousness, of the agent; and both ignore the kind of responsibility that arises just from having done something, whether intentionally or not, or from just being what one is – the responsibility, in the end, for what one is stuck with. Similarly, they both ignore the kind of moral ('ethical') considerations that do not embody a universal or univer-salizable rule; and of course they give no place to any notion of 'moral luck' or (to put it the other way) moral fate. Altogether, they take only a narrow view of the 'moral', and of which 'ethical reactions' (as Williams calls them) count as 'moral'.

For Williams, however, it is a major mistake of 'the morality system' to give a special meaning and a special prominence to the notion of obligation. Another is to regard all properly 'moral' reactions to be judgments, assessments, approval or disapproval: reactions that suggest 'a position of at least temporary superiority, the position of a judge' and merely 'binary' judgments – of guilt or innocence, for example. The 'system' has no use for what it regards as 'non-moral' reactions: dislike, resentment, contempt, or 'such minor revelations of the ethical life as the sense that someone is creepy'.[22] All of this makes 'the morality system' easily recognizable, of course; but the 'system' still seems to be only one version of what I call, more generally, conduct-morality, and a particularly objectionable one at that: objectionable, that is, on moral grounds. For it seems closer to the aggressively 'judgmental', *moralistic* notions of a Tom Tulliver, say, than to the operative conduct-morality of George Eliot at her best, for example, or of Pope, or of Henry James. Williams's 'ethics', after all, is centred on 'virtues', virtues being 'dispositions of character to choose or reject *actions* because they are of a certain ethically relevant kind' (my italics).[23] And why should we not call his 'ethical reactions' both 'moral' and 'judgments'? Why abandon the latter terms to those who conceive them too narrowly or simply abuse them? More to the point, is even a quasi-Aristotelian ethics sufficient for the whole scope of our moral thinking?

I say 'quasi-Aristotelian' because, in setting Aristotle up as a plausible alternative to 'the morality system', Williams actually has to jettison a good deal of Aristotle: not just his conception of what moral philosophy can achieve, or his 'mono-culturism' (as we might call it), or his views on slavery or on women, but also his teleological arguments, his conception of human nature, his supposedly exhaustive list of the virtues, and his beliefs in the unity of the virtues and in the doctrine of the Mean – to mention only the most obvious. But Williams finds Aristotle mistaken on at least two other matters; and as Williams's objections clearly tend in a life-moral direction (and incidentally underline how much of a conduct-moralist Aristotle really is), they are especially interesting to a literary critic.

One is that Aristotle's conception of human lives is too narrow in being merely sequential, and that his account of moral growth and education is too crude, as well as being rather at odds with his belief that people make their own moral 'characters'.[24] Certainly, it never crosses Aristotle's mind that the moral vigour and value of a life might show themselves in non-'moral', or even 'immoral', feelings, interests and be-haviour – as with Maggie Tulliver, for example, or Alcibiades. On the other hand, a good deal in Williams's own argument depends on his conceptions of human lives and human character; and to a reader used to thinking about character and how it is conceived and 'constructed' in particular works of literature, it seems rather odd that Williams does not much explore either idea, especially in relation to separating – or trying to separate – qualities and dispositions in the abstract into those that are 'ethical' in themselves and those that are not. The difficulty of separating them in actual people is not accidental; indeed this difficulty makes the abstract philo-sophical endeavour seem virtually impossible or pointless, or both. In fact, the difficulty marks one of the limits of philosophy.[25]

The second of Williams's objections to Aristotle I have in mind is to Aristotle's rather naive moral psychology, especially his failure to see how radically some virtues are affected by the agent's reflexive thoughts and feelings about possessing them: or to put it another way, how conduct may well take on a different complexion when seen in a life-moral context, which includes the nature and significance of a person's self-con-sciousness as well as consciousness. To describe a man as being courageous or generous, Williams notes (in the kind of analytic point that many literary critics might benefit from pondering), may mean several very different things, one of which (a morally 'primitive' one) is that he is 'concerned to conform his conduct to some paradigm of a generous man'.[26] This pinpoints, and quite rightly criticizes, what generations of Aristotle's readers have simply assumed: that achieving or practising a virtue is to regulate one's actions, to conduct oneself, according to an 'ideal': an already-established, accepted standard precon-ception of what the virtue consists in and looks like. For Aristotle himself, of course, there seemed nothing conventional or priggish or self-deceiving or of bad faith in deliberately cultivating a virtue or deliberately exercising it. For us, however, there often is, and the point applies perhaps especially to conflations of the life-moral with the conduct-moral. Thus it applies to Rorty's 'vocabularies' and 'images', for example, or to 'honour' and 'nobleness' in the mouths of some of Shakespeare's characters, or (most interestingly perhaps) to Pope's Flavia, who deliberately seeks 'while we live, to live' and ultimately dies of 'nothing but a Rage to live'.[27]

Although Williams says nothing about the 'ethical' importance of literature and literary criticism, it is obvious enough that they form one of the crucial social practices that establish, renew, reform and extend what Williams calls the 'thick concepts' on which 'ethical' thought depends: concepts such as *treachery*, *promise*, *lie*, *brutality*, *courage*, and *gratitude*, to which we should add *character* as well; and along with those concepts (if 'concepts' is the best word for terms so 'thick' with meaning and force) those beliefs about the social world which are, for Williams, an essential ingredient of a good life and enable people to use 'thick concepts' with a finer relevance and discrimination.[28] It is also pretty obvious that literature and literary criticism form one of the main ways, if not *the* main way, we try to discover mentally 'how truthfulness to an existing self or society is to be combined with reflection, self-understanding, and criticism', a question to which we 'cannot formulate the answer in advance, except in an unspecific way'.[29] As Williams says, philosophy cannot wholly answer it, nor (we must add) can works of literature; it has to be answered 'through reflective living'. Nevertheless, this sort of question, and possible ways of answering it in particular ways of being alive, are the natural concern of literature and criticism more than of philosophy. So too with Williams's belief that philosophy cannot realize 'a meaningful individual life...that does not reject society, and indeed shares its perceptions with other people to a considerable depth, but is enough unlike others, in its opacities and disorder as well as in its reasoned intentions, to make it *somebody's*'.[30] Here too, it seems to me that the door Williams closes on philosophy opens on to literature; one stops at the border where the other begins. It is rather like the relationship I have suggested between conduct-morality and life-morality: if both are too deeply built into the foundations of our culture for either to be abandoned, so too with both philosophy and literature in moral thinking. Very different as they are, the reach of one is insufficient without that of the other.

But there is yet another aspect of literature that transcends Williams's 'morality system'. In predicting the eventual decline of the 'morality system', Williams points to the fact that 'morality is under too much pressure on the subject of the voluntary',[31] to which he might well have added 'and the subject of the individual self'. Certainly, both concepts have been under heavy attack from structuralists and post-structuralists; indeed, they form the major part of what is now often cried down as 'humanism'. Williams, however, quite rightly sees both concepts as essential suppositions of ethical thought: 'that there be individuals with dispositions of character and a life of their own to lead', and that there are 'individuals who acquire certain dispositions and aims and express them in action'.[32] What needs to be emphasised, however, is that literature (and the critical 'humanism' that studies it) has from the very origins of Western culture carried other suppositions no less essential in moral thought, and has enabled people to think about the significance and consequences of those suppositions. I mean, for example, the supposition that 'dispositions of character' extend, in incalculable ways, beyond consciousness and will; that individual lives are individual not just in their 'opacities and disorder as well as in [their] reasoned intentions', but in the unpredictable forms into which they shape themselves as *this* individual life or as *that*; that not only do people 'express' their dispositions 'in action', but people also are 'expressed' in the dispositions that manifest themselves in activity and suffering; and that as well as having 'lives of their own to lead', people are also led by their lives – lives they may come to realize only in time to *be* theirs. As Williams sees, philosophy is limited when it comes to the irreducible individuality of people; it is literature, I want to add, that enables us to think of them as irreducible individuals as well as particular

collections of universal human virtues and vices – as lives as well
as agents.

IV

The other two Aristotelians I want to mention do discuss the
moral significance of literature, and do so, moreover, in relation
to specific works. What they also exhibit, however, are two
different but very common versions of a perennial weakness of
philosophers (and not only philosophers): I mean giving
priority, almost unwittingly at times, to recognizable ideas – to
already-formed concepts and universal principles, the kind of
thinking characteristic of philosophy and of conduct-morality –
over the individual, the unclassifiable, the *sui generis*, the kind of
thinking characteristic of moral life and of literature. Indeed, so
common is this assumption that *real* thinking, *real* knowledge,
are the preserve of philosophy, and poetry merely instrumental
to them, that it is worth looking in some detail at two
philosophers who actually want to argue (in some sense) against
that assumption, and invoke (of all people) Aristotle in whose
name to do so.

The first is Alasdair MacIntyre in his book, *After Virtue*. Here,
he argues for a return to an Aristotelian kind of moral
philosophy – one that takes 'a *whole human life* as the primary
subject of objective and impersonal evaluation, ... a type of
evaluation which provides the content for judgment upon the
particular *actions* or projects of a given individual ... a view of
human life as ordered to a *given* end' (my italics).[33] Of course,
MacIntyre is no uncritical Aristotelian either; he sees as well as
anyone what even a sympathetic modern reader must find
implausible in Aristotle, at least as it stands – including his
attitude to poetry.[34] As MacIntyre says, having 'no understanding of historicity in general', Aristotle naturally values
poetry as more 'philosophical' than history because he sees
poetry as dealing not with individuals but with types, and in
that, approximating much more to true *epistêmê* – knowledge of
essential natures and universal truths.[35]

Unfortunately MacIntyre does not elaborate on what an
understanding of historicity might have to do with a concern

with individuals, nor why this might be important in moral and literary-critical thinking; but it is a question that arises with one of MacIntyre's own leading ideas: that taking 'a whole human life as the primary subject of objective and impersonal evaluation' is – as Aristotle also assumed – to take a life lengthwise, so to speak, as a history, or in MacIntyre's term, as comprising a single *narrative*. MacIntyre means 'narrative' in a loose sense – it includes conversation and drama, for instance – but it is only *as* narrative, he claims, that we can morally understand and evaluate human actions and (especially) a human life as a whole. And the special moral importance of literature is its age-old concern with whole human lives.

In some ways, MacIntyre is obviously right about this: often literature is concerned with whole human lives in the way he says. But as I have argued, it is quite common to think of the unity or wholeness of a human life vertically, so to speak: as the complex of inter-relationships between a person's functioning, behaviour, actions and activity, considered either over a large stretch of time, or at some particular moment (or moments) in some particular set of circumstances, or (most commonly) both. A 'narrative' life does not have any special veridical advantage over, say, the imaginatively explorative analysis of the life; indeed, many narratives imply or point out how many and how different are the 'narratives' that could claim to tell the same life. What is more, any adequate 'narrative' has to consider a life under one of the essential conditions that make it a *human* life: that is, it has to respond to and capture not just the general features of a character, but also the particular distinctiveness of a life, its individual *anima*, its characteristic 'spirit' or 'principle', with its unique historicity. Pope is a case very much in point here, and his work also demonstrates how much constructing a lengthwise 'narrative' is largely a matter of discovering the inter-relationships over time between many vertical analyses and evaluations of the life – which means that we are talking about something less like a 'narrative' or even a 'story' than a 'dramatic action'. But here we mean 'drama' in the non-Aristotelian sense that denotes not just an unfolding structural series of events, but also the necessary correlative process of their being seen and understood as a vital structure of events and states, which articulates meanings *in* what it shapes and unfolds *as* it is being shaped and unfolded.

MacIntyre himself revives the old analogy between moral life and drama;[36] in doing so, however, he assumes what a literary critic would not, that a Shakespearean tragedy (*Hamlet* is MacIntyre's own instance) is the *hero's* drama, as if the dramatic action, the point and 'logic' of the play, lay simply in the hero's experience rather than in ours as we answer to it. In deciding, at every moment of the play, what is central to us and what is subordinate, we too in our moral perceptions are morally engaged; and in that process, the possible relationships we 'see' between one character's experience in the play and another's are far more multiple, complex and elusive than MacIntyre allows. At other points, MacIntyre seems to suppose that we begin to be moral beings only as we enter upon an 'action' which (in some largely unproblematic way) is already single and already defined, which (again in some largely unproblematic way) we see to be ours, and which ideally realizes a 'given end'. Again and again, MacIntyre sounds as if it is really conduct, better or worse regulated actions within a given plot, he is thinking of. It is, he argues, an agent's 'intentions, motives, passions and purposes' in terms of which we have to characterize occurrences as actions, and it is actions which form the substance of narratable lives. Narratives are the medium in which moral questions and answers have to present themselves to an agent, just as narrative is the only way one can consider a life as a whole so as to get some teleological purchase on it and thus be able to judge it morally. Conscious integrity or constancy has a crucial place in a life; for it is the quest for 'the good life for man' that is the *telos* by which dispositions can be measured as useful and therefore virtues, or obstructions and therefore vices. The 'good life for man is the life spent in seeking for the good life for man, and the virtues necessary for the seeking are those which will enable us to understand what more and what else the good life for man is'.[37] As MacIntyre insists, this has to be understood in social and historical terms as well as personal ones: 'the story of my life is always embedded in the story of those communities from which I derive my identity'. But it is still 'the *search* for the good, for the *universal*' that is the core of '*the* good life for man' (my italics).[38]

The implicit self-reference in these remarks makes it hard to know what to say to their general claim without a certain embarrassment. In one way, it is obviously a version of Aristotle's belief that there is one, single 'good life for man' and that philosophical contemplation is the highest form of it. In another way, it partly anticipates Thomas Nagel's argument for the need to go beyond any particular personal moral viewpoint to the moral 'view from nowhere'.[39] In yet another way again, it is not unlike Milton's view that the good man is the 'true wayfaring Christian' – he who can 'apprehend and consider vice with all her baits and seeming pleasures, and yet abstain, and yet distinguish, and yet prefer that which is truly better'.[40] But for all that, it is also so clearly self-referential as to seem like another version of 'Do as my book and I do.'

Altogether, MacIntyre seems to me virtually a pure conduct-moralist; and a further sign of it, I think, is his account of constancy or integrity. With the first, his conception of what the 'unity' or 'integrity' of a life might consist in seems, set beside Pope's career as a poet, for example, or Deronda's mother, as restricted as his conception of the possible 'wholeness' of a life: 'we may understand the virtues as having their function in enabling an individual to *make* of his or her life one kind of unity rather than another' (my italics).[41]

The problem about this essentially conduct-moral conception of constancy, integrity and 'wholeness' of life, becomes vividly clear in MacIntyre's account of Jane Austen's *Mansfield Park*, an account which is meant to specify and sustain that conception. For MacIntyre, the key episode is Fanny Price's rejection of Henry Crawford; and it seems to me a significant weakness in the moral theory that it should get the novel so remarkably wrong. For not only does the theory fail to account for what is there in the novel, but (more importantly) the novel is treated as simply exemplifying or instantiating the prior moral ideas Jane Austen is supposed to share with Aristotle and MacIntyre. The novel is never allowed to put any critical pressure of its

own on those ideas, as if it were not actively thinking about
matters highly relevant to MacIntyre's own views: thinking, I
mean, not just about those prior conduct-moral concepts or
ideas, but about the moral lives of which they are part, lives
irreducibly particular and individual.

Wanting to see Jane Austen as an 'Aristotelian' moralist like
himself, MacIntyre gives little or no weight to all the pointed
references to 'principle' throughout the novel. But it is in
relation to Fanny Price, whom he sees as the morally exemplary
figure of the narrative, that he has most to say.

He begins with a couple of patent inaccuracies: that at the
time the novel was written (1814), 'to refuse even a bad
marriage is an act of great courage, an act that is central to the
plot of *Mansfield Park*'.[42] It is made absolutely clear in the novel
itself that no one in it would expect a girl, even with Fanny's
'mediocre' social position to look forward to, to marry without
feeling love or some semblance of it – the point of some of Jane
Austen's most sardonic observations in the novel being the
shoddy, self-deluding, socially-advantageous semblances of love
that pass muster with many women. For Fanny to refuse Henry
Crawford is not an act of great courage: Sir Thomas certainly
leans on her rather hard, but it is clear that no one would, or
threatens to, force her into the marriage. What does take some
courage on her part, in fact, is the *suppressio veri* and the *suggestio
falsi* about Crawford's previous conduct that Fanny has to
practise with Sir Thomas, having to suffer in silence Sir
Thomas's charge of ingratitude, and having to endure Mary
Crawford's solicitude. As for the proposal's importance in the
plot, it is no more 'central' than, say, Fanny's visit to her family
at Portsmouth, which also occurs in the third volume of the
novel; and if it is central to anything, it is to the realization of
Fanny's spirit, her flowering into a beautiful and 'practically
wise' woman who can lead the (rather fatuous) Edmund into
the moral life of marriage as he once led her into the moral life
of Mansfield Park. For MacIntyre, however,

Fanny Price ... has been found positively unattractive by many critics.
But Fanny's lack of charm is crucial to Jane Austen's intentions. For
charm is the *characteristically modern* quality which those who lack or

simulate the virtues use to get by in the situations of characteristically modern social life...And the charm of an Elizabeth Bennett [*sic*] or even of an Emma may mislead us, genuinely attractive though it is, in our judgment on their *character*. Fanny is *charmless*; she has only the virtues, the genuine virtues, to *protect* her, and when she *disobeys* her guardian, Sir Thomas Bertram, and refuses marriage to Henry Crawford *it can only be because of what constancy requires*. In so refusing she places the danger of losing her *soul* before the reward of gaining *what for her* would be a whole world (my italics).[43]

It is hard to know where to begin with objections to this. Was the charm of Alcibiades a 'characteristically modern quality' useful for 'characteristically modern social life'? Then again, why must we reserve 'character' for the conduct-moral agent, and relegate the so-called 'charm' of Elizabeth Bennet and that of Emma Woodhouse – both 'charms' lumped together in the same catch-all basket and neither examined nor properly valued – to mere 'attractions'? (Even Hume on 'a manner, a grace, an ease, a genteelness, an I-know-not-what, which some men possess above others...and which catches our affection' is more searching and plausible than this.) But MacIntyre's account of Fanny seems more like moral melodrama than *Mansfield Park*. She is supposedly 'charmless'; but while she is rather priggish, and not everyone's favourite heroine, it is something like her particular charm that fascinates Henry Crawford and catches the affection of his sister, Mary. The Crawfords have the kind of 'charm' that MacIntyre has in mind, of course, which is perhaps better called 'vivacity'; but like the kind of affections they have, it is not the same kind of charm as Fanny's, which is rather like a sensitive steadiness. Indeed, Henry feels the attraction of Fanny's so much that he presents, to his sister at least, a rare example of a 'constancy' answering to that steadiness in his pursuit of it.

As for Fanny needing protection from Sir Thomas's commands, it seems as if MacIntyre's memory has misled him about the whole episode. There is no command, no disobedience, and the relevant protection comes from Sir Thomas himself. Indeed, one of the interesting things about the episode is the revealingly consistent play of Sir Thomas's moral conduct here (for example

his action over the fire being lit in Fanny's room) with his whole
spirit, his life as a whole; as against the no less revealingly
inconsistent play of Henry Crawford's moral conduct here (for
example his action in getting Fanny's brother a commission)
against his whole spirit, his life as a whole. Nor is there any
mystery about why Fanny refuses him; I cannot see what
MacIntyre means by 'it can only be because...'. An ideal
'constancy' does not come into it. Fanny does not love Henry
Crawford, or trust him, or even like him very much, no matter
what his social advantages. More to the point, she loves
Edmund, even though it looks (to her, not to us) as if she might
lose him to Mary Crawford. And although Jane Austen herself
seems to suggest in the last chapters of the novel that Fanny
might have come round to Henry in time, and that it might
have been the making of Henry if she did, the reader has no
doubt at all, from everything else in the novel, that Fanny will
not come round, and that, for *her*, marriage to Henry would be
nothing but a disaster. As for the Christian sentiment in the last
sentence I have quoted from MacIntyre, he must be thinking of
some other book. Not only does Fanny never come within a mile
of thinking that Henry represents 'a whole world' (in fact, no
one in the novel does, except perhaps for Mrs Norris); the point
about Fanny is that she is a moral being who could never *see* any
man's social 'advantages' in that way, let alone be tempted to
marry for them.

    What MacIntyre gets wrong, in short, is not just the actual
details of the episode, or even the social and conduct-moral
issues involved in it. His basically conduct-moral and exemplary
conception of 'narrative' causes him to miss what necessarily
complements the conduct-moral ideas and issues in the novel
and forms an essential part of its whole action (not simply its
plot): I mean the sense the novel captures of Fanny (and indeed
of many of the other characters too) as moral lives as well as
moral agents. Matters of sensibility, feeling, attraction, grace
and ease, hoping and fearing, and desiring, even some sense of
fatedness, become inter-twined in each character with matters
of judgment, choice, principle and deliberate intentional action;
and responsibility is found (by those capable of caring about it

and finding it) to apply to the whole of what one is, to how and what one sees things to be, to the life in one as one lives it out. To miss how Fanny's life takes root and begins to realize itself (like her sister, Susan's, later on) even in her parents' home in Portsmouth before she comes to Mansfield Park; how its roots catch hold at Mansfield Park (as they must) on what she can find vitalizing in what she is given – the kindness of Edmund and the civilities, ambiguous as they may be, of the big house; and how she comes to experience and engage with the world less defensively, with a freer, deeper and fuller animation, and so realizes, in the very way she is alive, the emerging attractiveness MacIntyre denies her: to miss all this is, in a very plain sense, to miss at least half the novel.[44] It is also to miss what a novel can capture of moral lives that the moral philosopher, even one who thinks he values literature very highly, cannot capture in 'discourse', which inevitably gives priority – logical and evaluative priority – to its own kind of conceptual terms and argument, and consequently sees literature as simply exemplifying or instantiating them.

V

Much the most perceptive, elaborate and far-reaching account by a contemporary moral philosopher of the relationship between moral philosophy and literature seems to me that of Martha C. Nussbaum – partly in her book on classical Greek thought, *The Fragility of Goodness*, and partly in a number of papers discussing a few modern literary works.[45] What I have in mind here are not so much the particular theses she argues, about moral luck, the vulnerability of goodness, and Greek attitudes to these, or (in some of her papers) about the nature of love; these call for specialist arguments of a kind I cannot pretend to. But underlying those theses are more general views about literature and moral philosophy, which are so extensive that they deserve a much fuller discussion than those views I have mentioned so far, and which are often put with such clarity and force that it is tempting simply to quote them. On many points, indeed, Nussbaum puts far better some of the things I have been trying to say in this book. And yet while I agree with a great many of her views, I must add that there are some I should nevertheless want to question or qualify, most especially on the two matters I raised earlier: her (unwitting) tendency towards merely conduct-morality, and her corresponding tendency (equally unwitting) to give in practice moral ideas in literature primacy over the moral *life* of literature. In fact, her work would be worth examining in some detail if only for the instructive example it provides of the differences between moral philosophy, however sympathetically attuned to literature, and literary criticism, however sympathetically attuned to moral philosophy.

Nussbaum's Aristotelianism involves an unusual view of Aristotle's *Ethics*. For her (as for Gadamer) Aristotle's conception of 'practical wisdom' dominates the foreground, while his (limited) conception of human nature and his (equally limited) table and account of 'the' virtues recede into the background, becoming (as Nussbaum seems to see it) something like a personal hedge against relativism.[46] This view of Aristotle has important advantages, of course. Nussbaum's account of 'practical wisdom' draws out the implications of what remains nowadays much the strongest and most persuasive side of Aristotle's ethics; and she insists that for Aristotle it is the person of practical wisdom who is 'the appropriate *criterion* of *correct* choice' (my italics):[47] which seems to mean in practice that 'correctness' is what is in accord with that conception of 'practical wisdom' which Nussbaum sees as Aristotle's.

Thus the crucial point of Aristotle's moral thought, Nussbaum argues, is his conception of moral practice – of the way one understands a situation and makes (as she puts it) 'correct' choices and decisions – as against a very widely held conception of moral practice that she calls 'Platonic' or 'scientific'. Each conception gives a different account of the role and importance of the particular and individual, as against the general and the universal. The 'Platonic' conception takes the most important features of a situation to be those that are general and repeatable; it sees the situation as only a case, an instantiation, of abstract general ideas and principles, so that the situation requires only universal rules or precepts for appropriate action. The Aristotelian conception, on the other hand, regards moral rules and precepts as no more than rules of thumb, useful in helping one to see the salient features of a situation, but always subordinate to the authority of the contingent, particular features of the situation. Indeed, it looks as if the Aristotelian conception is that which *can* capture the individual and unclassifiable:

> There is... room for surprise, room for both the cognitive insecurity and the human vulnerability that the Platonic scientific conception is seeking to avoid. A particular beloved person's particular salient properties can have ethical value when they are not anticipated by the [universal] principle – even when they *could not* because of their very nature be captured in any general formulation. Thus we must always be on the lookout for what is there before us in the world: we cannot rest secure in the thought that what we are to see and respond to is something that we have already seen before. And we must also be prepared for loss – for the valuable does not necessarily stay with us just on account of being exemplified in a universal principle that continues to be elsewhere instantiated.[48]

This is an unusual Aristotelian speaking, but it is worth noticing that, although the passage begins with what *seems* a matter of life-morality, it ends very differently when it gets spelt out. At the start, the difference between the 'Aristotelian' over the 'Platonic' is apparently a matter of two whole modes of life: a contrast Nussbaum traces most fully and forcefully in her discussion of Sophocles' *Antigone* in chapter 3 of *The Fragility of Goodness*. But even there, the difference seems at times what it clearly becomes here with Nussbaum's universal prescription. 'Thus we must always...': a difference merely of ('correct') conceptions – a matter, that is, of ideals of intellectual action, voluntary cognitive choices, universal cognitive precepts, in a word, a matter of *conduct*. It is as if Plato should have thought harder and become an Aristotelian. Nussbaum sees, of course, that a 'particular case would be surd and unintelligible without the guiding and sorting power of the universal... There is in effect a two-way illumination between particular and universal... [though] the particular takes priority.'[49] Nevertheless, a life-moralist would have to add to this that, if the particulars of a person, for instance, 'illuminate', it is not only the universal they illuminate, but also that which the universal may tacitly allow but which it cannot capture: those particulars – including the particulars of moral understanding, moral conduct and moral virtues, of course – in which a life or a mode of life, personal or social, manifests itself. Nor do the relevant particulars merely 'illuminate' this moral life; they evince it.

In one way, Nussbaum sees this too – that, indeed, being part of her notable insight about the moral dimensions of literature. She cites Aristotle's remark that, from his doctrine of the Mean, it follows that

The person who diverges only slightly from the correct is not blameworthy, whether he errs in the direction of the more or the less; but the person who diverges *more* is blamed: for this is evident. But to say to what point and how much someone is blameworthy is not easy to determine by a principle...: nor in fact is this the case with any other perceptible item. For things of this sort are among the concrete particulars, and the discrimination lies in perception. (1109b 18–23)[50]

What interests Nussbaum about this passage is not Aristotle's obvious concern with blame and conduct-morality, but his phrase, 'the discrimination lies in perception'. She regards this point (though it applies to judging wines no less than to judging guilt) to be a basic moral principle. A person's 'vision', how he or she sees things – whether 'correctly', as she puts it, or 'incorrectly' – is for her a crucially significant kind of moral action. For the kind of moral perception Aristotle means, she argues, is 'both cognitive and affective at the same time'; it is 'a complex response of the entire personality, an appropriate acknowledgement of the features of the situation on which action is to be based, a *recognition* of the particular'. And she explains what is meant by a 'correct' perception: full realization.

To have correct perception of the death of a loved one...is not simply to take note of this fact with intellect or judgment. If someone noted the fact but was devoid of passional response, we would be inclined to say that he did not really *see, take in, recognize,* what had happened; that he did not acknowledge the situation for what it was.[51]

This kind of realization, with its faithfulness to the particulars of a person or a situation, itself speaks the moral agent. It is also, we should remember, the conduct we expect of a literary work, which ought to realize what it claims to see, to feel and to think. But one of the interesting features of Nussbaum's commentary here is its silence about the other possibility in the case she outlines – the possibility on which modern dramatic literature depends: that we might be inclined to say that his 'love' was pretty notional or pretty exiguous, or perhaps that he could not yet endure taking in what had happened. As Nussbaum herself insists, in dramatic literature as in life we do not usually *know*, and know in advance, that 'a loved one' is the correct description and that this or that perception is therefore 'correct' or not. Aristotle's dictum is therefore significantly unlike Blake's, that 'as a man is, so he sees'. Aristotle's does not – as Nussbaum takes it, and as Aristotle no doubt meant it – open the possibility of innumerable ways and degrees both of seeing 'correctly' and of seeing 'incorrectly', numberless modes of human life, countless forms of moral being, among which we must dis- criminate – discriminate not only the correct from the incorrect, however, but the better from the worse. This, it seems to me, is what Nussbaum's stress on particulars should be directed towards – the life-moral sphere, not just the qualifications to be made in conduct-moral judgments. The latter, in fact, is no more than the way George Eliot the moralist saw the im- portance of particulars; the former, the more radical way George Eliot the novelist did.[52]

Nevertheless, despite any reservations one might have about Nussbaum's line of thought here, it leads to her most basic insight about literature. As she puts it in *The Fragility of Goodness*, Greek tragedies are to be regarded as 'ethical reflection in their own right'; indeed, she explicitly rejects the kind of exemplary use that philosophers (like MacIntyre) often make of literature. Literature is not, she rightly insists, merely a storehouse of examples for use in traditional philosophical discourse – the very style of that discourse betraying the assumption that ideas are prior to art and that 'the inquirer knows ahead of time what rationality is and how to express it in writing'. Unlike

philosophical examples, a tragic drama – read as a whole and in
its full poetic complexity – can trace

the history of a complex pattern of deliberation, showing its roots in a
way of life and looking forward to its consequences in that life. As it
does all of this, it lays open to view the complexity, the indeterminacy,
the sheer difficulty of actual human deliberation … [Unlike a philosopher's example], a tragedy does not display the dilemmas of its
characters as pre-articulated; it shows them searching for the morally
salient; and it forces us, as interpreters, to be similarly active.
Interpreting a tragedy is a messier, less determinate, more mysterious
matter than assessing a philosophical example; and even when the
work has once been interpreted, it remains unexhausted, subject to
reassessment, in a way that the example does not … [It provides] a
picture of [practical] reason's procedures and problems that could not
readily be conveyed in some other form.[53]

That says something important and not said often enough. In
another context, it is true, it leads Nussbaum into the
extravagant claim that a novel like *The Golden Bowl* is 'a
major … [and] irreplaceable work of moral philosophy, whose
place could not be fully filled by texts which we are accustomed
to call philosophical'.[54] As it stands, that claim seems to me
untenable, the differences between philosophy and literature
being what they are. But in pointing to the limits of moral
philosophy as it is commonly conceived, Nussbaum does seem to
me to be (quite rightly) getting at the way that this novel, like
any literary work, articulates and prompts (perhaps requires)
what is better called a process of 'ethical reflection', or as I
would prefer, of moral *thinking* – thinking of a kind, particular,
metaphorical and enactive, necessitated by the very nature of
the moral sphere, and not readily available to us except in works
of literature. This seems to me to help explain why different
readers, responding out of their different modes of life, reach
different views of the depth, import and force of the thinking in
particular literary works (*The Golden Bowl* being a case in
point). And Nussbaum is also right, I think, in fastening on the
gap in *The Golden Bowl* and (more obviously) in *The Ambassadors*,[55] between merely acting in accordance with moral rules
and ideals, even the highest, and doing that but also living out
the life that is in one, without fixed boundaries and markers in

a world of chance, of irreducible and deeply-valued particulars, and of vulnerability to moral danger – the danger of doing wrong to others or harm to oneself, or of moral confusion or bewilderment, or of having to wait on events to show their pattern,[56] or of compromising one's own conduct-moral integrity or purity. Indeed, this gap for Nussbaum *is* the moral import of James's (and his responsive reader's) 'sense of life'.[57] It is also this, as she says elsewhere, that 'literary theory' (at least that which wants only to liquidate the moral subject) has consistently ignored but will eventually have to reckon with.[58]

And yet, for all this, Nussbaum's view of literature is likely to strike a literary critic as limited in being expressly cognitive: literature is (unproblematically) 'about' recognizable moral problems, and it shows us, holds up before us, cases of 'practical wisdom'. Like Rorty, though in a far more substantial sense than his, she regards literature as speaking about people – '*about us*, about our lives and choices and emotions … about our social existence and the totality of our connections'. Our interest in it 'becomes (like Strether's in Chad [in Henry James's *The Ambassadors*]) cognitive: an interest in finding out (by seeing and feeling and otherwise perceiving) what possibilities (and tragic impossibilities) life offers to us, what hopes and fears for ourselves it underwrites or subverts'.[59] This is why moral philosophers ('and, in general, people pursuing "wisdom" about the practical') 'need to include in their study texts that have the appropriate form. If philosophy is a search for wisdom about ourselves, philosophy needs to turn to literature.'[60] What Nussbaum means by 'the appropriate form' is explained in several places; and here again a literary critic may well register some unease. Nussbaum sees that literary 'form' precludes the common habit of moral theorists to 'mine the work for a set of propositional claims'. On the other hand, what she thinks philosophers ought to do instead is to conduct 'an investigation of that which is expressed and "claimed" by the shape of the sentences themselves, by images and cadences and pauses themselves, by the forms of the traditional genres, by narrativity, themselves'.[61] Why only 'claimed by'? Why not also 'manifested in'? In *The Fragility of Goodness*, she speaks of

the distinctive moral content of Greek tragic poetry as 'not
separable from its poetic style'. The Greeks did not think it was
an 'ethically neutral matter', nor should we, whether someone
wrote poetry. 'Stylistic choices – the selection of certain metres,
certain patterns of image and vocabulary – are taken to be
closely bound up with a conception of the good.'[62] In other
words, the 'appropriate form' is that which best serves, and is
meant to serve, as a vehicle of formulable ideas of the good,
'correct' moral perception and wisdom; and it is evidently
analysable into a set of universal stylistic features that are
already known, defined and available for the writer's choice
and exploitation. This is a view of moral import and of 'form'
that a literary critic must have reservations about.

In so far as literature does explore the possibilities of human
life as these present themselves to practical moral wisdom in
Nussbaum's sense, her account of it is on the whole pretty
convincing, and also pretty heartening, at least to literary critics
who may have often thought something like this, but never seen
it expressed with such philosophical vigour. Nevertheless, there
are by now certain questions that a literary critic will want to
press – as one critic, Charles Altieri, has[63] – about her concentration on a cognitive and mimetic conception of literature
(without also allowing for, say, an expressive one): a bias that,
as Altieri says, clearly goes (along with her conceptions of moral
good and moral experience) with her reliance on Aristotle. The
difficulty here, Altieri points out, is not only that she concentrates on 'the traditional novelistic and dramatic functions'
(forms?) of literature at the expense of other literary modes and
styles; she also tends to ignore the moral power of literature to
affect the way a reader imagines what he or she *is*. But these
reservations seem to me to arise from a deeper problem:
Nussbaum's failure to consider literary works, let alone to value
them, for the '*anima*', the 'soul', the particular mode of life, they
manifest, as well as for the ('correct') conceptions and views
they depict and recommend to the properly attentive reader by
means of affective formal and stylistic techniques.

To a literary critic, for example, it is striking how little
Nussbaum makes of the ways that literature at its best (which is

what is being considered) creates (or 'constructs') the individual *lives* it thinks about: creates, I mean, not just the moral
situations, perceptions and actions of the characters, and the
responsive attention to particulars in which the character's or
the author's moral wisdom resides, but creates that of which
these *are* the particulars, what it is that *makes* them irreducible,
what it is that makes the particulars *matter* so much. It is
impossible, as Nussbaum argues, to capture an individual life or
mode of life in the universals of moral philosophy; and in
literature, different ages and cultures have conceived individual
lives in very different ways.[64] So, of course, does our own eclectic
age. And Nussbaum is clearly right to ask any moral philosophy
to acknowledge and leave room for just such crucial moral facts.
But, although she does not say so, it has always been the
(morally necessary) undertaking of literature to create or
construct some convincing sense of individual lives *as* lives, no
matter how many different conceptions and kinds of construc-
tions it has expressed over the centuries in doing so. Nussbaum's
account of literature gives much too little emphasis to those
sensuous and dynamic features of literature, in any genre and in
any style, that can bring the reader not merely to a correct
(perhaps new, perhaps deeper) perception or understanding of
human life as an object, but to a fuller, more intense, larger
mode of life itself – providing, of course, that the reader's moral
being can open itself to that of the work. (It hardly needs saying
that literature does not necessarily make the reader a better
moral agent or improve his or her life, any more than moral
philosophy does. In both cases, there are also other conditions to
be met.) It is not just the reader's five senses that literature can
awaken, or the reader's self-conception; more importantly, it
can also awaken and sharpen the reader's most basic sense of the
'spirit' of people, of vitality and decay in them, of when (in
Lear's phrase) 'one is dead, and when one lives'.

Some of Nussbaum's phrases do point in the right direction:
'possibilities of *life*', for instance, or the novel's capacity for 'the
sustained exploration of particular lives ... [or] the length and
breadth of a life' – or the term Nussbaum adopts from Aristotle
in speaking of the way in which the *Antigone* examines an entire

'course of life'.[65] In her recognition of the special 'cognitive' capacities that literature requires, and its concern with the possibly tragic conflicts between moral ideals, she might well seem to have said – or at least left room for – everything that a literary critic could reasonably want her to say. But although she does make these points, it is often more in a general or theoretical way than in cogent accounts of particular literary works. With literature, in fact, it is her own 'practical', individual perceptions and deliberations that are not always wholly convincing.

For one thing, her cognitive and mimetic conception of literature usually leads her to give primacy to the idea, and to look to a work for the 'correct' views or attitudes or mental processes the work depicts for us: or in Nussbaum's words, those it 'shows' us, 'leads us to think', 'invites us to see', and so on: terms characteristic of those who want to read a work as exemplifying or instantiating ideas and principles we already know, on other, 'philosophical' grounds, to be 'true' or 'correct'. Thus it is hard at times to distinguish what Nussbaum says about a work from what might be said by a philosopher or a critic who *was* 'mining the work for a set of propositional claims'. She usually seems to perceive actual literary works too much in the same light as her claim in *The Fragility of Goodness*, that 'we could exemplify Aristotelian perception using texts of many different sorts. I think, above all, of the novels of Henry James', although on this occasion she takes a speech from Euripides' *Trojan Women* 'in order to avoid anachronism' (as if *that* were a relevant issue).[66] There is nothing wrong, of course, in using literature for such examples. The danger lies only in suggesting that the ideas in a literary work form a separable, identifiable element in it, and that the moral significance and value of the work lie in the 'correctness' with which it depicts, in appropriate form and style, the 'correct' kind of ideas, deliberation and action. Nussbaum probably does not mean to suggest either of these, but if so, she sometimes takes too little care to block them off.

Her tendency to give primacy to moral ideas, and to perceive and analyze literature primarily in terms of such ideas, affects even her best, most explorative criticism of Greek tragedy in *The Fragility of Goodness*: her discussion of Sophocles' *Antigone* (in her chapter 3) and Euripides' *Hecuba* (in her chapter 13). The former, she begins,

> examines two different attempts to close off the prospect of conflict and tension by simplifying the structure of the agent's commitments and loves. It asks what motivates such attempts; what becomes of them in a tragic crisis; and, finally, whether practical wisdom is to be found in this sort of strategy or in an entirely different approach to the world.
>
> The *Antigone* is a play about practical reason and the ways in which practical reason orders or sees the world.[67]

These abstract issues are what Nussbaum assumes the play is about; it is certainly what most of her discussion of the play is about. At the end, it is true, she does strike a very different note: 'By invoking Dionysus as "chorus-master of the fire-breathing stars" (1147), the Chorus reminds us that we are watching and responding to just such a choral dance at a Dionysian festival. They suggest that the spectacle of this tragedy is itself an orderly mystery...'[68] Nussbaum always tends to interpret texts warmly and generously; but how could the invocation she quotes really have, by itself, the profound effect she ascribes to it here? The critical issue is, 'how does the drama create such a view of itself?' Our life-moral sense of the tragedy as a *mystery* springs from various dramatic elements and qualities in the play, but how are these related to the play's concern with practical reason and conduct? What is it in the dynamic 'spectacle' of this tragedy that brings us to see it as an 'orderly mystery'? And what mystery is it; and why and how is its mysteriousness important?

Nussbaum does try to tell us:

> It is this quality of loving affirmation that both Euripides and Aristotle (along with the parts of Plato who speak as Protagoras and the interlocutors of the *Phaedrus*), wish, in their different ways, *to hold before us* as an adult way of being excellent...But the Aristotelian argument, which continues and refines the insights of tragedy, reminds us that we do not achieve purity or simplicity without a loss in richness and fullness of life – a loss, it is claimed, in intrinsic value. (my italics)[69]

Clearly, the moral wisdom Nussbaum means, and perhaps also the mystery she means, are not at all simple or commonplace or comforting. As she puts them, they actually focus on one of the ways in which ideals of moral conduct can sometimes, in some people, preclude certain qualities of moral life. But Nussbaum's assimilation here of drama, treatise and philosophical dialogue drastically minimizes the differences between the various senses of 'hold before us'. A drama does not 'hold before us' depersonalized insights or ideals or even mysteries. It holds before us (in the sense of manifesting) a particular mode of life in the very way it imagines the lives and insights of particular individuals; and a drama holds particular individuals before us (in the sense of depicting them) rather than just the formulable views they express and 'represent'. It is significant, I think, that Nussbaum seems to have a limitingly instrumental view of poetry and of its importance in drama: once again, the idea takes primacy. Speaking of Aeschylus' *Agamemnon*, for example, she seems to be interested in the characters' conflicts for the sake of the moral positions those conflicts express, rather than, as a dramatic poet usually is, in the conflicting moral positions for the sake of the modes of life these conflicts manifest. Aeschylus 'shows' us not so much a solution to 'the problem' of practical moral conflict as 'the richness and depth of *the problem* itself'; and his 'poetic resources' put 'the scene *vividly* before us, *show* us *debate* about it, and evoke in us responses important to its assessment'.[70] In face of the words I have italicized, it is worth reminding ourselves that the value of the dramas as moral thinking does not consist merely in the ascertained wisdom, the 'correct' insights, they 'hold before' or 'show us vividly', but far more in the depth, energy and honesty with which they consider what it is to be, to be fated to be, to have to suffer as, and to have to live out the life in, this and that particular moral being. *The Fragility of Goodness* (like Aristotle's moral philosophy) generally leaves it unclear what a 'richness and fullness of life' would be in any particular individual; and yet surely the clearest and most convincing sense of such a life in Greek drama is not what is pre-determined and then 'shown' us in its characters, but what manifests itself in each play itself taken as a whole. And if so, then surely a prime task for the critical reader is to articulate as best he or she can the quality and value of *that* life.

In subtle ways, Nussbaum gives the moral idea primacy in dealing with Henry James too. At first glance, she seems very aware of the danger of doing so. As she reads *The Golden Bowl*, for example, the vessel of moral insight is an 'ideal' Maggie Verver, who encapsulates not just the highest ideals of moral conduct, but more, a still finer moral *life* that, at the end, recognizes that it must sacrifice the absolute purity and integrity of conduct as the necessary price of its own fullness. To be the ideal reader of the novel is therefore to be like the ideal Maggie in the second part of the book:

keenly alive in thought and feeling to every nuance of the situation, actively seeing and caring for all the parties concerned – and therefore safely right in the perfection of his or her attention. But we know already that this 'ideal' is not the work's entire story about human practical wisdom. We know that where there is great love in one direction there may also be, in another direction, a tragically necessary blindness. We now want to know whether this feature of our moral life also finds its place in the author's way of being responsible to his created story and in the reader's way of responding to his text. In other words, does the text itself acknowledge the flawed nature of the consciousness that produced it and elicit from us in turn, as readers, an acknowledgment of our own imperfection?[71]

What looks like an appeal to moral life again runs aground. The relevant moral ideas and the relevant moral 'correctness' are already 'known', it seems; Nussbaum can therefore answer her own question with a 'yes': 'with this text, as perhaps with few others in English literature, we are struck at every point by the incompleteness and inadequacy of our own attention'; and this incompleteness and inadequacy of ours highlights the well-nigh perfect adequacy of the authorial persona in relation to his 'more or less bleeding participants', as he calls them. If Maggie (and we) are revealed as morally 'superficial and impoverished with respect to Charlotte' at the end of the book – for into Charlotte's 'isolation and pain and silence' neither the author's nor (supposedly therefore) the reader's 'intelligent conversation and response' enter – this is the morally responsible, *self-imposed* limitation of the author's consciousness. Which is to say that the 'spirit', the moral life, manifested by the novel consists in nothing but James's perfectly 'correct' moral *conduct* as an observer and practitioner of practical wisdom.[72]

As a whole, Nussbaum's account of *The Golden Bowl* is governed by this unargued valuation of James's 'spirit', so that her emphasis falls on the *content* of his supposedly perfect 20/20 moral 'perception'. At first glance, once again, Nussbaum's account seems to be exactly of the kind that might be prompted by the distinction between moral conduct merely and moral life, and the irreconcilable conflicts possible between them. In fact, she argues that this novel (like *The Ambassadors*) is intentionally *about* that distinction and that conflict; and she traces how Maggie is brought (by the author) from innocently relying on moral rules and ideals, and innocently assuming that all moral values harmonize with one another, to relying on her practical wisdom, until, in the very last sentence of the book, Maggie comes to realize something of the tragic incompatibility of some conduct-moral values and some life-moral ones:

> It kept him before her therefore, taking in – or trying to – what she so wonderfully gave... [He] presently echoed: '"See"? I see nothing but *you*.' And the truth of it had, with this force, after a moment, so strangely lighted his eyes that as for pity and dread of them she buried her own in his breast.

Nussbaum sees a great deal in this passage.

> Maggie, seeing this singleness of vision, reacts to her sight of Amerigo as to a tragedy – with 'pity and dread.' For she sees, in truth, that he *does* see only her, that she and he together have brought about, within his imagination, an extinction of vision and a failure of response; and that this has happened of tragic necessity because of the requirements of his commitment to her.

For Nussbaum, the novel thus provides 'something like a persuasive argument' that (as we otherwise *know*) 'our loves and commitments are so related that infidelity and failure of response are more or less inevitable features even of the best examples of loving'.[73] And it is from this starting point, which once more gives primacy to the idea, that her second paper on *The Golden Bowl* describes what the novel shows: it shows what being 'finely aware and richly responsible' consist in, which extends even to the limitations she believes the author consciously and responsibly imposes on his own narration. It is a characteristically generous account of the novel – generous both to the author and to the Ververs, father and daughter. On the other hand, it does not envisage, let alone answer, other possible accounts of the novel; in fact, it seems to me (as to other readers, no doubt) over-generous to the Ververs and also to James. Her account of the last sentence of the book is a case in point. Its moral complexity really depends on seven words – '*as for pity* and *dread* of them' (my italics) – and two of those words, it is worth noticing, are 'as for'. Whatever that phrase means, apart from some unspecified likeness, it is surely not a substantial enough peg on which to hang large conclusions about the moral import of the novel as a whole. Tragic realizations made in a vaguely-lit turn in the very last sentence of a very long book seem to me neither realizations nor tragic, quite apart from other, equally plausible, things the four words could refer to: Maggie seeing a reflection in his eyes of complicity in her manipulations and some well-deserved guilt about them, for instance.

Another highly relevant case is a passage from chapter 37 of the novel that Nussbaum makes much of in her second paper. In this chapter, the 'acts to be recorded', as she puts it, are Mr Verver's sacrifice of his need of Maggie by choosing (for her sake: unspecified) to return to America with Charlotte; Maggie's 'preservation of his dignity' in making this choice (i.e. not letting on that she thinks she knows why he is really making it); and his 'recognition of her separate and autonomous life' as so large and so fine (as he supposes) as both to require and to justify his renunciation. Nussbaum's account of the moral complexities here, and of the Ververs' actions, is itself fine and eloquent; and as she says, an essential element in the Ververs' moral manoeuvring is recorded in the passage in question. For the passage pictures Maggie in crucially life-moral terms; and Nussbaum takes it both that the picture is Adam Verver's, and that the picture is in some sense true. For Nussbaum, one might say, the picture is rather like Cleopatra's 'dream' of Antony: 'His legs bestrid the ocean...'; but here, it is surely relevant to add, there is no Dolabella to answer, 'Gentle Madam, no'. The passage she discusses is the following:

The mere fine pulse of passion in it, the suggestion as of a creature consciously floating and shining in a warm summer sea, some element of dazzling sapphire and silver, a creature cradled upon depths, buoyant among dangers, in which fear or folly, or sinking otherwise than in play, was impossible – something of all this might have been making once more present to him, with his discreet, his half shy assent to it, her probable enjoyment of a rapture that he, in his day, had presumably convinced no great number of persons either of his giving or of his receiving. He sat awhile as if he knew himself hushed, almost admonished, and not for the first time; yet it was an effect that might have brought before him rather what she had gained than what he had missed... It could pass, further, for knowing – for knowing that without him nothing might have been: which would have been missing least of all. 'I guess I've never been jealous', he finally remarked... 'Oh, it's you, father, who are what I call beyond everything. Nothing can pull *you* down.'[74]

For Nussbaum, – intent on what is 'claimed' by the 'shape of the sentences', and by images and cadences and pauses and so on – this picture of Maggie captures a 'sense of lucidity, expressive feeling, and genuine lyricism', which positively move us. For Verver to see his daughter in just this way is 'to know her, to know their situation, not to miss anything in it – to be, in short, "a person on whom nothing is lost"'. The passage 'records a moral achievement of deep significance', and one that has 'a pivotal role' in all of Verver's subsequent moral activity.[75]

If we read this passage in its context, however, it is much less clear that the picture of Maggie is to be taken as her father's rather than that of the 'authorial voice'; and as for the picture itself, it is also hard to see it as encapsulating such a great moral truth and such a great moral achievement. For one thing, if we attend not just to what is 'claimed' by the shape of the sentences, the images, cadences, pauses and so on, but also to the 'authorial' life that manifests itself in them, the 'picture' seems to me to have a rather factitious, not to say laboured, air about it. (Comparison with the Cleopatra passage only makes this glaringly obvious.) Even more to the point, if the sentences 'claim' to form a true 'picture', their shape is actually a web of hypothetical conjectures, suppositions and possibilities: 'the suggestion as of', 'might have been making', 'her probable enjoyment', 'had presumably convinced', 'as if he knew', 'might have brought', 'as he might feel', 'could shine', 'could pass', 'might have been seeing' and so on. This is not the only passage in the novel suggesting or conjecturing moral depths and subtleties, of course; there is, for example, that 'as of' in the very last sentence. But this passage, even taken at face-value as a sketch of a highly idealized Maggie, seems beyond any clear moral (and sexual) perception that Adam Verver could articulate, even to himself. What he explicitly says in this scene, or what he is given explicitly to say – including such gems as 'Look here, Mag, ... I ain't selfish. I'll be blowed if I'm selfish', and 'Oh shucks' – is not more than might be said by a sensible, thoughtful, but rather commonplace man. His much subtler daughter has a very high, idealized conception of him, it is true, a conception that becomes more explicit (and more excited) towards the end of this scene, when he does exactly what she wants him to do; and the 'authorial voice' may be registering a similar Maggie-projected valuation of him here. But if so, the reader has to do a good deal of complaisant projecting of his own in order to see in Verver a dramatic reality, a moral life, that could convincingly express its perceptions in such fine conjectures and subtle possibilities. In fact, if the fancied picture of Maggie does express any such fine moral perception of great significance (and I for one do not think it does), the perception is surely less Verver's than James's, even if James may be thought to be ascribing it to his character in some vague and uncommitting degree. Certainly, it is all too possible to take this picture of Maggie as manifesting the basic limitation of this novel: James seems to be trying here, as he does so often in the book, to weave a web of fine, life-moral significance around characters, actions, and situations that are either dramatically too thin or morally too dubious to manifest it in themselves.

Hence, I think, the rather unfocused comic irony in the passage Nussbaum cites – if it *is* comic irony – of 'passion', 'rapture', 'bliss' and 'balm' (not to mention 'the beauty of her condition'). Any such transcendence of the conscious conduct-moral self as these words suggest seems to me highly uncharacteristic of either father or daughter, which is one moral difficulty about the novel. But the problem goes further: the novel seems to lack any substantial life-moral value, made manifest in any of the characters or in any of their relationships or in any of their projects, which can be placed against their questionable conduct-morality. If the novel 'claims' to show how Maggie's sufferings and actions – actions life-morally necessary though conduct-morally dubious – realize some finer, freer, deeper, nobler mode of life and love in her (and perhaps in others as well), I am surely not the only reader who finds any such moral life conspicuously unrealized: unrealized dramatically because unrealized in any freer energy, any strong vital pulse, manifesting itself in the prose that 'renders' the drama. James's moral consciousness is intense, subtle, elaborate, self-aware and all-absorbing, but it is also often self-absorbed, and it is always moral *consciousness*. Such life-moral, trans-conscious possibilities as passion, rapture, bliss, seem highly uncharacteristic not only of the Ververs, but of the novel itself. But whatever the reader makes of the novel's '*anima*' or 'spirit', its distinctive moral life – and that 'spirit' may well seem darker, more obscure, or at least more ambiguous, than a state of 'correct' moral perception and 'responsible' moral action – it is like any mode of human life: it has a nature, powers and also *limitations* of its own. Nussbaum rarely engages in such critical inquiry of the life-moral strengths and limitations of the various works or writers she discusses, though Beckett, it is true, does seem a notable exception. But even there, Nussbaum's life-moral criticism actually turns on the truth or falsity (the 'correctness') of Beckett's beliefs about the world.

To make moral sense of a life or a mode of life, it is necessary to capture some sense of it *as* a life – not just a linear narrative of contingent circumstances and events and voluntary actions from birth to death, nor just a collection of general traits and qualities, nor just a locus for the inter-action and 'discourse' of impersonal biological, social, cultural, psychological, linguistic and other structures or forces. It is part of Nussbaum's distinction as a moral philosopher that she sees why and how this applies with people; and yet with literature she often seems in practice to share the characteristic failing of the philosopher: to think of a life, as Aristotle also does, in too restrictingly sequential and too normative a way (with one eye, that is, on '*the* good life for man' and '*the* virtues'), and consequently with too simple and unproblematical a sense of what individual lives consist in. It is this that seems to underlie the philosopher's tendency to give priority to ideas: to regard fictional and dramatic works of literature, not as articulating a process of moral thinking, but as a kind of moral philosophizing. Hence, I think, Nussbaum's tendency to treat the moral beings depicted in such literature, despite her own much more cogent general understanding, too simply as 'correctly', *philosophically*-understood moral cases; her account of them is consequently unqualified by a sense of other moral possibilities, other moral considerations, other moral complexities, manifest in the work.

Nevertheless, if Nussbaum shows some of the failing of the moral philosopher, it is also part of her distinction as a moral philosopher that she can provide a striking counter-example to this tendency in her accounts of literature. However convincing her account of Plato's *Symposium* (chapter 6 of *The Fragility of Goodness*) may be to classical philosophers, it seems to me a vivid and telling example of a critic seeking to capture a sense of the particular lives depicted in a work, and because of that – or rather, *in* that – to capture a sense of the life of the work itself. Her account of Alcibiades, and to a lesser extent of Socrates, as they figure in the dialogue is built up from character-analysis, narrative and story, picture and image, historical scholarship, logical analysis, analysis of argumentative motive and a sensory responsiveness to a life in activity ('bursting'), not just in action: 'Alcibiades the beautiful, the marvel[l]ous nature, presents himself to our sensuous imagination, an appearance bursting with color and all the mixed impurity of the mortal flesh.'[76] Nussbaum distinguishes Alcibiades' views very sharply from Socrates', and therefore both from Plato's; and in the process we are led, not just to see, but in seeing to grant, what Nussbaum's critical argument is driving at: the life-moral importance (which is philosophical as well as – or rather, because – experiential) of loving, founded as it is in the particularity, indeed the uniqueness, of human beings and therefore in the impermanent and the certainty of loss, as against the importance of reason, which is founded in the permanent and universal. Finally, there 'dawns on us the full light of Plato's design, his comic tragedy of choice and practical wisdom. We see two kinds of value, two kinds of knowledge; and we see that we must choose.'[77]

It may be relevant to Nussbaum's critical insight here that this is not a case of drama being assimilated to philosophical argument, but of philosophical argument being assimilated to drama: to what she calls Plato's 'comic tragedy'. The characters' views about the world are not important for what they manifest of their moral beings, but their moral being for how this shapes their views about the world. It may also be relevant that this text is not by Aristotle and therefore expository, but by Plato and therefore dialogical – as well as challenging to Nussbaum's earlier view of Plato, who now, in this 'harsh and alarming book', 'starkly confronts us with a choice, and at the same time...makes us see so clearly that we cannot choose anything'.[78] Perhaps it is only the last infirmity of a philosophical mind to look for 'choices' and for the general truths about the world that the book 'makes us see'. On the other hand, Nussbaum herself shows us how the book's cogency as a process of moral thinking rests on its life-moral sense of the very different modes of life (seen here really *as* lives) it depicts and explores: in the subtle, attentive particularity of that lies its own 'spirit' or life. And if it is Nussbaum the conduct-moralist who sees Alcibiades' story as 'in the end, a story of waste and loss, of the failure of practical reason to shape a life',[79] it is Nussbaum the life-moralist who, having described how Alcibiades died, captures something of the life that was in him in a dramatic picture set against that death: 'When Alcibiades finished speaking, they burst out laughing at the frankness of his speech, because it looked as though he was still in love with Socrates (222c). He stood there, perhaps, with ivy in his hair, crowned with violets.'[80] To grasp this, as well as 'the failure of practical reason', and their bearing on both the argument and the spirit of the work, is the kind of critical life-moral insight she argues for.

As I hope is obvious, I think the main point of considering Nussbaum's work in such detail as this is to understand how a highly thoughtful and sympathetic philosopher sees the moral significance of literature. If the way she traces out that significance in particular works seems to me not always wholly convincing, I do think that she does at least underline a real problem for the literary critic – especially one who sees, as I do, the moral life of a work as manifesting itself in (among other things) a distinctive kind of moral thinking. As she insists, the awareness and the attitudes with which a reader begins a tragedy or a substantial novel, for instance, are not those with which he or she ends it; something about the work – what I would call its whole 'dramatic action' – brings the reader from one state to the other. To call the process an argument or, as Nussbaum sometimes does, moral 'philosophizing' will not do; but even to call it moral 'thinking' – a term that still claims it to be, in a wide but legitimate sense of the word, rational – leaves the critic with the difficulty of specifying and tracing it out so as to incorporate all of the sensory, enactive, dynamic elements both of its life-moral force and its rationality, without distorting either it or the reader's answering to it. For it is a distortion to treat it, in effect if not in theory, as a matter of recognizable ideas that the work presents to the reader's mind in a 'vivid' and 'practical' form and thereby persuades the reader to share its own moral 'knowledge', its own 'correct' moral understanding.

Much the same problem arises when it comes to explaining the specific ways in which a particular work is 'about' people. What, precisely, is it about people that *War and Peace*, for instance, or *Antony and Cleopatra*, is about? Once again, Nussbaum underlines the problem here by making it seem easier to solve than it is. The works she discusses, it turns out, are

about the same philosophical issues and 'correct' philosophical
insights that she (with or without Aristotle) thinks morally
crucial. There is nothing unusual about this kind of answer, of
course; we are all drawn to works that express or embody our
fondest wisdom. But it is also commonly assumed, as Nussbaum
tends to assume at times, that the 'themes' of a work, what it is
specifically 'about', are just such abstract moral truths,
'correct' ideas even about having moral ideas, which it gives us
to 'see'.

In practice, that assumption is probably the most common
way that the idea is given priority, both in moral thinking
generally and in literature particularly. In moral thinking, one
may conceive the idea as an 'ideal', or an 'image', or a
'vocabulary', or principles of 'correct' judgment, action, and
even practical reason; and doing this is to give primacy to
conduct-morality. With literature, it is most often abstract ideas
that are treated as if they preceded the work (perhaps in time,
but certainly in logic) and as if (in interpretation and criticism)
they are the terms in which the work should be discussed. Once
again, literature is reduced to 'discourse'; and what gets left out
is precisely the power of a literary work to *create* or '*construct*' the
objects of its thinking, very often by creating moral agents who
are also moral lives: the particulars in which the life exhibits
itself, and the particulars in which the relationships between
agency and life exhibit themselves, being not only main objects,
but also main manifestations, of that thinking.

To say what an intensely complex novel or a Shakespearean
tragedy is 'about' is, as Nussbaum sees, not at all easy. The
answer is certainly not self-evident, even after we reach the state
of mind to which the work finally brings us. Nor, given our
actual experience of such works, can we believe any answer to
be more than provisional, always open to revision: even, indeed,
the answer that a work is 'about' the impossibility of saying
definitely what any complex 'narrative' or 'drama', whether in
art or in life, is 'about'. In seeing this, and seeing too that
rational moral thought is not necessarily nor even often the kind
practised by philosophers or ethical casuists, Nussbaum's
theoretical insight is somewhat at odds with her practice; but

her practice still presents another challenge to the literary critic. For it is a question whether any critical account of the moral life, and the complex moral thinking that manifests it, of a novel like *The Golden Bowl* or of a drama like *Antony and Cleopatra* – thinking that is creative, 'constructive', sequential and rational – can really avoid making that thinking seem, by the very exigencies of critical practice, argumentative and rational in the same way as philosophy is. I am not sure if it can; – but that is clearly matter for another inquiry.

Notes

1 Bernard Williams, *Ethics and the Limits of Philosophy*, London, 1985, p. 93.

1 'PERPETUALLY MORALISTS'...'IN A LARGE SENSE'

1 Francis Bacon, *The Advancement of Learning*, in *The Works of Francis Bacon*, ed. J. Spedding, R. L. Ellis and D. D. Heath, 14 vols., London, 1870, III, p. 421.

2 Matthew Arnold, 'Wordsworth' in *Essays in Criticism, Second Series*, in *Complete Prose Works of Matthew Arnold*, ed. R. H. Super, 11 vols., Ann Arbor, 1960–77, X, 1973, pp. 36–55.

3 Samuel Johnson, *Lives of the English Poets*, ed. G. B. Hill, 3 vols., Oxford, 1905, I, pp. 99–100.

4 Cf. Matthew Arnold 'On the Modern Element in Literature', *Prose Works*, I, 1960, *pp.* 18–37. It is interesting that, about the same time as Arnold gave this lecture (1857), another thinker in London was also pondering why some literature survived the age in which it was written and which it therefore reflected; but in the *Grundrisse*, Marx could only come up with a rather weak and commonplace answer (probably derived from Schiller): Karl Marx, *Grundrisse*, trans. Martin Nicolaus, Penguin edn, 1973, pp. 110–11. On the equation of writing and 'violence' common in contemporary 'theory', and on the moral views implicit in such 'theory', see Tobin Siebers, *The Ethics of Criticism*, Ithaca and London, 1988.

5 Cf. Mary Midgley, *Heart and Mind: the Varieties of Moral Experience*, Brighton, 1981, pp. 103ff: 'Is "Moral" a Dirty Word?'.

6 For some examples of this attitude see *PN Review*, XII, iv, 1985.

7 Arnold, 'Wordsworth', p. 46.

8 This point is nicely illustrated in the cases discussed by James S.

Fishkin, *Beyond Subjective Morality: Ethical Reasoning and Political Philosophy*, New Haven and London, 1984, chapter 3. For another discussion of judging, see Wayne C. Booth's stimulating book, *The Company We Keep: An Ethics of Fiction*, Berkeley and Los Angeles, 1988, especially pp. 70–7.

9 Ronald Beiner, *Political Judgment*, London, 1983, chapter 7. A much more thorough and widely known discussion of the matter is, of course, Hans-Georg Gadamer's *Truth and Method*, N.Y., 1975.

10 Arnold, 'Wordsworth', p. 45.

11 Cf. Thomas Nagel, *Mortal Questions*, Cambridge, 1979, p. 51: 'We make judgments about people's beauty or health or intelligence which are evaluative without being moral.' But surely we also make judgments about these matters which are moral in being evaluative?

12 Mill on Bentham, in *Collected Works of John Stuart Mill*, ed. J. M. Robson *et al.*, Toronto and London, x, 1969, pp. 112–13.

13 Mill, *Collected Works*, x, pp. 95ff.

14 Mill's *Logic*, in *Collected Works*, VIII, 1973, p. 949. For another discussion of Mill's distinctions between the moral and the aesthetic, see John Gray, *Mill on Liberty: a Defence*, London, 1983, pp. 40ff.

15 Mill, *Logic*, in *Collected Works*, VIII, 1973, p. 952.

16 See, for example, R. M. Hare, *Freedom and Reason*, Oxford, 1963, p. 186; Bernard Williams, *Ethics and the Limits of Philosophy*, p. 6. For another literary critic's view of the matter, however, see Wayne C. Booth, *The Company We Keep*, pp. 8–11.

17 Gadamer, *Truth and Method*, p. 5.

18 Cf. Midgley, *Heart and Mind*, p. 117: the meaning of 'moral' is, in some usages, 'much like *spiritual*, but without the ontology'.

19 Alan Ryan, *The Philosophy of John Stuart Mill*, London, 1970, p. 216.

20 J. S. Mill, *Utilitarianism*, chapter 2 in *Collected Works*, x, 1969. By 'his own experience' I mean, of course, the famous crisis described in chapter 5 of his *Autobiography*.

21 Henry Sidgwick, *The Methods of Ethics*, London, [1874], 1901, pp. 107–8, n. 1.

22 Leon Rosenstein, in *Critical Inquiry*, 3, 1976–7, pp. 543–65.

23 Hare, *Freedom and Reason*, pp. 150ff. On the point of terminology here, Hare is arguing against P. F. Strawson's paper, 'Social Morality and Individual Ideal', *Philosophy*, 36, 1961, pp. 1–17. I discuss some of Strawson's other ideas in the next chapter.

24 Hare, *Freedom and Reason*, pp. 153–4.

25 Hare, *Freedom and Reason*, pp. 147ff.

26 J. L. Mackie, *Ethics: Inventing Right and Wrong*, Penguin Books, 1977, pp. 106–7.

27 J. B. Schneewind, *Sidgwick's Ethics and Victorian Moral Philosophy*, Oxford, 1977, pp. 243–4.

2 '*HOW* TO LIVE' AND 'HOW TO *LIVE*'

1 Matthew Arnold, *Literature and Dogma* in *Prose Works*, VI, 1968, pp. 404 and 407–11.

2 Samuel Coleridge, *Biographia Literaria*, ed. J. Shawcross, 2 vols., Oxford, 1907, II, chapter 18, p. 65.

3 P. F. Strawson, 'Social Morality and Individual Ideal', *Philosophy*, 36, 1961, especially pp. 1–3.

4 Coleridge, *Biographia Literaria*, II, p. 50.

5 Boswell's *Life of Samuel Johnson*, Everyman edn, 2 vols., London, [1906], 1935, I, p. 159 (Aetat. 45).

6 Matthew Arnold, *Culture and Anarchy*, Preface.

7 Bernard Williams, *Morality: An Introduction to Ethics*, Pelican Books, 1973, pp. 75–6.

8 E. H. Gombrich, *Meditations on a Hobby Horse*, London, 1963, especially p. 29.

9 Coleridge, *Biographia Literaria*, II, p. 20.

10 Peter Winch, 'Human Nature', in *The Proper Study*, Royal Institute of Philosophy Lectures, IV, 1969–70, London, 1971, p. 10.

11 J. S. Mill, *On Liberty*, chapter 3, in *Collected Works*, XVIII, 1977, pp. 265–6.

12 Johnson, *Lives*, III, p. 101.

13 Milton, *Paradise Lost*, IX, ll. 894–916; quoted from John Carey and Alastair Fowler (eds.), *The Poems of John Milton*, London, 1968, pp. 908–10.

14 Jane Adamson, '*Othello*' as Tragedy, Cambridge, 1980, p. 310.

15 The fact that it recurs in Adam's morally wishful and evasive speech to Eve (l. 956) does not seem to me to justify it here.

16 A. J. A. Waldock, *Paradise Lost and Its Critics*, Cambridge, 1947, p. 56.

3 AGENTS AND LIVES: MAKING MORAL SENSE OF PEOPLE

1 James Joyce, *Ulysses* ('Scylla and Charybdis'), Penguin edn, 1968, p. 194.

2 I have discussed this aspect of Joyce's work in *The Classical Temper*, London, 1961, chapters 2 and 3; and in *Joyce* (Writers and Critics Series), Edinburgh and London, 1962, 1965, 1967, chapters 1 and

3. See also C. H. Peake, *James Joyce, The Citizen and the Artist*, London, 1977, chapter 2.

3 James Joyce, *A Portrait of the Artist as a Young Man*, London, 1968, p. 207. Cf. 'A man of genius makes no mistakes. His errors are volitional and are the portals of discovery': Stephen Dedalus in *Ulysses*, p. 190.

4 Joyce, *Portrait of the Artist*, p. 60.

5 Joyce, *Portrait of the Artist*, pp. 102, 104.

6 Joyce, *Portrait of the Artist*, pp. 149–50.

7 Joyce, *Portrait of the Artist*, pp. 176–7.

8 Joyce, *Portrait of the Artist*, p. 257.

9 Joyce, *Portrait of the Artist*, p. 219.

10 Letter to Trusler, 23 August, 1799, in William Blake, *Poetry and Prose*, ed. Geoffrey Keynes, Nonesuch edn, London, 1948, p. 835.

11 Johnson, 'Life of Milton', in *Lives*, 1, pp. 165–6. The Joyce formulation is Stephen's in *Ulysses*, p. 213.

12 A recent good example concerned with literature and literary criticism especially is Charles Altieri, *Act and Quality*, Brighton, 1981.

13 I have in mind here such arguments as that of Gray, *Mill on Liberty: a Defence*, pp. 73ff.

14 Thomas Hardy, *Tess of the D'Urbervilles*, chapter 15, *ad fin*. Penguin edn, 1978, pp. 150–1.

15 The best account of this phenomenon is Maurice Mandelbaum, *History, Man and Reason*, Baltimore and London, 1971.

16 George Eliot, *The Mill on the Floss*, Book 6, chapter 6. Cf. the much more interesting view in Book 3, chapter 1, which is focused on Mr Tulliver rather than on Maggie.

17 Aristotle, *Nicomachean Ethics*, 1144b.

18 The best discussions of the issues here that I know are: Jon Elster, *Ulysses and the Sirens*, Cambridge, 1979, especially sections 3 and 4; *Sour Grapes*, Cambridge, 1983, especially section 2; and Michael Slote, *Goods and Virtues*, Oxford, 1983, especially pp. 43, 77–8, 107, 118–19.

19 Cicero, *De Officiis*, 1, section 108ff.

20 David Hume, *Enquiries*, ed. L. A. Selby-Bigge, rev. P. H. Niddich, Oxford, [1975], 1982, p. 322.

21 David Hume, *A Treatise of Human Nature*, Book 3, part 3, section 2.

22 David Hume, *An Enquiry Concerning the Principles of Morals*, section 9, part 1; in Hume, *Enquiries*, p. 277.

23 Hume, *Enquiries*, p. 267.

24 Cf. the blurring in 'when I make plain my anger or joy, in facial or verbal expression... [this] is not... the dropping of clues which

enable you to infer. This is what manifestly anger or joy *is*. They are made evident not by or through the expression but in it … [E]xpressive activities involve using signs, gestures, spoken or written words…'. Charles Taylor, *Human Agency and Language*, *Philosophical Papers* I, Cambridge, 1985, p. 91.

25 Tolstoy, *War and Peace*, trans. Louise and Aylmer Maude, Book 12, chapter 2; World's Classics edn, 3 vols., London [1922–3], 1970, III, p. 174.

26 *Johnson on Shakespeare*, in the Yale Edition of the *Works of Samuel Johnson*, vols. VII and VIII, ed. Arthur Sherbo, New Haven and London, 1968, VII, pp. 523–4.

27 *Antony and Cleopatra*, V, ii, ll. 79–92. I have quoted the Peter Alexander text, London, [1951], 1968.

28 Coleridge, *Biographia Literaria*, II, ch. XIV, p. 12.

29 *The Poems of Alexander Pope*, ed. John Butt, one-volume Twickenham edn, London, 1963, p. 310. The reference in lines 1 and 3 is of course to Pope's early and important poem, *Windsor Forest*.

30 Ortega y Gasset, 'In Search of Goethe from Within' [1949], in his book, *The Dehumanization of Art and Other Essays on Art, Culture and Literature*, Princeton, 1968, p. 143. I am grateful to Frank Cioffi for this and some other examples.

31 *Absalom and Achitophel*, ll. 543–68, in *The Poems of John Dryden*, ed. James Kinsley, Oxford, I, 1958, p. 231.

32 Alexander Pope, Epistle 'To Allen Lord Bathurst' ('Of the Use of Riches'), ll. 299–314; Pope, *Poems*, p. 583.

33 A notable recent example is Alasdair MacIntyre, *After Virtue*, London, 1981, chapters 10–18.

34 An excellent account of the mimetic ways needed to convey 'what a particular person is like' is Stuart Hampshire's in *Freedom of Mind and Other Essays*, Oxford, 1972, pp. 149ff.

35 *The Winter's Tale*, IV, iv, ll. 135–46.

36 From Burnet's *History of His Own Time*, in David Nicol Smith, *Characters from the Histories & Memoirs of the Seventeenth Century*, Oxford, [1918], 1936, pp. 235–6.

37 Keats, Letter to Richard Woodhouse, 27 October 1818, in *The Letters of John Keats*, ed. Maurice Buxton Forman, Oxford, 1935, p. 228.

38 First Epilogue, chapter 8; Tolstoy, *War and Peace*, III, pp. 445–6.

39 A. C. Bradley, *Shakespearean Tragedy*, London, 1904, p. 7 (chapter I, 'The Substance of Shakespearean Tragedy').

4 'DOING GOOD TO OTHERS': SOME REFLECTIONS ON *DANIEL DERONDA*

1 F. R. Leavis, *The Great Tradition*, London, 1948, p. 42.

2 Friedrich Nietzsche, *Twilight of the Idols*, trans. R. J. Hollingdale, Penguin Books, 1968, p. 69. Cf. Nietzsche, *The Will to Power*, trans. Walter Kaufmann and R. J. Hollingdale, N.Y., 1967, pp. 199, 204, 211, and elsewhere.

3 Gordon S. Haight, *George Eliot: a Biography*, Oxford, [1968], 1978, pp. 465–6. Her famous remarks to F. W. H. Myers in Cambridge (also quoted by Haight, p. 464) illustrate the same point: 'she, stirred somewhat beyond her wont, and taking as her text the three words which have been used so often as the inspiring trumpet-calls of men, – the words, *God*, *Immortality*, *Duty*, – pronounced, with terrible earnestness, how inconceivable was the *first*, how unbelievable the *second*, and yet how peremptory and absolute the *third*. Never, perhaps, have sterner accents affirmed the sovereignty of impersonal and unrecompensing Law. I listened, and night fell; her grave, majestic countenance turned toward me like a sibyl's in the gloom; it was as though she withdrew from my grasp, one by one, the two scrolls of promise, and left me the third scroll only, awful with inevitable fates. And when we stood at length and parted, amid that columnar circuit of the forest-trees, beneath the last twilight of starless skies, I seemed to be gazing, like Titus at Jerusalem, on vacant seats and empty halls, – on a sanctuary with no Presence to hallow it, and heaven left lonely of a God.'

4 Jane Austen, *Emma*, vol. 3, chapter 13.

5 George Eliot, *Daniel Deronda* Book 2, chapter 16; p. 136. *Page references are to the standard Blackwood edition of the novel.*

6 Indeed, as George Eliot recognizes, Grandcourt's life-moral qualities could possibly have been seen as positive conduct-moral virtues in other circumstances: 'If this white-handed man with the perpendicular profile had been sent to govern a difficult colony, he might have won reputation among his contemporaries. He had certainly ability, would have understood that it was safer to exterminate than to cajole superseded proprietors, and would not have flinched from making things safe in that way' (Book 6, chapter 48; p. 446). Could George Eliot have thought such extermination was a good thing in 'difficult' colonies? Cf. her innocence about the ardour of nationalistic and other 'world-historical' movements: for example Deronda's remark to Mordecai: '"Nations have revived. We may live to see a great outburst of force in the Arabs, who are being inspired with a new zeal."

"Amen, amen," said Mordecai...' (Book 6, chapter 42; pp. 394–5).

7 P. F. Strawson, 'Social Morality and Individual Ideal', pp. 15–17.

8 Mill on Bentham, in *Collected Works*, x, p. 112.

9 *Daniel Deronda* Book 3, chapter 23; p. 189.

10 *David Copperfield*, chapter 39.

11 Leavis, *The Great Tradition*, pp. 106–7. There is a remarkable shift to a more life-moral view of Gwendolen in a later essay by Leavis: 'Gwendolen Harleth', in *The Critic as Anti-Philosopher*, ed. G. Singh, London, 1982, especially p. 75.

12 *Daniel Deronda* Book 4, chapter 32; p. 272.

13 *Daniel Deronda* Book 7, chapter 51; pp. 470–1, 497, 499, and elsewhere.

14 Leavis, *The Great Tradition*, p. 109.

15 *Daniel Deronda* Book 5, chapter 35; p. 322.

16 *Daniel Deronda* Book 1, chapter 3; p. 14.

17 *Daniel Deronda* Book 1, chapter 9; pp. 69–70.

18 The word is Henry James's, in his '*Daniel Deronda*: A Conversation', reprinted in Leavis, *The Great Tradition*, especially p. 259.

19 *Daniel Deronda* Book 5, chapter 36; p. 340.

20 Cf. Henry James, '*Daniel Deronda*: A Conversation', p. 256: 'He *is* rather priggish, and one wonders that so clever a woman as George Eliot shouldn't see it.'

21 *Daniel Deronda* Book 7, chapter 56; p. 520.

22 *Daniel Deronda* Book 7, chapter 56; p. 519.

23 *Daniel Deronda* Book 7, chapter 56; p. 521.

24 *Daniel Deronda* Book 8, chapter 65; p. 580.

25 It is unclear in the last sentence of the first paragraph quoted above whether the 'they' in 'glad they were born' refers to the best of women or to those who are glad. It may not seem to matter much, but it makes some difference to the kind of moral effect Gwendolen might have on others.

26 *Daniel Deronda* Book 8, chapter 65; p. 580.

27 *Daniel Deronda* Book 8, chapter 69; p. 600.

28 *Daniel Deronda* Book 8, chapter 65; p. 580.

29 *Daniel Deronda* Book 7, chapter 51; p. 479.

30 *Daniel Deronda* Book 7, chapter 51; p. 474.

31 *Daniel Deronda* Book 7, chapter 51; p. 478.

32 *Daniel Deronda* Book 8, chapter 69; p. 608.

33 The episode in which the portrait of a corpse suddenly appears is in *Daniel Deronda* Book 1, chapter 6; pp. 42–5, along with some

reflections on Gwendolen's 'fits of spiritual dread' and the 'fountain of awe' in her.

34 *Daniel Deronda* Book 5, chapter 36; p. 330.
35 *Daniel Deronda* Book 7, chapter 54; p. 510. The 'nameless something' seems to be much the same as Hume mentioned.

5 MORAL THINKING IN *THE MILL ON THE FLOSS*

1 *The Mill on the Floss* Book 1, chapter 5; pp. 25–6. *Page references are to the standard Blackwood editions of George Eliot's novels.*
2 *The Mill on the Floss* Book 6, chapter 13; pp. 424–6.
3 *The Mill on the Floss* Book 5, chapter 3; p. 302.
4 *The Mill on the Floss* Book 6, chapter 12; p. 423.
5 *The Mill on the Floss* Book 3, chapter 3; pp. 186–7.
6 *The Mill on the Floss* Book 6, chapter 14; pp. 436–45.
7 *The Mill on the Floss* Book 7, chapter 2; p. 462.
8 *The Mill on the Floss* Book 3, chapter 1; p. 179.
9 D. H. Lawrence, *The Rainbow*, chapter 6.
10 *The Mill on the Floss* Book 6, chapter 6; p. 372.
11 *The Mill on the Floss* Book 5, chapter 4; p. 306.
12 *The George Eliot Letters*, ed. Gordon S. Haight, 7 vols., London and New Haven, I, 1954, p. 277; also quoted in Haight, *George Eliot: a Biography*, p. 60.
13 *Daniel Deronda* Book 7, chapters 51 and 53; pp. 470, 500.
14 *The Mill on the Floss* Book 6, chapter 10; pp. 408–9.
15 Eliot, *Letters*, III, p. 374.
16 *The Mill on the Floss* Book 7, chapter 5; p. 479.

6 FINDING CONGENIAL MATTER: POPE AND THE ART OF LIFE

1 *An Essay on Man*, IV, ll. 111–2; *The Poems of Alexander Pope*, ed. John Butt, London, 1963, p. 539. All references to Pope's poems are to this one-volume edition of the Twickenham text.
2 *Epistle to Arbuthnot*, ll. 340–1; Pope, *Poems*, p. 608. Pope's editor, John Butt, refers at this point to the gloss afforded by a passage in the *Essay on Man*, IV, ll. 391–3; Pope, *Poems*, p. 547, which underlines the 'wide' meaning, and which is very close to the third quotation above. The phrase in Spenser that Pope was perhaps echoing (*Faerie Queene*, I, Invocation, l. 9) also uses the term in its wide meaning.
3 *Imitations of Horace*, Epistle II, i, ll. 75–8; Pope, *Poems*, p. 638. The title 'Moral Essays' was provided by Pope's editor, Warburton.

4 The present essay develops some of the points I have made in two earlier essays: 'Pope: The Drama of the Self', in *The Critical Review*, 23, 1981, pp. 66–81; and 'Integrity and Dramatic Life in Pope's Poetry', in R. F. Brissenden and J. C. Eade (eds.), *Studies in the Eighteenth Century*, Canberra, 1976; reprinted in Boris Ford (ed.), *The New Pelican Guide to English Literature, 4: From Dryden to Johnson*, Penguin Books, 1982.

5 *Literary Criticism of Alexander Pope*, ed. Bertrand A. Goldgar, Lincoln, Nebraska, 1965, pp. 108, 161.

6 'Prologue to Mr Addison's Tragedy of Cato', ll. 1–4; Pope, *Poems*, p. 211.

7 Epistle II. To a Lady, 'Of the Characters of Women', *Moral Essays*, II, ll. 116–20; Pope, *Poems*, p. 564. For the phrase from the Preface to the 1717 volume see Pope, *Poems*, p. xxvi.

8 This is of course a reference to Stephen Greenblatt's study, *Renaissance Self-Fashioning*, Chicago and London, 1980, especially chapter 1 on Thomas More, and chapter 3 on Wyatt.

9 A useful book here is Penelope Murray (ed.), *Genius, The History of an Idea*, Oxford, 1989, especially pp. 17, 46–9, 67–75. Cf. Gadamer, *Truth and Method*, pp. 46ff.

10 Johnson, *Lives*, III, p. 217.

11 *Lines added to Wycherley's Poems*, ll. 3–6; Pope, *Poems*, pp. 272–3.

12 The best attempt to take it seriously in this way is A. D. Nuttall, *Pope's 'Essay on Man'*, London, 1984.

13 *Essay on Man*, IV, ll. 227–76; Pope, *Poems*, pp. 542–4.

14 *Essay on Man*, II, ll. 117–22; Pope, *Poems*, p. 520.

15 *Epistle to Arbuthnot*, ll. 83–8; Pope, *Poems*, p. 600.

16 *Epistle to Arbuthnot*, ll. 193–214 and 305–33; Pope, *Poems*, pp. 604–5 and 608.

17 'Eloisa to Abelard', ll. 359–66; Pope, *Poems*, p. 261; see also 'Elegy to the Memory of an Unfortunate Lady', ll. 75–8, *Poems*, p. 264. Woes that can be sung and then painted are perhaps appropriately referred to so colloquially as ''em'.

18 *The Rape of the Lock*, v, ll. 115–22; Pope, *Poems*, p. 241.

19 *The Dunciad Variorum*, I, ll. 83–92; Pope, *Poems*, pp. 355–6.

20 *The Dunciad in Four Books*, (1743), IV, ll. 5–8; Pope, *Poems*, p. 766.

21 *Logic*, chapter 12, in Mill, *Collected Works*, VIII, 1973, pp. 943ff.

22 *The Dunciad*, IV, ll. 445–52; Pope, *Poems*, p. 788.

23 *Imitations of Horace*, Sat. II, i, ll. 11–14; Pope, *Poems*, p. 614.

24 The lines quoted are from *Arbuthnot*, l. 1, Pope, *Poems*, p. 597; *Imitations of Horace*, Sat. II, i, 14, Pope, *Poems*, p. 614; *Arbuthnot*, ll. 358–9, Pope, *Poems*, p. 609; *Epilogue to the Satires*, *Dialogue* II, ll. 208–9, Pope, *Poems*, p. 701; and ll. 8–9, *Poems*, p. 695.

25 *Arbuthnot*, ll. 321–2; Pope, *Poems*, p. 608.
26 *The Dunciad*, I, ll. 115–34; Pope, *Poems*, p. 726. The earlier version of this passage, in which the hero is Theobald, not Cibber, is *The Dunciad Variorum*, I, ll. 109–126; Pope, *Poems*, p. 360. The wit in the later passage has obviously found more 'matter' congenial, and therefore more life in answering to it.
27 *The Dunciad Variorum*, Appendix 1; Pope, *Poems*, p. 433.
28 *Epilogue to the Satires*, Dialogue II, ll. 212–19, 247; Pope, *Poems*, pp. 702–3.
29 *Imitations of Horace*, Ep. I, i, ll. 19–20; Pope, *Poems*, p. 625.
30 *Epilogue to the Satires*, Dialogue II, ll. 197–8; Pope, *Poems*, p. 701.
31 *Imitations of Horace*, Ep. II, ii, ll. 203–205; Pope, *Poems*, p. 655.
32 *Imitations of Horace*, Ep. I, vi, ll. 26–7; Pope, *Poems*, p. 631.
33 *Imitations of Horace*, Sat. II, ii, l. 180; Pope, *Poems*, p. 624.
34 *Imitations of Horace*, Ep. I, i, ll. 167–8; Pope, *Poems*, p. 629.
35 *Imitations of Horace*, Ep. II, i, l. 262; Pope, *Poems*, p. 644.
36 *Imitations of Horace*, Ep. II, i, ll. 341–7; Pope, *Poems*, p. 647.
37 *Imitations of Horace*, Ep. II, ii, l. 115; Pope, *Poems*, p. 653.
38 *The Dunciad*, IV, ll. 65–7; Pope, *Poems*, p. 770.
39 *Essay on Man*, II, l. 133–4; Pope, *Poems*, p. 520.
40 *The Dunciad*, IV, l. 627–34; Pope, *Poems*, p. 799.
41 *Essay on Man*, II, ll. 172–4; Pope, *Poems*, p. 521.

7 LITERARY JUDGMENT: MAKING MORAL SENSE OF POEMS

1 F. R. Leavis, *The Common Pursuit*, London, 1952, pp. 213–14.
2 Michael Tanner, 'Literature and Philosophy', *New Universities Quarterly*, 30, 1975–6, pp. 54–64.
3 For example, Plato, *Ion* 533ff, *Republic* 605ff.
4 *Miscellaneous Prose of Sir Philip Sidney*, ed. Katherine Duncan-Jones and Jan Van Dorsten, Oxford, 1973, pp. 78–9.
5 *The Works of John Dryden*, Vol. XVII, *Prose 1668–91*, ed. Samuel Holt Monk, Berkeley and Los Angeles, 1971, pp. 55, 58.
6 *The Poems of Alexander Pope*, Twickenham edn, VII, *The Iliad of Homer Books I–IX*, ed. Maynard Mack, London and New Haven, 1967, p. 4.
7 Johnson, *Lives*, III, 165–6.
8 F. R. Leavis, *Revaluation*, London, 1949, p. 58.
9 Mill's Inaugural Address in *Collected Works*, XXI, pp. 252, 254.
10 *Autobiography* in Mill, *Collected Works*, I, p. 151.
11 *The Poems of Matthew Arnold*, ed. Kenneth Allott, London, 1965, pp. 225ff, lines 42–57.

12 Arnold, *Prose Works*, IX, p. 51.
13 Dudley Young, *London Review of Books*, 19 September 1985, p. 9.

8 AFTERWORD: SOME LIMITS OF PHILOSOPHY?

1 See, for example, Jane Adamson, 'Who and What is Henchard? – Hardy, Character and Moral Inquiry', and David Parker, 'Evaluative Discourse and the Return of the Repressed', in *The Critical Review*, 31, 1991, pp. 47–74 and pp. 3–16.
2 Cora Diamond, 'Having a Rough Story about What Moral Philosophy Is', *New Literary History*, 15, 1983, 160–3. The phrases by Iris Murdoch are from her paper, 'Vision and Choice in Morality', *Proceedings of the Aristotelian Society*, supplementary volume 30, 1956, especially p. 39.
3 John Sabini and Maury Silver, 'Emotions, Responsibility, and Character', in Ferdinand Schoeman, (ed.) *Responsibility, Character, and the Emotions*, Cambridge, 1987, pp. 172–4, and n. 2.
4 Mary Mothersill, *Beauty Restored*, Oxford, 1984, pp. 170–1.
5 Mothersill, *Beauty Restored*, p. 199.
6 Mothersill, *Beauty Restored*, p. 197. Cf. pp. 313ff, where Mothersill discusses Aquinas' term, *apprehensio*.
7 Mothersill, *Beauty Restored*, pp. 422–3; 425. Cf. Booth, *The Company We Keep*, p. 138, n. 13.
8 Mothersill, *Beauty Restored*, pp. 425–6.
9 Richard Rorty, *Contingency, Irony and Solidarity*, Cambridge, 1989, p. 82.
10 Rorty, *Contingency*, p. 80.
11 Rorty, *Contingency*, p. 81.
12 Rorty, *Contingency*, pp. 141–4.
13 Rorty, *Contingency*, p. 107; cf. p. 108, n. 8.
14 An interesting modern attempt to do what Aristotle is often supposed to have done is Michael Slote's project in his forthcoming books, *From Morality to Virtue* and *Agent-Based Virtue Ethics*.
15 Stuart Hampshire, *Two Theories of Morality*, Oxford, 1977, p. 44.
16 Stuart Hampshire, *Thought and Action*, London, [1959], 1982, pp. 249–50.
17 Hampshire, *Thought and Action*, pp. 251ff.
18 Stuart Hampshire, *Innocence and Experience*, London, 1989, especially pp. 97, 115–17, 125ff.
19 Aristotle, *Politics*, 1339b ff.
20 Williams, *Ethics and the Limits of Philosophy*, pp. 174, 196.
21 Williams, *Ethics and the Limits of Philosophy*, pp. 34–6.
22 Williams, *Ethics and the Limits of Philosophy*, pp. 37–8.

23 Williams, *Ethics and the Limits of Philosophy*, pp. 8–9.

24 Williams, *Ethics and the Limits of Philosophy*, pp. 37–8.

25 Williams, *Ethics and the Limits of Philosophy*, pp. 30ff. Here, I think Charles Taylor's idea of 'strong evaluation' is helpful in suggesting why a larger, or at least a more elaborate, conception of character is needed even for conduct-morality. See his paper, 'What is Human Agency?' in vol. I of his Philosophical Papers (2 vols.): *Human Agency and Language*, Cambridge, 1985, especially pp. 25, 34, 39, 41–3.

26 Williams, *Ethics and the Limits of Philosophy*, pp. 10–11, and his *Moral Luck*, Cambridge, 1981, pp. 45–7. The distinction between being a person who acts out of a genuine (virtuous) attitude towards another, and acting out of a concern with being oneself that (virtuous) sort of person, is made much of by Paul Seabright in 'The Pursuit of Unhappiness: Paradoxical Motivation and the Subversion of Character in Henry James's *Portrait of a Lady*', *Ethics*, 98, 1988, pp. 313–31. As Seabright observes, 'If there were rules for achieving character, rules that could be followed by anyone who had character formation as a goal, the content of character-based ethics could be expressed simply in terms of those rules…' (p. 321).

27 'Epistle…To a Lady', ll. 87–100; Pope, *Poems*, one-vol. Twickenham edn, p. 563.

28 Williams, *Ethics and the Limits of Philosophy*, pp. 139, 140, 154, 200. The same applies, of course, to what Iris Murdoch calls 'the secondary moral vocabulary' (*The Sovereignty of Good*, London, 1970, pp. 17–20), of which I take Williams's 'creepy' to be an instance. As one writer puts it, the vocabulary Murdoch means includes the terms for 'traditional virtues and vices, and also an indefinitely extendable range of terms we may have to draw on in trying to characterise those myriad "elusive activities" and other ways of being alive which escape any such traditional vocabulary. To Murdoch's "pert, familiar, brusque, juvenile, narrow-minded, snobbish, jealous, simple, spontaneous, undignified", we could go on adding: "prickly, repressed, nasty, candid, sinister, brutal, brittle, brash, noble, graceful, elegant, shallow, pompous, trivial, evasive, sentimental, crass, subtle, tactful, spare, rigid, (un)-imaginative…" Not only is this list of terms indefinitely extendable, but…frequently…we can find that *no* readily available terms will suffice to render our sense of another. There may not be simple names in the language for all the morally significant configurations we encounter. And then we may have to draw on metaphor to do the job, or perhaps tell a story…'. Christopher Cordner, 'F. R.

Leavis and the Moral in Literature', in Richard Freadman and Lloyd Reinhardt (eds.), *On Literary Theory and Philosophy: A Cross-Disciplinary Encounter*, London, 1991, p. 77.

29 Williams, *Ethics and the Limits of Philosophy*, p. 200.

30 Williams, *Ethics and the Limits of Philosophy*, pp. 201–2.

31 Williams, *Ethics and the Limits of Philosophy*, p. 194.

32 Williams, *Ethics and the Limits of Philosophy*, p. 201.

33 Alasdair MacIntyre, *After Virtue*, London, 1981, p. 32.

34 MacIntyre, *After Virtue*, p. 32, also chapters 11 and 12, and pp. 169ff.

35 MacIntyre, *After Virtue*, p. 149.

36 MacIntyre, *After Virtue*, p. 199.

37 MacIntyre, *After Virtue*, p. 204.

38 MacIntyre, *After Virtue*, p. 205.

39 Thomas Nagel, *The View from Nowhere*, N.Y. and Oxford, 1986.

40 Milton, *Areopagitica*, paragraph 7.

41 MacIntyre, *After Virtue*, p. 189.

42 MacIntyre, *After Virtue*, p. 223.

43 MacIntyre, *After Virtue*, p. 225.

44 For an interesting account of *Mansfield Park* along such lines, see three articles published in *The Critical Review*: John Wiltshire, 8, 1965, pp. 121–8; David Ellis, 12, 1969, pp. 107–19; and most relevantly, Robin Grove, 25, 1983, pp. 132–50.

45 Martha C. Nussbaum, *The Fragility of Goodness: Luck and Ethics in Greek Tragedy and Philosophy*, Cambridge, 1986; and most especially the following papers: 'Flawed Crystals: James's *The Golden Bowl* and Literature as Moral Philosophy', *New Literary History*, 15, 1983, pp. 25–50; 'Fictions of the Soul', *Philosophy and Literature*, 7, 1983, pp. 145–61; '"Finely Aware and Richly Responsible": Literature and the Moral Imagination', in Anthony J. Cascardi (ed.), *Literature and the Question of Philosophy*, Baltimore and London, 1987, pp. 169–91; 'Narrative Emotions: Beckett's Genealogy of Love', *Ethics*, 98, 1988, pp. 225–54; 'Love's Knowledge', in Brian P. McLaughlin and Amélie Oksenberg Rorty, (eds.) *Perspectives on Self-Deception*, Berkeley and London, 1988, pp. 487–514; 'Perceptive Equilibrium: Literary Theory and Ethical Theory', in Ralph Cohen, (ed.) *The Future of Literary Theory*, N.Y. and London, 1989, pp. 58–85. These papers have now been collected in Nussbaum's book, *Love's Knowledge: Essays on Philosophy and Literature*, N.Y. and Oxford, 1990 (*referred to below as L.K.*).

46 Nussbaum, *Fragility*, p. 305.

47 Nussbaum, *Fragility*, p. 290.

48 Nussbaum, *Fragility*, p. 300.

49 Nussbaum, *Fragility*, p. 306; cf. Nussbaum's paper on 'Love and

the Individual: Romantic Rightness and Platonic Aspiration', in Thomas C. Heller, Morton Sosua and David Wellberg, (eds.) *Reconstructing Individualism: Autonomy, Individuality and the Self in Western Thought*, Stanford, 1986, pp. 253–77; *L.K.* pp. 314–34.

50 Nussbaum, *Fragility*, p. 300. The translation here is evidently Nussbaum's own, which differs in several ways from the more familiar translation by W. D. Ross: 'But up to what point and to what extent a man must deviate before he becomes blameworthy it is not easy to determine by reasoning, any more than anything else that is perceived by the senses; such things depend on particular facts, and the decision rests with perception.'

51 Nussbaum, *Fragility*, p. 309.

52 For George Eliot, see the end of Book 7, chapter 2 of *The Mill on the Floss*.

53 Nussbaum, *Fragility*, p. 14.

54 Nussbaum, 'Flawed Crystals', p. 39; *L.K.*, p. 138.

55 Nussbaum, 'Perceptive Equilibrium', pp. 66ff; *L.K.*, pp. 176ff.

56 Nussbaum, 'Perceptive Equilibrium', p. 75; *L.K.*, p. 184.

57 Nussbaum, 'Flawed Crystals', pp. 34ff; *L.K.*, pp. 134ff.

58 Nussbaum, 'Perceptive Equilibrium', pp. 59–62; *L.K.*, pp. 168–72.

59 Nussbaum, 'Perceptive Equilibrium', p. 61; *L.K.*, p. 171.

60 Nussbaum, 'Narrative Emotions', p. 230; *L.K.*, p. 290.

61 Nussbaum, 'Perceptive Equilibrium', p. 83; *L.K.*, p. 192.

62 Nussbaum, *Fragility*, p. 15.

63 Charles Altieri, 'From Expressivist Aesthetics to Expressivist Ethics', in the same volume, *Literature and the Question of Philosophy*, as 'Aware and Responsible' first appeared (see n. 45 above), pp. 132–66, especially p. 164.

64 An instructive study bearing on this is Christopher Pelling, (ed.) *Characterization and Individuality in Greek Literature*, Oxford, 1990, especially Pelling's own 'Conclusion'.

65 Nussbaum, *Fragility*, p. 51.

66 Nussbaum, *Fragility*, p. 313.

67 Nussbaum, *Fragility*, p. 51.

68 Nussbaum, *Fragility*, p. 82.

69 Nussbaum, *Fragility*, pp. 420–1.

70 Nussbaum, *Fragility*, p. 49.

71 Nussbaum, 'Flawed Crystals', pp. 45–6; *L.K.*, pp. 143–4.

72 Nussbaum, 'Flawed Crystals', p. 47; *L.K.*, pp. 144–5. A good discussion of this and other moral aspects of the novel, though from a different point of view from mine, is Richard Freadman, *Eliot, James and the Fictional Self*, London, 1986, especially chapter 4.

73 Nussbaum, 'Flawed Crystals', pp. 37, 41; *L.K.*, pp. 136–7, 139–40.

74 Henry James, *The Golden Bowl*, Penguin Modern Classics edn, n.d., pp. 476–7.
75 Nussbaum, 'Aware and Responsible', pp. 172–4; *L.K.*, pp. 150–2.
76 Nussbaum, *Fragility*, p. 184.
77 Nussbaum, *Fragility*, p. 198.
78 Nussbaum, *Fragility*, p. 198.
79 Nussbaum, *Fragility*, p. 166.
80 Nussbaum, *Fragility*, p. 199.

Index

Works cited in the text are generally indexed under the author's name. However, when there are a substantial number of references, they are indexed under their title.

personal mode of life, and life-morality
121–2
Petrarch (Francesco Petrarca) 191
philosophy,
  attitude to poetry 150
  distinguished from literature 262–3,
    276–7, 306–7
  and understanding of love 100
Plato,
  on behaviour 80
  conception of moral practice 286–7
  on 'how to live' 36
  moral language 229
  on music 270
  on power of poetry 234–5, 252
  Symposium 303–5
poetry,
  as acts of responsible agents 231
  aesthetic judgment of 225–6
  as agent in itself 231–4
  Aristotle on 270
  attitude of philosophers to 150
  Bentham on 17, 26
  Coleridge on 39
  distinction from philosophy 226–7
  fear of 234–6
  as functioning of impersonal system
    229, 230
  integrity of 189
  judged in terms of human activity
    228–9, 230–1
  making moral sense of 229–42
  as manifesting lives 234–42
  models for 39–40
  and moral ideas 10
  and moral judgment 111
  moralistic attitude to 250
  practical judgment of 227–9
  theoretical criticism of 226–7
  and understanding of love 100
politics, influence on judgment 239
Pope, Alexander 274
  adoption of poetic guises 212–14
  art of life 197, 201–2, 208, 221–2,
    265
  attitude to genius 193–4, 196
  attitude to poetry 231
  on Buckingham 108, 110, 209
  on business of poet 188
  'centripetal' and 'centrifugal' modes
    of life 219–21
  conflicts of moral thinking 113

  defence of moral conduct 119–200,
    202–3
  as dramatic poet 189–90
  ideals as system of objective 'truths'
    and rules 187–8
  influence of changes of outlook in
    seventeenth century 192
  Johnson's 'Life' of 242–4
  on life as narrative 279
  moral beliefs 194–8
  moral defence of poetry 189
  poetic self-consciousness 187, 192–3,
    207, 211
  on poetry and prose 217
  view of satire 188–9, 216
  The Dunciad 186, 202, 206–8, 211,
    214–16, 219–21
  'Elegy to the Memory of an
    Unfortunate Lady' 55, 61, 194, 204
  'Eloisa to Abelard' 194, 204
  Epilogue to the Satires 211, 216
  'Epistle: To Allen Lord Bathurst' 103
  Epistle to Arbuthnot 198–203, 207, 212
  'Epistle to Miss Blount...after the
    Coronation' 205
  Essay on Criticism 204–5, 208, 233, 237
  Essay on Man 194–8, 208, 220
  'Hymn Written in Windsor Forest'
    101–2, 194
  Imitations of Horace 207, 210, 211
  Moral Essays 198, 208–9, 211, 220
  Preface to translation of *The Iliad*
    237–8
  Prologue to Addison's *Cato* 188
  The Rape of the Lock 205–6, 220
  The Temple of Fame 194
  translation of *The Iliad* 197
Portrait of the Artist as a Young Man, A 31,
  64–9, 70–5, 77, 93
  on conduct 83
  'dramatic' mode 71–2
  and unity of moral life 72–5
  and vocation 102
  see also Joyce, James
practical criticism 9–10

rationality, as part of mode of life 221
religion, and judgment 239
responsibility, Aristotle on 270
Richards, I. A. 9–10
Romanticism, and poetry reflecting
  organic unity 101